AF740401

THE INVISIBLE ORIGINS OF LEGAL POSITIVISM

Law and Philosophy Library

VOLUME 52

Managing Editors

FRANCISCO J. LAPORTA, *Department of Law,*
Autonomous University of Madrid, Spain

ALEKSANDER PECZENIK, *Department of Law, University of Lund, Sweden*

FREDERICK SCHAUER, *John F. Kennedy School of Government,*
Harvard University, Cambridge, Mass., U.S.A.

Former Managing Editors
AULIS AARNIO, MICHAEL D. BAYLES†, CONRAD D. JOHNSON†,
ALAN MABE

Editorial Advisory Board

AULIS AARNIO, *Research Institute for Social Sciences,*
University of Tampere, Finland
ZENON BANKOWSKY, *Centre for Criminology and the Social and Philosophical*
Study of Law, University of Edinburgh
PAOLO COMANDUCCI, *University of Genua, Italy*
ERNESTO GARZÓN VALDÉS, *Institut für Politikwissenschaft,*
Johannes Gutenberg Universität Mainz
JOHN KLEINIG, *Department of Law, Police Science and Criminal*
Justice Administration, John Jay College of Criminal Justice,
City University of New York
NEIL MacCORMICK, *European Parliament, Brussels, Belgium*
WOJCIECH SADURSKI, *European University Institute,*
Department of Law, Florence, Italy
ROBERT S. SUMMERS, *School of Law, Cornell University*
CARL WELLMAN, *Department of Philosophy, Washington University*

The titles published in this series are listed at the end of this volume.

THE INVISIBLE ORIGINS OF LEGAL POSITIVISM

A Re-Reading of a Tradition

by

WILLIAM E. CONKLIN

Faculty of Law, University of Windsor,
Visting Fellow, Clare Hall, Cambridge University

KLUWER ACADEMIC PUBLISHERS

DORDRECHT / BOSTON / LONDON

A C.I.P. Catalogue record for this book is available from the Library of Congress.

ISBN 0-7923-7101-1

Published by Kluwer Academic Publishers,
P.O. Box 17, 3300 AA Dordrecht, The Netherlands.

Sold and distributed in North, Central and South America
by Kluwer Academic Publishers,
101 Philip Drive, Norwell, MA 02061, U.S.A.

In all other countries, sold and distributed
by Kluwer Academic Publishers,
P.O. Box 322, 3300 AH Dordrecht, The Netherlands.

Printed on acid-free paper

All Rights Reserved
© 2001 Kluwer Academic Publishers
No part of the material protected by this copyright notice may be reproduced or
utilized in any form or by any means, electronic or mechanical,
including photocopying, recording or by any information storage and
retrieval system, without written permission from the copyright owner.

Printed in the Netherlands.

CONTENTS

Acknowledgements

This book has been long in the making. Millie Bakan saw what I was doing at a very early stage during the late 1980s and my concerns would not have taken the form of a manuscript without her encouragement and piercing questions. When the book seemed complete during the mid-1990s, I delivered various sections and chapters at conferences on the Continent and in the U.K. and in philosophy or law faculty workshops at Edinburgh's Law and Society Centre, Birkbeck College, Queen Mary College, Liverpool University, and University College London. I am grateful to the participants who took the time and effort to comment on my presentations. William Christian, Walter Skakoon, Bert van Roermund, Ernie Weinrib, Jonathan Lavery, Mark Thornton, Louis Wolcher, Janet Ritch, Kent Enns, Robin Jackson, Wally McLeod, and Sabine Grebe read particular chapters and this invariably initiated conversations that helped me to clarify my claims and arguments. I am grateful for the time and effort they took in offering me feed-back. The referees also made me conscious of shortcomings. I am especially grateful to Henry Pietersma and Sol Nigosian, who, throughout the years when I was writing the manuscript, joined me in wide-ranging conversations about its themes and, by so doing, encouraged me to continue the long project. John King copy-edited the final draft, offering invaluable comments relating to content and style. Without his help as copy-editor, this book would not have seen the light.

The manuscript simply would not have been completed, however, except for the opportunity to spend my summers and long weekends in the civilized environment and library facilities of Victoria College at the University of Toronto. I am especially grateful to Jean O'Grady and Margaret Burgess of the Northrop Frye Centre at the College for their support over the years and to Brian Merrilees and Roseann Runte for allowing me to work at the Centre.

I am grateful to my mother, who, over the years, frequently read my manuscripts. It is to her spirit that I dedicate this book.

William E. Conklin
10 February 2001

About the Author

William E. Conklin has authored *In Defence of Fundamental Rights* (1979), *Images of a Constitution* (1989) and *The Phenomenology of Modern Legal Discourse* (1998). Having co-edited four volumes in the fields of third-world jurisprudence and access to justice, he has also written extensively in different fields of the humanities and of law. He received his doctorate in Social and Political Thought from York University in 1992 after having received graduate degrees in Law from Columbia University and in International Relations from the London School of Economics.

Introduction

Since the Renaissance, societies have been organized with the sovereign state as the centre. Internally, the authority of the sovereign state is plenary. In the exercise of this authority, the state may define who is a legal person, assign rights and duties to the person, create or terminate legal relationships between the persons, and prescribe social behaviour in terms of legal norms. The legal norms enclose social behaviour inside conceptual boundaries. The enclosure is potentially total. Ultimately, the institutions of the state may coerce one to comply with the normative prescriptions. And, in the coercive act of a state institution, much good may be accomplished as well as much evil. Concerning the latter, persons may be incarcerated, tortured, cleansed of their citizenship, expelled from their territory, and executed; their property may be confiscated and their means of a livelihood terminated. Publicists and teachers redefine social events from the viewpoint of the state, and the new political leaders and legal officials displace the old Founding Fathers with new Founding Fathers whose intent legitimizes all acts of government officials. The laws of the state are said to bind all persons who live within the territorial boundaries of the state. The substantive content of a law remains authoritative despite the apparent injustice of the content. No institution – neither a religious institution nor political party nor a corporation – possesses the authority to posit and enforce binding laws unless the state's legal institutions have authorized such authority. The state alone possesses a monopoly of force: no social organization may impose force without the authority of a state institution.

The sovereign state also possesses an external aspect. A state is immune from scrutiny from other sovereign states. A state is autonomous (*auto*, meaning 'self' and *nomos*, meaning 'law-making'). No one state may exercise authority in a manner that interferes with the sovereignty of another state.

The big question is 'why are the laws and regulations in such sovereign states authorized when the acts of petty and organized criminals are not?' This issue does not necessarily go to the justice of the acts of state. Nor does it go to the factors that officials may authoritatively incorporate into their deliberations about the actions of the state. Rather, this critical question addresses the nature of legal authority itself. Why is a rule or norm of a state's officials binding upon the social behaviour of residents within the territory of the state: that is the question of the day. If one could only resolve that question, one might begin to understand the apparent inhumanity of state institutions that authoritatively expel long-standing residents, torture others, authorize the disappearance of many others, and execute many more, all in the name of the authority of the state. If one could understand why a human law is binding, one might finally appreciate why the state possesses a monopoly of coercive authority.

Jurists have generally offered two perspectives from which to respond to this issue. The one, the natural law tradition, has claimed that officials must evaluate the substantive content of a rule in order for the rule to be authoritative. In this act of evaluation, the law would be binding if its content were consistent with universal principles that transcended the particular law. Such universal principles are considered unwritten. They are so considered because they have not been authored by the institutions of the state. Instead, natural law theorists have claimed that the source of the transcendental principles is one's "heart" or conscience. Perhaps it would be best to consider the universal standards as intuitive. The universal standards seem natural – so much so that they have been called 'natural laws.' The mere posit of a rule by a civil institution does not render the rule authoritative and binding. The content of the rule must be measured against the natural universal laws. It is not surprising that, given the Judaeo-Christian influence in western culture, especially since the Renaissance, natural laws have been associated with a still further transcendent and self-starting source, independent of the content of the natural laws: namely, a divine Author. The Author has been considered invisible. As I shall argue in Chapter Two, this invisibility has been considered synonymous with a sense of the divine.

The second approach, the tradition of legal positivism, dominated the thought of the sophists of the fifth-century *polis* as well as the legal thought of the newly formed sovereign city-state of the Renaissance. The assumptions of legal positivism have so permeated legal thought even to this day that I eventually describe this dominant strain of thought as 'the Tradition.' The tradition of legal positivism has insisted that the authority of a rule is not determined by reference to the substantive content of the rule. This is not to say that morality and anthropology and politics and psychology do not enter into deliberations about the substantive content of a binding rule. But the legal positivist tradition has insisted that the substantive content of a rule is separate from its authority. What makes a rule authoritative is its source or grounding or *arche*. I shall argue in Chapter Three that such an impersonal trace of the authority of a rule to its distant *arche* has dominated European legal thought since the Roman times, perhaps even since the later Greek. At times, this impressive tradition has associated the *arche* with a founding author of the civil institutions; at other times, with an *a priori* concept untouched by human passion; and at still other times, with the felt experience of bonding that officials share towards the civil institutions.

Contemporary commentators have reinforced the demarcation of binding laws into natural law theory and legal positivism for too long. The deliberative stage of the legislative and adjudicative incorporate factors that even in the recent past would have been considered morality or non-law. Statutes, constitutional texts, and international treaties have incorporated prescriptive moral norms. Human rights statutes, constitutional bills of rights, and international conventions exemplify such a phenomenon. Even commercial law codes and common law doctrines in the fields of private and administrative law have required officials to articulate moral standards of fairness and justice in day-to-day decisions. Evidence rules have been widened and, in aboriginal cases, for example, what courts have considered legal evidence has become less formal. Higher courts in the common law countries now expect competent counsel to be familiar with the anthropological researches concerning the pre-European tribal legal cultures. Both jurists and judges are increasingly sensitive to the possibility that laws have hitherto represented the voices of men, especially privileged men, and that the legal voice should be more inclusive of women. So too, the highest courts in the land have ordered that public institutions include personnel with diverse ethnic-religious backgrounds. And officials have deferred to alternative modes of decision-making that aspire to avoid the legalism and formalism of adjudication so that the parties may address the substantive content of their disputes. The broadening of the factors incorporated into deliberative content of law, even so short as a decade ago, would have been rejected in many common law countries as moral, as political, as improper for the judicial function, and as inappropriate for pedagogy in a professional law school. The separation of law from non-law has been undermined in the deliberative stage of the adjudicative process.

When one turns to the question 'why are laws binding?' or 'why is a decision authoritative or valid?' one also faces a striking similarity in theories of law that are self-described as legal positivism and natural law, for both approaches to law share a common inquiry into the authorizing origins or *arche* of the authority of humanly posited laws. For natural law theory, the *arche* has been considered, until relatively recently (with the writings of Lon Fuller and possibly Ronald Dworkin, for example) to be the invisible Author or Nature.[1] For legal positivism, the *arche*, I argue in Chapters Three to Nine, is also invisible. By 'invisible,' I mean that the *arche* is inaccessible through the humanly constructed language of officials such

1 In *The Structuralism of Analytical Jurisprudence* (forthcoming), I argue that Dworkin's works do presuppose an invisible author and an invisible juridical paradise.

as judges, lawyers and legislators.[2] Both the tradition of natural law and the tradition of legal positivism search for an *arche* of the grounding for their human laws.

I take up the latter line of inquiry in this book. As I explain in Chapter Three, I put to the side the character of moral factors that officials incorporate into their deliberative process.[3] I address a different question. Instead of asking 'what factors (political, social, ethical, psychological, or statistical) are members of a legal structure?' I examine what lies at the authorizing origin of binding laws. With the possible exception of Joseph Raz, whose work I examine in Chapter Nine, the concern of recent legal philosophers has been the identity of law. Here, the identity of the factors that constitute membership within the phenomena of "law" has entered into the deliberations of legislatures and courts. Here, officials have asked whether statutes, regulations, precedents, jurists' treatises, or unwritten customs, for example, constitute laws. The nature of a binding law, however, is a different issue. Here, the issue is 'why is a law binding, whatever factors enter into the deliberation about the substantive content of a binding law?' The central claim of the tradition of legal positivism, again, is that the latter issue of the authority of law is separate from the issue of the identity of the factors that enter into the deliberation about a binding law.

My method of analysis is to read the canons of legal positivism seriously. I shall retrieve what each important thinker has understood as the ultimate authorizing origin of binding rules and norms. I shall retrieve the thinkers' resolution of the latter issue, though, by re-visiting how the canons understand the nature of legal language. In particular, what do the canons define as legal language? And does such a view of legal language provide insight into the question, 'what is the authorizing origin of a binding law?' Is the origin outside language?

The issue of language is not new to the discourses of the humanities and of law. It is especially an issue that permeates Hegel's phenomenology during the nineteenth century, the recently translated and highly original works of the Russian thinker Mikhail Bakhtin (1895-1975), the German and French elaboration of the phenomenology of language (especially the writings of Edmund Husserl and Maurice Merleau-Ponty), the social and literary criticism of French and German writers during the 1960s and 1970s (especially Michel Foucault, François Lyotard, and Jacques Derrida), English literary criticism since the 1970s, and unsystematic

---

2 I draw from Emmanuel Levinas, *Totality and Infinity*, trans. Alphonso Lingis (Pittsburgh: Duquesne University Press, 1961, 1969) and Maurice Merleau-Ponty, *Visible and Invisible*, ed. Claude Lefort, trans. Alphonso Lingis (Evanston: Northwestern University Press, 1964, 1968).

3 This is the subject of my book, *The Structuralism of Analytical Jurisprudence* (forthcoming).

writings by legal theorists during the 1980s and 1990s.[4] In short, there is a deep and rigorous context from which I retrieve the importance of language in the tradition of legal positivism.

Indeed, in Chapters Four to Eight, I retrieve how language is indispensable for an appreciation of how each of Thomas Hobbes, Jean-Jacques Rousseau, John Austin, Hans Kelsen, and H.L.A. Hart grounded the authorizing origins of humanly posited binding laws. The tradition of legal positivism can only grow richer if one connects these thinkers' insights about legal language with their understanding of why is a posited norm or rule binding.

In particular, the canons in the tradition of legal positivism have generally understood language in a very special manner. For one thing, the canons have assumed, I shall argue, that legal language is primarily written. What is meant by 'written' is not just that humanly posited laws are written on a page. After all, the writings of poets and novelists are also written on a page. What is important for the thinkers of legal positivism is that a script is authored by an appropriate official or institution in civil society. The institution is related with other institutions, and together they form an interdependent hierarchical structure modelled on a pyramid. For some centuries, the legislature was understood as the important institutional author. Much of the common law is unwritten, one might say, in that legislatures have not authored many common law rules. But the 'unwritten' common law rules and principles are expressed in texts that courts and quasi-judicial tribunals have authored. Since the influence of American realism in the 1920s and of Jeremy Bentham in the nineteenth century, judges have been considered the authors of the 'unwritten' common law principles.

Accordingly, the authoritative writing of legal officials has been associated with very special authors. The authors, as contemplated by Thomas Hobbes (as I argue in Chapter Four), originate an institutional structure whose rules, in turn, bind all the populace within the state's territory. The authors, in the case of Jean-Jacques Rousseau or John Austin (as I argue in Chapters Five and Six), may be 'the People' whose will transcends the rules of the civil institutions. Or, as in the case of Joseph Raz (as I argue in Chapter Nine), the authors may be the institutions themselves. The above philosophers postulate that authors begin legal language.

No matter how one understands the identity of the authorial source of written laws (whether a transcendent General Will, 'People,' or civil institution), such an author is considered self-starting, autonomous, originary, or a creator of written expression. The author's expression represents the author's concepts. Jurists and

---

4 I provide an annotated bibliography of these contributions in Conklin, "Alternatives to the Study of Law: An Annotated Bibliography of Legal Phenomenology and Legal Semiotics," *Current Legal Theory* **16**: 3-61. Bakhtin also wrote under the name of V. N. Volosinov.

officials call the concepts legal doctrines or legal rules. One may be familiar with some such doctrines from daily life: criminal intent, consideration, fee simple, freedom of speech, and the like. The author may authorize institutions to posit such concepts. A distinct and assignable author, placed on the institutional hierarchy, legislates the doctrines. It is even a common practice in common law countries to cite the date and place of the author's creation of the expression at the end of a statute or the start of the judicial decision.

If there were a time and place when an author of the legal doctrines could not be identified, as suggested most forcefully by Hobbes, Kelsen, and Hart, then the unwritten would characterize such a condition. Since law is written by distinct and assignable authors, a non-law would characterize a condition of the unwritten. Officials reject the unwritten pre-language world as a pre-history, pre-morality, and pre-legality. Officials cannot recognize the social or moral norms of such a world as binding because they exceed the expression authored by civil institutions. By interpreting the classics of modern legal positivism, we shall discover that legal existence is associated with a special authored or written language that officials on the institutional hierarchy recognize as authoritative.

What cannot be authored in this sense of an autonomous, self-creating author, I shall show, is excluded as non-law, as outside 'the Law,' as morality, as anthropology, as subjective. Hobbes and Locke describe such an unrecognizable, languageless world as "barbaric" and "savage." Kelsen and Hart describe such an unwritten world as "primitive" and "pre-legal." It seems that without self-conscious authors to will legal doctrines, there cannot be authoritative, binding laws. The exclusionary character of legal language addresses the subject-matter of 'what is law?', the evidence admissible in court, the factors that a particular official may incorporate into her/his deliberations, and the nature of the official's decision itself.

What the great thinkers of legal positivism consider legal language – an authored written expression and a special sense of an author at that – makes both inclusions and exclusions.

Traditionally, legal positivism claims that a legal language represents or stands for categorical objects. Hobbes calls such representations "signs." Today and put simply, we call the object of a sign a referent: the sign refers to an object. The referent may be a physical object of nature. Or, as in the case of legal discourse, the referent may be a concept which, again, is called a doctrine or a rule. Hobbes' understanding of posited laws, as I argue in Chapter Four, privileges the legal sign. Officials can only recognize an object – a physical tree or a concept – if they possess words or phrases to represent the object. Again put simply, the words and phrases are signs of objects. The words and phrases signify the objects. The objects are, in a sense, absent from the signs. Legal officials signify the object by differentiating one word or phrase from another, thereby hoping to give a denotative signification to the word or phrase.

A written language, though, also makes exclusions.[5] What remains unwritten in the sense of being untraceable to some identifiable author in a contingent time and place is external to legal language. The most important excluded elements of language, perhaps, are experiential or lived meanings that an official brings *into* a statement or phrase that signifies a legal doctrine. Such experiential meanings have been considered unwritten and, therefore, non-law. Instead, legal language has been confined to the written statements of the authorized institutional authors: legislatures, courts, municipal councils, and all their officials.

Paul Ricoeur's helpful distinction bears repeating here.[6] A sign represents or signifies an object or referent. A symbol, in contrast, is experienced without the thought or reflection that mediates between sign and utterer. A symbol does not represent a further object. An immediacy joins symbol with the experiential body of the person who identifies with the symbol. The consequence is that myth contextualizes a symbol. A symbol fuses the public with the legal institutions without reference to some transcendent authorizing origin. A mysticism or spiritualism colours the symbol.

So officials, preoccupied with the rational trace of the grounding of a binding law, are prone to exclude the symbol as legally non-existent. Officials are constrained by legal statements, and these statements stand for or represent the concepts that the author – usually a legislature or court – intended as authoritative. Officials can only approximate or represent the ultimate grounding of legal reasoning. We shall observe in later chapters that, according to the canons of legal positivism, legal officials generally take the authorized signs to be created by self-starting civil authors. Officials consider such written authored expression as the sole component of legal language. Only the concepts that legal signs represent – only such concepts are believed to constitute legal existence. The experienced symbols, to use Ricoeur's term, are just not part of the authoritative legal language. Rather, authoritative concepts differentiate law from non-law, law from morality, legal existence from non-existence, truth from falsity – or so the tradition of legal positivism suggests.

We shall see in Chapters Four to Nine that the nature of binding laws depends upon the special manner in which jurists and officials consider legally binding

5 I offer examples in Conklin, *The Phenomenology of Modern Legal Discourse* (Aldershot, U.K.: Dartmouth/Ashgate, 1998), 69-102 and *passim*.

6 Paul Ricoeur, *Hermeneutics & the Human Sciences*, ed. & trans. John B. Thompson (Cambridge: Cambridge University Press, 1981), 32-40. *The Conflict of Interpretations*, ed. Don Ihde (Evanston: Northwestern University Press, 1974), 28-9, 58-9.

signs. Without a specially authored language to signify their concepts and their "facts," officials would relapse into an unrecognizable world. I read the tradition of legal positivism in a manner that suggests that, without such a written language, there cannot be binding doctrines to which legal signs could refer. The exterior to language – or, more correctly, to what officials consider legal language – would be unrecognizable because officials are only familiar with the written signs with which we have learned to represent legal concepts. Without a language, the realm exterior to language is objectless – objectless because objects (or referents) only exist if there is a term or sentence or other mark of writing that stands for an object. The blind spot or *aporia* of legal positivism is that the exteriority of language lacks any term or sentence or other series of marks whose referent officials can analyze. The exteriority is a non-knowledge. Like the outer space of our earthly world, we remain uncertain as to what is 'out there' beyond the legal statements.

Legal statements (or norms), however, rely upon an explicit or implied regress to a prior and stable original object or intent. The latter object functions as an *arche*. Thus, in the tracing of one grounding of a norm to another, there needs to be finality. Without the finality, the tracing would continue *ad infinitum*. The finality brings closure to the tracing and, with that closure, a norm can be said to be posited or set down. It is the final ultimate grounding that is the subject of my investigation in this book. Once one returns to the issue of the language through which officials represent or signify their doctrines, rules, principles, and other concepts, the need for an ultimate authorizing origin of such concepts is apparent. The great thinkers of the legal positivist tradition, I claim, have found it necessary to project the ultimate grounds of binding laws into the very unanalyzable exteriority to the recognizable legal language. The blind spot of the tradition of legal positivism is that officials have had to exclude the authorizing origin from legal existence despite the need to assume an originary source or grounding for laws to be considered binding on others. The binding laws, which authorize the acts of officials, refer to an unanalyzable and, in a sense, languageless realm of non-law or legal non-existence as the authorizing origin of the laws.

The legal positivist tradition has attributed different identities to the ultimate *arche* of binding laws. The tradition describes the ultimate *arche* as an author. In the works of Hobbes (Chapter Four), the authors, once they authorized the creation of the state's civil institutions, are excluded from the question of what commands are authoritative. Jean-Jacques Rousseau (Chapter Five) claims that one author, the General Will, grounds the authority of all legislated rules. The final authors of Hobbes and Rousseau are, in a sense, invisible. During the nineteenth century, the author was projected as historically contingent. In this case, the legislature or a court, or the people were considered the historical authors of binding rules. During the twentieth century, though, the tradition of legal positivism further attempted to explain why a rule is binding, whatever its substantive content. The first attempt, associated with Hans Kelsen (Chapter Seven), draws from the notion of an *a priori* concept presupposed by officials. The second, elaborated by H.L.A. Hart (Chapter Eight) draws from the written statement about the officials' unwritten sense of bonding with a social convention. A third, brilliantly argued by Joseph Raz (Chapter Nine), suggests that a rule is binding because of its institutional source in a structure of interdependent institutions of the sovereign state. Whatever the suggested ultimate source of a binding rule, its source lifts the subjectivity of the posit of a rule or value into an objective realm of binding laws, its substantive content come what may.

The crucial point here is that important versions of legal positivism, like natural law theories, have postulated an originary authorizing origin to humanly posited binding rules/norms.[7] The important difference between the two general approaches has been that, for natural law theory, some uncontrollable and uncontrolled transcendent source constitutes the origin, and, for legal positivism, human beings or humanly created institutions posit the ultimate *arche* of authoritative laws in the unanalyzable and unrecognizable externality to humanly posited laws.

According to the canons of legal positivism, the authorizing origin of humanly posited, binding laws is a mere possibility. The origin is a mere possibility, the origin being postulated as exterior to legal existence, and only this legal existence is true or real. The tradition has associated the *arche* of a legal structure with some one unrecognizable and unknowable object exterior to legal language. The origin dwells in the very objectless realm which, by virtue of the understanding of language as written by authors, is objectless. Being a mere possibility, officials must possess faith in the existence of the origin. The whole of the positivist project hangs upon a faith in the possibility of the invisible. Such an invisibility is essential for the origin to terminate the trace of the authority of humanly posited norms, and that termination is essential for the humanly posited norms to be more than mere linguistic fragments, the one unconnected with the other.

This authorizing origin of binding humanly posited laws is coloured with an invisibility that both philosophers of the natural law tradition and the legal positivist tradition have heretofore attributed to the divine *arche* of natural laws. For the humanly posited norms, to be binding, need some other author, norm, social experience, or experiential disposition to obey the law, which is radically different from an ordinarily posited norm. To meet this requisite of a radically different origin, the tradition of legal positivism, I show in Chapters Three to Nine, situates the origin outside the officials' language of posited norms. Legal existence, though,

---

7 I use the terms 'rules' and 'norms' synonymously at this point, although we shall see in Chapters Seven and Eight that Kelsen and Hart have very different connotations for each term.

is only constituted from such a language. So the very authorizing origin of the language of legal existence is inaccessible or, perhaps better, invisible to that language.

I claim, in sum, that the great thinkers of the legal positivist tradition were conscious of the need for finality to the posit of rules and norms, that they appreciated the importance of language in one's understanding of the nature of law and that, given their understanding of what constitutes legal language, the authorizing origin of humanly posited laws is understood as prior and external to legal language. Being external to legal language, the origin is inaccessible through the familiar statements of legal officials. Again, I describe such an inaccessibility to language as invisible. The point, then, is that the canons of legal positivism have acknowledged the need for an invisible authorizing origin to the posited laws. The origin, however, exceeds what has been taken as legal language. This origin, utterly foreign to the officials' recognizable written statements about posited rules and norms, ends the trace of humanly posited norms from the grounding of one norm to another.

The officials' unquestioning faith in the possibility of an absent invisibility as the ultimate *arche* of nature of binding laws begs the question, then, as to whether the substantive content of such laws is, indeed, separate from the authority of the laws. How can binding posited laws remain humanly posited if their ultimate grounds are excluded from what is taken as legal existence? Does not legal positivism postulate the very self-creating origin that the natural law tradition, until recently, has attributed to the Judaeo-Christian Author? Is the only difference between the two traditions of natural law and legal positivism that officials create the need for the invisible *arche* in order to complete the project of authoritative posited laws whereas the natural law theorist claims *sui generis* that the *arche* is self-created?

More generally, whether the *arche* is self-starting or created by the officials of civil institutions, can officials and jurists maintain the separation of the authority of posited rules from the substantive content of the rules? I shall argue in the following chapters that the nature of legal authority, according to the tradition of legal positivism, postulates an authorizing origin that takes on different senses of the invisible. What could be more related to the non-legal realm, as defined by legal positivism, than the invisible? And what could be more related to the substantive content of a binding rule than a religious claim or presupposition about the content of the whole positivist legal structure?

Indeed, if the ultimate authorizing origin of humanly posited laws is an invisible *arche*, then do the self-imposed boundaries between natural law theory and positive law theory collapse? Has the boundary been maintained only at the cost of forgetting the invisible character of the ultimate authorizing origin of posited human laws? Do officials insist upon tracing the authority of one norm from another, of one institutional source from another, only at the risk of forgetting the most important postulate of their own theory? Do officials maintain the totality and autonomy of the legal structure of a sovereign state (and its consequential coercion) by forgetting the invisible character and the dire importance of their necessary creation and then by forgetting that they had forgotten such an important element to the nature of law? Have we finally reached an explanation of the role of the modern legal order in the authorizing of evil as well as of good?

1

The Positive Law – Natural Law Dichotomy, Aristotle and the Greek Totemic Legal Culture

1. The Rise of the Positive Law–Natural Law Dichotomy

One can readily appreciate that the tradition of legal positivism has defined itself in terms of an antagonist: natural law theory. Binding laws are considered cognitive objects (rules, principles, doctrines, policies) that human authors have posited. Natural laws are said to transcend such humanly posited objects. If inconsistent with the natural law, a humanly posited rule is void or unauthorized. As such, the humanly posited rule does not exist.

This juxtaposition of legal positivism against natural law theory is not a recent event. The dichotomy makes its first entry into European culture with the rise of the Greek *polis* during the fifth century (B.C.E.). Teachers, historians, orators and philosophers depended upon the city-state for their prestige, recognition and income. Perhaps because they were dependent upon the city-state, the professional teachers (called sophists) privileged the laws that the city-state authored even against the seeming uncontrollable forces of *physis* or nature.

On the one side, the laws or *nomoi* of the city-state are variable, historically and socially contingent, and often arbitrary. The positive laws may be coded in the form of a script, or they may be considered unwritten in the form of customs. Social life is constructed vertically: higher and lower, supreme and subordinate, gods over men, men over women and children, masters over slaves, writing over the unwritten. As with the family,[1] a ruler presides at the pinnacle of the *polis*. The *polis* is believed to posit the laws. The officials may amend or even repeal the *nomoi*. The *nomoi*, whether written in (authored) codes or unwritten in customs, create a legal existence.

1 This is generally discussed in John M. Cooper, "Aristotle on Friendship," in ed. Amelie O. Rorty, *Essays on Aristotle's Ethics* (Berkeley: University of California Press, 1980), 301-40, fn. 35, and in F.M. Cornford, *From Religion to Philosophy: A Study in the Origins of Western Speculation* (New York: Harper, 1957) , 93.

The professional philosophers of the day juxtapose the laws of the *polis* against a radical other: *physis*. Humans may control the *nomoi*; the laws of *physis* are uncontrollable. In contrast with the historically contingent and variable *nomoi*, *physis* is considered determinative of social events. *Physis* arises from forces and events that are independent of human contrivance.[2] *Physis* is something primal, unchanging, and universal. *Physis* transcends human acts and thereby brings stability and order to an ever-changing social and physical world. Political leaders construct religious shrines in the form of human bodies. For the Athenians, divine sources are located at the Delphi. The gods and goddesses enforce the laws of *physis*. Zeus sits at the pinnacle of the hierarchy of gods. Even chance or *moira* is subordinate to Zeus's will. A secret religious group of priestesses is elevated to a status higher than that of living mortals. Mystery and mysticism surround the priestesses. Though the *polis* also served as a guardian of the laws of Zeus, *nomoi* and *physis* struggled for supremacy.

The sophists found little difficulty in justifying why the *nomoi* should be given a binding force over the laws of *physis*. Their arguments took two forms. The first form, which reaches its full fruition in Aristotle, claims that the *polis* is the ultimate source for virtuous living. Socrates states the point in the *Theaetetus*, for example, that

> [a]nd again in social matters, the theory will say that, so far as good and bad customs or rights and wrongs or matters of religion are concerned, whatever any state makes up its mind to enact as lawful for itself, really is lawful for it, and in this field no individual or state is wiser than another.... But ... in right and wrong and matters of religion – people are ready to affirm that none of these things is natural, with a reality of its own, but rather that the public decision becomes true at the moment when it is made and remains true so long as the decision stands.... (*Theaetetus* 172a-b)

Mindful of the "Ode to Man" in Sophocles' *Antigone*, Protagoras privileges the moral supremacy of human action when he declares that man, not *physis*, is the measure of all things (*Theaetetus* 152a). Protagoras makes the same point in Plato's *Protagoras* when he equates ethics with "good judgment" (*euboulia*) in one's own affairs, not with *physis* (*Protagoras* 318d). That is, one would be better able to order one's household and one's city, not by deferring to *physis*, but by receiving a course of instruction. After positing his claim, Protagoras proceeds to describe how civil society originates from the elements of *physis*, how creatures take on speech and names, how men make war against each other in the state of nature (*physis*), and how they must create a *polis* as the formidable way to organize social relations against *physis* (*Protagoras* 320d-322c).

---

2 Glenn R. Morrow, "Plato and the Law of Nature," in eds. Milton R. Konvitz & Arthur E. Murphy, *Essays in Political Theory* (New York: Kennikat Press, 1948), 17-44, 19.

Gorgias goes on to associate a special type of knowledge, a forensic rhetoric, with the *nomoi* (*Gorgias* 449d-454c). The rhetoric is forensic in that, unlike the permanence and order associated with *physis*, the teacher has learned rhetorical techniques to make the audience hear what it wants to hear.[3] Lawyers especially use forensic rhetoric very well (*Theaetetus* 172d-173b). Along these lines and not without some basis, Callicles complains that Socrates himself shifts back and forth between *physis* and *nomos*, depending on how it suits his particular claim (*Gorgias* 483). The bond of friendship offers a less cynical justification why the *nomoi* of the *polis* should prevail over the determinative laws of *physis*. The ultimate human construct, the social contract, justifies the supremacy of the laws of the city-state, a justification that remains to this day (*Republic* 359a-b). Even Socrates in the Speech of the Laws in the *Crito* defers to such a contract as the reason why Socrates himself was ethically bound to accept his verdict rather than to escape to an island (*Crito* 50a-51c).

The sophists justified the supremacy of humanly posited laws in a second manner. Here, philosophers frame their arguments in terms of a determinative *physis*. Callicles himself appeals to a controlling *physis* because *physis*, he claims, dictates that it is just for the better to rule the worse and that the strong should rule the weak (*Gorgias* 483b-484b). Thrasymachus too takes up the importance of *physis* in the *Republic*, only to argue that *physis* coincides with the *nomoi* of the *polis* (*Republic* 338e). Glaucon also privileges *physis* only to claim that *physis* warrants that the strongest men legislate human laws (*Republic* 359c). The *nomoi* of the *polis* manifest just such a natural law. One ought to obey the *nomoi*, however unjust. And the moral content of the *nomoi* of one *polis* will vary from the content of the *nomoi* in another. Even if there were some intrinsic Good, legislators could not impart their virtues to others (*Protagoras* 320). This was so because *physis* overrides wisdom and *physis*, in particular, tends to produce strong men. Hippias declares, for example, that everyone present, and perhaps all Greeks, are kinsmen and fellow citizens *by nature*, not by despotic *nomos* (337c-d). Accordingly, in order to constrain the naturally strong men, the sophists argue, it is necessary for a city-state to enact and enforce binding laws. As to the claim that the *polis* is created from a social contract, it was countered that the cosmos had been created by Fate or what the Romans later called *fortuna*. As such, the substantive moral content of laws exceeded the scrutiny of human agents; yet, the content remained relative to the particular interests of the rulers of a sovereign *polis*.

In sum, *nomoi* manifested the supremacy of *physis*; yet, precisely because *physis* required that it was in the interest of citizens to constrain the strongest men, the

---

3 See the analysis of R.E. Allen, *Socrates and Legal Obligation* (Minneapolis: University of Minnesota Press, 1980), 10-13.

nomoi were considered supreme over *physis*. Whether the authorizing origin of the *polis*'s laws was located in convention or in nature, the substantive content of the *nomoi* was separate from the authority of the *nomoi* themselves. The contemporary Anglo-American professional law school did not create the theory and practice of legal positivism.

By the time that Plato (428–348 B.C.E.) and Aristotle (384–322 B.C.E.) arrive on the cultural scene, the aim of the laws of the city-state is to teach the ruled how to be just in social relations. The laws are considered human constructs rather than objects determined by *physis*. Indeed, Aristotle claims that Socrates (469–399 B.C.E.) had, in the construction of his arguments about the Good life, entirely ignored *physis (Metaphysics* 987b1). In the *Apology*, Socrates admits that he finds it unnecessary to theorize about the laws of the heavens or the laws of the gods in the netherworld (*Apology* 18b). *Nomoi* are believed to constrain and guide the inexorable laws of nature so as to inculcate virtuous conduct by ruler and ruled alike. So Socrates' student, Plato, shifts the study of law from the inexorable laws of *physis* to the question 'what virtuous conduct is necessary for the human creation of a Good life?' Even when philosophers appeal to some originary social contract as the ultimate authorizing ground of posited laws, they realize that such a contract does not actually describe a past or present state of affairs. Rather, as Protagoras argues, the 'social contract' is introduced as an analytic tool to disentangle the constituent elements of the *polis*. What exists by *nomos* does not exist by *physis*, and what exists by virtue of *physis* does not exist by *nomos*. The rise of *nomoi* brings with it the division of the cosmic order into only two possibilities: contingent human laws and uncontrollable natural laws. A void dwells between humanly posited laws and natural laws.

2. The Constraint of the Positive Law–Natural Law Dichotomy

The positive law–natural law dichotomy remains with us today. It represents an either–or structure of possibilities within which one interprets the works of jurists and the reasoning of officials. Since Augustine and Aquinas, some jurists and officials have associated natural laws with a First Author who has created the natural and human worlds according to a thought plan. Those human laws that contradict the natural laws are considered invalid and, therefore, non-existent. With Thomas Hobbes, if not earlier writers, positive laws have been grounded in an author's writing. Action that lacks a trace to the author is without authority. If one cannot trace an official's action to such an author, then the action is illegal and unjust. The problem is that, once one reads legal phenomena in terms of the dichotomy, other possibilities as to why are laws authoritative are excluded. And particular philosophies that attempt to explain why human laws are authoritative are over-simplified.

Such an over-simplification characterizes commentaries about Aristotle's texts concerning law, for example. Leading scholars have associated Aristotle with both legal positivism and natural law. Once so labelled, the interpreter has ignored some passages, privileged others and read the privileged passages in a particular manner that reinforces the wisdom of the label.

On the one hand, for example, Thomas Aquinas, John Locke, Frederick Pollock, John Salmond, and Alasdair MacIntyre draw upon book V of the *Ethics* in order to elaborate a hierarchy of laws with natural law at the apex.[4] Leading scholars of the natural law tradition have located Aristotle in this tradition. One can retrieve such a view from A.P. d'Entrèves, Anton-Hermann Chroust, John Finch, and Paul Sigmund.[5] Hinting at a problem which will be encountered in my reading of Aristotle's works in a moment, however, Sigmund adds that "[h]owever, aside from the references to the *Antigone*, his work contains no attempt to spell out the details of this universal natural law nor to use it to invalidate existing laws."

4 Thomas Aquinas (1225–1274) is often understood, for example, as articulating 'classical' natural law. Claiming only to be an interpreter of Aristotle, Aquinas elaborated a theory of divine and natural laws that posited a supreme invisible Author as the creator of nature. Natural laws were subordinate to divine laws and these, in turn, to eternal laws. Eternal laws governed God and divine laws were the translation of the eternal laws to human behaviour. Without a doubt, Aquinas associated natural laws with a determinative sense of nature. Natural laws constituted legal existence. They were not the 'oughts' attributed to natural laws by contemporary legal theory. Thomas Aquinas, *Summa of Theology* I-11, q. 90, ad. 3, ed. Mary T. Clark, *An Aquinas Reader* (Garden City, New York: Image, 1972), 368. From the Book V passage of Aristotle's *Ethics*, Locke concludes that "it is rightly inferred that there exists some law of nature, since there exists some law, which obtains everywhere." John Locke, *Questions concerning the Law of Nature*, folio 13 (Ithaca: Cornell University Press, 1990). Also see Frederick Pollock, "The History of the Law of Nature" in *Essays in the Law* (London: Macmillan, 1922), 31-79, esp. 32-45. Salmond concludes from the Book V passage as well as from Aristotle's reference to *Antigone* in the *Rhetoric* that "[i]n these passages we see natural law recognized in its various aspects." John W. Salmond, "The Law of Nature," *Law Quarterly Review* **11** (1895): 121-43, 127. Alasdair MacIntyre argues that the reference to natural laws "everywhere having the same force" in the *Ethics* does not contradict the claim that natural justice makes certain human conduct bad in itself. MacIntyre, *Whose Justice? Which Rationality?* (Notre Dame, Indiana: University of Notre Dame Press, 1988), chap. 7, 121.

5 A.P. d'Entrèves, *Natural Law: An Introduction to Legal Philosophy* (London: Hutchinson University Library, 1970), 13-16. More recently, Anton-Hermann Chroust, a past editor of *Natural Law Forum*, locates Aristotle in a long established tradition which "contrary to some ill-advised opinions . . . can definitely be traced back to the teachings of the so-called 'Pre-Socratics'." Chroust "On the Nature of Natural Law," in ed. Paul Sayre, *Interpretation of Modern Legal Philosophers: Essays in Honor of Roscoe Pound* (New York: Oxford University Press, 1947), 70-84, esp. fn. 5. John Finch claims that Aristotle gave "a new found philosophical impetus to the doctrine of the law of nature and had avoided and eliminated the mystery which had characterized certain of the earlier doctrines." John Finch, *Introduction to Legal Theory* (London: Sweet & Maxwell, 1979; 3d ed.), 31. And, after a close study of natural law theory, Paul Sigmund concludes that "[f]rom all these cases it seems clear that Aristotle believed in the existence of some common legal principles which are universal and based on nature." Sigmund, *Natural Law in Political Thought* (Cambridge, Mass: Winthrop, 1971), 10.

On the other hand, Aristotle has also been interpreted as a foremost philosopher of positive law. Perhaps, the closest reading along these lines was offered by Hans Kelsen, who claimed that Aristotle had glorified positive law.[6] Heinrich Rommen offered that although Aristotle was considered the "father of natural law," "the natural law does not dwell in a region beyond the positive law."[7] C.K. Allen relied upon the same passages noted above in the *Ethics* and *Rhetoric* as support for a natural law theory, only to conclude that a "particular equity," which supplied the deficiencies of positive law, should not be construed as subordinating positive law to moral principles.[8] More recently, Fred Miller has argued that Aristotle does not leave a place for natural rights independent of a pre-political state of nature.[9] And the foremost English-speaking text in jurisprudence concludes that although

> natural law thinking has occupied a pervasive role in the realm of ethics, politics, and law from the time of Greek civilization ... even Aristotle, for whom nature played a cardinal role in the unfolding of man's social development, was so little interested in natural law in the form of normative rules that he contented himself with a passing reference to the distinction between natural and conventional justice, while immediately qualifying this by pointing out that, among men, even natural justice is not necessarily unchanging.[10]

How is it possible that such leading scholars associate Aristotle's works with both the natural law and the legal positivism traditions? Is it possible that the interpreters themselves have worked within a paradigm that excludes the precise understanding which Aristotle himself had intended? Returning to the *nomos/physis* distinction of the sophists, for example, is it possible that interpreters have associated positive laws with writing and natural laws with the unwritten? Aristotle refers to "natural justice," "general laws," "universal laws," "the law of nature,"

---

6 Kelsen, "Aristotle and Hellenic-Macedonian Policy," in *Ethics* **48-9** (1937-39): 1-64, esp. 28-51. Also see Kelsen, "Aristotle's Doctrine of Justice," in *What is Justice?* (Berkeley: University of California Press, 1971), 110-36.

7 Heinrich A. Rommen, *The Natural Law: A Study in Legal and Social History and Philosophy* (St. Louis & London: B. Herdu, 1949), 16-18.

8 C.K. Allen, *Law in the Making* (Oxford: Clarenden, 1964; 3d ed.), 390.

9 Fred D. Miller, *Nature, Justice and Rights in Aristotle's* Politics (Oxford: Clarendon, 1995). Miller explains in "Aristotle and the Origins of Natural Rights," *Review of Metaphysics* **49** (June 1996): 873-907 that there is no sense of rights against the *polis* in Aristotle. Richard Kraut has argued that Aristotle does have a concept of natural rights, although it plays no role in his theory of the state. Richard Kraut, "Are there Natural Rights in Aristotle?" in *Review of Metaphysics* **49** (June 1996): 755-74.

10 Lloyd of Hampstead and M.D.A. Freeman, *Lloyd's Introduction to Jurisprudence* (London: Stevens; Toronto: Carswell, 1985, 5th ed.), 92, 106, citing *Ethics* V, 1134b. Edgar Bodenheimer expresses a similar caution when, after identifying the theory of natural justice with Aristotle, he continues that "the Aristotelian notion of natural justice has been obscured by the passages." *Jurisprudence: The Philosophy and Method of the Law* (Cambridge, Mass: Harvard University Press, 1962; 1974), 12.

and "equity." Do these universal laws draw from the sophists' *nomos/physis* dichotomy or, instead, from an earlier culture that had preceded the *nomos/physis* dichotomy?

3. The Determinative Sense of Natural Laws

Let us take an initial look at Aristotle's works in order to appreciate how he might have understood natural laws in terms of a *physis*. Here, Aristotle takes *physis* as a biological and physical determinism. It is a determinism from which Aristotle draws in the early part of the *Politics*, for example, when he describes the natural difference between men and women. Male and female are united "not of choice, but because, in common with other animals and plants, mankind have a natural desire to leave behind them an image of themselves" (I, 2, 1252a 25-27). This determinative *physis* leads to a natural impulse for men and women to procreate. Aristotle even considers the family as a natural institution in that biological needs and desires cause the family to grow. Secondly, Aristotle adopts a determinative signification of nature when he suggests that nature grants some beings foresight "by the exercise of mind" and others, bodily strength. This biological difference leads "by nature" to slavery and to a ruler/ruled relationship, according to Aristotle. And so, a "natural slave" is a slave "everywhere" in all societies when a human creature's body is naturally inferior in brute strength (I, 5, 1254b 25).[11] Thus, there is a natural impulse to dominate physically over others. Thirdly, Aristotle appeals to a determinative *physis* when he describes the physical need for food, shelter and clothing. Such physical needs include "men's everyday wants" (I, 2, 1252b 14), "the supply of daily needs" (1252b 17), and "the bare needs of life" (1252b 30). Biologically determinative needs for food, shelter and clothing impel human beings to associate with each other in a family.

Aristotle takes the determinative sense of *physis* further when, in the *Politics*, he associates the final end of a human organism, *eudaemonia*, with *physis*. *Eudaemonia* involves the capacity to flourish in characteristically human capacities. Speech and reason are such natural capacities.[12] *Eudaemonia* is an activity that one exercises *with others* over a lifetime.[13] In order to make one's thought practical vis-à-vis others, one must exist socially with other human beings. Even if *eudaemonia* were reached through pure contemplation, as he suggests in the

11 Aristotle contrasts a natural slave with a slave by convention, such as exists after a Greek city-state has conquered another city-state in a just war (*Politics* I, 6, 1255a 23-4).

12 In the *Politics*, Aristotle defines *eudaemonia* as "the realization and perfect exercise of excellence, and this not conditional, but absolute." VII, 13, 1332a 9-10.

13 "For one swallow does not make a summer, nor does one day." *Politics* I, 7, 1098 a18.

final book of the *Ethics* (X, 7, 1178b 29),[14] a human organism needs other humans in order to reach a purely contemplative state.[15] Without food and the other necessaries provided by others, for example, the organic body would not survive and, without the organic body, the mind would not survive (X, 7, 1179a 25-b13). Put another way, pure contemplation, without others, is for God alone. Nature intercedes between man and his thoughts so as to render human thought impure or, at least, to produce a more complex *physis*. Drawing from Aristotle's characterization of human beings as "rational animals," one part is higher and more god-like (the rational part of one's soul) and the other is lower and biological (the animal part of one's soul). As the nature of the *cosmos* is responsible for the exaltation of the *cosmos*, *physis* is not an impediment. The human organism, accordingly, possesses an incomplete *eudaemonia*. A complete or divine-like *eudaemonia* is absent from the human organism precisely because of the intervention of *physis*. Being incomplete, a human being must strive to reach *eudaemonia* with others. The quest to fulfil what is absent from an organism leads to the conclusion that "man is a political creature and one whose nature is to live with others" (IX, 9, 1169b 18). As he puts it early in the *Politics*, "[b]ut he who is unable to live in society, or who has no need because he is sufficient for himself, must be either a beast or a god: he is no part of a state" (I, 2, 1253a 27-28).

Aristotle joins this determinative sense of *physis* with natural justice in book V of the *Ethics*. Natural justice is said to be "unchangeable" and "by nature," having "the same force everywhere" (V, 7, 1134b 24-25). His example, again, is the natural phenomenon that fire burns both in Athens and in Persia. In sum, many of Aristotle's writings reflect a determinative sense of nature.

4. The Exclusionary Character of the *Nomos-Physis* Dichotomy

So far, Aristotle's works seem to support the view that the historically contingent laws of the state may clash with the determinative laws of *physis* and that the former were subordinate to the latter. But, working within the *nomos-physis* paradigm, a certain problematic comes to the fore. If one accepted the determinative character of nature and if the human laws of the *polis* were subordinate to the determinative natural laws, there would be no need for legal institutions to depart from the pre-determined course directed by *physis*. *Nomos* could only supplement the universal laws of *physis*.

---

14 He argues that "he who exercises his intellect and cultivates it seems to be both in the best state and most dear to the gods." X, 7, 1179a 23.

15 This is discussed generally in John M. Cooper, "Aristotle on Friendship," in ed. Amelie O. Rorty, *Essays on Aristotle's Ethics* (Berkeley: University of California Press, 1980), 301-40, esp. 327, 330-34; and in John M. Cooper, "Aristotle on the Forms of Friendship," *Review of Metaphysics* **30** (1976-77): 619-48, esp. 645-48.

But the problem is that Aristotle's theory of law is incoherent if one understands his view of universal, natural laws as manifestations of an uncontrollable *physis*. Aristotle's theory of laws just does not fit either with human laws or with *physis*.

The first set of problems arises from Aristotle's claim that the universal natural laws are the consequence of an art, not *physis*. First, law-making is an art not unlike education, he writes in the *Ethics* (X, 9, 1181a 12-1181b 10). As an art, "a previous training and habituation" help the citizen to practise excellence (*Politics* VIII, 1, 1337a 20-21). So laws inculcate the unwritten and unspoken assumptions of the citizen in contrast with the laws of a *physis* which, as an internal source of movement of change, human beings cannot control. Unwritten customs are inculcated through human conduct; *physis* is uncontrollable. A human being is vulnerable to uncontrollable external natural forces, although some natural phenomena are internal to the organism. The problem that Aristotle presents is this: if law-making is an "art" or inculcated rather than the consequence of *physis*, how is it possible to describe such laws of an art as "universal" and "natural"? Further, if the universal laws are "unchangeable," how can they remain an "art," for an art infers that the laws evolve over time? Further, Aristotle claims that the coded laws of the *polis* depend upon the unwritten customs for their efficacy. If the state's laws depend upon the unwritten for their efficacy, how can one still maintain that the state's authority is sovereign and that the ruler's consciously posited commands alone constitute binding laws? Surely, there must be something more originary than the *polis* in order to ground the authority of humanly posited laws.

These issues cannot be resolved if one remains within the *nomos-physis* binary. For the binary excludes the possibility that there are universal laws that are, first, not from a determinative *physis,* and yet, second, are constructed by human beings. Because of the unwritten character of laws, it is difficult to speak of an author of them. And a written or coded enactment of the *polis* is presumed to possess a pre-existing author. A custom emanates internally from *within* the consciousness of a citizen, not from a distinct and assignable legislature. The unwritten goes to the content of the laws: the unwritten is believed, not reasoned nor posited. The binary of natural law–positive law thereby structures the sorts of questions that one may ask. The alternative to the written laws of the sovereign *polis* is left confused and incoherent.

It is difficult to label Aristotle a legal positivist or a natural law philosopher because of a second set of problems. Aristotle is often quoted for the claim that the laws of nature are universal. For example, he describes "natural justice" in the *Ethics* as "everywhere having the same force" (1134b 24-25). Further, he writes in the *Politics* that natural justice "does not exist by people's thinking this or that" (*Politics* VII, 7, 1334b 18-19). In the same vein, he writes that natural justice is "common to all, even to those who have no association or covenant with each other" (I, 3, 1373b 3-6). Aristotle assures us in the *Rhetoric* that Antigone had these laws in mind when she stated that the law to which she felt bound was "not of to-day or yesterday it is, But lives eternal: none can date its birth." Aristotle also cites Empedocles, who had claimed that the law against murder manifested "an all-embracing law through the realms of the sky unbroken it stretcheth, and over the earth's immensity" (*Rhetoric* I, 13, 1373b 16-17).

The problem is that, even though Aristotle describes the natural laws in such a strong universalist character, he also insists that they are historically and socially contingent. In the *Ethics*, for example, he claims that natural justice is changeable when applied to citizens. He exemplifies the point in *Magna Moralia* (1194b 30-1195a 8) when he reminds one that the right hand is stronger by nature, although it is possible that all men could become ambidextrous. Though nature determines human action to be one thing, the action is capable of being otherwise. And in the *Rhetoric*, Aristotle admits that natural justice depends upon social censure for its efficacy (1374a 21-23).[16] Also, natural justice depends upon written codes. Without writing, it would be difficult to speak of gaps that equity could fill (1374a 26). These social contingencies render suspect any interpretation of the universalist laws in terms of a universal determinative *physis*. How can natural laws be determinative if they are also socially contingent? And how can they be written, if they transcend the contingencies of the written?

Aristotle's works offer a third problem if one remains within a paradigm that attributes the nature of law in terms of either determinative universal laws or socially contingent authored codes. If the universal laws, which ground the codes of the *polis*, are universal and unchangeable, how can the determinative laws allow for revolutionary change? Indeed, is there a necessary relationship between the universal laws and social contingency? If *physis* is the determining factor of the universal laws, may social-cultural practice diverge from the universal laws? For example, although Aristotle describes sexual difference in terms of a determinative nature, in *The Constitution of Athens,* he also describes sexual difference as an important issue in understanding the constitution of a *polis*. The form of a constitution may remain the same even though its particular content may evolve to the point that the content is unrecognizable. The content of a constitution shifts like the chorus of a tragedy and a comedy even though the chorus remains the same (*Ethics* III, 3, 1276b 5). Similarly, though the form of music may remain the same, different musicians will produce the form differently. The melody will depend upon whether its compositional scheme is Dorian or Phrygian (*Ethics* III, 3,

16 Conduct may spring from "exceptional goodness or badness" and yet, meet "with censure and loss of honour, or with praise and increase of honour and decorations." He offers the example of "gratitude to, or requittal of, our benefactors, readiness to help our friends, and the like."

1276b 9). A *polis*, like the actors or musicians, is "a partnership." When the partnership evolves into a new compound, its content projects a different *telos*. The *telos* is drawn from the social practices (or matter) of the compound. The laws no longer remain the same. In sum, though the form seems determinative of the content of the laws, the socially contingent laws actually construct the form. One oversimplifies Aristotle's universal laws by understanding law either as determinative or, alternatively, as posited by human rulers. Universal laws are not determinative if socially contingent practices mould the content of the universal laws. Nor are they determinative if the same populace may evolve to the point that its government varies in form. Some other sense of 'law' must be considered to explain Aristotle's texts.

5. The Figurative Sense of Natural Laws

The key to the problematic of the *nomos-physis* dichotomy is that the paradigm excludes a figurative sense of nature that Aristotle had in mind when he elaborated his general theory of universal laws. Here, Aristotle considers laws which, though constructed by human beings over time, seem natural because ruler and ruled alike fuse or identify immediately with them. Such laws seem so natural that Aristotle, following Plato in the *Laws*, describes them as of "a second nature." What binds a society together, according to Aristotle, is the sense of immediacy with which the citizen feels bonded with a social practice: "[t]he state, as I was saying, is a plurality, which should be united and made into a community by education," he suggests in the *Politics* (II, 5, 1263b 36-37). Without such a sense of immediate bonding, "[t]he best laws, though sanctioned by every citizen of the state, will be of no avail unless the young are trained by *habit* and *education* in the spirit of the constitution" (V, 9, 1310a 14-17).[17] The laws of a second nature, unlike the *physis* of a first nature, are not uncontrollable and uncontrolled by human beings. "Let us remember," he emphasizes in the *Politics*, "one should not disregard the experience of the ages" (II, 5, 1263b 42-1254a 4).

A custom seems uncontrolled and uncontrollable precisely because of the identity of the citizen with the custom's content, Aristotle writes. The immediacy of a custom disguises the coercive character of an authored law. A custom makes the coercion less painful, he argues in the *Ethics* (X, 9, 1179b 33-34). The *nomos* part of the natural law/positive law excludes a figurative sense of natural law because the *nomoi* are supposed to be consciously authored by the rulers of the *polis*. However, the customs are un-authored. The customs are lived in the unconscious. They are taken for granted. They are not the subject of identification, articulation

17 Emphasis added.

and conscious reflection. Ruler and ruled feel constrained by the universal laws, yet the laws are unwritten and, therefore, un-authored by some ruler. The unwritten laws need no hierarchy of juridical officials with an author at the pinnacle to render its binding character.[18]

Aristotle is not alone here in his elaboration of natural laws "in the second sense." Plato hints at such a figurative sense of nature in the *Laws* when he too describes the universal laws of "a second nature." Here, unwritten and unspoken customs are accepted by ruler and ruled alike *as if* they were 'natural.' The very immediacy or felt bonding with the customs prevents the social practice from being distinguished from the citizen's actions. In the *Laws*, for example, Plato refers to the unwritten laws against incest as possessing this very immediacy. As the Athenian puts it in the *Laws*, a citizen's "lawless natures" feel strictly and precisely restrained by unwritten laws which are "not at all against their will, but entirely with their will" (VIII, 838d).

Hegel too aspires to retrieve just such a natural law in the second sense in his philosophy of *Recht*. Hegel calls such a social bonding between citizen and laws, a *Sittlichkeit*. Early Greek tribes, according to Hegel, experienced what Hegel calls a primitive *Sittlichkeit*.[19] Though there was hardly a sense of an autonomous individual in the tribal culture, the consciousness of the tribal member united with the tribal community. Customs were a critical element of *Recht*. This immediacy between tribal member and community contrasts with a reflective *Sittlichkeit*, such as may have existed amongst the citizenry of classical Athens according to Hegel. In a reflective *Sittlichkeit*, a citizen self-consciously and deliberately acts in accord with Goodness as nested in the community's culture. An authored code manifests such a self-conscious and deliberate reflection.

With this second sense of natural laws in hand, Aristotle's commentaries about universal, natural, general laws appear more coherent. Unwritten customs do change over time and yet, they do not change "by people's thinking this or that" in some self-reflective manner as occurs with respect to an authored code. Unwritten customs are unauthored in that they do not possess an identifiable source. The un-

18 I shall argue in subsequent chapters that this pyramidal hierarchy permeates the writings of Austin, Kelsen, Raz and others. Foucault describes the pyramid as the 'royalty model of sovereignty' in Michel Foucault, "Two Lectures" in *Power/Knowledge: Selected Interviews and Other Writings, 1972-1977* (New York: Pantheon, 1980), 91-97, and connects the pyramid to the modern bureaucratic state in "Governmentality" in eds. Graham Burchell, Colin Gordon and Peter Miller, *The Foucault Effect* (Chicago: University of Chicago Press, 1991), 87-104. Foucault discusses how a discourse constructs the externally situated author in "What is an Author?" in ed. Paul Rabinow, *The Foucault Reader* (New York: Pantheon, 1984), 101-20.

19 Hegel describes a primitive *Sittlichkeit* in *Phenomenology of Spirit*, trans. A.V. Miller, fwd. J.N. Findley (Oxford: Oxford University Press, 1977), para. 440, 441 and 444.

written laws seem "natural" precisely because the rulers and ruled feel bonded with them. The determinative laws of *physis* lack such an internal sense of bonding for the laws of *physis* are posited beyond the control of citizen and official. Although natural justice may be invariant, Aristotle supports the thinner claim that human beings treat justice as variable. This is so even with matters about which justice may not be variable.

Contrary to the sophists' distant objective *physis*, Aristotle describes how natural laws emanate from the social experiences of a particular *polis*. Aristotle does so both in his theoretical expositions of universal laws in the *Politics* and the *Ethics* and in his descriptive account of the Athenian constitution in *The Constitution of Athens*. Each society – at least the rulers of each society – strives to attain or to fulfil the form (end) embedded in its matter (social practices). Upon reaching its end, the matter changes to such a point that the form of the legal structure shifts into a new form. Thus, a society's legal order is "perverted" or unnatural if its rulers pursue a legal form that has not emanated from its social practices in their historical context. This is so even if the rulers were to superimpose an ethically better legal form upon the society.[20] Conversely, a constitutional form is natural if it is embedded within the existing social practices and the historical context of a particular society.[21] So, for example, a monarchical constitution is natural if its social practices elevate one citizen as pre-eminently more virtuous over all others. But a monarchial constitution, as a legal form, is unnatural or "perverted" for a particular society if all of its citizens are equally virtuous with an equal capacity to rule and to be ruled. Aristotle can only speak of the best constitution in the circumstances, not of an ideal constitution. One is left to conclude that natural laws, just as a natural constitution, do not evolve in as involuntary a manner as does a flower, let alone *physis* generally. Rather, laws evolve naturally when a citizen is immediate with the legal forms in that the forms are drawn from social practices with which the citizen identifies.

So one errs if one reads Aristotle as supporting some determinative sense of nature just as one also errs if one reads Aristotle as supporting some authorial or

20 This point is discussed in A.C. Bradley, "Aristotle's Conception of the State," in ed. Evelyn Abbott, *Hellenica: A Collection of Essays on Greek Poetry, Philosophy, History and Religion* (New York: Longmans, Green, 1907; 2d ed.), 166-222, at 205-06. As Bradley puts it, an imperfect constitution is the best which a society can achieve "because it is the natural outcome of a given social condition. Given a certain material, a population of a certain kind and in a definite degree of civilization, and there is a form or order naturally fitted for it; and no other order, however superior it would be in better circumstances, is better for *it*" (205). However, Curtis Johnson argues that the best constitution is reached when the good citizen is a good man. "Who is Aristotle's Citizen?" in *Phronesis* **29** (1984): 73-90.

21 For an analysis of Aristotle's forms of democracy see Mortimer Chambers, "Aristotle's 'Forms of Democracy'" in American Philological Assoc., *Transactions and Proceedings* **92** (1961): 20-36.

legislative sense of positive law. "But some qualities [of human virtue]," he asserts in the *Politics*, "there is no use in having at birth" (VII, 13, 39-40). That is, a determinative *physis* does not produce virtues. Why not? Because virtues are a human art, "altered by habit." The laws of the *polis* mould and influence what is unwritten. Habit turns some naturally endowed gifts (in the determinative sense of 'naturally') into good or bad conduct (VII, 13, 1332b 2). The good or bad conduct is thereby socially contingent, not a permanent fixture of *physis*. One had best understand the nature of law in terms of unstated habits that inculcate the virtues of the good citizen. "Let us remember," Aristotle emphasizes in the *Politics*, "one should not disregard the experience of ages" (II, 5, 1263b 42-1254a 4). Even legislatures enact codes with education in view: "[a]ll else is the work of education; we learn some things by habit and some by instruction" (1332b 10-11). So Aristotle adds habit and reason to the requisites of a well-governed *polis* in the *Politics* (VII, 13, 39-40).

6. The Laws of the Totemic Culture

Now, what is important in appreciating the limited and exclusionary character of the positive law/natural law paradigm is that the dichotomy only arose *after* the *polis* had displaced a culture when the unwritten customs had unified both *nomos* and *physis*. During the earliest period of Greek philosophy, that of totemic religions of the Minoan (2000 B.C.E.) and Mycenean (1500 B.C.E.) cultures, the *nomoi* and *physis* were one and the same. Legal authority did not ultimately rest in a pyramidal hierarchy of officials in a city-state nor in a similar hierarchy of gods and goddesses in the netherworld. The *nomos-physis* binary was unnecessary as an explanatory or justificatory tool. Laws just *seemed* to be all-controlling. They were not written down in scripts such as Solon's Code. The unwritten laws could not even be identified with a personalized author or source. Being unwritten and authorless, the laws could not be traced to some higher authority. Indeed, legal authority did not rest with an authorizing origin or *arche* to which conventions could be traced. Nor were they the subject of reflection when enforced.

And yet, the unwritten laws were believed to constrain both the gods and tribal members. The constraints seemed natural, universal, everlasting and uncontrollable. No mortal could ignore or override the universal spirits of the netherworld. Even the gods, including Zeus, were subject to the justice of the netherworld.

The closest word we have to associate with this non-modern sense of legal authority is Fate or *Moira*. *Moira* was impersonal, without an identity, without a will and without a particular origin in time and space. *Moira*, in a sense, was prelegal if one takes the *nomoi* of the *polis* of fifth century (B.C.E.) Greece as manifesting 'the legal.' Preceding the language of the *nomoi*, indeed preceding the speech of the public realm of the *agor*, *Moira* was inaccessible to the later language of the *polis*. Perhaps the closest to which a human being could access *Moira* was through the oracles of the priestesses. Women played important ritualistic roles in the reverence to this invisible *Moira*.[22] Women presided over totemic religious ceremonies. Women were deified. Women entertained and participated in festivals. But because day-to-day experiences were so overwhelmed with natural events, rituals exalted natural events as a manifestation of *Moira*. Magic coloured the human effort to understand the uncontrollable. Droughts, military disasters, and disease were explained as nature's reaction to the errors of human *hubris*.

Antigone appealed to just such a unifed view of *nomos* and *physis*, for example, when she claimed that she was bonded to the "unfailing and unwritten laws of heaven." One would invariably be unsuccessful in attempting to overcome the power of such *Moira* in the totemic culture. What was the sanction for disobedience of *Moira*? After all, as the *polis* did not yet exist, the *polis* could not enforce *Moira*. *Moira*, instead, spoke through the unconscious of the tribal member. If a god exceeded the limits imposed by *Moira*, *nemesis* wrecked havoc upon the Hellenes. Anguish overcame a member who violated the universal laws of *Moira*. The spirits of a netherworld meted out justice through the human experience of dread.

Cornford points out that the *Moira* in the *Illiad* allotted jurisdiction to each god.[23] The word 'destiny' is derived from this sense attributed to *Moira*. *Moira* (destiny), *Nemesis* (avenging anger) and *Dike* (justice) were associated with the allotted place of a god in the cosmic order. So too, all human beings and all tribes were allotted a place in this cosmic order. Since the unfailing laws of heaven controlled all human action, all tribal members were equal before the law: the spirits applied *Moira* universally to each human being and to each god/goddess. Aristotle expresses this earlier sense of legal equality under *Moira* when he writes that the laws of the netherworld were "common to all, even to those who have no association or covenant with each other" (*Rhetoric* I, 13, 1373b 8-9). In contrast with the later posit of (authored) codes as exemplified in the codes of the great legislator Solon, tribal rulers did not put the laws of *Moira* into written form. Nor did any invisible author create *Moira*. *Moira* placed all human rulers in a special role in the cosmic order. Even the chief of a tribe or clan was subject to the impersonal *Moira* that was enforced by the spirits of the netherworld. A tribal chief could not claim to have authored the laws of the tribe.[24] Nor could one locate a time and place

---

22 See generally, Georg Thomson, *Studies in Ancient Greek Society: The Prehistoric Aegean* (London: Lawrence & Wishart, 1954; 1949), esp. chap. 5-7; B.C. Dietrich, *The Origins of Greek Religion* (Berlin, New York: Walter de Gruter, 1974), chap. 2 & 3.

23 Cornford, *From Religion to Philosophy*, 93, 103.

24 Jean-Pierre Vernant, *Myth and Society in Ancient Greece*, trans. Janet Lloyd (New Jersey: Humanities Press, 1974), 16.

when and where a particular law had been promulgated. Even Zeus was subject to *Moira* during this early period.[25] Zeus dispensed the laws; Zeus did not author them. Zeus was identified as the author of the universal laws at a far later date, with the rise of the *polis* and the legislative acts of the *polis*'s rulers.

Moira was impersonal. *Moira* exceeded the control of the ruled as well as of the ruler. A tribal member did not reflect about *Moira* before acting: Antigone just went out and buried her brother's corpse because the unwritten customs required that she do so. She faced a very serious sanction if she did not do so. The ruled felt constrained by *Moira*. The ruled lacked the freedom to choose or to legislate moral rules for oneself as is claimed for the individual in a modern liberal state. *Moira* situated the tribal member in a cosmic order, not just in a special role in a tribe. The inexorable emotive power of *Moira* left human striving futile. *Moros* meant 'appointed death.' The goddesses, called *Moirai*, appointed death. The *Moirai* were not personified in the *Agam*. Because *physis* (nature) unified the human and divine worlds so as to reinforce an homogenous order, *Moira* seemed inevitable, impersonal, and natural. *Moira* dwelled beyond the control of human agents. *Moira* was uncontrolled and uncontrollable.

It is not surprising that the tribes and clans should consider that nature – the nature of desert storms and plagues and epidemics – manifested *Moira*. The overpowering control of nature was assimilated into the rituals and social practices of the tribe. Magical ceremonies exalted nature. The survival of the tribe itself depended upon the constraints of natural phenomena so much so that fifth-century sophists transformed the impersonal authorless sense of *Moira* into an external determinative *physis*.[26] In this displacement of *Moira* with *physis*, the sophists forgot that the early Greek tribes had considered *nomos* and *physis* as one and the same.

From the collapse of this totemic culture toward the end of the second millenium (B.C.E.) until the rise of the city-state in the middle of the first, the sense of the

---

25 Ibid., 104.

26 Empedocles was one such philosopher. John Burnet explains that Empedocles began with Parmenides' view of an indestructible 'what is' as the sole reality. But Empedocles argued that this indestructible 'what is' was not entirely homogeneous and continuous. Rather, substance was created from four natural elements: fire, air, earth and water. These elements were eternal. But because they constituted a heterogeneous mixture, "strife" permeated them. Burnet, *Early Greek Philosophy* (London: A and C Black, 1930; 4th ed.), 227-33.

According to Guthrie, Empedocles translated this interpretation of nature through the lens of *Dike* or Justice. Guthrie, *A History*, 346. As a complement of *Moira*, *Dike* forbade the generation or termination of any physical object. Divine laws were associated with *Moira*. Thus, they were eternal and immutable. According to Guthrie, Parmenides, Empedocles, Heraclitus and Anaximander shared the belief that *physis* was associated with *Moira*. Ibid., 353.

Also see Guthrie, *In the Beginning: Some Greek Views on the Origins of Life and the Early State of Man* (Ithaca: Cornell University Press, 1957), chap. 1-3.

divine, as a radical other to the *nomoi* of the *polis*, was ambiguous. With the sense of the divine shared by the pre-Dorian clans, an inexorable authorless destiny was attributed to *Moira*. This impersonal destiny constrained all acts of the gods and goddesses as well as all human acts. Tribal members worshipped female divinities who interpreted *Moira*. With the sense of the divine associated with the Dorian warrior tribes, the warrior god, Zeus, presided over the universal laws: *Moira* was now considered subordinate to the pyramidal structure of gods and goddesses. Athena, the daughter of Zeus, represented both *Moira* and Zeus. *Moira* comes to be manifested through the signs of the gods. The invading warrior clans believed that human beings could create laws, the *polis* was understood as the ultimate such creator, and men, with the aid of the *polis*, could alter the course of the gods through prayer, sacrifice and obedience to human laws. Against this background, Aristotle could eventually define the *polis* as "the union of families [sometimes translated as clans] and villages" (*Politics* 1281 a1). The clans and families possessed a deep history with a radically different sense of law and of the divine than that which first meets the eye with the *nomoi* of the *polis*. The *polis* unified two very different legal cultures.

With respect to the role of the divine, the gods of the totemic culture contrasted with the later humanized warrior gods of the city-state.[27] In the religious context of the culture of the *polis*, Zeus sat at the pinnacle of a pyramid of gods. Indeed, during this period, Zeus was believed to have created or authored the universe. In the totemic culture, however, no such creator or author was understood to have authored the cosmos and its structure of gods and civil authorities. The gods of the totemic culture were agents of *Moira*: they did not author *Moira*. The divine was reserved for *Moira* alone. *Moira* even controlled *physis*. What is, must be. Neither humans nor nature exercised choice. Without choice, human beings and gods did not possess a will. *Moira* controlled and determined what the sophists later attributed to the separate worlds of *physis* and *nomos*. *Moira* manifested boundaries beyond which no god or human official might authoritatively act.

As a consequence, the early Greek tribes shared a very different sense of legal authority than did the later sophists who justified the supremacy of the *nomoi* of the *polis*. For the sophists of the *polis*, counsellors and soldiers represented a person, perhaps a king. The king declared edicts at an identifiable place and time. The king finalized any dispute in the city. In contrast, in the earlier Minoan and Mycenean totemic cultures, however, *Moira* lacked an identifiable origin that could be quantified in time and place. After all, no gods had created *Moira*. Nor were the laws of *Moira* the object of deliberation or reflection. There was no deference

27 See generally, A.C. Bradley, "Hegel's Theory of Tragedy" in eds. Anne Paolucci and Henry Paolucci, *Hegel on Tragedy* (Garden City, New York: Doubleday, 1962), 367-88.

by the tribal member to some hierarchic structure of higher/lower gods. Indeed, Jean-Pierre Vernant suggests that Zeus and the other gods were "powers," not "persons," in the earlier cultures.[28] The gods represented or signified a 'jurisdiction.' All gods were subordinate to the impersonal *Moira* or destiny.[29] *Moira* transcended the gods. Even Zeus could not foresee the future. As such, Zeus could not determine the future, however much he desired such control and however much he desired a knowledge of the future. *Moira* existed before history. Neither Zeus nor any other god had authored *Moira*. Nor might Zeus and the Greek gods contradict or withstand the hold of *Moira*. *Moira* destined the jurisdictional boundaries of each god.

Unlike the abstract transcendent natural laws that contemporary legal theorists have attributed to natural laws, *Moira* was lived through the day-to-day experiences of tribal members. Tribal members felt a sense of immediacy or presence with *Moira*. Tribal members read the experiences of their bodies into the dictates of *Moira* as they faced their crises, most often natural crises. The laws of *Moira* were not the object of intellectual reflection and construction. Such laws were not created by some human or divine author. Rather, the laws were lived through the experiential bodies of the tribal members. The ritualistic gestures "communicated" customs through experiencing bodies. It was Antigone's brothers who were killed on the battlefield. It was *her* older brother's corpse that was the subject of Creon's edict. King Creon was *her* uncle. It was *her* little sister who initially urged Antigone to disobey the universal law in favour of the edict of the men in the tribe. It was Antigone *herself* who was sentenced to a stoning to death and subsequently to starvation for following the universal law. And it was *her* father who had bedded her grandmother. Upon gaining this knowledge, it was *her* father who was banned from the territory of Thebes. And *her* father had blinded his own eyes upon learning that he had bedded his mother. Though her law was considered universally shared, she believed, Antigone *experienced* the universal law through *her* body. Like Antigone, all tribal members read their experiences *into* the unwritten laws as they survived nature from day to day. The universal laws of the Greek tribes were alive. The laws "live[d] eternal," as Aristotle put it in reference to Antigone's own defence of her action (*Rhetoric* I, 13, 1373b 12-13).

By reading the universal laws through the experiences of tribal members, tribal experiences, not some determinative *physis*, created the unwritten laws of the tribes.[30] Nature may have actually conditioned the need for this or that convention.

---

28 Vernant, *Myth and Society in Ancient Greece*, 98. Interestingly, the early Amerindian tribes also lacked any sense of a hierarchy of higher and lower gods and civil authorities. See Walter B. Miller, "Two Concepts of Authority" in *American Anthropologist* 57 (1955): 271-89.

29 Vernant, *Myth and Society in Ancient Greece*, 12. Also see the discussion in R.P. Winnington-Ingram, *Sophocles: an Interpretation* (Cambridge: Cambridge University Press, 1980), 150-55.

30 This is examined in detail in Cornford, *From Religion to Philosophy*, chap. 1-3.

The rhetoric of rulers and ruled may have deferred to the uncontrollable laws. The laws may have been universally shared by all tribes in the Hellenic world. Tribal members may have universally attributed the enforcement of the customs to invisible spirits. Nonetheless, the universal laws were humanly constructed from the social practices of particular Greek tribes. The practice that the eldest sister bury the corpse of a deceased brother killed in battle was one such custom. What rendered a universal and determinative character to customs was that they had existed for so long. As Antigone put it, "no one knows when they were first put forth."[31] Contrary to the view of the later sophists who justified the *nomoi* of the *polis*, unwritten tribal customs – not *Moira* nor even a determinative *physis* – constituted the universal 'natural' laws of the early Greek totemic culture. Though the customs were unwritten, unauthored, and without an origin, human beings had created the customs over time.

The critical characteristic of the universality of *Moira* was the unwritten character of *Moira*. Neither ruler nor ruled could identify the time and place when *Moira* was promulgated. Nor could rulers and rules deliberate about the unwritten laws since they were left unarticulated. Indeed, unlike the formal public procedure surrounding the promulgation of Creon's stipulated law in Sophocles' *Antigone*, Antigone felt intuitively bound to the unwritten laws. As the chorus explains in *Antigone*, "[t]hy power, O Zeus, ... a ruler to whom time brings no old age, dwellest in the dazzling splendour of Olympus. And through the future, near and far, as through the past, shall this law hold good" (611-13). Indeed, one's bodily experience with the unwritten laws carried a very different sense of space and time than did the *nomoi,* which could be identified with a distinct and assignable author, the *polis*. The promulgation of the *nomoi* of the *polis* could be measured by a quantitative and abstract conception of space and time. In contrast, Greek tribal culture could not abstract a conception 'space' from the bodily experience of space/time.[32] Tribal experience was concrete. The customs of a tribal member possessed "an emotional colour." Space did not possess an unambiguously fixed locus. And time did not have a uniform duration, like a clock, of qualitatively indifferent moments. Each phase of 'time' in the context of unwritten laws was charged with a unique emotional value and significance for a tribal member. Thus, one cannot adequately describe un-authored customs as having been "enacted" or "promulgated." Again, as Antigone described in her defence, "[f]or their life is not of to-day or yesterday, but from all time, and no man knows when they

31 Sophocles, *Antigone*, in *The Three Theban Plays: Antigone, Oedipus the King, and Oedipus at Colonus*. Trans. Robert Fagles (New York: Penguin, 1982, 1984), line 457.

32 H. and H.A. Frankfort, "Myth and Reality," in H. Frankfort, H.A. Frankfort, John A. Wilson, Thorkild Jacobsen, *Before Philosophy: The Intellectual Adventures of Ancient Man* (Harmondsworth: Penguin, 1949), 29-36.

were first put forth" (455-57). A mortal simply could not recognize divine laws as having been created by a prior author in a quantitative and abstract space/time spectrum as did the natural law theory of a later day.

After all, unlike authored *nomoi* of the *polis*, the customs of the totemic culture could not be discovered in a code or in an utterance. How could the unwritten/unspoken customs be learned, then? Were the customs learned cognitively? The customs were lived through personal day-to-day bodily experiences. The most important experiences were lived through ceremony and ritual. In contrast to the sense of a transcendental god as the creator/author of the universe of later Judaeo-Christian thought, the gods of the totemic tribes did not transcend social life.[33] One generation transferred the divine laws to the next through gestures of the experiential body, not merely through the forms of the mind. Ritual battles, though they served warlike consequences, purified the tensions of the tribe. A social equilibrium was reached in the tribe. The ritualistic battles pitted men against men, men against women, women against women. Age groups and territorial units were also at play in the rituals.[34] The rituals and festivals induced feelings of communion amongst antagonists. Participants bonded together. For example, during one festival, the *Apatouria*, the *phraters* accepted adolescents (the *ephebe*) into adulthood after the *ephebe*, along with his peers, had been forced to survive nature beyond the tribe's frontier. Having returned to the tribe strong willed, a ritual bonded the adolescents with their peers and with the community members who had already experienced the rites. Girls also participated in these initiation rites. If a girl refused to marry, she became a warrior. If she were physically overcome in a ritual battle, she was considered a true virgin. Through the rituals, a tribal member came to bond with the collective.

Now, the experienced unwritten laws of the totemic culture contrast sharply with the natural law–positive law dichotomy within which scholars have interpreted Aristotle. First, commentators have usually associated natural laws with an invisible Author who is believed to have created the determinate laws of nature. The invisible Author is believed to dwell in a transcendent supersensible world which the citizen cannot possibly access, let alone experience bodily. In contrast, the Greek tribal member experiences *Moira* through symbolic events and rituals.[35] Secondly, the *nomoi* of the *polis* are debated and justified in the *agora* of the

---

33 Vernant, *Myth and Society in Ancient Greece*, 100-01, 220-21. Also see generally, J. Huizinga, *Homo Ludens: A Study of the Play-Element in Culture* (Boston: Beacon, 1950), chap. 4.

34 See esp, Jean-Pierre Vernant, *Myth and Society in Ancient Greece*, 20-23.

35 I capitalize 'greek' although the 'Greek' as an ethno-nationality is associated with the much later *polis* and still later nation-state.

city just as the human laws of a modern state are debated in the parliament.[36] The *Moira* of the Greek tribes, in contrast, is intuitively 'known,' without reflection or debate. For example, after a battle, the survivors collected and buried the dead without discussion. And, as described above, the initiated young men (*Kouroi*) were recognized as adults through rites or sacred performances.[37] Third, the experiential body of the young carried out the ritual without interposed categories, reflection or deliberation. Forms and reflection arrived on the scene after the *agora* had become the cultural centre of the village and after the urban social life had displaced the rural. Speech was now differentiated between a private space and the fixed rules of a public rhetoric, public speech being expressed in the *agora*. A rhetorical struggle or agonistics characterized the public speech. An intellectualism configured the public speech. Fourth, the public language of the *polis* privileged referents that were external and separate from the signs: one could think about a referent as if the referent were an independent product of the author. For the tribe, in contrast, natural events took on a *symbolic* character: the symbol had no referent beyond the symbol. Without a referent, a natural event could be merely experienced as important. Like the flag to the American citizen or hockey to Canadians of old, the symbol was at one with the tribal member: an attack against the symbol amounted to an attack against the tribal member's very person. The tribal member fused with the symbol. Finally, in the former tribal life, the tribal member brought her/his body *into* the apparent natural signs, despite the belief that *Moira* controlled the signs. The embodiment of meaning brought life *into* the universal laws.

It seems reasonable to conclude, then, that the discourse that privileged *Moira* as constitutive of natural laws reflected a very different discourse than that of the *nomoi/physis* dichotomy of the city-state. The radically different discourses drew from radically different senses of legal authority.

On the one hand, the discourse of the city-state searched for an authorizing origin of the humanly posited laws. The Greeks used the word *arche* to signify this grounding. The city-state was considered the authorizing origin of human laws. The sophists justified the authority of the laws of the *polis* by arguing that the laws of *physis* were very unsatisfactory compared with the laws authored by the sovereign *polis*.

On the other hand, one can retrieve from early Greek tribes a radically different sense of legal authority than that associated with a quest for an *arche*. Unwritten customs did not possess an *arche* or authorizing origin, not even some father-god such as Zeus.

---

36 The importance of the *agora* to the culture of a *polis* can best be gleaned in Jacques Marseille et al., *Histoire 2e* (Nathan, 1996), 8-25.

The *Moirai*, whom the female elders of the clan represented, presided over initiation, marriage and death ceremonies. Such rituals allocated 'portions' or 'divisions' of wealth and labour. Taking Paul Ricoeur's distinction, natural events were interpreted as symbols rather than as signs that represented an absent referent.[38] *Moira*, meaning 'division' or 'portion,' evolved from the female spinners of a tribe.[39] *Nomos* similarly denoted 'division' or 'portion.' But *nomos* applied to pasture, the preserver of *men*. As the *Moira* of the clan disintegrated into family holdings with male heads, the unwritten customs continued to regulate pastures. The pastoral culture remained tribally centred. Men disguised themselves with women's clothes in order to gain access to the priestess-dom of the tribal divine.[40]

With the rise of the *polis*, though, the *nomos*, which village male elders authorized, displaced the authorless *Moira* of the pastoral clans. The *nomoi* reached their full maturity with the written codes of the city-state.[41] In contrast to the authorless natural laws associated with *Moira*, the authority for the *nomoi* was believed to rest in a distinct super-author, the *polis*. Being authored, the *nomoi* could be authored, amended and repealed at will and the authority of the *nomoi* excluded as scrutiny of their content.

7. The Positive Law–Natural Law Dichotomy as Suspect

Conditioned as we are to read legal and philosophic texts through the lens of our own cultural assumptions, we oversimplify our understanding of legal authority by working within the 'all or nothing' possibilities of either a determinative natural law or a contingent humanly authored law. Natural laws are not determinative if civil laws may mould how human agents act. Nor may one take nature as determinative if so many different forms of government differ one from the other. Some other sense of natural law must be taken into account in order to explain the educative, diverse and socially contingent character of legal phenomena that appear universally shared. Some other sense of the invisible, rather than Augustine's and Aquinas's transcendental author, must be attributed to the authority of binding laws.

As an example, and only as an example, a close study of the texts of Aristotle suggests that the natural law–positive law dichotomy oversimplifies the possibilities of 'what is the authorizing origin of human laws.' That dichotomy has long associated natural laws with a divine Author and positive laws with a human

37 Gilbert Murray, *Five Stages in Ancient Greek Society: A Study of the Origins of Western Speculation* (New York: Harper & Bros., 1957), 29.

38 Thomson describes the symbolic character of natural events in *Studies in Ancient Greek Society*, 339.

39 Ibid., 334-339.

40 Ibid., 486.

41 Ibid., 346-47.

author. The divine Author's will is manifested through the natural laws which, in turn, authorize all humanly posited laws. The human author's will is manifested through the author's written expression that is usually associated with a code. Aristotle's texts can best be interpreted as drawing from a sense of legal authority which is unauthored, though the un-authored laws appear universal and yet humanly constructed.

Aristotle understood unwritten customs as the authorizing origin of humanly authored codes in the unwritten and the unconscious. On the one hand, unwritten laws could hardly be described as having been authored at a distinct time and place by an assignable author. On the other hand, the unwritten laws were not determinative in the sense of being uncontrollable. Though universal, the natural laws were the consequence of human interpretation and human experiences over a long period of time. Though created by human beings, they were unwritten. The universal natural laws were natural laws in a figurative sense. It is not surprising, though most ironic, that many contemporary legal philosophers who identify with legal positivism have claimed that the very unwritten conventions that Aristotle described as universal and natural, do, indeed, authorize posited laws. The claim is doubly ironic in that Aristotle retrieved the conventions from an earlier epoch which had attributed an invisibility to binding humanly posited laws.

The problem is that the unity in the totemic culture of humanly posited laws on the one hand and of the natural laws of *physis* on the other is forgotten once the philosophers of the *polis* have had their day. Or so it seems. For the construction of a theory of *nomoi* leaves little room for the possibility that the laws of *Moira* were not really determinative but rather that they manifested humanly created unwritten customs. Re-defining the cosmos in terms of *physis* and *nomos*, the laws of *physis* could do little but supplement the over-reaching humanly authored laws of the *polis*. Legal authority thereby took on a new character with the *polis*.[42] *Nomoi* were believed to voice the will of the city-state. *Nomoi*, in contrast with the newly constructed laws of *physis*, were variable, socially contingent and, ultimately, violent, although the apparent objectivity of the *nomoi* and the association of the *nomoi* with the gods disguised such violence. With the creation of the *physis/nomos* dichotomy by the apologists of the city-state, the laws of the earlier totemic culture were considered pre-legal or primitive, if they were ever recognized.

---

42 F.M. Cornford, *From Religion to Philosophy*, 74-5. W.K.C. Guthrie expresses the same opinion in Guthrie, *A History of Greek Philosophy*, 6 vols. (Cambridge: Cambridge University Press, 1969), vol. 3, 55-134.

2

Invisibility in Modern Legal Thought

The Introduction juxtaposed natural law thought with legal positivism as the two main responses to the question 'why are humanly posited laws binding?' I have just described how Aristotle elaborated a theory of natural law, a theory, though, which took nature as "a second nature." Unwritten customs were so immediately felt that they were considered 'natural.' The early Greek tribes shared such an unwritten sense of law, although, as we have just observed, the natural unwritten laws and the humanly posited laws were considered one and the same. I now wish to take up the notion of invisibility and examine how modern legal thought has identified several very different senses of invisibility.

The tradition of legal positivism has associated legal existence with the human posit of binding laws. With the Judaeo-Christian influence, such a human posit of binding laws has been opposed to the laws of an invisible Author or God. The explanations offered for the question 'why are laws binding?' have generally worked within the possibility that the alternative to humanly posited law is the will of some invisible Author. Aurelius Augustine (354–430) and Thomas Aquinas (1225–1274) expounded the latter view.

The problem that medieval legal philosophers, such as Augustine and Aquinas, faced is not unfamiliar to the tradition of legal positivism, however. Do the human laws defer to civil institutions for the ultimate authorizing source of the human laws? If civil laws are authored by human agents (as opposed to being un-authored), what authorizes the officials to posit binding laws? Is the authority located in the content of the human laws? Or do the officials have to measure the content against a transcendental standard? Do non-legal factors enter into the deliberations of the officials? Alternatively, although non-legal, transcendental factors may enter into the deliberations, does the authority of a binding law exclude such factors from the law once the law has been posited?

And yet, if one is to maintain the binding character of human laws, what would ultimately authorize the human laws to be posited? Is the quest for legal authority itself a circular project? Does it depend upon the givenness of the institutional source/author as a premise in the logic of analysis? Or do the institutions themselves depend upon an inaccessible origin beyond the institutions?

These questions are very important. Their importance, though, has been forgotten because the positive law–natural law dichotomy has delimited the two possibilities – laws are authored either by human agents or ultimately by a divine Author – as exclusive of what constitutes the nature of law: either legal authority rests with human authors or legal authority rests with an invisible author who has posited a determinative nature that transcends humanly posited rules. Until the twentieth century, the nature of law was understood in terms of the two options. But are there other senses of the invisible than that of a divine Author? If so, does each sense of the invisible follow Aquinas's Author of natural laws?

1. The Invisible Author

a) *The author as expressive of a thought plan*

In order to appreciate Aquinas's contribution to discussions about the nature of law and the assimilation of his view of natural law by the tradition of legal positivism, one needs to return to my remarks in the Introduction about the notion of an 'author.' When one uses the word 'author,' one usually thinks of a novelist, essayist, playwright, poet or composer, for example. The novelist, immersed in historically contingent circumstances, creates a story. A novelist or legislator is an 'historical' author. Words signify or represent what the author intends. The historical author is believed to create or originate a cognitive object or web of objects. The author posits a sign that represents the absent object. The author's act of creation emanates external to the objects that are signified in a script. The script is a product of the author. The author wills a cognitive object by expressing her/his thoughts in the script.

Today, we are immersed in a culture that privileges the notion of the 'author.' The legislature is usually pictured as the primary author of legal statements. In a sense, the reader may read a statutory provision as if the original author of the text, situated externally and chronologically prior to the reader, gazed down upon the reader. The reader feels constrained by the gaze of the author. When the legislature is understood as the primary author of legal statements, the judge, as the enforcer of the author's expressed will, has little choice but to apply that will as if the author controlled the judge's decision. The judge reads a script as if the historical author – a legislature or judge or the founding fathers of the basic text – had intended the particular interpretation. The judge interprets as if he or she were inside the thought plan of the historical author. The interpreter must purge his or her interpretive act of all subjective feelings in order to fully access that thought plan of the historical author. The interpreter impersonally re-reads an ordinance or a judicial decision as if the 'Law' or 'Justice' or an imagined spirit of the Law or Justice controlled the interpreter.

But if statutes and regulations are understood as having been authored by a prior legislature, what grants that author its authority to express its mind and to expect its intent to be obeyed? From whom does the author gain its authority? Is it good enough that some later judge merely cites the place and time of a prior author – some earlier legislature or 'the Founding Fathers' – as the authority for the judge to render an interpretation? Must we remain within the trace of scripts in order to find the ultimate authority for the legal rules? But what institution or convention authorizes the very existence of the legislature? Can there be a finality to the search for an authorizing origin? If there can be such a finality, must it remain inside the trace of writing that human authors – or the institutions created by human authors – posit?

b) Thomas Aquinas's Author

Thomas Aquinas (1225–1274), the late medieval exponent of natural laws, takes up this notion of an author as the creator of the material world. In contrast to our contemporary sense of an author as socially and historically contingent, though, Aquinas considers the author as invisible. The invisible Author is better known as the Judaeo-Christian God.

The invisible Author creates nature as its product.[1] Aquinas's supreme Author precedes its product. Since nature is the product of physio-chemical causes, Galileo later explains, there must be one first cause and that one cause must lack any further cause as a referent. Such a first cause of the material world takes the form of a creative invisible Author, according to Aquinas. The Author implants a design into the material world. So Aquinas describes the Author as "the primary efficient cause of things." Since such an Author is the first cause of the production of the material world, the Author exists.

Here, Aquinas gives the divine author a theistic character. By this, one means that the divine is a self-determining source that transcends any individual human being's knowledge or experience. Though such a source exists of its own accord, the source produces all that exists in the material realm. In contrast, deism holds that the first Author is unrelated to the finite material realm. A deity is an unknowable Being without particulars. Aquinas rejects the deistic view of God. As an Author, God designs or intends the material world *as its product*. God, as Author, "foreknows" the eternal laws and all human objects that emulate God's plan.[2] Like the sense of the human author elaborated above, God dwells external

1 Aquinas, *Treatise on Law*, as translated from the First Part of the Second Part of the *Summa Theologica* in *Basic Writings of Saint Thomas Aquinas*, ed. Anton C. Pegis (New York: Random House, 1945; 1266-73) Q. 90; Q. 91, Art. 1; Q. 93, Art. 5.

2 Aquinas, *Treatise*, Question 90, Preface; Question 96, Art. 5, Reply Obj. 3.

and prior to God's products. God, the inaccessible Author, instils natural laws into man's mind.[3] God is *external* to its product. God's product is nature: "Just as in every artificer there pre-exists a type of the things that are made by his art, so too in every governor there must pre-exist the type of the order of those things that are to be done by those who are subject to his government."[4] So too, Aquinas writes, divine wisdom possesses a plan or ideal type that it desires to posit onto the earthly world. All the plans of inferior governors are caused by the First Mover or the "governor-in-chief," as author of the whole. So the products of a human institution, being the agent of the Holy Ghost, are the products of the Holy Ghost, not of the human agent.[5] The first principles of natural law are "indemonstrable" because their justification lies within the thought-plan of the First Author and that plan remains inaccessible through the language of statutes and written reasons for judgment.

God expresses its thought plan in nature. Put differently, the Author's intent is immanent within the finite matter of the world. Despite its immanence inside all material structures, the Author is independent of and external to the world of matter, knowledge and experience. Such a divine Author is a radical other to its material product, and yet, all natural entities are dependent upon the Author. The Author/Creator creates a finite world from no-thing. The created world is separate from or other to the Author. That is, again, the created world is God's product. God is the Author of the material world. Accordingly, the Author is the First Cause and, therefore, can do nothing but exist.

As the first cause of existence, the Author is omnipotent in the sense of being able to do everything. Being omnipotent, the Author creates the world without the Author even possessing a body. That is, the Author is Mind or, better, Consciousness. The Author acts without an intermediary in the human world. The Author's limitless power renders all other beings dependent upon the Author.

Against this background of an omnipotent First Cause that exists, all humanly posited laws are supplemental to the Author's thought-plan. Humanly posited laws that contradict the intermediate principles of the Author's will are void. That is, they do not exist. As Aquinas puts it in a well-known passage in response to the question whether every law is derived from the eternal law:

> Human law has the nature of law insofar as it partakes of right reason and it is clear that, in this respect, it is derived from the eternal law. But insofar as it deviates from reason, it is called an unjust law and has the nature, not of law, but of violence.[6]

3 Aquinas, *Treatise*, Question 90, Art. 4, Reply Obj. 1.
4 Aquinas, *Treatise*, Question 93, Art. 1, Answ.
5 Aquinas, *Treatise*, Question 93, Art. 5, Answ.
6 Aquinas, *Treatise*, Question 93, Art. 3, Reply Obj. 2.

Aquinas responds to the question whether every human law is derived from the natural law a few pages later with:

> *I answer that,* As Augustine says, *"that which is not just seems to be no law at all."* Hence the force of a law depends on the extent of its justice. Now in human affairs a thing is said to be just from being right, according to the rule of reason. But the first rule of reason is the law of nature, as is clear from what has been stated above.[7]
>
> Consequently, every human law has just so much the nature of law as it is derived from the law of nature. But if in any point it departs from the law of nature, it is no longer a law but a perversion of law.[8]

Aquinas's point is clear: legal existence dwells with the Author's natural laws. Humanly posited laws do not exist if contradictory with such natural laws.

c) *Hans Kelsen's invisible Author*

Aquinas is not alone in his privileging of an invisible Author as the authorizing origin of all human laws. As an example and only as an example, I wish to turn to the works of Hans Kelsen (1881–1973) for, of all the leading exponents of legal positivism of the twentieth century, Kelsen has written extensively about natural law theory. Kelsen takes up Aquinas' theistic sense of the divine. This is important because Kelsen elaborates his pure theory of legal positivism in juxtaposition to a theistic account of a determinative natural law.[9] As a consequence, Kelsen, in his justification and description of legal positivism, implicitly excludes two other senses of the invisible, which I shall identify below. What is important for my purposes is Kelsen's re-statement of his straw-person, natural law theory, not the intent of Augustine, Aquinas or others.

Kelsen restates natural law theory as follows. The Author, imputing its will into the material universe, is a "Being of natural, sensibly perceptible, reality," Kelsen insists.[10] According to Kelsen, the divine Author in natural law theory moves everything. The Author creates the material world as its product. As with Aquinas, Kelsen understands the Author as preceding its product. Since the Author designs nature, nature manifests the Author's design.

What is the relationship between the Author's nature and the posit of human laws, according to Kelsen's view of natural law theory? On the one hand, Kelsen emphasizes the determinacy of natural laws. The natural universe is ordered according to determinate, unchangeable physico-chemical causes of all natural phenomena. These causes are 'laws' in that they universally guide all creatures

7 Aquinas, *Treatise*, Question 91, Art. 2, ad 2.

8 Aquinas, *Treatise*, Question 95, Art. 2.

9 Hans Kelsen, *The Pure Theory of Law*, trans. Max Knight (Berkeley: University of California Press, 1967; originally published as *Reine Rechtslehre*, Vienna: Deuticke, 1934), 193-217.

10 Kelsen, *Pure Theory*, 56.

despite the particular desires of human agents. The law of gravity is just such a law. One can recognize Kelsen's restatement of natural law as influenced by Newtonian theories about nature: namely, that the effect must be equal to the cause; that a cause can have only one effect; that an effect is only traceable to one cause; that a chronologically preceding cause relates to a chronologically succeeding effect; and that mechanical phenomena can be determinately pre-determined in their prescribed course upon one's knowledge of the initial state of motion. Against the objectivity of such interrelated physio-chemical causes, the physical universe exists independently of contingent human action. Accordingly, the universal natural laws constitute an 'is' world. Human action is considered practical, in Kelsen's view of natural law theory, to the extent that human action fulfils the determinate 'givens' that the Author has created.

The Author of natural law theory, according to Kelsen, is omniscient in a limitless intentional power. The Author knows all that happens. All beings exist by virtue of their dependence upon the sustaining power of the Author. The posit of human laws is no exception to this dependent relationship. A human law gains its authority by virtue of its consistency with the Author's intent as manifested in determinative natural laws. What 'ought' to be depends upon the 'is' of the natural physical world that the Author has created. That is, the source of moral laws or 'oughts' draws from the 'is' world of nature. Human agents cannot alter the 'is' of natural laws for natural laws are determinative. But because physical-chemical laws lie immanent *inside* human agents and *inside* all social contingency, the 'oughts' of a human agent dwell inside the 'is' of determinative laws. Nature, as a network of physico-chemical laws, alone determines the 'is' and the 'oughts.' If a human law contradicts a determinative natural law, then it just does not exist, and the official who acts in its name does so in excess of jurisdiction. The authorizing origin of contingent human laws, then, dwells in the universal, determinative natural laws. Kelsen himself rejects the claim that legal existence begins with determinative natural laws. In the process of understanding nature in an adjectival sense, though, he does not address other senses of the invisible absent origin that the tradition of legal positivism postulates. He thereby constructs the easier case to rebut. As a consequence, his theory of legal positivism is particular to Kelsen.

Contrary to the claim of Aquinas, Kelsen associates the universal natural laws with moral 'oughts.' The 'is' realm begins and ends with the norms that human agents, not some invisible Author, posit, and the Author posits ideal-directed 'oughts.' As Kelsen (erroneously) puts it, the determinative sense of the physio-chemical nature is "an essential element in the doctrine of *Natural Law*."[11] A human

11 Hans Kelsen, *General Theory of Norms*, trans. Michael Hartney (Oxford: Clarendon Press, 1991; 1979), 70.

agent cannot will, amend or direct nature. Rather, a human agent wills a norm. A norm is situated in a *Sollens*-sentence, which living beings will. A 'natural' order arises, in contrast, "from a basic fact somehow *objectively* given, and thus existing independently of man's subjective willing."[12] Kelsen describes the Author of physical nature in similar terms: that is, God, as the supreme cause of the material universe, wills the universal "as a basic fact." Kelsen adds, though, that God – presumably the Judaeo-Christian God as Author – also constitutes the highest justice. So, Kelsen's critique of natural law theory hinges upon his reading of the is/ought distinction *into* natural law theory. Having done so, Kelsen identifies natural laws with an 'ought,' not the 'is' world, which Aquinas actually claimed for the natural laws. Natural laws are 'oughts' that human agents aspire to reach. At the same time that Kelsen accepts and then reads the is/ought distinction into natural law theory, he categorizes the authorizing origin of natural laws through the Judaeo-Christian sense of a divine Author. He erroneously privileges the author as exclusive of the possibilities of an invisible origin.

The universal natural laws, in particular, lose historical contingency. Contingency characterizes human acts of will. Natural laws lie immanent within all human action, in Kelsen's view of natural law theory. And God, as the First Cause of the causes and effects of physio-chemical movement, authored all movement. So, divine reason imputes a design that human norms express and replicate. Accordingly, all human norms always remain subordinate to the 'is' of divine reason, in Kelsen's version of natural law. Divine reason embodies the 'is' as well as the 'ought' of human action.[13] Human laws are practical or exist to the extent that they participate in divine reason. The 'ought' and 'is' worlds are one and the same in natural law theory, according to Kelsen.

In a later work, *Society and Nature*, Kelsen modifies this determinative view of nature by taking into account mid-twentieth-century quantum physics. Kelsen acknowledges that Mach, Laplace, and Heisenberg had found each of the Newtonian postulates mentioned above wanting. Kelsen concludes from their work that we must replace the simplistic deterministic view of nature with a probability theory of science. However, once done, Kelsen still maintains that natural laws require a determinative cause for every event.[14] Again in a later essay, "The Idea of Natural Law" (and entirely ignoring Aristotle's sense of natural laws as unwritten, intuitive and indeterminate), Kelsen understands nature as determinative: "everything real which actually occurs in a manner directly or indirectly perceivable

12 Kelsen, *General Theory of Norms*, 29.

13 Kelsen, *General Theory of Norms*, "Note 61," 310.

14 Hans Kelsen, "The Law of Causality in Modern Natural Science," in *Society and Nature* (New York: Arno Press, 1974), 249-62, at 257.

to the senses and must take place according to the *causal* law."[15] Kelsen does modify his theory of natural laws in this manner, however: what he had earlier taken as an 'ought' – the universal natural laws – he now reads *into* the notion of a norm. Natural laws, not just human laws, are norms. But in Kelsen's version of natural law, they remain invisible norms that the supreme Author has willed. Because of their invisibility, one can neither describe nor predict such universal norms, Kelsen reiterates.

In sum, Kelsen reads a particular sense of nature into natural law theory.[16] Kelsen projects a theory of natural law that accepts a determinative sense of nature. Secondly, he projects into natural law theory the view that accepts an invisible Author as the creator of such determinative laws.[17] Having set up his straw person in the way he has, Kelsen is left with only one alternative: legal positivism. By setting up his straw person in the way he does, Kelsen avoids the possibility that the tradition of legal positivism may have postulated alternative senses of the invisible than that of the invisible Author that Kelsen had retrieved from Thomas Aquinas.

2. The Invisible as an Inaccessible Immediacy

Modern legal thought has privileged a second sense of invisibility. Preoccupied with associating the natural law tradition with an invisible Author, I have just suggested, the tradition of legal positivism has understood its opposing theory, natural law theory, in terms of the invisible Author of a determinative nature. But there is another sense of natural law, a figurative sense, as I suggested in Chapter One. Instead of manifesting determinative causes of the physio-chemical universe, universal laws are understood in terms of a figurative nature. Officials or citizens

---

15 Kelsen, "The Idea of Natural Law" (1928), in *Essays in Legal and Moral Philosophy*, ed. Ota Weinberger, trans. Peter Heath (Dordrecht: D. Reidel, 1973), 27-60, at 28. His emphasis.

16 Kelsen also re-reads Kant so as to describe him as a natural law theorist. Why? Because *Recht*, for Kant, dwells in an ideal realm without human authors. The closest that Kant comes to privileging a human author is his notion of an autonomous rational person. Kant, *The Metaphysical Elements of Justice*, trans. John Ladd (New York: Macmillan, 1985; 1797) intro., line 227, pp. 28-9; *Grounding of the Metaphysics of Morals*, trans. James W. Ellington (Indianapolis: Hackett, 1981; 1785) sect. 2, line 414, p. 24; sect. 3, 463, p. 61. But that person is purged of all inclination or bodily desire. See e.g., Kant, *Religion within the Limits of Reason Alone*, trans. Theodore M. Greene & Hoyt H. Hudson (New York: Harper, 1934, 1960; 1794, 2d. ed. 1793), bk. 3, p. 87. For Kant, the claim that an invisible author has created the material world is "theological," not philosophical. An objective method, pure practical reason, produces the universal laws of *Recht*. Such an objective method contrasts with the human authors who will arbitrary objects, according to Kelsen. *Recht* takes on an uncontrolled character much as Kelsen describes of natural laws.

17 An invisible Author wills and reasons "the ultimate source of the moral law" in natural law theory, according to Kelsen. Hans Kelsen, "The Foundation of the Theory of Natural Law" (1964), in *Essays in Legal and Moral Philosophy*, 114-53, at 136-40.

are so bonded with customs that the laws seem 'natural.' An immediacy joins ruler/ruled to the laws of a second nature. One does not need to codify, reflect, or deliberate about them in order to ascertain their authoritativeness. The behavioural gestures of the body – also important aspects of a language, though unrecognized as such by the canons – attest to the existence of binding laws.

The early Greek tribal culture associated just such pre-scriptive conventions with divine laws. Unwritten laws seemed to tribal members to be uncontrollable and uncontrolled. One may reconcile the apparent contradictions of Aristotle's theory of laws only by realizing that the universal laws of which Aristotle writes are generally shared customs. In the *Laws*, Plato coined the phrase "of a second nature" to describe the unwritten customs. Here, Plato departed from the theory of forms that he had enunciated and justified in his earlier dialogues, especially in the *Republic*. But the unwritten customs of the *Laws* shared something with the forms of the *Republic*. First, the unwritten laws and the form of the Good were both held out as the *arche* of humanly posited laws. Secondly, the *arche* in both cases was unwritten and unspoken. Plato considered them as pre-language. As such, the unwritten customs as well as the form of the Good possessed a divine character in that no human being could ever gain a presence with them through legal language. We could only mimic them through the metaphors of poetry and music and the arts. Even Plato himself could only approximate the origin by using metaphors and similes to manifest the existence of the form of the Good. The allegory of the cave, the myth of Er, and the similes of the sun and of the line were his foremost examples in the *Republic*. And however hard he tried, even Socrates, the wisest of all persons, could never access the divine sign that led him to question who was the wisest person on earth. As such, he rested content in the *Crito* with a social contract, to which he himself had implicitly agreed, as the authorizing origin of the crimes of which he stood accused.

Along the same basis, one may recall how Antigone felt that she had no choice but to bury the corpse of her brother after battle. The custom with which she felt bonded could well be described as a natural law in the figurative sense of "a second nature." Some legislature did not create or author the custom: the custom was authorless. The custom lacked a distinct and assignable time and place of promulgation. Once again, as Antigone says, these laws "live forever." Their authorizing origin rested "from the first of time, and no one knows when they first saw the light."[18] Such a custom, she quite rightly exclaimed, had no origin in time or space, at least as time and space are measured by a clock and a physical locus. No one knows when these laws of a "second nature" first saw the light of day

18 Sophocles, *Antigone*, in *The Three Theban Plays: Antigone, Oedipus the King, and Oedipus at Colonus*. Trans. Robert Fagles (New York: Penguin, 1982, 1984), line 457.

because they were authorless, without an *arche*, without a Creator or Author, even without a unifying first cause that could be said to originate the trace of authority. Laws "of a second nature" seemed natural because they were lived as they were interpreted. Creon, Teiresius, Haemon, and the chorus did not, at least initially, experience the unwritten laws: they could only speak *about* the customs because their loyalties deferred to the *polis* as the *arche* of binding laws.

Antigone embodied meaning as she gestured to spread dust onto the corpse. Like Oedipus, who felt that he had no choice but to blind himself when he learned that he had bedded his mother, Antigone felt that she had no choice but to follow the unwritten law, whatever the consequence or content. Antigone's and Oedipus's experiences with the unwritten laws made the unwritten laws seem natural. Antigone did not search her memory as to whether the custom had existed. She was not taught the custom in a classroom or in a book. She did not seek advice from some elder as to whether the particular custom exists. She did not debate with others nor reflect upon the goodness of the custom. She acted from a bond with the custom. She felt that she had no choice but to follow the custom. Now lifted from its corporeal identity, her brother's spirit would continue to live in the netherworld.

It may seem strange to consider unwritten laws as the invisible authorizing origins of humanly authored binding laws. For, we may be in the habit of associating an invisibility with a divine Author. After all, that was how Hobbes, Rousseau, and Kelsen understood invisibility. In addition, the conventions are posited in a sense by human beings, albeit in a manner that has no distinct and identifiable author. Is it possible that unwritten customs share an invisible character with such a view of the Author of nature?

Georg Wilhelm Frederick Hegel (1770–1831) suggested as much. Hegel's central concern in his studies of law was to retrace how social life had evolved from the primitive Greek tribal legal culture to the modern nation-state.[19] When the citizen is at one with the community, an ethical life or *Sittlichkeit* characterizes social relations. The Greek life of fifth century Athens manifested such an immediacy of citizen and community, in Hegel's view. Hegel called the Greek manifestation of an immediacy a primitive *Sittlichkeit*. With the advent of the modern nation state, the project of the philosopher was to describe a reflective *Sittlichkeit*. Here, the citizen was self-conscious and yet, at the same time, bonded with the community.

---

19 Hegel, G.W.F., *The Phenomenology of Spirit*, trans. A.V.Miller, analysis of text and forew. by J.N.Finday. (Oxford: Oxford University Press, 1977; 1807). Translated from *Phanomenologie des Greistes*. 1952. Edited by J. Hoffmeister). *Natural Law*. Trans. T. M. Knox. Oxford: Oxford University Press, 1975). *Philosophy of Right*, trans. T. M. Knox. (Oxford: Oxford University Press, 1952). This point is explained in Conklin, "Hegel, the Author and Authority in Sophocles' *Antigone*" in ed. Leslie Rubin ed., *Justice v. Law in Greek Political Thought* (New York: Rowman & Littlefield, 1997), 129-51.

Now, Hegel was quick to emphasize that Western culture had been a project to represent earlier lived historical moments. A representation could never gain access to such a lived moment when one was bonded with the other. Philosophy and only enter the scene after the experience of immediacy. The moment of immediacy was always a moment of lost memory. One just could never experience the bondedness as the bondedness had originally been experienced. The immediacy or oneness of self and others may never be recovered or re-lived, except through a second-order representation of the experienced event.

When Hegel analyzes this spirit of self-knowledge in the *Philosophy of Right*, he describes how legal consciousness evolved into two senses of a sovereign state. The one, the state of a civil society where individuals possessed legal rights and duties, postulates the state as external to the individual, family, or corporation. Here, the external state, much like the state today, posits rights and duties through written statutes and judicial decisions. The second, 'the state proper,' fuses individual rights, the family, and intermediate organizations into a oneness. This latter state proper is a reflective *Sittlichkeit*. Such a state assimilates all differences within society. In this state, there is no object beyond the community. Since an immediacy characterizes the relation of individual and state, the laws are not coded in the writing of some legislature. Rather, the laws are unwritten because all individuals, families, and corporations are at one with the laws. In addition, the state is greater than the sum of its parts – its parts merely representing an object. Religion, for Hegel, involves a quest for a unity that bonds the whole together. But such a oneness, always one step away from the posit of written laws, is inaccessible. For that reason, Hegel describes the state proper as "divine." The divine, then, remains the methodical trace of various forms of legal consciousness in western culture, no one form ever satisfied in what is written as a law. The written laws of a sovereign state always enter the scene too late. For the juridical language of a modern state can only re-present the moment of immediacy that exuded from an earlier experienced social life when the individual and official bonded with the laws into a community.

3. The Invisible as an *a priori* Concept

Now, I have argued that Hans Kelsen associated natural law with an invisible Author of nature. Kelsen rejected natural law theory precisely because such an Author was non-human. For Kelsen, all that existed were prescriptive statements about human acts of will. He constructed what he described as a 'pure' theory of law to describe such a legal existence. But his theory was not so pure. For he too needed an external authorizing origin, inaccessible from within the language of binding human laws. The origin, for Kelsen, was an *a priori* thought that human officials presupposed when they willed norms. That is, the authorizing origin of norms, as a pure idea, was left unexpressed in legal language. How can a concept exist *ab origine* without a sign to represent the concept? And yet, such an *a priori* concept, which Kelsen calls a *Grundnorm*, carries a sense of the invisible in that the juridical agent cannot gain a proximity with the *a priori* concept except one stage removed in the form of a sign. I pointed out in Chapter One that the *nomos/physis* dichotomy of the sophists excluded the possibility of a sense of law that focussed upon the experiential body rather than the cognitive, the unstated rather than the stated, the immediate rather than a mediating language. Such a sense of law was shared amongst the members of the early pre-*polis* Greek tribes. I now wish to argue that the paradigm of humanly authored/determinative natural laws excluded a further sense of the invisible origin of binding laws.

Immanuel Kant best elaborates this third sense of the invisible in modern legal thought. The key to his theory is, of course, his distinction between a phenomenal realm of human experience and the noumenal realm purged of all human inclination. The ultimate grounding of morality, assuming one wishes to be moral, is a perfectly pure will purged of all human inclinations. Because all human agents possess a mixture of inclinations and conceptions, human agents can never access the perfectly pure will. Perhaps only one being, a holy and irresistible Being, may access the perfectly pure will, though we lesser humans will never know if such a Being exists or whether a human being has accessed the pure will. Kant's sense of the divine, then, is not associated with some single all-knowing, all-good, and all-powerful Creator/Author. The divine is a lack in our knowledge of humanly authored rules. That lack conditions both the legal and the phenomenal realm.[20] The lack is invisible in the sense of being inaccessible from within the language of the structure of civil institutions.

The authorizing origin of human laws is an idea rather than an historical event. Indeed, deeply nurtured in a pietistic home, Kant considered the attribution of divinity, such as later by Kelsen, to an invisible Author as "theological."[21] Such an Author desired glory and dominion, according to Kant, and these attributes combined, in turn, "with the awful conceptions of might and dominion."[22] Kant dis-

20 See Kant, *Critique of Judgment*, trans. with intro. Werner S. Pluhar; forw. Mary J. Gregor (Indianapolis: Hackett, 1987; 1790), "Comment to sect. 86," line 446, p. 335-36.

21 This is not surprising, given the criticism of the scholasticism and formalism that Pietism made against the contemporary Lutheran Church during the late seventeenth century. For an excellent overview of the influence of Pietism on Kant, see Theodore M. Greene and Hoyt H. Hudson, "Introduction," in Kant, *Religion within the Limits of Reason Alone*, Cloister Library (New York: Harper & Row, 1960), xii-xxii. Pietism focussed upon the practice of Christianity, especially empathy towards the needy, kindliness towards other denominations, and interest in the heathen abroad.

22 Kant, *Grounding of the Metaphysics of Morals* [hereinafter cited as *Grounding*], trans. James W. Ellington (Indianapolis: Hackett, 1993, 3d. ed.; 1785), sect. 2, line 443, p. 47.

placed the invisible Author with an *a priori* idea. Authored laws, authored that is by human agents, are grounded in some authorizing origin, first, if the origin lacks a further referent for its own authority. An invisible Author does not authorize an authorizing origin: if the Author did so, the origin would not be an origin, Kant argues. The authorizing origin must be valued in and for itself.

Kant's theory of the origin failed to account for the representative character of language. Once one introduces the sign, however, there is a problem. A sign represents or stands for an object. But the authorizing origin of civil laws, according to Kant, cannot signify some further object. If it did so, the origin would no longer finalize the trace: the object represented by the sign would be the origin. The origin, therefore, must be signless or a pure concept.

The civil laws, Kant argued, are instrumental in that they are synthetic propositions.[23] In an analytic proposition, the subject contains the proposition's predicate. An analytic proposition abstracts from all contingent conditions relating to space and time. For example, the legal concept of possession is *possessio noumenon* rather than *possessio phaenomenon*, Kant writes. One may possess a material object juridically without possessing it physically in contingent circumstances.[24] An *a priori* proposition may be necessarily true and yet not be based upon observation, nor upon induction from experience, nor logic. In contrast, in a synthetic proposition, one cannot produce a predicate without a "third term." The third term justifies the predicate. Civil laws are synthetic *a priori* propositions in that, though drawn from the intelligible realm, they require a 'third term' to produce the predicate of a legal proposition. The third term joins the subject to the predicate in a cognitive relationship. The third term is an *a priori* concept that is prior to and apart from the realm of material possession and human experience. The cognitive relationship is synthetically constructed, not intuited.[25]

The will is part of this cognitive relationship. The will is rational in that it is purged of emotive inclination. The rational will brings a material object under the legal category. Kant notes in one legal tract, for example, that an "unbridgeable conceptual chasm" between human laws and the phenomenal realm is so wide that legal equality is consistent with the utmost material inequality.[26] As a consequence, the *physis* of the sophists is no longer a premise of legal reasoning. To the contrary. Yet Kant considers such a cognitive enterprise practical or real. The

---

23 Kant, *Grounding*, sect. 2, line 417, p. 27.

24 Kant, *Metaphysical Elements of Justice*, trans. with intro. John Ladd; Library of Liberal Arts (New York, Macmillan, 1985; 1797), sect. 6, line 250, p. 57.

25 Kant, *Grounding*, sect. 3, line 457, p.57.

26 Kant, "On the Common Saying: 'This may be True in Theory, but it does not apply in Practice'" [hereinafter cited as "Theory and Practice"], in *Kant's Political Writings*, ed. Hans Reins (Cambridge: Cambridge University Press, 1970; 1792), 61-92, at 74-5.

cognitively constructed juridical categories are practical in that they enclose experience and material property when they are applied to experience or matter.[27] Legal reasoning should not, Kant claims, "flap its wings impotently, without leaving the spot, in a space that for it is empty, namely, the space of transcendent concepts that is called the intelligible world, and thereby lose itself among mere phantoms of the brain."[28]

Kant adds a second characterization to the invisibility of the authorizing origin of civil laws. The authorizing origin of civil laws dwells in an idealized kingdom of ends. A will is a member of this kingdom if it is purged of all inclination and empirical desires. But because all human beings inevitably bring inclinations into their actions, there is only one possibility of who is a member of such a kingdom: namely, a person which has a pure will where all human inclination has been erased. The kingdom is an "ideal," a mere "idea," he writes.[29] So too, purged of all experience, inclination, and emotion, the rational autonomous will is also a mere idea. A price, which is only assigned to an instrumental good in a contingent circumstance, cannot be allocated to such a rational will. Nor can such a kingdom describe how human beings actually behave. Accordingly, Kant words the third formula of the categorical imperative in this manner: "Act according to the maxims of a universally legislative member of a *merely potential* realm of ends." If there is such a rational person, there will only be one such person in contrast to the multiplicity of particular persons in the phenomenal realm where inclination has its sway. The transcendent One in the kingdom unifies the heterogeneity of the phenomenal.

Against this background, the authorizing origin of civil laws cannot be located inside the language of the structure of the civil laws of a modern state. The origin is absent from ordinary statutes and judicial decisions. Why is the origin absent? For one thing, legal officials, inevitably infused with inclination, are immersed in a phenomenal realm. But the origin is situated in an intelligible world beyond the limits of the phenomenal. In addition, because of the locus of the origin in the intelligible realm, a legal official cannot 'know' what constitutes the origin. All certain knowledge terminates when one reaches the limit of the sensible world. Yet, we must keep open the possibility that there exists a perfectly good will on the other side of the limit in order to ensure an authorizing origin for human laws.

At this point, Kant offers a further insight. Precisely because the authorizing origin of legal authority is absent from the structure of human laws, juridical agents forever *desire* to reach the origin. That is, the motivating force of legal desire does not originate in the inclinations of the human body. Desire emanates

---

27 Kant, *Metaphysical Elements of Justice*, Appendix, line 372, p. 139-41.

28 Kant, *Grounding*, Sect. 2, line 428, p. 35-6.

29 Kant, *Grounding*, sect 2, line 433, p. 39.

from the body's *lack* of an absent origin. The legal official can only approximate such an absence as a sign. The official cannot access the authorizing origin because, located as it is in an intelligible or supersensible realm, purified of all contingent experiences, an enormous untranslatable chasm persists between the legal official's experiences and the intelligible realm of the official's reasoning.[30] Legal reasoning is thereby forever frustrated. As Kant explains in his *An Introduction to the Metaphysics of Morals*, "[i]n this way, however, the satisfaction of reason is only further and further postponed by the continual inquiry after the condition [of a grounding in an intelligible realm]."[31] Legal reasoning restlessly desires what it cannot access. At best, such reasoning can only postulate the authorizing origin as a possibility.

A juridical agent, then, certifies the authoritativeness of a humanly posited rule "through the tracing back of its origin."[32] Kant likens such a backward-looking project, so remarkably similar to the reasoning of a common law lawyer, with the interpretation of the Christian Scripture. Here, the interpreter of the Scripture must search out, little by little, ancient reports about the invisible Author through languages long dead. Such an interpretive project is infused with a faith that the "first teacher" of the Scripture, though located on the other side of the religious society and its institutions, actually lived. Such a faith also imbues the Kantian search for the pure idea that is believed to ground human laws. Why? Because a wide untranslatable *differend* separates the language of the civil laws from the one externally situated *a priori* grounding of such a structure. As legal officials can only think an idea if they possess a sign to represent the idea, they must possess faith that the *a priori* idea at the authorizing origin of posited rules actually exists.

Since the maxims by which human agents act already conform with the universal laws of the pure will, a perfectly good will does not possess duties, Kant remarks in the *Grounding for the Metaphysics of Morals*. The 'oughts' are already 'woulds' for the pure will.[33] He confirms this view in "Perpetual Peace" when he suggests that "God is the only being for whom the concept of duty ceases to be valid."[34] So too, in *The Metaphysical Elements of Justice*, Kant suggests that "the sovereign in the state has many rights with respect to the subject, but no (coercive) duties."[35] Why? Duty ceases to be appropriate if one's action is

30 Kant begins *The Metaphysical Elements of Justice*, intro., line 211, p. 10, with this point: "the faculty of desire is the capacity to be the cause of the objects of one's representations by means of these representations." Accordingly, legal reasoning is an "intellectual pleasure."

31 Kant, *Grounding*, Sect. 3, line 463, p. 61-2.

32 Kant, *Religion within the Limits of Reason Alone*, bk. 3, p. 103.

33 Kant, *Grounding*, sect. 2, line 414, p. 24.

34 Kant, "Perpetual Peace" (1795; 2nd enlarged edn., 1796), in *Kant's Political Writings*, 93-130, at 99, fn.

35 Kant, *Metaphysical Elements of Justice*, "General Remarks", line 319, p. 85.

uninfluenced by the inclinations of the phenomenal realm. When our actions are influenced by inclinations, we remain in an imperfect realm. The universal laws of the noumenal realm are 'oughts' to such an imperfect world.

What follows is that the supreme civil institution possesses many rights but no duties towards the citizen.[36] Just as legal reasoning, purified of all human inclination, would lack any further duties, so too the structure of institutions in civil society places one institution at the pinnacle in order to represent the possibility of a perfectly good will. If the nominal head, say a president or king, of the structure of civil institutions could be coerced by some other institution, the nominal head would be subordinate to the enforcer. The trace of subordination would continue *ad infinitum* from institution to institution, higher and higher up the ladder of institutions. So, the highest civil institution would lack duties to the citizenry.

Moreover, the citizen may not criticize the actions of the highest civil institution. For to critique or punish the officials who represent the supreme civil head of the state institutions would imply that another institution overrode the head. The head, to be head, must be intrinsically valued in and of itself. Only the pure concepts of a supersensible realm qualify for such a situs and status. Since the externality is a cognitive realm of universals, unconditioned by particular empirical contingencies, the institutional structure of legislature, courts, and executive act "as a universal suzerain."[37] The supreme head of the state "is, as it were, *invisible*, and is not an agent but the personified law itself."[38] The head shares this intelligible world with the invisible *arche* of legal authority: the head is an "abstract object of thought."[39] Since the supreme civil institution, a king or parliament, is an *abstract* object of thought and, as a consequence, a "universal suzerain," the head is believed to guard the juridical condition where the intelligible controls the phenomenal.[40]

Here, in the *Metaphysical Elements of Justice*, Kant goes one step further. Because the sovereign lacks duties, the subject may only complain of, not challenge, the sovereign's actions. To critique the head is to critique the faith in the possibility of a grounding in the metaphysics of morals (law). That is, to critique the civil head undermines the very possibility of a perfectly good will. And to execute the head of state constitutes an eternal crime for such a treasonous act, an act of the phenomenal realm, swallows up the intelligible. Kant cautions that the civil constitution represents an authority that is "so holy and inviolable that it is a crime even to doubt it or suspend it for an instant."[41] Instead of the phenomenal swallowing up the intelligible, the universal

36 Kant, "Perpetual Peace" in *Kant's Political Writings*, p. 99, fn.
37 Kant, *Metaphysical Elements of Justice*, sect. 7, line 253, p. 61-2.
38 Kant, "Theory and Practice," 77. Emphasis added.
39 Kant, *Metaphysical Elements of Justice*, sect. 51, line 338, p. 109.
40 Kant, *Metaphysical Elements of Justice*, 80.
41 Kant, *Metaphysical Elements of Justice*, "General Remarks", line 319, p. 84.

laws of the intelligible should enclose the contingent acts of the phenomenal. Juridical propositions and "the holiest" right and justice are situated in the intelligible realm.[42] One can appreciate Kant's proscription against any inquiry into the origin of authority once one conceives the possibility that, like the perfectly good will, the sovereign civil head possesses no duties.

Indeed, Kant describes the origin of sovereign public laws as "holy."[43] He describes "the Idea of a political constitution" as "holy and irresistible" in that the Idea is "an absolute command of practical reason judging in accordance with concepts of justice."[44] The key, for Kant, is that the authority for a civil constitution originates in the noumenal realm, independent of historical contingencies. Such an authorizing origin lacks a further referent beyond the origin: that lack explains why it is an origin rather than an instrumental means to another referent/origin. The authorizing origin of a civil constitution, then, may not refer to some further referent as a grounding of humanly authored laws. The authorizing origin, purged of all inclination, constitutes a kingdom of ends that all ought to share.[45] The popular wills of historical authors gain their authority from the pure practical reason of such a noumenal realm. Such a metaphysics, though, risks distancing a civil constitution from the social practices of a civil society. H.L.A. Hart, as I explain in Chapter Eight, acknowledges such a risk. And so, in order to avoid an association of posited laws with naked violence, he grounded the authority of binding humanly posited laws in something beyond such rules: the unstated judicial conventions.

The problem is that, perhaps because of the influence of the conception of the divine as an invisible Author, the tradition of legal positivism has ignored or excluded competing senses of the invisible. Kant argues, however, that legal officials must *protect the secret of the invisible origin of humanly posited laws.* Put bluntly in Kant's own words, "[t]he origin of the supreme authority is, from the practical point of view, not open to scrutiny by the people who are subject to it; that is, the subject should not be overly curious about its origin as though the right of obedience due it were open to doubt (*jus controversum*)."[46] Humanly authored rules may punish, execute or exile even if one were to "ruminate" about the originary moment of

42 Kant, *Metaphysical Elements of Justice*, line 321, p. 87, fn. 8.

43 Kant, *Metaphysical Elements of Justice*, "General Remarks," line 335, p. 105.

44 Kant, *Metaphysical Elements of Justice*, "Appendix," line 372, p. 140. Kant privileges a divine end in synthetic *a priori* reasoning when he argues that all persons, except a murderer, possess a dignity. The murderer lacks dignity and must suffer death because "pure juridical legislative reason (*homo noumenon*)" submits the criminal to the penal law. In contrast to the people considered as individuals, the court acts through pure practical reason. The criminal, as such an individual, cannot possess a voice in legislation. Thus, the murderer has willed punishable acts that undermine the dignity of all rational beings and thereby the structure of legal authority itself. *The Metaphysical Elements of Justice*, "General Remarks," line 335, p. 105, and generally at pp. 99-107.

45 Kant, "Theory and Practice," 73.

46 Kant, *Metaphysical Elements of Justice*, "General Remarks," line 318, p. 84.

authoritative human laws.[47] It is even "futile" to try to trace the authority of legal rules backwards beyond historical records to the invisible authorizing origin of the rules. The subject must passively accept the invisible spirit of the posited rules.[48]

Why must the authorizing origin of humanly posited laws remain a secret, according to Kant? Universal juridical rights and duties rationally enclose the inclinations of a subject. A juridical right, like the right to possession, is an *a priori* category that constitutes "an objective, practical reality," independent of social relations inter-se.[49] Social relations must conform to the transcendent juridical relations. United under the legislative will of the sovereign, the citizen should not be "overly curious" about the authorizing origin of civil laws, Kant claims in the *Metaphysical Elements of Justice*.[50] For to resist supreme institutions, Kant continues, calls into question the very unconditionality that characterizes the authorizing origin of legal authority. Indeed, because juridical rights originate in a prior intelligible realm, to ask whether legal authority preceded civil law involves "pointless questions that threaten the state with danger if they are asked with too much sophistication by a people who are already subject to civil law." Or, as Kant put the point in a supplementary explanation, it is punishable for any citizen to inquire whether violence originates legal authority.[51] Only issues related to the intelligible realm are relevant to the authority of humanly posited laws.

4. The Invisibility of the Absent Origin

The natural law–positive law dichotomy has excluded two very important senses of invisibility: first, the invisible immediacy that bonds one's body to a pre-scriptive convention; secondly, the invisible *a priori* concept that transcends historically contingent institutional and cognitive structures. But these invisible origins of legal authority are forgotten in order to ensure the sovereignty or autonomous character of the interrelated human laws. I shall argue in the following chapters that at the same moment that the canons of the Tradition (of legal positivism) have acknowledged a faith in the mystical invisible origin about binding humanly authored laws, the canons have also maintained that, from the viewpoint of the officials who work internally through legal language, this mystical absent origin must be forgotten in order for norms to be binding.

The issue that permeates the Tradition is this: what could be more antithetical to the nature of a humanly posited law than that such a law itself depends upon a

47 Kant, *Metaphysical Elements of Justice*, line 319, pp. 84-5.

48 Kant, *Metaphysical Elements of Justice*, sect. 49, line 317, pp. 82-3.

49 Kant, *Metaphysical Elements of Justice*, "Theory and Practice," 86.

50 Kant, *Metaphysical Elements of Justice*, sect. 49, line 318, p. 84.

51 Kant, *Metaphysical Elements of Justice*, line 371, p. 139.

faith in a mystical invisible grounding for its authority? If no such invisibility characterized the authorizing origin of humanly posited rules, would there be any desire for officials to seek a grounding for their posited norms? Would officials be able to claim an impersonal authority for their laws? Would legal reasoning, so bent upon tracing the grounds of one norm from another, conceal the invisibility of the authorizing origin of posited laws? Would officials forget that the very sense of authority inherited from the Romans contradicted other senses of authority, including the experiential legal authority of early Greek tribes? Would authoritatively sanctioned evil of the twentieth century, with all its horror, confront the official face-to-face?

3

The Tradition of Legal Positivism in Modern Legal Thought

Why do jurists and officials consider certain norms/rules as legally binding? How is it possible for officials to insist that their role is not to question the political wisdom or substantive moral content of norms/rules? Why do lawyers and judges, to be more specific, observe from the sidelines, as it were, as if their norms/rules were impersonal and their decisions distanced?

1. The Impersonality of Posited Laws

Such an impersonality has not always coloured the authority of a 'law.' When early Greek legal culture shifted from the rural clans and tribes to a more urbanized *polis*, as I noted in Chapter One, law came to be associated with the role of a particular personality in the *polis*. Such a personality co-ordinated action. One 'rose' to be king. The king was considered the fountain or source of all laws. Sophocles' King Creon manifested such a personal ownership of the laws, for example, when he exclaimed to his son, "The city is the king's – that's the law!"[1] Authority was associated with altitude, with superior and inferior, upper and lower, supreme and subordinate. All citizens and members of the royal circle were expected to obey the king. Initially, blood lineage identified who should be king. At some point, probably during the early fifth century (B.C.E.), the election of the ruler by a council of elders displaced blood lineage. Greek plays struggled with what personal virtues should be expected of such a chosen ruler: courage, beauty, wisdom, temperance, holiness or justice, for example.[2]

The quest for some one authorizing origin of binding laws is not an isolated inquiry amongst the early Greeks, though. One can retrieve such a quest, for

1 Sophocles, *Antigone*, in *The Three Theban Plays: Antigone, Oedipus the King, and Oedipus at Colonus*, trans. Robert Fagles (New York: Penguin, 1982, 1984), line 825.

2 This association of legal authority with the personal virtues of a ruler continued even to early modern times, as one may observe in Machiavelli's *Prince* and his *Discourses*. For Machiavelli, the *virtu* of the ruler combined with *fortune* or chance to ensure the obedience of the citizenry to the ruler of a city-state. Machiavelli's sense of *virtu*, though, differed substantially from fifth century Athens for the ruler's 'goodness' was measured in terms of his ability to remain in power in the city.

example, from the fifth century sophists who claimed that humanly posited laws were binding because such laws had been posited by the *polis,* and the *polis* was sovereign over all competing social institutions and groups, including the family and the clan. Unhappy with the moral relativism of the sophists, however, Socrates insisted in the *Apology* that something logically prior to the laws of the *polis* – a divine sign – had led him to challenge the sophists' claims about the ultimate virtue of the *polis*. That divine sign arguably emanated from the pre-*polis* gods who had played a supplemental role to the over-determinative *Moira*.[3] In the *Crito*, Socrates argued, somewhat at odds with his deference to a divine sign, that a social contract, independent of the goodness or evil of a particular law, had grounded the authority of the laws of the *polis*.

Plato carried this inquiry in a transcendent grounding of the ruler's authority one step further. The virtuous person, for Plato, should exhibit Goodness, although, in some dialogues, Plato privileged Beauty over the Good. Goodness was a form valued intrinsically. That is, Goodness was valued in and for itself. The ruler, to be good, desired the form of Goodness. Bodily experiences merely replicated the form. The good person sought the invisible forms of knowledge: the absence of the form from human inclination provided the engine for the love of wisdom. The good ruler, educated to desire the form of an absent Goodness, alone possessed the authority to found a just state. Plato even named his lovers of wisdom in the *Republic*, 'the Founders,' because a knowledge of the Good life would ground or originate the authority of all laws in a just state.

When Plato's student, Aristotle, began to teach, Aristotle too associated legal authority with the personal virtues of the ruler. But the virtuous ruler sought a complete Good. A complete Good was "self-sufficient." Such a "self-sufficient" Good ended "that which when isolated makes life desirable and lacking in nothing." (*Ethics* 1097b15). A "self-sufficient" Good constrained the otherwise infinite series of adding other goods to any one good. For Aristotle, though, pure contemplation of the forms was secondary to *phronesis* or practical reason. The good ruler knew how to connect his knowledge of forms with the particulars of human experience. Aristotle attributed such a *phronesis* to the good ruler. Instead of one's blood line or one's virtues or one's contemplation of pure forms, then, the laws of the *polis* depended upon the personal virtues of the ruler for their authority.

Although Plato in the *Laws* and Aristotle in the *Politics* certainly privileged the 'rule of law' in a just *polis*, this appeal to some impersonal *auctoritas* is

3 In the *Apology* (24c), Metetus accuses Socrates of doing "injustice by corrupting the young, and by not believing in the gods in whom the city believes, but in other *daimonia* that are novel. *Four Texts on Socrates* trans. Thomas G. West and Grace Starry West, intro. Thomas G. West (Ithaca: Cornell University Press, 1984; 1998 rev'd. ed.).

crystallized with the Roman lawyer. Such an *auctoritas* displaces the personal virtues of the ruler as the guiding factor of a binding law. The Roman ruler, who exercised legal authority, did not need to be wise nor courageous nor beautiful nor good. Rather, the legal official only had to trace the ruler's action to some grounding or source or origin. This appeal to a grounding elevated the virtuous act of the juridical official (or lack of a virtuous act) to the *auctoritas* of the act. The trace of authority to a ground also ensured that, once an official acted within his jurisdiction, one could not question the substantive content of his acts. An impersonality cloaked the application of the Roman laws. Such an impersonality, supported by military strength, helped the Roman rulers to legislate and to adjudicate over such culturally and linguistically diverse peoples as the Latins, Egyptians, Greeks, Gauls, Anglo-Saxons, Germans, and Slavs. By the end of Augustus' rule (14 C.E.), Roman legal authority presided over 70 million inhabitants, of whom three-quarters lived in the twenty-four or twenty-five provinces. Once categorized as a citizen of the state, each legal person was equally entitled to certain rights and benefits. The impersonal character of the Roman legal order reached its culmination in what Hegel describes as a moment of stoicism when formal legal categories were considered constitutive of social/cultural practice.[4] The consequence of such stoicism was that Emperors Tiberius (14-37 C.E.) and Caligula (37-41 C.E.), for example, could terrorize the populace as if bodily pain were not part of legal/social reality. The linkage of an official action to a legal institution which, in turn, could be grounded in some higher institution such as the Roman Senate: such a trace of authority through an institutional hierarchy immunized the official from any legal suit against him personally. Even when aliens increasingly became litigious during the second century B.C.E., the praetors borrowed elements of law from sources other than the *ius civile* (the Twelve Tables, compiled in 450 B.C.E., and subsequent statutes) and overlaid the *ius civile* with a *ius gentium,* which transcended the conduct of all officials.[5] The impersonality of the *ius gentium* assured a rule of laws, rather than of men, until naked coercion, under Tiberius and Caligula, usurped the impersonality of law.

The Roman jurists distinguished *auctoritas* from the *potestas* and *potentia* of a ruler. *Potestas* and *potentia* went to the *de facto* efficacy and acceptability of the ruler's actions. On the one hand, the fear of the Roman army and police invariably lay in the background behind an official's action. On the other hand, one obeyed an official even if one disagreed with the substantive content of the official's

---

4 G.W.F. Hegel, *The Phenomenology of Spirit*, trans. A.V. Miller (Oxford: Oxford University Press, 1977; 1807), para. 198-201.

5 M. Cary, *A History of Rome: Down to the Reign of Constantine* (London: Macmillan, 1957; 2d ed.), 145-46.

utterance or conduct. *Auctoritas* went to the issue of legitimacy. In contrast to the legal culture of classical Greece, where legal authority was associated with the virtuous ruler, the Romans considered an action authoritative if the action could be traced through writing to a ground or source, however evil the person who represented the source was. So, what Plato had formerly considered mere 'opinion' was now authoritative if the opinion were grounded within the metaphysical boundaries of the official's jurisdiction. If an official acted within prescribed boundaries and according to special manner and form procedures, his acts were considered *intra vires*; if beyond the scope of the prescribed boundaries, the actions were considered *ultra vires*. The *vires* transformed an action (or speech act)[6] into a juridified event with a legal consequence.

What did the Roman lawyers mean by the notion of *auctoritas*?[7] First, a trustee was said to possess an *auctoritas* vis-à-vis the trustee's beneficiaries. Beneficiaries were said to possess duties to obey the trustee. Sometimes, secondly, Roman poets, philosophers, and scholars were acknowledged as authorities. Here, the *auctoritas* of a poet's utterance, for example, depended upon the truth claims of the utterance. The authority of a law, though, concerned a third sense of *auctoritas*. Here, *auctoritas* transposed an act of naked violence into legality. The poet could only express an emotive inclination to admire the conduct of the ruler. Both republican senate and emperor, in contrast, could authoritatively marshall legions against rebellious nationalities. When they did so, the legions would obey the emperor because of the *auctoritas* of the emperor's acts.[8]

Why did the word of the Roman official authoritatively command obedience? The key here was the notion of an *auctor* or creator. Such a notion seemed to take hold with the Romans. Like the trustee and poet, the senate or emperor were considered an *auctor*. Their signed declarations commanded obedience independent of the wisdom or substantive moral content of the declarations. The *auctor* imprinted his intent or thought plan into an ordinance or statute. The *auctor* produced cognitive objects that the ordinance represented. As such, the *auctor* was believed to pre-exist the product in time. The statute was believed to control the trustee's acts. Such a statute empowered the juridical agent. All officials were

---

6 The notion of a speech act in the context of legal discourse is best elaborated in Robert Alexy, *A Theory of Legal Argumentation: The Theory of Rational Discourse as Theory of Legal Justification*, trans. Ruth Adler and Neil MacCormick (Oxford: Clarendon Press, 1989), 53-58, 104-07.

7 See generally Leonard Krieger, "Authority," in Philip P. Weiner, *Dictionary of the History of Ideas: Studies of Selected Pivotal Ideas*, vol. 1 (New York: Charles Scribner's Sons, 1968; 1973), 141-62.

8 Augustus (27 B.C.E.–14 C.E.) represented each sense of *auctoritas*: he acted as the public trustee of the Senate, the private counsellor of the people and the guardian trustee of the Commonwealth (*pater patriae*); secondly, his statements possessed the *auctoritas* of truth and; thirdly, he *authored* or created incomplete ideas in those statements.

agents of the *auctor* of the statute. By the second century C.E., an impersonal 'authority of the laws' or 'the authority of the Senate' coloured the acts of the *praetorae*, military commanders, senators, and emperors. Even in oppressive actions against the citizenry, such as under Tiberius, the Emperor would cite the authority of the Senate for the Emperor's oppressive actions. Of course, great debates and, indeed, civil wars centred around the issue 'who is the legitimate *auctor*: the Senate or the Emperor?' Or 'is the Roman state the *auctor* of the laws and, if so, what institution or official – senate or emperor, Roman emperor or the Eastern emperor, one blood line or another – best represents the will of the state?'

The Romans were not content with locating the institutional *auctor* of civil society. There had to be a finality to the authorizing origin of the whole structure of institutions. At times, that finality was believed to rest with the Senate, then with the Emperor and, finally, with a divine Emperor. Without such a finality to the trace of authoritative signs, particular ordinances, statutes, or utterances of the official would lose their impersonality. So too, the reasoning of the officials would lose its impersonality. And without an impersonality to colour the utterances and conduct of the officials, the utterances and conduct would manifest a crude violence when a ruler posited his cognitive objects or categories upon the ruled. As a consequence, the ruled only obey the rulers because of the military might with which the rulers may enforce their utterances and conduct. The utterances and actions, though 'posited,' can hardly qualify as 'legal' if only violence explains their authority. Indeed, the utterances and actions can hardly be described as posited for, like the ebb and flow of Heraclitus' river, they lack the permanence and fixity that goes with a posited object.

What is important for our context is that legal authority evolved from bodily rituals in the early Greek tribes to the virtuous actions of the ruler of the *polis* of classical Greece to the impersonality of the source or grounds of the Roman *auctoritas*. With the latter, officials searched for a grounding or source of a posited command. Binding laws were authored by civil institutions or officials who were authorized to act inside the jurisdiction of such institutions. Ultimately, there had to be one grounding of the whole legal structure. Such an ultimate grounding can best be described as the *arche*. The postulate of an *arche* assured the official that the posit of a command or norm was impartial if the grounding of the norm could ultimately be traced to the *arche*. The association of authority with a ground or origin was absorbed into medieval legal thought.[9]

---

9 Otto Gierke, *Political Theories of the Middle Ages*, trans. with intro. Frederic William Maitland (Beacon Hill/Boston: Beacon Press, 1900; 1958), 76-100.

2. Is there a Tradition of Legal Positivism?

The thrust of my inquiry is to tease out the different senses of the *arche* of legal authority from the tradition of legal positivism. But such an inquiry begs whether there is even a tradition of legal positivism. When one re-reads the canons of legal thought, for example, they address the nature of law with different emphases. Indeed, some leading contemporary philosophers of law conclude that the term 'legal positivism' should be excised from the vocabulary of legal philosophers because there is so little agreement as to what one means by the term.[10] Have jurists, over time, shared a set of values which, because there is little agreement, could even be described as a tradition? Are there some one or two core ideas to legal positivism? If one focuses upon one theme of legal positivism and then defends (or criticizes) that theme, however, both apologist and critic may well succeed against the privileged theme. But they may not succeed against another version of legal positivism or even against some generally shared theme of legal positivism. Is there any shared theme of legal positivism, then?

Just such a problematic might be said to characterize Ronald Dworkin's critique of H.L.A. Hart's positivism. According to Dworkin, Hart's positivism focuses upon rules as constitutive of law. Dworkin's critique of a rules-oriented positivism does not succeed necessarily against, say, Kelsen's version of legal positivism, a version that focuses upon statements about rules as acts of will. Similarly, Lon Fuller associates American realism with legal positivism.[11] And yet, realists themselves, such as H.E. Yntema, dissociate realism from positivism, interpreting the latter as formalism.[12] Legal positivism is associated with logic and form; realism with the social and economic substance and consequences of rules. As the realist Roscoe Pound (1870–

10 See, e.g., Robert Summers, "The New Analytical Jurists," in *New York University Law Review* **41** (1966): 861-96, 869; and 'Legal Philosophy Today – An Introduction,' in Summers ed., *Essays in Legal Philosophy*, vol. 1 (Berkeley: University of California Press, 1968), 1-21, 16: "it would be best in legal philosophy to drop the term "positivist" for it is now radically ambiguous and dominantly pejorative." In "Beyond Positivism and Law," Ota Weinberger writes that "[i]t is altogether questionable whether there even exists a class of characteristics common to all positivist theories." The best that one can do is to offer a "family resemblance." Neil MacCormick and Ota Weinberger, *An Institutional Theory of Law* (Dordrecht: Reidel, 1986), 111-26, 113. Also see Kent Greenawalt, 'Too Thin and Too Rich: Distinguishing Features of Legal Positivism' in Robert P. George, ed., *The Autonomy of Law: Essays on Legal Positivism* (Oxford: Clarendon Press, 1996): 1-29, 24: "If we could achieve recognition of some central truths and limitations of legal positivism, then perhaps we could reduce the confusion and misconceptions that attach to that label, and see more to clearly substantial issues about law and about courts that interpret law. Until that happy day arrives, we may do better to discuss issues on their own, not relying so much on labels that now mislead and irritate more than they clarify."

11 Lon Fuller, *The Law in Quest of Itself* (Boston: Beacon Press, 1940), 46-7.

12 Hessel E. Yntema, "Jurisprudence on Parade," in *Michigan Law Review* **39** (1941): 1154-1181, 1164. Also see Edgar Bodenheimer, "Analytical Positivism, Legal Realism, and the Future of Legal Method" in *Virginia Law Review* **44** (1958): 365-78, 365

1964) puts it, "[a]s the analytic jurist insisted on the pure fact of law, the new realist seeks the pure fact of fact."[13] Clearly, different philosophers mean different things by the term 'legal positivism.' More clearly, the critics of legal positivism have sometimes attacked a position attributed to legal positivism even though claimants of legal positivism do not hold such a position.

In a sense, each chapter of this book slowly elaborates these characteristics of legal positivism as I re-read the canons of the Tradition in an effort to retrieve how the canons acknowledge the necessity for the authorizing origin of posited rules. Although the term 'legal positivism' did not appear in recent legal discourse until the mid-nineteenth century and was rarely used until the 1940s, one can trace important elements of legal positivism to the seventeenth century work of Thomas Hobbes and to the eighteenth-century works of Jean-Jacques Rousseau and Immanuel Kant. Hegel too might be associated with the Tradition, although his by-pass of the traditional natural law/legal positivism dichotomy warrants a separate book.

Can legal positivism only be understood in term of its binary, natural law theory? How is a theory of legal positivism distinguished from a theory of natural law? Is the distinguishing issue that of the validity or authority of a rule or other standard? If so, is positive law characterized by the posit of laws by human authors in contrast with the posit of laws by a non-human author, a god or transcendent Author? Does the 'state of nature' or the 'primitive' or the 'pre-legal' or a 'law beyond law,' all considered at different times as the grounding of humanly posited rules, share the same authorizing function of human laws as do the universal, external "self-evident" or "indemonstrable" natural laws of Aquinas? Does the structure of human laws depend upon an 'outside' for its authority or do human laws define the outside non-law?

When one examines the identity of the authorized members of 'law,' what is the nature of those members? Are positive laws rules? If a judge must decide in a penumbra beyond the core signification of the rule, is the judge positing non-law? Or does positive law include the judge's values? Must the interrelated rules and/or values be located in a cognitive structure that is self-legislating or autonomous vis-à-vis other structures? Or does legal positivism accept that posited laws represent the Newtonian sense of 'reality' or 'facts' and that the natural laws represent the 'oughts' of subjectivity? Does legal positivism ultimately rest upon a postulate that an autonomous self-referring structure of legal concepts is authoritative, exclusive of the substantive, moral content of the concepts? Or, in a related manner, does the Tradition postulate a self-referring structure of institutions whose personnel posit the categories? What, more generally, have the canons of modern legal thought defined as the chief characteristics of legal positivism?

---

13 Roscoe Pound, *Jurisprudence* 5 vols. (St Paul: West, 1959), vol. 1, 258.

3. Three Inquiries

In order to better respond to such an inquiry, it is helpful to isolate three very different inquiries that jurists have undertaken.

The first goes to the issue of whether one may draw from other disciplines, such as anthropology, ethics, sociology, and other human sciences, in order to understand the nature of law. Hans Kelsen suggested in the very first page of *The Pure Theory of Law* that one may understand the nature of law independent of these disciplines, for example.[14] H.L.A. Hart, however, rejected the "absurd views that law in its proper functioning needs no recourse to other disciplines and that 'correct' legal decisions can simply be deduced by strictly logical means from purely legal premises."[15] Indeed, Hart went so far as to describe his theory of law as a "sociological" one. And Frederick Schauer has described as "slander" any claim that analytic jurisprudence is an amoral enterprise.[16] It would seem that the issue of what disciplines (or discourses) an official may include in the analysis of law depends upon how one responds to the next two issues. For if officials do not include ethical, political, anthropological, or other 'non-legal' values in their deliberation about the identity of 'what is law,' then there is a weak basis for including non-legal studies in the analysis of law. And even if non-legal values are incorporated into the deliberation about 'what is a binding rule,' the incorporation of non-legal disciplines into the study of law would also seem inappropriate if the nature of a binding law excludes non-legal factors.

The second inquiry goes to the identification of the authoritative members of a legal system. This might be understood as an issue about legality or identity: which rules are legal as opposed to non-legal, which are justicible as opposed to non-justicible, which are members of the structure? This second issue takes one to the deliberation during adjudication. What standards are identifiable as being incorporated into legal existence? What values, norms, rules, or other standards are incorporated into the content of law? Is there a limit to which an official may deliberate about such standards? Neil MacCormick has forcefully argued, for example, that the separation of law from morals does not entirely preclude a role

14 Hans Kelsen, *The Pure Theory of Law*, trans. Max Knight (Berkeley: University of California Press, 1967).

15 Hart, "Analytical Jurisprudence in Mid-Twentieth Century: A Reply to Professor Bodenheimer," in *University of Pennsylvania Law Review* **105** (1957): 953-75, 955-56. Having said that, Hart also goes on to claim that "the time the student can afford to spend on jurisprudence is likely to be better spent on the close and careful analysis of fundamental legal notions and those lying on the boundary of a legal system than in assimilating what he can of other social disciplines."

16 Frederick Schauer, "Positivism through Thick and Thin," in ed. Brian Bix, *Analyzing Law: New Essays in Legal Theory* (Oxford: Oxford University Press, 1998), 65-78, at 70.

for morals in the elaboration and justification of laws.[17] In particular, drawing from Lon Fuller, MacCormick suggests that there are certain moral aspirations that are intrinsic to law: that law be certain, for example, or predictable or universally applied. Another such moral aspiration is the expectation that judges give practical reasons for their actions. So too, H.L.A. Hart suggests that there is a minimum moral content to a modern legal order.[18] Jules Coleman suggests that the legality of a norm may depend upon its "substantive merits" or morality, but then it might not.[19] Joseph Raz argues that one incorporates moral arguments into the deliberative stage of law creation and, further, that rules may direct judges to incorporate moral standards.[20] Even John Austin accepts that a judge may legitimately "build" a new legal rule from one's "own views of what law ought to be," whether of utility or some other standard.[21] So, if such a 'strict' exponent of legal positivism as John Austin admits to the incorporation of moral factors into adjudicative deliberation, one can hardly understand the nature of posited law in terms of the identity inquiry.

So we are left with a third inquiry. This is what is properly called the 'separability thesis,' according to Raz.[22] Here, the issue does not address whether 'non-legal' disciplines may offer insight as to 'what is law.' Nor whether moral sentiments, moral reasoning, subjective values, or social practices are incorporated into the content of binding rules/norms. These issues go to the deliberation about 'what values and standards are members of legal existence.'[23] Rather, whatever the content of law, the question is 'why is the rule/norm authoritative?' The same rule, identified and articulated, may be located in both a moral structure and a legal structure; the one may be authoritative morally and the other authoritative legally. But why is one rule moral and the other legal? What makes the rule legally binding? Why

17 MacCormick, "Natural Law and the Separation of Law and Morals," in ed. Robert P. George, *Natural Law Theory: Contemporary Essays* (Oxford: Clarendon Press, 1992), 105-33.

18 H.L.A. Hart, *The Concept of Law* (Oxford: Clarendon, 1961, 1994, 2d ed.), 193-200.

19 See, e.g., Jules Coleman, "Second Thoughts and Other First Impressions," in ed. Brian Bix, Analyzing Law: New Essays in Legal Theory (Oxford: Clarendon, 1988), 257-322; "Incorprationism, Conventionality and Practical Difference," in *Legal Theory* **4** (1998): 381-425.

20 See, e.g., Joseph Raz, "Authority, Law and Morality," in *Ethics in the Public Domain* (Oxford: Clarendon, 1994).

21 Austin, *Lectures on Jurisprudence* vol 2 (New York: Burt Franklin, 1970; reprint from Robert Campbell ed., London: John Murray, 1885, 5th ed. rev'd; originally published in 1861), Lecture 37, 337-38.

22 Joseph Raz, "The Nature of Law," in *Ethics in the Public Domain*, 195-209; "Authority, Law and Morality."

23 This notion of the 'discovery' of a rule is juxtaposed with the justification of a rule in Richard Wasserstrom, *The Judicial Decision* (Stanford: Stanford University Press, 1961). Raz makes a similar distinction between deliberation and a decision. See Raz in "Reasons for Action, Decisions and Norms" in ed. Joseph Raz, *Practical Reasoning* (Oxford: Oxford University Press, 1978), 128-43; and *Ethics in the Public Domain.*

may coercion legitimately enforce such a binding rule/norm? That question, according to the separability thesis, excludes a consideration of moral values and moral reasoning even though the rule/norm has the same content in both contexts.

The question as to what non-legal factors enter into a judge's decision, then, concerns a theory about adjudication – a particular subject of interest in American legal thought.[24] The question as to what disciplines a legal theorist may examine addresses the theories about how laws are made. The third issue, the question about legal validity (or authority), concerns the nature or essence of law: what makes one rule authoritative and another rule moral?[25] The tradition of generic legal positivism has consistently maintained that the nature of a binding law separates the authority of a rule/norm from its substantive moral content. Here, the Tradition has staked out its imperial claim. I intend to argue that such a general claim of the separability of legal authority from a non-legal knowledge manifests a naive loss of legal memory when one appreciates the invisible as the authorizing origin of humanly posited rules/norms.

4. The Authorizing Origin of Posited Rules/Norms

Now, the separability thesis hinges upon the construction of an enemy, what the Tradition calls morality. 'What is a binding posited law?' depends upon the separability thesis and the separability thesis depends upon a response to 'what is morality?' Much is taken for granted in the separability thesis for we are left with many complex issues. Both the questions 'what is morality?' and 'what is legality?' depend upon something deeper than some grand reference to 'morality' or some implicit association of morality with 'oughts.' What is it, for example, that authorizes rules to create institutions which, in turn, may enact authorizing rules? What is the nature of legal authority? What gives an authorizing rule its authority? Is the 'morality' of the separability thesis those values, assumptions, rules and other standards that lack legal authority? Are the latter factors the 'oughts' of moral reasoning in that they are 'outside' the self-referring legal existence?

If the separability thesis hangs upon a claim about the authority of a posited rule or value, what underlies the nature of the binding authority of a rule? And what gives the authority-making procedures and institutions their authority? Does the structure of rules/norms depend upon membership criteria that officials accept inside the structure? Do the membership criteria authorize the creation of institu-

24 Anthony J. Sebok, *Legal Positivism in American Jurisprudence* (Cambridge: Cambridge University Press, 1998).

25 See generally Joke Klein Kranenburg, "Legal Positivism Divided" in *Current Legal Theory* **15** (1997): 3-23.

tions, and do those institutions then constitute legal existence? If such institutions constitute legal 'existence,' then do the standards that guide behaviour, located inside the language of norms/rules, make for the test of authority? If so, then is the test for authority ultimately grounded in the social behaviour that legal language signifies? If officials are guided by the test for membership in the group of officials, does that test alone render them 'officials' of a 'legal system'? Does the acceptance by officials of a rule of class membership itself make law possible? If the authorizing origin of law is external to legal existence, must legal officials believe in the origin or *arche* as a matter of faith? Is social acceptance by officials of *that* faith coercively posited upon non-officials?

The authorizing origin of legality may well include a community's mores or basic experiential attitudes of respect towards legal institutions. There may be no constraints as to what can and cannot be the content of the authorizing origin. Although there may be no necessary connection between the authority of a posited rule and non-law, non-law may be incorporated into the originating rule of a legal structure. That is, the 'oughts' external to the cohesive structure of legal categories and the values implicit in the categories may well be included in this one authorizing origin or source of the rules/norms. There needs to be some grounding that can be said to ascertain which rules or values are legal and which are not. And if this full authorizing origin were located from inside the language of humanly posited rules, what would give the legal official an assurance that the inside rule/norm differed from non-law? Would the forceful posit of such a rule alone be sufficient to ensure that all other ordinarily posited rules were authoritative? What would render the 'inside' rule final and binding? Are we reconciled to returning, once again, to coercion – implied or explicit – as the ultimate authorizing source for the authority of a posited rule? Does the appeal to an absent invisible authorizing origin of posited rules/norms relieve the official of facing the violence of posited rules/norms?

Even the exponents of a more 'inclusive' positivism do not carry their claim about the authorizing origin of legality far enough. Jules Coleman admits, for example, that the authorizing rule *may* not necessarily be located from inside the chains of rules that are known as 'legality.'[26] But an inquiry into the authorizing origin is not a question of 'may.' I intend to argue in subsequent chapters that the Tradition postulates that the authorizing origin of humanly posited rules *must* be

26 Jules Coleman, "Authority and Reason" in ed. Robert P. George, *Natural Law* (Oxford: Clarendon Press, 1992), 287-319; and "Incorporationism, Conventionality, and the Practical Difference Thesis," in *Legal Theory* **4**: 381-425, at 407-12. However, in "Second Thoughts and other First Impressions" in ed. Brian Bix, *Analyzing Law: New Essays in Legal Theory* (Oxford: Clarendon Press, 1998), 257-322, at 266, Coleman writes that legal positivism claims that there must be one "logically possible legal system [structure]" where there is no ought value or moral worth which conditions the structure.

located *external* to binding rules/norms. The sense of legal authority that requires that there be an authorizing origin does not even end with the rule of recognition inside the language of the legal structure. For even the rule of recognition signifies a pre-law, unstated founding judicial convention. The quest to reach such a pre-law *arche* conditions the posited rules/norms and the tradition that we have inherited from the sophists who justified the binding norms of the *polis*.

The critical issue of a modern legal order since the Roman times is that the posit of norms or values be considered impartial or objective. Each leading philosopher of legal positivism has offered a different resolution of this problem. Generally, the Tradition has suggested three very different avenues of argument. Officials, working within the legal order search for a grounding or origin of any one legal rule or norm. By tracing each ground from one to another, the official postulates that one final grounding exists. It is that one final grounding that is the subject of the balance of this book. Thomas Hobbes and Jean-Jacques Rousseau associated the final grounding with an invisible nature that was inaccessible to the statutes and precedents of legal officials. John Austin grounded the binding laws with the external habits of the peoples as an indeterminate author. Hans Kelsen introduced a second theme when he claimed that the origin of the binding norms rested in an *a priori* concept that the officials presupposed. And H.L.A. Hart initiated a third strain of thought when he grounded the rule of recognition in the unwritten judicial practices that he excluded from the posited norms/rules of a modern state as "pre-legal."

Each strain of legal thought, though, raises a series of very important issues. What is it that makes a rule of recognition or a social practice an authorizing rule of a modern legal order? Is there some invisible nature, an author, *a priori* concept, social convention, or attitude of respect – invisible to the legal official's view of legal existence – postulated in order to ensure that humanly posited rules/norms are binding? Is the *arche* accessible through the officials' legal language? Or does the language itself – the language of lawyers and judges – at best approximate the *arche*? Must one journey into a non-existence, to some complex heterological externality that legal officials cannot possibly recognize as legally authoritative in order for norms/rules to be binding? Must officials have faith that the externality is a oneness? Is the authorizing origin of posited rules/norms accessible from the language of the rules/norms? And can one know what is the identity of the external origin if only objects, recognizable through the official language, can be said to be known? If the origin is unsignifiable through legal language, is the origin unknowable? Is, then, the origin invisible to the legal officials who may only recognize what they take to be legal existence?

We are left, then, with a faith that the *arche* exists. Is this faith logically necessary in order to ensure that the heterology of voices of officials unified into a single voice with a single will? For example, Hans Kelsen writes about a single *Grundnorm,* which is left unarticulated in a structure of legal norms. H.L.A. Hart is usually taken as claiming that *one* rule of recognition grounds the legal structure. Although many conventions may underlie a legal structure, it is assumed that one special convention can be inscribed as the founding rule of a constitution. Not all philosophers of legal positivism have claimed, though, that there is one rule of recognition with a single content. Joseph Raz and Jules Coleman, for example, maintain that there may be several master rules of recognition.[27] According to Coleman, however, judges, lawyers, and legislators share a single unifying grounding when they give reasons or justifications for their actions. The single grounding is that practical reason matters in the search for a binding rule, according to Coleman. Even the grounding of practical reason, though, has another far deeper authorizing origin to the effect that a certain ideal model of a legal structure ought to support practical reason. The authority of a rule/norm is not the practical reason itself but an authorizing postulated ideal, independent of the exercise of practical reason. Autonomy, equality and public justification are such ideals. These ideals postulate the grounding of practical reason. Once again, though, the official is reconciled to believing in such a grounding as a matter of faith. The official, believed to be constrained by the posited norms/rules, cannot recognize the *arche* as legally existent.

5. The Problematic of Modern Legal Positivism

The question of the absence of an authorizing origin vis-à-vis posited rules/norms raises another set of issues. How is this absence manifested? Is the absent object believed to be a transcendent author of the structure? But how could such an author's will be accessible if the author transcends posited norms/rules? Is the absent object a pure *a priori* concept unencumbered with human inclination? If such a concept were untainted with the reasons and inclinations of lawyers and judges or with the language of such officials (upon whom is conferred the authority to recognize rules and other standards inside the structure), how can such lawyers and judges access such a pure idea external to the posited rules/norms? Perhaps the absent object, then, is a convention. If so, how can that convention be recognized as a legitimate or justicible standard from recognizable signs if it is unwritten and unspoken? After all, a convention is unwritten and unspoken. Is it the unwritten conventional behaviour that is absent from the language of the legal structure? Or is legal language one step removed from such a behaviour? Can our language only approximate such behaviour? Finally, perhaps the absent origin is

27 Joseph Raz, *The Authority of Law*, 95. Coleman, "Second Thoughts," 261.

an experience of immediacy where the official is bonded with a legal institution. But may posited rules/norms, to remain separate from non-law, recognize such an immediacy? Does the immediacy exist from the legal point of view? If the immediacy cannot be recognized as legally existent, then can the authorizing origin as an immediacy be true? If not, must the legal officials reason about their faith in the existence of the origin?

The problematic of modern legal positivism is that officials postulate in their reasoning that there must be a finality in their quest for the authority of humanly posited rules/norms. Again, the quest has taken the form of the trace of one intellectual grounding of a rule/norm from another. The legal official assumes, as a matter of faith, that some one ultimate grounding or *arche* is absent from the trace. That trace to an *arche* is believed to objectify what would otherwise be considered an arbitrary subjective value. The trace of the grounding of posited rules/norms to an authorizing origin in an *arche* separates the content of the rules/norms from non-law. The trace also immunizes posited rules/norms from a charge that their posit manifests an arbitrariness or, perhaps, a violence. I shall argue in the forthcoming chapters, though, that important canons of legal positivism privilege the language of the trace. I intend to retrieve a phenomenon of language from the Tradition. Such a language has been understood in terms of written statements or sentences and the authors of such statements. The statements have often been projected as a transparent medium for the trace of one grounding to another to the ultimate *arche*. But legal language is not transparent. If legal understanding incorporates the official's forestructures of meaning as well as the official's expectations *into* the statements that signify the content of the rules/norms or if legal understanding incorporates the understood role of the institutional source of the rule/norm, is this embodiment of meaning rejected as non-law, as non-existent? If so, does this forgotten phenomenon of language necessitate that the *arche* be inaccessible to the language?

Does the authorizing origin, then, become merely some unrecognizable object or, more correctly, some no-thing once legal language takes hold amongst officials? Is the absence believed to be prior to legal language? May the officials recognize the *arche* as existent? If so, do lawyers and judges possess, at best, a 'vision' of the invisible source, which their norms/rules can never access for the authorizing origin to be an origin? Is Hobbes' natural condition or Rousseau's general will just such a vision? Does faith in the existence of the authorizing origin condition legal reasoning? Is it the image of the authorizing origin that constrains the official?[28] Does that image induce the official to believe that he or she is bound by a posited rule/norm? Is

28 See William E. Conklin, *Images of a Constitution* (Toronto: University of Toronto Press, 1989).

the official language of the structure closed from other languages, such as the languages of anthropology, ethics, and music? Must officials forget that the image is a necessary, rather than just a possible, postulate for legal existence? Must officials forget the image of the absent object, however named by judges and lawyers (whether as the 'Rule of Law' or 'Justice' or 'the Law'), as a secret lost inside the officials' language. Does the law/non-law, law/morals dichotomy follow from the postulate of an invisible origin of the authority of the norms/rules? That is, are rules posited as authoritative only on the condition precedent that the authorizing origin of the trace of authority is invisible?

4

An Invisible Nature: The Origin of Thomas Hobbes's Civil Laws

1. The Paradox

Thomas Hobbes' theory of law carries through the paradox of supporting binding civil laws which depend upon an invisible authorizing origin.

Hobbes (1588–1679) describes a humanly created sovereign legislator whose legal authority is comprehensive over all social behaviour within the jurisdiction of the sovereign. No other independent office in civil society may over-ride the laws of the sovereign legislature. Nor may any other state do so. Nor may any Author, nor moral principle nor custom transcend the authority of the civil laws. The sovereign is self-legislating or autonomous (*auto nomos* meaning 'self' 'legislating'). A judge must ground his decision by reference to another civil law and its legislative source without regard to the substantive moral content of the particular law. Even Justice begins and ends with the structure of civil institutions. The self-legislating scope of the civil laws is total in that no one citizen nor government official is immune from the tentacles of the sovereign's laws. Justice and ethics arise on the scene after the sovereign has posited its laws. Even then, justice refers to the rigorous application of the posited laws, not to the moral content of those laws.

The paradox is this. Despite the total enclosure of all human action inside a structure of civil laws, the authority of the civil laws is grounded upon an invisible condition with invisible creatures which dwell external to the institutional structure. This dependence upon an externality for the authority of civil laws is manifested in natural duties which the sovereign legislator owes towards the citizenry. The most important natural duty is respect for life and for liberty. The natural duties owed by the sovereign legislator transcend the civil laws. In addition, the citizen maintains certain rights independent of the civil laws. First, the citizen may not be compelled to confess a crime. Secondly, the citizen possesses the natural right not to kill, wound or maim oneself even if so ordered by the sovereign legislator. Thirdly, if the legislator's actors convict "a great many men together" of a capital crime for which they will receive capital punishment, the convicted persons retain the liberty "to joyn together, and assist, and defend one another."[1] Fourth, this natural right to protect one's physical being "can by no Covenant be relinquished." Once the legislator can no longer protect the subject, the subject is no longer obligated to the sovereign legislator.[2] The natural duties of the state and the natural rights of the citizen originate from an inaccessible *externality* to the self-legislating sovereign. The sovereign legislator and the citizen carry these natural duties and rights into the institutional structure of civil society. What is critical, though, is that in order to maintain the totality of the legislator's authority, the legal officials, working internally through a vertical hierarchy of offices, must forget their dependence upon the externality in order to maintain the authority of civil laws.

Now, this paradox, the paradox of a totality of civil laws which depend upon an invisible externality for their authority, has been the subject of many interpretations and attempted reconciliations. M. M. Goldsmith read a Galilean view of nature into Hobbes' arguments.[3] Ever-moving causes and effects, characteristic of the natural condition, hovered in the background of the creation of a sovereign state. Another series of efforts to reconcile the paradox focused upon the historicist image of the human subject which Hobbes allegedly brought into his arguments. Leo Strauss claimed that Hobbes presupposed an autonomous, rights-oriented subject in contrast with the pre-modern view of an uncontrolled and uncontrollable fate.[4] Hobbes' sovereign exemplified such an autonomous subject. C.B. Macpherson claimed that Hobbes read a bourgeois individual into his arguments.[5] Such an individual possessed an unlimited desire to possess private property. Michael Oakeshott offered a third form of interpretation, one which concentrated upon Hobbes' new notion of political obligation.[6] Unlike the radically solitary individual of the natural condition, the individual impliedly authorized the creation of the state's laws.[7] The citizen was free to the extent that civil laws were silent.

---

1 Thomas Hobbes, *Leviathan*, ed. with intro. C.B. Macpherson (London: Penguin, 1968; 1651), chap. 21, 270.

2 *Leviathan*, chap. 21, 272.

3 M.M. Goldsmith, *Hobbes' Science of Politics* (New York and London: Columbia University Press, 1966). Also see R.S.Peters, *Hobbes* (Harmondsworth: Penguin, 1967).

4 Leo Strauss, "The Spirit of Hobbes' Political Philosophy," in *Natural Right and History* (Chicago: University of Chicago Press, 1953), chap. 1. Also see Strauss, *The Political Philosophy of Hobbes: Its Basis and Genesis*, trans Elsa M. Sinclair (Chicago: University of Chicago Press, 1952).

5 C.B. Macpherson, *The Political Theory of Possessive Individualism: Hobbes to Locke* (Oxford: Clarendon Press, 1962).

6 Michael Oakeshott, "Introduction to *Leviathan*" in Hobbes, *Leviathan*, ed. Oakeshott (Oxford: Blackwell, 1946), vii-lxvi. Reprinted in *Hobbes on Civil Association* (Oxford: Basil Blackwell, 1975), 1-74. References will be made to the *Civil Association* edn.

7 Oakeshott believes that such a solitary individual does exist and is a real individual being. Ibid 34. This is erroneous, I suggest, because one must ask 'how is it possible for an individual human being to exist without a language?'

David Gauthier carried this issue of legal obligation further by distinguishing between the psychological sense of 'being obliged' in the natural condition and the deontological sense of 'having an obligation' in civil society. Although human agents were obliged to obey God, they possessed moral duties in civil society by virtue of their consent to the authority of civil laws.[8] A fourth and final set of interpretations has claimed that Christian values underlie Hobbes' arguments. For example, A.E. Taylor argued that the obligation to obey the civil sovereign rested upon the prior obligation to keep promises, an obligation which the Christian God had commanded.[9] Howard Warrender then claimed that Hobbes' sense of God in the natural condition continued into a political obligation in civil society.[10] F.C. Hood went further still by claiming in *The Divine Politics of Thomas Hobbes* that Hobbes had postulated Christianity as crucial to understanding the civil laws.[11]

I wish to re-read the relation of civil laws to the natural condition by privileging Hobbes' theory of language. For Hobbes, an author creates a product – a text, a contract, an idea – through a name or sign. A sign represents an object. A chain of signs constitutes a language. Only civilized human beings possess a language, Hobbes insists. Beasts, "savages," children and idiots, in contrast, dwell in a natural condition where, "without SPEECH, consisting of *Names or Appellations*, and their Connexion; whereby men register their thoughts; recall them when they are past; and also declare them one to another for mutuall utility and conversation," we would have "neither Common-wealth, nor Society, nor Contract, nor Peace, no more than amongst Lyons, Bears, and Wolves."[12] Only when creatures have acquired shared significations (that is, a language, in Hobbes' view) for their grunts and marks, only then are they able to author expressions whose signified objects others may understand. As Hobbes puts it in the *Elements of Law*, "[a]s in the discerning faculties, man leaveth all community with beasts at the faculty of imposing names."[13] Where signs to signify one's thoughts are lacking, desires must emanate from the individual's physical body rather than from the thoughts of her/

8 David Gauthier, *The Logic of Leviathan: The Moral and Political Theory of Thomas Hobbes* (Oxford: Clarendon Press, 1969).

9 A.E.Taylor, "The Ethical Doctrine of Hobbes" in *Philosophy* (1938) **13**: 406-24, reprinted in ed. K.C. Brown, *Hobbes Studies* (Oxford:Basil Blackwell, 1965), 35-55.

10 Howard Warrender, *The Political Philosophy of Hobbes: His Theory of Obligation* (Oxford: Clarendon Press, 1957), 7, 10, 322. Also see Warrender, "A Reply to Mr. Plamenatz," in *Political Studies* **8** (1960): 48-57, reprinted in Brown, *Hobbes Studies*, 89-100.

11 F.C. Hood, *The Divine Politics of Thomas Hobbes: an Interpretation of Leviathan* (Oxford: Clarendon Press, 1964).

12 *Leviathan*, chap. 4, 100.

13 Thomas Hobbes, *Elements of Law: Natural and Politic*. Ed. with pref. and critical notes, Ferdinand Tonnies and with intro. by M. M. Goldsmith (London: Frank Cass; 2nd ed. 1969; 1889). Critical ed'n by Howard Warrender, (Oxford: Clarendon Press, 1983), part 1, chap. 2, sect. 12, (hereinafter cited as 1.2.12).

his mind. Without the external constraint of language, desires are unlimited. Without a language, there is no possibility for the arts, for culture or for law. Language is the mark of civilization, according to Hobbes. Life is nasty, brutish and short. Hobbes describes such a condition without language as 'natural.'

Hobbes privileges authors who emerge from such a language-less condition. The authors found the authority of all civil laws. But neither an author nor the laws can access the logically prior language-less condition in that one can only access an object, according to Hobbes, through a language. The natural world which Hobbes describes lacks any such language, let alone a language which the juridical officials in civil society can recognize. Neither juridical agents nor citizens may return to a condition where language is absent. For Hobbes, language is like a prison house from which one cannot escape. The world which Hobbes describes as grounding legal authority in civil society, then, is invisible in the sense of being inaccessible to human language. It is not surprising that Hobbes should be preoccupied with the role of the divine in such an inaccessible condition.

The acquisition of conventions about the signification of signs reconciles the paradox of the dependency of the totality of binding civil laws upon an origin which is invisible to the legal officials in civil society.

From the standpoint of a juridically appointed actor working inside an office of the Representer, the civil laws are omnipotent vis-à-vis the subjective values and desires of all citizens of the state. The civil laws transcend the subjective desires of all actors. Citizens may not rebel against the laws. A citizen or an actor may not question the political wisdom of the substantive content of the laws. Citizens may not even own property independent of the state's authoritative structure. The *Common*-wealth, as Hobbes called the sovereign legislator, has no legal capacity until all creatures in the natural condition join to create a supreme representative through their shared signs. But they cannot do so until they share conventions about the significations of signs. At that point, the creatures have become authors of expression. Hobbes calls the supreme representative of the authors, the Representer. The Representer is the sole legislator. The Representer may abrogate a civil law because the Representer alone possesses authority to enact a civil law. The Representer may abrogate any one civil law by enacting another civil law. The Representer, in addition, is not subject to the civil laws of its actors. Why not? Because as the sole Legislator, the Representer may repeal any civil law which hinders the Representer. If the Representer could not repeal its laws, it would not be supreme.[14]

14 *Leviathan,* chap 26, 313.

The supremacy of the Representer is manifested in a structure of institutions which emulate a pyramid or patriarchy. Some office, preferably that of the king, is the supreme office of the pyramidal organization of institutions (the Crown, the parliament, the common law courts, the equity courts, the police, and subordinate officials). Institutions are vertically hierarchized under the supreme office. The offices of all lower-level officials are rationally connected in vertical lines to the supreme Head of the pyramidal organization: judge is subordinate to legislature, legislature is subordinate to king. The citizenry is external to such an organization of offices. The citizenry may act from valid religious or moral factors. But they are outsiders to the institutional structure. Such outsiders may not impose legal rules authoritatively. Their opinions are 'ought' considerations without the authority of a law. Legal existence depends upon the authority alone of a rule as applied by an official on the hierarchy of offices of the sovereign state. The inter-connected commands are total in that no personal action and no private thought is potentially immune from the commands.

On the other hand, these complete, theoretically all-inclusive commands possess an escape hatch or opening to a very alien world. Not unlike the open door to the castle of law in the parable of the 'man from the country' at the end of Franz Kafka's *The Trial*, the self-referring structure of governmental institutions has a gap. The gap opens outward to a realm unrecognizable from within civil laws. In this alien realm, the expression of one's desires is marked by the movement of one's physical body. Only beasts reign in this world. Hobbes himself emphasizes at the start of the *Leviathan* that from the standpoint of an official on the civil hierarchy of institutions, this alien world is unrecognizable because such officials can recognize a perceived object or understand a concept only if one can associate a name or sign with the object.[15] If there is no shared language in the alien world beyond the boundaries of jurisdiction of the civil institutions, then the officials positioned in the "offices" cannot recognize such an alien world. Lacking shared conventions as to what their noises and marks signify, Hobbes describes the individuals as "creatures" and "beasts" rather than as human beings, for they may only express their desires through their physical bodies rather than through the language constitutive of culture. The dread of returning to such a brutal realm without language dominates the beasts once they begin to acquire conventions about signs. The dread drives all creatures to desire peace. The desire for peace is replicated in civil society. When the beasts begin to share conventions about what this or that mark or sound signifies – only then are the creatures capable of reaching agreements with each other. They become authors of their own expressions.

15 See esp. *Leviathan*, chap 1-7.

2. Why is Language Important?

Why is language important? After all, is not Hobbes considered part of an empiricist tradition which presupposes a transparent medium between observer and perceived object? Hobbes begins the *Leviathan* with the disclaimer that it is necessary to know the natural causes of sensation. Since objects, external to the human body, cause movement in the determinative sense elaborated in Chapter One, reasoning can never reach beyond its own representations of the external objects.[16] Signs represent such objects. One becomes conscious of one's representations through the act of naming them. The act of naming natural and artificial objects preconditions all reasoning in that reasoning can never pass beyond names. So, one generates rational knowledge by abstracting names from experience. Names register or represent our thoughts. Accordingly, we reason by joining names into an interconnected web of names. Such a web of names Hobbes calls a language.

Hobbes claims that signification inheres in a name. Each name signifies what it says: that is, the name denotes a fixed, certain, objective concept. An author of a sign, then, expresses a thought or cognitive object. An author creates or originates the sign which represents the thought. Along the lines of Ockham,[17] Hobbes claims that whereas the object named is singular and individual, the name itself is a universal of particulars. According to Hobbes, a name imposes a universal upon a multiplicity of objects.[18] Truth lies in the right ordering of names, not in the essence embedded in an external object which the name represents. A name stands for or represents a particular. If an actor correctly associates a particular with the appropriate universal name, he or she exercises sound reasoning. Since signification is denotative, Hobbes associates a definition with Truth. As Hobbes puts it:

> By this it appears how necessary it is for any man that aspires to true knowledge, to examine the Definitions of former Authors; and either to correct them, where they are negligently set down; or to make them himselfe. For the errours of Definitions multiply themselves, according as the reckoning proceeds; and lead men into absurdities, which at last they see, but cannot avoyd, without reckoning anew from the beginning; in which lyes the foundation of their errours.[19]

Hobbes suggests that one begins to acquire scientific knowledge when, in conjunction with the scientific method, one correctly assigns a name to an

16 *Leviathan*, chap. 1, 85.

17 See generally, Frederick Copleston, *A History of Philosophy*, vol. 3, bk. 1 (New York/London: Doubleday, 1946; 1985), 39-42, 46-48.

18 *Leviathan*, chap. 4.

19 *Leviathan*, chap. 4, 105.

object.[20] He claims that one understands "when a man upon the hearing of any Speech, hath *those thoughts* which the words of that Speech, and their connexion, were ordained and constituted to signifie."[21] However, when we bring our passions (the experiential body) into an action, the names take on "inconstant" signification which "can never be true grounds of any ratiocination."[22] This "wrong speech" occurs on three occasions: first, when an author's name does not correctly correspond with the designated object; secondly, when an interpreter uses a name as a metaphor; and thirdly, when the names do not declare the precise will of their author. Metaphors and tropes are "less dangerous because they profess their inconstancy."[23]

So what is a language, according to Hobbes? How is a language connected to knowledge? A language is composed of "Names or Appellations, and their Connexion; whereby men register their Thoughts."[24] By uttering peculiar sounds, beasts come to recognize the sounds as words and, then, as sentences. The words, when combined into sentences, signify or represent the utterer's thoughts. Hobbes' point is that we do not just have pure thoughts. Thoughts must be signified by signs or "names." The special relations of signs with thoughts constitute a language, according to Hobbes. The primordial relation of beasts lacks this special relationship between signs and thoughts. Fear and anxiety dominate their actions, as a consequence. The worst fear is that of the brutal war of beast against beast. The greatest desire is that each and all will respect each other as each would wish to be treated. Once the beasts begin to speak and write, they come to agreements which bind the contractees into the future.[25] The beasts, once they begin to share conventions about the significations of signs, become authors and thereupon constrain their fears and desires through their contracts. The fears and bodily desires are what Hobbes calls "natural laws." The corresponding duties to ensure peace and to respect each other as good neighbours fulfil "natural duties."

---

20 For Hobbes' view of the scientific method, see esp. Copleston, chap. 5, 115-17. Hobbes is quick to note that the faculty of "reckoning" for the Romans lay in the *Nomina* or names for the *Rationcinatio* or accounting of money (*Rationes*). *Leviathan,* chap. 4, 106. It is interesting and ironic that contemporary legal analysis in common law jurisdictions gives great weight, at least in form, to the *ratio decidendi* of a legal judgment.

21 Copleston, 109. Emphasis added.

22 I have argued in *The Phenomenology of Modern Legal Discourse* (Aldershot/Brookfield: Dartmouth/Ashgate, 1998), chap. 5, that this view has a Husserlian flavour to it although, for Husserl, the subject intuitively thinks. Accordingly, meaning is provisional and subject to revision for Husserl. For Hobbes, one has a concept rather than a thought of a referent. Hobbes' view is more Platonic in this respect.

23 Copleston, bk. 1, vol. 3, 109-10.

24 *Leviathan,* chap. 4, 100.

25 *Leviathan,* chap. 14, 197-98.

3. Nature as a Condition Lacking a Shared Language

The beasts of the primordial condition may physically resemble human beings. Indeed, Hobbes writes that the natural condition includes "naturall fooles, children or mad-men" in that they are incapable of understanding the terms and consequences of language.[26] Fools, children, and the insane are no more than lions, bears, and wolves because they lack conventions as to what objects signify or represent their verbal noises. Some beasts, such as bees and ants, do live "sociably" with one another, Hobbes admits.[27] Such beasts do have "some use of voice, in making knowne to one another their desires, and other affections."[28] Yet, without "that art of words by which some men can represent to others," bees and ants cannot differentiate good from evil conduct. Lacking signs, beasts can only move in a direction driven by their particular bodily appetites and intuitive judgments. They cannot signify their thoughts, one to the other. So they cannot express what is expedient for the common benefit. Without shared signs to represent their thoughts, there is no society, peace, or the arts. Only savagery, solitude, and habitation in caves characterize the natural condition. Although Hobbes describes the natural condition as a literary device for the purpose of imagining away legal authority, he makes the anthropological claim on several occasions that the "savages" of North America lived in such a natural condition.[29] According to Hobbes, a concord amongst Amerindians depended upon natural lust, not upon reflection or discourse. Without a government or civil society, Amerindians remained in the natural condition.

Why would there be no peace amongst the beasts who cannot speak or write to each other in such a natural condition? Because, without shared conventions about what any one sound or mark signifies, no thoughts would be possible and, without thoughts to constrain one's action, only one physical body would constrain another body's movement. A body's desires would be unlimited. "To make Covenants with bruit Beasts, is impossible" because the beasts would not understand the terms of the contract. In such a condition, "every man has a Right to every thing; even to one another's body."[30] So, a culture retrospectively and artificially imposes a language upon the body's unlimited desires. Prior to culture, nature prevails. Nature, Hobbes understands as a condition where beasts are unable to express their desires except through the movement of their physical bodies. Though such movement, of course, offers gestural significations, Hobbes understands language as verbal and written rather than as gestural. This language-less condition logi-

26 *Leviathan,* chap. 26, 317.
27 *Leviathan,* chap. 27, 225.
28 *Leviathan,* chap. 17, 226.
29 See, e.g., *Leviathan,* chap. 13, 187; chap. 30, 378.
30 *Leviathan,* chap. 14, 190.

cally and chronologically precedes culture. The natural condition is primordial. Human beings progress towards civil society.

Most importantly, without signs to signify their bodily desires, there can be no contracts between the beasts. If a 'civilized' person contracts with a beast, the latter cannot understand the contract because the beast does not share a language with the civilized contractee. The beasts lack shared conventions as to what a sign signifies to each party to the contract: "to make covenant with bruit Beasts, is impossible; because not understanding our speech, they understand not, nor accept any translation of Right; nor can translate any Right to another; and without mutuall acceptation, there is not Covenant."[31] Without a shared language, a creature, alone amongst a multiplicity of individuals, lacks friends or associates. Raw power relations amongst the individuals determine the outcome of their disputes. Without language, "there had been amongst men, neither Common-wealth, nor Society, nor Contract, nor Peace."[32] Nor is there a culture, nor understanding, nor arts nor letters. Indeed, there is no account of time. Worst of all, there is "continuall feare, and danger of violent death; And the life of man, solitary, poore, nasty, brutish and short."

A beast's acquisition of a language is a slow process.[33] Hobbes best describes the process in Part 1, chapter 5, of the *Elements of Law*. Speech begins as the physical motion of the tongue: "[a]nd men desiring to show others the knowledge, opinions, conceptions, and passions which are in themselves, and to that end having invented language, have by that means transferred all that discursion of their mind ... by the motion of their tongues, into discourse of words." Once the tongue develops recognizable sounds, the sounds indicate words and sentences, and the words, in turn, represent invisible thoughts. Once beasts gain "the benefit of words" and thoughts signified by those words, they "exceed brute beasts in knowledge."[34] Language and thought go hand in hand: creatures invent language in order to express their "knowledge, opinions, conceptions, and passions which are within themselves."[35] Conventions about the significations of words precede reasoning: "and *ratio* now is but *oratio*, for the most part, wherein custom hath so great a power, that the mind suggesteth only the first word; the rest follow habitually, and are not followed by the mind."[36] And at the point when beasts accept the linguistic conventions, the beasts become authors:

---

31 *Leviathan*, chap. 14, 197. In *De Cive*, vol. 3 of Clarendon Edition of the Philosophical Works of Thomas Hobbes, critical edn. by Howard Warrender (Oxford: Oxford University Press, 1983; 1651), Part 1, chap. 2, sect. 12. Entitled in 1st edn. as *Philosophical Rudiments concerning Government and Society*. Hobbes explains that one cannot contract with another unless the party accepts an offer. But beasts can neither make nor accept an offer.

32 *Leviathan*, chap. 13, 186.

33 *Elements of Law*, 1.5.5.

34 *Elements of Law*, 1.5.13.

35 *Elements of Law*, 1.5.14.

36 Ibid.

they are able to express their thoughts to each other and to promise to fulfil their mutual undertakings. In sum, the motion of a tongue is slowly transformed into a discourse about the thoughts signified by the tongue's movement.

A society and culture begin to take form. The linguistic conventions induce members to communicate *inter-se*. Once they share such conventions, they become *authors* of their expressions and a culture takes hold. The authors can promise certain undertakings through their expressions. Language constrains the unlimited desires of their physical bodies. Indeed, the authors become self-conscious as if their cognitive objects mirrored their new identities as authors. They come to understand each other: "[u]nderstanding being nothing else, but conception caused by speech."[37] Even reasoning comes on the scene with linguistic conventions: "where Speech is not, there is neither *Truth* nor *Falsehood*."[38] Hobbes is impressed that the Greeks used the same word, *logos*, for both speech and reasoning because, without shared conventions about the signification of words, one could not reason: "not that they [the Greeks] thought there was no Speech without Reason; but no Reasoning without Speech."[39] With such shared significations of words, formerly language-less creatures are drawn together into social relations. The acquisition of a language thereby lifts beasts from a natural condition into an artificially created condition characterized by a language and, with language, a public reason.

4. The Actors of a Language

a) The artificial persons of a language

When authors begin to express themselves, they are "makers" or "artificers." Man is an artificer and language is the medium through which an artificer creates products. One thought succeeds another thought in a private or mental discourse, according to Hobbes. And yet, without words, one could not even possess a "private discourse." With words, authors may create an artificial person or agent to represent them for certain purposes. The sovereign state is one such artificial agent.[40] So too, an author produces *thoughts* about good and evil by representing the thoughts in expressions: "[f]or Morall Philosophy is nothing else but the Science of what is Good, and Evill *in conversation*, and Society of mankind."[41] Justice and injustice only enter the scene once creatures share conventions about the signification of words and sentences.

---

37 *Leviathan*, chap. 4, 109.
38 *Leviathan*, chap. 4, 105.
39 *Leviathan*, chap. 4, 106.
40 *Leviathan*, "Introduction," 81.
41 *Leviathan*, chap. 15, 216. Emphasis added.

Hobbes distinguishes between the artificers of expression and the natural persons who lack words and sentences to signify thoughts. One is given a name in a culture. The name of a person signifies a "Feigned or Artificiall person." An artificial person is "the *disguise*, or *outward appearance,* of a man."[42] It is as if on the stage of a theatre, an actor, in turn, impersonates or re-presents the authentic or "natural" person through language.

Now, Hobbes describes two types of artificial persons. First, there is an "author" who creates a sign to signify his private thoughts.[43] Secondly, Hobbes describes an "actor" who represents the authors' intent. Yet, the author is not natural or authentic because the author communicates his desires through artificially constructed signs rather than through bodily violence as one finds amongst the beasts of the early natural condition. Emotive inclinations rule the actions of natural persons. The actor "feigns" the will of the author who owns the words. By "feigned," Hobbes means that the actor "invent[s] something with no basis in fact." Like an actor on the stage of a theatre, Hobbes' actors play with the authors' words. Actors mimic or copy or mock the authentic world of natural persons by acting through the words owned by the playwright or author.[44] "The disguise or outward appearance" of the actor "counterfeited [the natural person] on the Stage."

But once the author speaks, the author, not the actor, owns the words. The author's words grant authority to the actor to act on behalf of the author. The actor represents the author. That said, the actor cannot exceed the boundary or *vires* of the author's commission of authority to the actor. The actor's actions may not exceed the author's train of thought which his words signify. In a sense, the actor mediates between the author's words and intent on the one hand and the addressee of the author on the other. The actor may even mediate between God, as the author of the Scriptures, and God's "children."

The state too is such an actor, according to Hobbes. The state is neither a natural beast which lacks signs to signify its desires nor an author who expresses ideas through such signs. An artificial person, the state is created by the words of other artificial persons, the authors. The state's authority to enact expression is total. That totality of authority renders the state autonomous or sovereign. As Hobbes describes in *De Cive*, the City "hath no being but by their Supreme Power."[45]

The many authors possess dominion over the words by which the state is produced. A multiplicity of authors create the state. This multiplicity of authors

42 *Leviathan,* chap. 16, 217.

43 I refer to the male gender because Hobbes intends that his claims only concern men. Hobbes continually describes the pyramidal organization of offices as "patriarchal." So, even if women ever occupied an office, their role, which determines their decisions, would come from a patriarchal context.

44 *Leviathan,* chap. 16, 217.

45 *De Cive,* 2.12.4.

own their words of creation. But the state, as an actor, feigns the intent of the authors. The unilingual voice of the state transcends the contradictory voices of the multiplicity of authors. The simple and supreme actor speaks down towards its own actors on the patriarchal structure. So too, the state monologically speaks towards the addressees/citizens while the latter passively listen. The voice of the state, as representative of the authors, binds the original authors even though the state, the supreme actor, is created by such authors.

b) The authors

Hobbes is obviously preoccupied with the *auctoritas* of the actors who feign the words of authors. The authority of the actors to mimic the authors lies with the original intent of the authors when they created one special actor, the state, to represent their interests.

The derivation of the state's authority from this transference of authority from author to actor leads to two consequences.[46] First, an actor's play with an author's original words may contradict the unwritten customs which had conditioned the lives of beasts. The main requirement here is that the actor has been authorized to invalidate such a custom. How is it possible that an actor may legitimately override the very beasts whose desire for peace the actors artificially replicate? The important point is that all actors fulfil the will of the authors who had commissioned the actors to act.

Secondly, if the actors refused to override the unlimited desires of languageless natural persons when the authors authorized the actors to do so, the actors would thereby contradict the natural laws. Why? Because the beasts of the early stage of the natural condition cannot enter into contracts for they do not understand each other, lacking a language with which they can enter into contracts. As such, by a contract, authors authorize actors to contradict the manner by which natural persons act in the natural condition.

One promise, then, transcends all actions. By that promise, the authors agree to create a single super-actor to represent all authors. Hobbes calls such a super-actor, the Representer. One actor will ensure peace, a peace which was found wanting amongst the beasts who had acted according to the emotional inclinations of unlimited bodily desires. Once subordinate actors posit civil laws, the civil laws place boundaries about possession with the effect that property becomes private or exclusive to the owner of the property. The Representer of the authors retains a pure legal title over all material objects in civil society. The Representer's subordinate actors will not be able to rescind such title. But in agreeing to delegate

46 *Leviathan*, chap. 16, 218.

their authority to their single representative, the many authors agree to alienate their sovereignty to the Representer. They do so wholly and forever in order to prevent a return to the natural condition when beasts roamed the earth and when those beasts, because they could neither speak nor write through a shared language, imposed their natural wills upon competing bodies. Having transferred their sovereignty to their Representer, the multiple authors are thereby obligated to obey the laws of their Representer *as if* the Representer were the supreme actor in the plays of human creation.

So, the subordinate actors located down the lines of the institutional hierarchy bind the multiple authors who had created the supreme Representer. The actors effectively dominate the play, though the authors created the play. The authors may not renege upon their promise to follow the commands of their super-actor, the Representer. In a sense, the authors owned title to the copyright, but the actors effectively control the use of the words. For, if any one individual complains about an enactment of the Representer, that individual effectively complains about her/himself because each individual, as an author, impliedly authors all acts of the Representer by agreeing to abide by the Representer's acts. The basic contract signed "of every man with every Man" operates "as if every man should say to every man, 'I authorize and give up my Right of Governing my selfe, to this Man [the Representer/agent], or to this Assembly of men, on this condition, that thou give up the Right to him, and Authorize all his Actions in like manner.'"[47]

Thus, a "reall Unity" transcends the discordent voices of the multiple natural persons in the earlier natural condition. The unity also transcends the particular wills of the authors when they first acquired conventions about signs. This juridically constructed "reall Unity" is an artificially created unity, crystallized from a shared language and superimposed upon the real, fractious relations of the beasts of the natural condition. Hobbes names the Representer, the "Common-wealth," in that the agent represents the common general good of all beasts. Once created, the Representer may "use the strength and means of them all, as he shall think expedient" in order to ensure the fictitious unity.

c) *The monologic voice of the Representer*

But who is this artificial person in whose name judges and legislators and all other subordinate actors must feign? The Representer is neither a private individual human being nor a king nor a judge nor a legislator. The Representer does not even possess the "private reason" of a natural person. The Representer is that artificial person who mimics authors. The Representer does not create products,

47 *Leviathan*, chap. 17, 227.

such as subordinate offices and laws: the many authors do that. The Representer merely represents the intent of the authors who owned the expression which had created the Representer. Through their expression, the authors agree to create an artificial person who speaks on their behalf. All civil laws will be guided by "the Reason of this our *Artificiall* Man, the Common-wealth, and his command, that maketh Law."[48] Such a reason signifies the unified transcendent will of the multiplicity of the authors who had expressed themselves by their contract.

Now, the "essence of the Common-wealth" is "One Person," Hobbes writes. Unless there is a single supreme sovereign, there would remain discord in civil society. Two (or more) competing supreme persons would struggle for supremacy: "[a]nd the Common-wealth being in their Representative but one Person, there cannot easily arise any contradiction in the Lawes; and when there doth, the same Reason is able, by interpretation or alteration, to take it away."[49] Even the judges are subordinate to the One representative. The judges must have regard to the intent of the One representative when they interpret a statute or ordinance. Indeed, Hobbes speculates in *De Cive* that the claim that several authorities embody the supreme authority is seditious.[50] The single representative is supreme even over the judges who apply the Representer's will in diverse circumstances, Hobbes points out in *De Cive*.[51] He likens the Representer to the father in the "little city" of a family. A citizen owns no right against the sovereign Representer except to the extent that the sovereign has assigned a right to the citizen.[52] One must trace authority to some supreme and absolute office which may function as the *terminus ultimus* of the citizenry as a whole.[53] In order to ensure a finality to the posit of a statute or a common law precedent, any particular statute or precedent must be rationally linked to the one ultimate representative of the whole populace.

One Representer speaks in a *single*, unilingual and monologic voice. The ideas of the Representer emanate from the Representer *to* the subordinate offices under the Representer. Hobbes' Representer neither listens nor responds to the citizen for the citizen speaks from an 'ought' world outside the legal structure of the Representer: the Representer's voice is monologic vis-à-vis the citizenry. The Representer's officials synthesize competing customs, voices and ideas into a single voice with "exact definitions."[54] The civil laws embody such a unilingual voice. Precisely because of its Oneness, the representative of the many authors cannot

48 *Leviathan*, chap. 26, 317. Emphasis added.
49 Ibid.
50 *De Cive*, 2.12.5.
51 *De Cive*, 2.6.8.
52 *De Cive*, 2.8.5.
53 *De Cive*, 2.6.8.
54 *Leviathan*, chap. 5, 116.

allow for any discordant claimant to authority: "there cannot easily arise any contradiction in the Lawes; and when there doth, the same Reason [of the Artificiall Man] is able, by interpretation, or alteration, to take it away."[55] This "real" unity of civil laws is imposed upon the disparate contradictory voices in the natural condition. The monologic voice of the Representer finalizes all disputes in civil society.

The sovereign Representer speaks through institutional "offices" which are organized in the model of a pyramid. The supreme representative, like the other actors, is an office, not a person, at the pinnacle of the organization of authoritative offices. "I speak not of man but (in the Abstract) of the Seat of Power," Hobbes writes in his Epistle Dedicatory.[56] All actors, then, must passively listen to the monologic voice of the Representer. When interpreting a statute, a judge, for example, must search for the "reason," "sentence" or intent of the Representer. The search moves the judge to synthesize the texts of other actors into a rationally coherent whole as if the Representer had willed a linearly directed thought-plan which authoritative documents signify. The judge interprets such documents as if constrained by the omnipresent gaze of the Representer. All actors decide and act in the name of the Representer. The Representer is all-knowing and omniscent. But the Representer, as a metaphysical construct, lacks the body of a natural person. So long as a judge interprets a text as if the Representer had expressed the ideas behind the text, the judge's interpretation is valid or authoritative. But if a judge, as an actor, exceeds the supreme Representer's intended boundaries, the actor expresses a subjective value and thereby renders an unauthoritative and, therefore, an "unjust" opinion.

In contrast with other actors, then, the Representer can never act unjustly: "nothing the Soveraign Representative can doe to a Subject, on what pretence soever," Hobbes insists, "can properly be called Injustice, or Injury; *because every Subject is Author* of every act the Soveraign doth."[57] The sovereign does no wrong, for example, by putting a citizen to death. An interpretation of the contract can be considered just, then, only after the authors have authorized the basic contract and only after the subordinate officials have begun to enforce its terms. Actors enforce the contract's terms as if the original authors in the natural condition were making the decision. Justice does not lie in some universal laws which transcend the civil laws: "[b]efore there was any government *just* and *unjust* had no being, their nature onely being relative to some command, and every action in its own nature is indifferent; that it becomes *just*, or *unjust*, proceeds from the right of the

55 *Leviathan*, chap. 26, 317.
56 *"Epistle Dedicatory"* to *Leviathan*, 75.
57 *Leviathan*, chap. 21, 264-65. Emphasis added.

Magistrate."[58] Where there is no language, superstition, not justice, reigns. A language, backed by force, constrains the unlimited appetites of bodies in the natural condition. When the conventions about signs are enforced, property and contracts emerge. At that stage, the unlimited desire to possess physical objects becomes limited, subject to the caveat noted below. The basic contract elaborates the terms of justice. A law is authoritative if it has been posited by the appropriate office in the Representer's structure. If authoritatively posited, the rule is just: "no Law can be Unjust. The Law is made by the Soveraign Power, and all that is done by such Power, is warranted, and owned by every one of the people; and that which every man will have so, no man can say is unjust."[59] Without a contract, each creature possesses an unlimited right to possess every object. No action can be considered unjust if each creature possesses an unlimited right to possess every object. Injustice is the non-performance of a contract. Only with a contract can one speak of justice and injustice.

Hobbes describes texts as being alive and dead. A text is alive if it is created by the appropriate institutional actor on the stage. In a section entitled "Of Sovereign Power" in the *Dialogue*, Hobbes argues that, by itself, a sign is but a "dead letter." Even a statute or ordinance, without more, is "but a dead Letter."[60] But if the statute is linked with the voice of an actor vertically located under the highest office of the Representer, a dead sentence becomes alive. If a judge speaks within the *vires* or boundaries of authority, the statute remains "alive," although, ironically, the juridical actors are artificial persons. The institutional structure makes the statute alive because the structure can be traced to the 'live' natural creatures who, when they become authors, desire peace and who delegate their authority to the Representer.

Hobbes makes this point by distinguishing between the author of a document and one who "pens" the document.[61] An author intends the thoughts as signified in a document. But the intent of the one who pens the document – the draftsman, the king, the clerk of the privy council – is not relevant to the document's authority. The king's signature at the end of a document does not render the ordinance valid. What is critical is the king's authority to pen the ordinance. The ordinance is an act of the king, an actor. To render the king's ordinance valid, one must link the king's ordinance to the locus of the office of the king in the vertical hierarchy of other offices

58 *De Cive*, 2.12.1.

59 *Leviathan*, chap. 30, 388.

60 Hobbes, *A Dialogue between a Philosopher and a Student of the Common Laws of England*. Ed. & intro. Joseph Cropsey (Chicago: University of Chicago Press, 1971; 1681), "Of Soveraign Power," 58-9 (10). The page references will be to the Cropsey edn. with the original pagination in (...), as noted by Cropsey.

61 *Dialogue*, "Of Soveraign Power," 59 (11).

of the supreme Representer. Moreover, one must ensure that the king has penned the document within the boundaries posited by the Representer's civil laws.

d) The supremacy of the Representer

One point needs to be clarified. The authors create a legal existence by virtue of their creation of the sovereign Representer. If one exceeds the authoritative boundaries of action for any office inside the Representer's hierarchy of offices, one ventures into a personal world. Even though Hobbes insists that the actors speak and write on behalf of the intent of the multiple authors in the natural condition, this unity is feigned in that the unity artificially transcends the desires of the multiple actors. Such a transcendent unity is not experienced – or, at least, it is not experienced in the same manner as is a bodily struggle in the natural condition. The Representative's commands may impact upon the bodies of the actors and the citizens in civil society. After all, they will be enforced. Accordingly, the Representer represents a fictitious unity which becomes real despite its artificial or culturally constructed character. The multitude in the natural condition simply cannot be one.[62] The multitude needs a single agent, external to the multitude, in order for them to survive the unremitting, unrestrained war of body against body: "[t]here is therefore no other government in this life, neither of state, nor religion, but temporal.... And that governor must be one; or else there must needs follow faction and civil war in the commonwealth, between the *Church* and *State*."[63]

Hobbes' message is clear. In order to ensure peace, the single Representer must remain supreme over all other actors and all human subjects within its territory. All rights are transferred to the sovereign Representer. The Representer is greater than the sum of its parts. Hobbes describes the extent of supremacy in this way in *De Cive*:

> there is a *Supreme power* in some one, greater then which cannot by Right be conferr'd by men, or greater then which no mortall man can have over himself. But that power, greater then which cannot by men, be conveigh'd on a man, we call ABSOLUTE: for whosoever hath so submitted his will to the will of the City, *That he can, unpunisht, doe any thing, make Lawes, judge Controversies, set Penalties*, make use, at his own pleasure, of the *strength*, and wealth of men, and all this by Right, truly he hath given him the greatest dominion that can be granted.[64]

The closer the subordinate official reaches the gaze of the Representer, the closer does the official reach the Truth. "In the presence of the sovereign," Hobbes describes in the *Leviathan*, the citizen "shines no more than the Starres in the

62 *Leviathan*, chap. 16, 220-21.
63 *Leviathan*, chap. 25, 306. Cf. *De Cive*, 3.18.1.
64 *De Cive*, 2.6.13; 2.6.18.

presence of the Sun." When citizens appear beyond the Representer's sight, "they shine some more, some lesse."[65] First, the Representer is not bound by its own laws because the Representer may, over time, amend or repeal its statutes. Secondly, whatever the Representer does is unpunishable: the king can do no wrong.[66] Thirdly, a citizen possesses property only as a tenant of the Representer who, in turn, owns a pure absolute title to the property. A subject only owns *private* property in his relationship to others in civil society.[67] Fourth, no citizen may challenge the authority of the sovereign to make laws. Situated *under* the commands of the Representer's institutions, the citizen lacks authority traceable to the Representer. As John Austin would put it, the citizen merely expresses a subjective opinion.

Indeed, once the contractees agree to create the Representer, any minority which did not wish to enter that contract must now agree to its terms: "because the major part hath by consenting voice declared a Soveraigne; he that dissented must now consent with the rest; that is, he contented to avow all the actions he shall do, or else justly be destroyed by the rest."[68] For each and all voluntarily agreed to follow the will of the majority. Each natural person is implicitly the author of the sovereign's actions. So long as the Representer acts with authority, it can do no wrong upon any originary author, however stringent the punishment.[69] For to complain about the Representer is, in effect, to complain about oneself as the author of the sovereign Representer. If one enters into society only to later contravene its covenants, one may not rejoin society: such a violator is now outside the law, an out-law.

5. The Problematic of Hobbes' Theory of Sovereignty

The originary authors are situated external to their own product, the Representer. Once the civil institutions are constructed, even the multiplicity of authors who implicitly agreed to the contract, remain *external* to their own product. The external situs of the creative author places the author *under* its product, the Representer, and the Representer's products, the civil laws. Each author is equal *before* the laws of the Representer. Even the king or some other supreme office must act *under* the civil laws. Common law lawyers call this subordination to the Representer's voice, the 'rule of law.' All citizens, even those who strongly believe that the Representer's subordinate actors are violating the conditions of the contract which created the Representer, impliedly consent to the actions of the subordinate actors.

---

65 *Leviathan*, chap. 18, 238.
66 See *De Cive*, 2.6.13; 2.9.3.
67 *De Cive*, 2.8.5.
68 *Leviathan*, chap. 18, 231.
69 *Leviathan*, chap. 18, 232.

The total enclosure of the Representer's civil laws takes me to the critical problematic of Thomas Hobbes' theory of law. Hobbes builds an argument for the necessity of a sovereign or self-legislating state, the Representer, in order to ensure peace. But Hobbes grounds the authority of the state's laws in a primordial condition inaccessible to the official language of the state. We need a state with total authority in order to overcome the condition of perpetual struggle where creatures did not share a language. Once such creatures gain a language, they become the authors and owners of their own words. The authors desire a peace which they could not experience in the condition when they only had their physical bodies to resolve their disputes. The authors' desires for peace and for brotherly love (if there is such a thing) do not make sense without Hobbes' speculative belief that a primordial natural condition logically and chronologically precedes the civil laws. The goal of the civil laws is to institute the desires of authors who dread the condition when they could neither speak nor write. The authors enter the stage *after* they have acquired a language. Hobbes places their situs logically and anthropologically *post facto* a primordial condition. For to be an author or creator, one must share conventions with readers about the cognitive objects associated with an author's writing. At that point, authors and addressees will recognize each other's words. The primordial language-less condition prior to such a recognition, though, originates or grounds the acts of the authors.

But with the finality of this pre-linguistic moment, there arises a critical problem in Hobbes' philosophy of law. The pre-linguistic moment, because it cannot be accessed through a language, is unrecognizable to the officials who work in the Representer's offices. How can one recognize a condition when the condition lacks signs to signify its own identity or when our own language (that is, the language of the officials) lacks signs with which to recognize such a language-less condition? Hobbes' actors can only recognize thoughts or physical objects which are signified through speech and writing. Once the beasts recognize conventions about the signification of names, they become authors who just cannot escape from language. They cannot return to a condition without language. To do so would be like returning to one's infancy when one could only babble (although we know now that even an infant can express a pain or a desire by the tone of her cry). Without signs with which to speak and write, the beasts could not even express their private thoughts except through their brutish bodies. Interestingly, without signs to signify their private thoughts, it is unlikely that Hobbes' beasts even had private thoughts. Indeed, Hobbes' beasts are less than what we understand as a mammal today since we know now that many mammals and fish do possess verbal and gestural languages. The unmediated bodily acts of the beasts are left as a remainder outside the language of the civil laws.

6. The Natural Condition

a) Are there laws in the natural condition?

In their application of the Representer's will, legal officials forget the very possibility of a gap in the interconnected institutions and their laws. Hobbes maintains, however, that even the natural condition is governed by laws. How is this possible? And what is the nature of these laws in the natural condition? How can there be laws if there are no linguistic conventions to signify the voices and marks? If there are 'laws,' what is the character of the 'laws' in the pre-language condition?

Because the beasts in the natural condition lack conventions about the signification of signs, they cannot communicate their thoughts with each other. They can communicate neither verbally nor in writing. The multiplicity of individuals possess their physical bodies. The inclinations of their bodies drive them to desire objects which they lack. Struggle or 'war' characterizes their desire to dominate each other's body. To the extent that laws govern this acquisitive world, the laws are 'natural' in that the strength of the natural or biological body determines the outcome of struggle. Neither the thoughts of the mind nor the signs of expression are important because thoughts are impossible without signs, Hobbes says, and signs are not possible in the pre-legal condition. The only constraint upon any one creature's actions is the countervailing power of the physical body of another creature. Neither reason nor language constrains bodily action in the natural condition.

Thus, at best, the intuitively grasped practices in the natural condition are "theorems." The theorems hypothesize the causes and effects of the never-ending movement of material objects. As such, the theorems are pieces of advice about the movement of creatures which can neither speak nor write. Hobbes rightly distinguishes theorems from the commands of an author. The theorems are not really laws. The theorems concern "what conduceth to the conservation and defence of themselves [of bodies]; whereas Law, properly is the word of him, that by right hath command over others."[70] The theorems speculate about the causes and effects of the movement of physical bodies in the physical-chemical universe. In contrast, Hobbes reserves the term 'law' to a command which is authored. Society is civil because language, not bodily movement, joins one individual with another.

Hobbes uses two corresponding senses of the word 'natural' in the *Leviathan*, then.[71] First, when one physical body is much more powerful than another body in a realm without language, the weaker body 'naturally' defers to the stronger. One body

70 *Leviathan*, chap. 15, 122-23.

71 A.P. Martinich, *The Two Gods of Leviathan: Thomas Hobbes on Religion and Politics* (Cambridge: Cambridge University Press, 1992), 93.

is always going to be more powerful than another. Individual bodies are scattered and isolated, there being no shared conventions as to what any one sign signifies.

The second sense of 'natural' arises when one has entered into a society where there is a shared language. Here, bodies can be considered equal. For the language signifies cognitive objects and these, by virtue of their universal character, transcend the unequal brutal bodies. An artificial equality encloaks the former unequal power relations between the bodies. In such a society of artificially constructed equality, there remains a natural duty of the Representer to defer to the desire for peace which was so absent in the natural condition. This natural duty is the second sense of 'natural.' Although the Representer exercises a totality of legal authority over all other beings in civil society, the Representer fulfils a natural duty of peace through the expression of its civil laws.

b) Two promises of the authors

Hobbes clearly sets out two very different stages in the evolution from the natural condition to civil society. In the first stage, creatures cannot speak or write. A perpetual struggle of moving bodies is played out. In the second stage, these creatures begin to share conventions about the sounds which their tongues express. With such conventions, the creatures appreciate the opportunity to escape from the former condition where force determined the outcome of disputes. When the multiplicity of individuals gain some facility to understand, according to Hobbes, they become sufficiently self-conscious to realize that it is in their self-interest to escape from the language-less condition of beasts and savages. They become creators or authors of sentences. They also are able to make promises to each other because they share meaning attributed to sounds.

Now, later in the *Elements of Law*,[72] Hobbes suggests that human agents may contract with each other in the language-less natural condition. Such contracts create rights which belong to the signatories of the contracts. Such rights can only be enforced by self-help. But in the *Leviathan*, *De Cive*, and the *Dialogue*,[73] human beings acquire property and legal rights only *after* they have passed through the natural condition. Before one shares conventions about the significations of signs, one may only possess a theorem about the movement of bodies. The natural laws in civil society are not really laws. As a language, civil laws may restrain and abridge natural laws in that the purpose of civil laws is to limit the natural unlimited liberty of each man to possess goods.[74] Only when the sovereign expresses its will in writing, only then is its will called a law.

72 *Elements of Law*, 1.15.8.
73 *Leviathan*, chap.15, 202; *De Cive* 2.6.1; *Dialogue* 73 (36).
74 *Leviathan*, chap. 26, 315.

Once the beasts share conventions as to what special words and sentences signified, the creatures, now authors, make two promises. Only at this point does Hobbes describe the theorems as 'laws.' Hobbes described the first promise in this manner: "Do not that to another, which thou thinkest unreasonable to be done by another to thy selfe."[75] Since the former beasts in the language-less natural condition have now acquired a language, signs may represent their desires. Each physical body now falls *under* and *inside* the invisible boundaries of the thoughts signified in the public language.

Hobbes describes the second promise in this manner: "that a man be willing, when others are so too, as farre-forth, as for Peace, and defence of himselfe he shall think it necessary, to lay down this right to all things; and be contented with so much liberty against other men, as he would allow other men against himselfe."[76] And so, motivated by the first promise, the authors agree to create an artificial person with an absolute sovereignty to ensure an equal liberty for all. The authors agree to a totality and autonomy for the sovereign in order to ensure that the unlimited natural liberty of objects be restrained and, if necessary, abrogated. And this restraint is necessary in order to ensure a peace which is forever lacking in the land of beasts. The duty of the artificially created Representer is to ensure that no one human being will ever return to the natural condition where physical strength determined the outcome of disputes. So the Representer, though an artificial actor, continues a natural duty to ensure peace from the dread which creatures would have experienced in the natural condition: "[t]he Office of the Soveraign, (be it a Monarch, or an Assembly,) consisteth in the end, for which he was trusted with the Soveraign Power, namely the procuration of *safety of the people*."[77] So, the multiplicity of authors, in their first act after acquiring a language, authorize the Leviathan to express and to protect the authors' interest through civil laws. The Leviathan cannot posit its own ultimate authority. For the authority emanates from the authors who pre-exist the Leviathan. As Hobbes writes in *De Cive*, "our obligation to civil obedience, by vertue whereof the civill Lawes are valid, is before all civill Law."[78]

In sum, the authority of the Leviathan's institutional structure is total vis-à-vis all other actors and all human subjects before the laws. And yet, the Leviathan owes natural duties to the creatures of the natural condition. When the Leviathan's

---

75 *Leviathan*, chap. 26, 318. When Hobbes described the first fundamental law of nature early in the *Leviathan*, he was referring to the early stage of the natural condition when creatures did not share a language. Because of the consequences of the language-less condition, the first principle of living should be "That every man, ought to endeavour Peace, as farre as he has hope of obtaining it; and when he cannot obtain it, that he may seek, and use, all helps, and advantages of Warre." *Leviathan* chap. 14, 190.

76 *Leviathan*, chap. 14, 190.

77 *Leviathan*, chap. 30, 376.

78 *De Cive*, 2.14.21.

laws are silent, the actors must consider the unwritten theorems (equity) for direction. What is important here is that the private conscience of all natural subjects, not of an actor in civil society, identifies the theorems of the invisible condition. And private conscience is responsible to God alone. Like the Leviathan, all human beings who have acquired linguistic conventions owe a natural duty. In their case, though, the natural duty is to obey the Leviathan's commands. In the enforcement of natural duties, all bodily authority, which each language-less beast had previously possessed as a possessive individual, is transferred to the supreme Representer. The authorization of the Representer to act on behalf of all human subjects within its territory, then, pre-exists the Representer and its offices. The Representer is the *product* of the deliberation of authors who, haunted by the memory of an invisible language-less condition, desire never to return to it.[79]

c) Natural duty

Hobbes writes of two senses of justice, then. The one is a natural justice which manifests theorems about the movement of the language-less creatures. The other is a justice which is only possible, we have noted above, after the authors have constructed a basic contract. The second sense of justice is not an *apriori* concept. Rather, it is conditional upon the terms of the historically contingent civil laws. Such civil laws are written in statutes and ordinances. The first sense of justice, natural justice, is unwritten in that it is imprinted into the hearts of the natural beasts who cannot speak or write. But in such a language-less condition, natural justice cannot be the subject of reflection for reflection is only possible through a language. Because natural justice remains unwritten, there is no language to access such a justice. A vague unwritten equity hovers behind the never-ending struggle of beasts. So, the Representer is not supreme vis-à-vis natural justice. Although the civil offices are subordinate only to the Representer, the Representer remains subordinate to the divine source of the conscience which is manifested in natural justice.[80] The Representer only represents juridically defined offices which can speak and write through statutes, ordinances and judicial decisions.

Unlike the many authors in the first stage of culture, the Representer possesses a special natural duty: namely, to ensure that all actors of the Representer never return

79 Even Howard Warrender misses the point that the natural duties arise before the creatures in the natural condition begin to understand each other through shared conventions about marks and sounds. Warrender, *Political Philosophy of Hobbes*, 1-79. Warrender does claim that the citizen's obligation to obey the state's laws arises prior to and independent of the creation of the state. But Warrender, missing the importance granted to language as the distinguishing factor between the natural condition and civil society, and associates the natural condition with the first act of culture when creatures make covenants with each other. Warrender ignores Hobbes' focus upon the inability of the creatures in the prior condition to speak or write through a language.

80 F.C. Hood, *The Divine Politics*, 145.

to the natural condition. This duty emanates from the dread of war in a language-less condition. The beasts, situated in the natural condition, may well have had an inclination or desire to terminate their never-ending struggle. But the duty of peace becomes a duty when the creatures have acquired a language. At that point, the creatures, as authors of expression, may differentiate good from bad action.

And yet, the duty is not a civil duty which the Representer, or its subordinate actors, may later posit. A creature may not transfer the right to receive peace, there being no right until after the authors have acquired a language through which to deliberate about the conditions of their promises. Even then, there is no right until the authors have created the Representer who, in turn, has constructed institutional offices whose officials may deliberate and decide. In addition, only with a shared language, can the creatures become self-conscious to the point of understanding what are their moral and legal duties. The natural duty of peace is not really a duty because human agents only become conscious of the duty, as a duty, when they can speak and write. At that point, they are in a position to realize that the natural duty to seek peace, though a subject of consciousness only when they have acquired a language, is inalienable because the duty emanated from a condition where desires were unmediated by thoughts and signs.

The duty is a natural duty, yet a duty which only the artificially created Representer owes. The Representer owes the duty to the many authors who had contracted with each other to create the Representer. Ultimately, the Representer functions here as the only natural person in civil society in that, though constructed as an artificial person through language, the Representer remains linked to the language-less natural condition where strife and dread prevailed.[81] Although the sovereign state is not subject to its own laws, it being sovereign vis-à-vis its offices and subjects, the Representer remains subject to natural duties because no actor, including the Leviathan, can retrieve a language-less condition.[82] Such a condition remains uncontrollable and uncontrolled except to the extent that institutions, motivated by the dread of the former condition, represent the event through a second-level narrative of enacted laws.

d) The natural duty to respect life

Liberty, Hobbes says, is the absence of opposition to the natural movement of a material body. In the natural condition, the movement of one body is unlimited except to the extent that the movement of another body constrains the movement of the first. Civil laws protect and restrict such liberty of movement when one extends the material bodies to include human agents. Civil laws are "artificial

81 See generally ibid., 210.
82 *Leviathan,* chap. 29, 367.

chains." An artificially constructed person, the sovereign Representer, fastens the chains of signs to subordinate juridical actors and to addressees who possess liberty. In the natural condition, there was "a full and absolute Libertie in every Particular man."[83] The artificial Representer of all authors transfers such a natural liberty into civil society: whether society is constructed by contract or by conquest, "[i]t is manifest, that every Subject has Liberty in all those things, the right whereof cannot by Covenant be transferred."[84]

What liberty of the movement of material bodies, precisely, may not be transferred to civil society? First, the citizen possesses a natural right not to kill, wound or maim her/himself even if the Representer orders the citizen to do so. A contract not to defend oneself physically, when challenged, is void.[85] Nor may the individual be ordered not to resist those who assault him, nor to abstain from "food, ayre, medicine, or any other thing, without which he cannot live."[86] Why not? Because "man by nature chooseth the lesser evill, which is danger of death in resisting; rather than the greater, which is certain and present death in not resisting."[87] Although the Representer's actors may be authorized to kill me, I am not obligated to kill myself when so commanded by the Representer's actors.

Hobbes offers that the citizen may not transfer a second natural duty into civil society: one may not be compelled to confess a crime. Why not? Because in the natural condition, each natural person judges the morality of her/his own actions. But in civil society, an involuntary confession may be followed by punishment. Since such civilly imposed coercion returns one to the dread of the natural condition, one may resist.[88]

Thirdly, if the Representer's actors convict "a great many men together" of a capital crime for which they will receive capital punishment, the convicted persons retain the liberty "to joyn together, and assist, and defend one another."[89] Why? Because each retains the natural right to defend her/his life, whether guilty or innocent. It is not unjust to bear arms after a series of unjust acts by the Leviathan, according to Hobbes.

Fourth, this natural right to protect one's physical being "can by no Covenant be relinquished." Once the Representer can no longer protect the subject, the subject is no longer obligated to the sovereign Representer.[90] In

83 *Leviathan*, chap. 21.
84 *Leviathan*, chap. 21, 268.
85 *Leviathan*, chap. 14, 199.
86 *Leviathan*, chap. 21, 269.
87 *Leviathan*, chap. 14, 198.
88 *Leviathan*, chap. 14, 199.
89 *Leviathan*, chap. 21, 270.
90 *Leviathan*, chap. 21, 272.

such a circumstance, the Representer, as the soul of the Common-wealth, has departed from its body – the body politic. Once the soul leaves the body, the body is left misdirected and on its own.

Hobbes' general point is that the literal words of a contract do not bind the subject. Rather, it is the intention of the authors behind their words that matters.[91] And the authors intend to respect the natural tendency of all bodies to protect their self-interest as they collide with each other in the natural condition.

In sum, the natural laws permeate the civil laws once the state is organized. For, the natural 'laws' dictate that covenants, once agreed, be performed. That is, theorems of nature underlie obedience to civil laws.

And yet, the *authority* or *validity* of civil laws is considered separate from the moral content of those laws. A text is valid as a source of law if its 'author' can be traced to the actors on the institutional hierarchy of actors. The manner and form by which the text is enacted is the crucible of authority. The prescriptive content of the text is immaterial to such manner and form of its enactment. I have just noted that such a prescriptive content may manifest the bodily desires in a natural condition. As Hobbes writes in *De Cive*, the laws of nature are "the summe of Morall Philosophy" (although in the *Leviathan*, moral philosophy is only possible *after* the Leviathan has established its subordinate actors).[92] And the moral philosophy (of *De Cive*) is the law of God as expressed by the Word of Christ.[93] God's will may be violated by either one's will or one's deed.[94] But such a violation dwells in a metaphysical realm external to the structure of commands of the supreme Representer in civil society.

7. The Authority of Written Laws

What is the distinguishing nature of law, then? All civil laws, to be considered authoritative, must be authored by a supreme artificial person, the Representer. But what gives the Representer its authority to command subordinate offices and citizens?

Not surprisingly, the crucial factor lies in Hobbes' distinction between the written laws and the unwritten laws. The written laws are authoritative. The unwritten are unauthoritative. Although the unwritten laws may technically be evidenced in writing, laws are only considered "written" if they have been authored by actors on the Representer's institutional structure. Hobbes accepts this theme through all his texts.

91 *Leviathan*, chap. 21, 268.
92 *De Cive*, 1.3.32.
93 *De Cive*, 1.4.11.
94 *De Cive*, 1.4.21.

The big question is 'what is writing?' Does Hobbes mean a script that is printed and published? Or does he mean something else? Can the human voice be considered 'writing,' according to Hobbes? Hobbes associates writing with a voice or "some other sign" which signifies the will of the supreme Legislator, the Representer.[95] It is not a penned or written script *per se* which manifests writing. Rather, the key to writing is "a voice." The signs of the voice must be published. The authoritative voice must emanate from the supreme Representer. So, the Representer's expression is not voiced in the sense of a sound. Rather, the expression voices a 'make-believe' sound. The statutes, ordinances, and judicial decisions of the subordinate actors manifest the Leviathan's singular voice. Such a voice transcends the many voices of the creatures in the natural condition. The Leviathan's voice even displaces the many voices of the authors except, of course, their writing in the form of a social contract.

Legislative assemblies, judges, and other officials represent the official voice of the Representer. Such an official voice contrasts with the natural condition. In the latter, there is no voice except the grunts and moans of beasts that do not share a language. A heterology of voices dominates the later stages of the natural condition when creatures come to understand conventions as to what particular noises of the tongue signify. Continuing along these lines in *De Cive*, Hobbes says that the unwritten laws express the voice of nature or natural reason.[96] If a philosopher published a book which summarized such unwritten laws, the philosopher, as author, would not render the unwritten laws 'written.' Though an author, such a philosopher, would lack the authority to state what is the law, the philosopher would write from outside the trace of authority to the supreme Representative.[97] A commentator or philosopher gains her/his authority from her/his expertise of the subject-matter of the book, not from her/his situs in an institutional hierarchy, according to Hobbes. Customs too, even if coded in some academic treatise, lack the authority of the supreme Representer. Indeed, lacking any distinct and assignable author, a custom cannot be traced to the Representer's voice. As Hobbes writes in the *De Corpore Politico* Part of the *Elements of Law*, "[w]ritten laws therefore are the constitutions of a commonwealth expressed ... custom *of itself* maketh no laws." Nevertheless, Hobbes explains, a custom may be given "the vigour of the law" "because the sovereign power is supposed tacitly to have approved such sentence for right, and thereby it cometh to be a law, and numbered amongst the written laws of the commonwealth. For if custom were sufficient to introduce a law, then it would be in the power of everyone that is deputed to hear

95 *De Cive*, 2.14.14.

96 Ibid.

97 This contrasts with Martin Luther (1483–1546) who had earlier claimed that God is infinite inwardness. Also see Kant, *Critique of Judgment*, trans. Werner S. Pluhar (Indianapolis: Hackett, 1987; 1790), Pt 1.

a cause, to make his errors law."[98] A custom is transformed into law when the offices of the sovereign Representer articulate the custom as writing.[99] The voice of the Representer is supreme over all philosophers, customs, and commentaries because the commands of governmental offices may be traced to the commands of the Representer.

Accordingly, if a script were written and published, it remains 'unwritten' for Hobbes if its author lacks an authority which can be rationally traced to the supreme legislature, the Representer. All natural subjects remain external to the Representer's institutional actors even though the natural subjects may be under and inside the enclosure of laws posited by the actors. Natural persons may not challenge the authority of the Representer unless the Representer violates the natural duties which the Representer owes to the authors and, ultimately, to the divine Author. Unless and until the Representer establishes the authoritative institutions of civil society, the natural subject retains the "liberty" to act as if it were a beast in the natural condition.

In theory, though, the Leviathan's actors may constrain such natural liberty – on condition, of course, that the Leviathan fulfils its own natural duty to respect the author's natural right to life, again as described above. When the actors do so, the private conduct becomes public, a public language displaces private languages, and unlimited desires succumb to the artificial constraints of civil laws. The public space of civil society supplements the private desires of the natural condition.

But the supplemental public space becomes primary once one shifts from the unwritten natural realm to the artificial culture of artificial persons. Only in the public space of writing may one speak of justice. "Where speech is not, there is neither *truth* nor *falsehood*," Hobbes writes.[100] Indeed, before there can be justice between creatures, we must share a language with each other. Language is thereby logically *antecedent* to justice and to civil laws.[101] Hobbes reaches this conclusion in the *Leviathan* when he defines civil laws as those rules commanded "by Word, Writing, or other sufficient Sign of the Will."[102] With a shared language, both authors and authority are possible and with authority, so too is justice. Hobbes reiterates the point in the *Dialogue* when he says that before there was justice and injustice, title or property or lands distinguished by *Meum, Tuum, Alienum*, there *had* to be a law-maker with authority.[103] Hobbes also makes this point in *De Cive* when he writes that one cannot contract with another unless the one party accepts

98 *Elements of Law*, 2.10.10.
99 *De Cive*, 2.14.15.
100 *Leviathan*, chap. 4, 105.
101 *Dialogue*, "Of Soveraign Power," 72-3 (41).
102 *Leviathan*, chap. 26, 312.
103 *Dialogue*, "Of Soveraign Power," 73 (36-37).

the offer. But beasts can neither make nor accept an offer because they do not understand the thoughts signified by another creature's sounds/moans.[104] And again in the *Leviathan*, Hobbes writes that "[t]o make Covenant with bruit beasts, is impossible; because not understanding our speech, they understand not, nor accept of any translation of Right; nor can translate any Right to another; and without mutuall acceptation, there is no Covenant."[105]

Put differently, the addressees of civil laws are neither natural persons in a natural condition nor the authors who have acquired linguistic conventions. As a precurser to H.L.A. Hart's view, Hobbes insists that civil laws speak only to the *juridical actors* in a civil society, not to the citizenry: the king's laws "speak not to all the Kings Subjects in general, but only to his Officers; implicitly forbidding them to Judge, or execute any thing contrary to the said Grants [of the King]."[106] Even when a judge interprets the theorems of the natural condition, the judge's interpretation is "Authentique" if rendered "by Authority of the Soveraign."[107] The judge artificially and authoritatively creates 'facts.' But these 'facts' are not the judge's subjective values. When a judge privileges 'the facts,' the 'facts' are considered objective because of the judge's situs as an office which the sovereign created under it. A judge would be unable to evaluate facts because Hobbes accepted the Galilean view that matter is in continual flux. So long as a judge interprets within the *vires* of the sovereign's will or "sentence," the judge's reasoning represents the sovereign's will. But if the judge exceeds such boundaries, the judge acts in his personal capacity as a citizen, and thereby renders an unjust judgment.[108] So, for there to be 'law,' the law must be "written and published; but also that there be manifest signs, that proceedeth from the will of the Soveraign."[109] The signs must provide sufficient evidence that the Representer had authorized the signs. The evidence must document the time and place when and where the Representer expressed its will. An actor's interpretation of the sign must possess "the Authority of the Common-wealth."[110] Such authority makes the interpretation "authentique."

So, from the vantage point of the judicature offices, the words and sentences of those outside the offices are "a dead letter, which of itself is not able to compel a Man to do otherwise than himself pleaseth, nor punish, or hurt him when he hath

104 *De Cive*, 1.2.12.

105 *Leviathan*, chap. 14, 197.

106 *Dialogue*, "Of Soveraign Power," 75 (41).

107 *Leviathan*, chap. 26, 323.

108 According to John Knox (c.1513-1572), if the sovereign itself were unjust, the citizenry had the right to depose the immoral sovereign. The citizen may interpret the civil laws in terms of 'who is saved' and 'who is damned.'

109 *Leviathan*, chap. 26, 319.

110 *Leviathan*, chap.26, 322.

done a mischief."[111] The trace of a sign to a subordinate actor renders a sign "alive." Just because a statute ends with a signature, though, this does not make the statute valid. The document must be traced to a distinct and assignable office. The office, in turn, must possess the legal authority to enact or 'write' the statute. And that depends upon whether the office can be rationally linked to a prior and higher source on the vertical hierarchy of offices and, further, whether the subordinate office has acted within the boundaries which the Representer 'intended.' Neither the king nor the legislature authorizes a law by virtue of its personality or social status or the virtue of its rulers.[112] Nor does a custom possess the aura of authority by virtue of its longevity of existence or precedential value.[113] Nor are laws made by "long Study, Observation and Experience," as Chief Justice Edward Coke had held on more than one occasion.[114] Rather, the reason of the artificial Representer authorizes "that *Anima Legis*, that *Summa Lex*."

But what is the nature of this 'reason'? The Representer's 'reason,' according to Hobbes, is the ability to trace a document, such as a statute, to its source in an 'author'/actor and, then, to trace that 'author'/actor to a still higher source and, from there, to the supreme legislature of the whole hierarchy. Ultimately, the king's reason begins and ends with the Representer. The trace of authority of any juridical decision or action is self-referential. The king is not a philosopher who questions the moral or religious content of the thought intended by the king's signs. Nor should he be. Nor should any of the artificial persons, the actors, question the substantive moral content of any rule. The king can neither pen a law nor defend his citizenry against an enemy nor raise an army without the authority to do so. The king, as a human subject, is *under* the civil laws, just as are all citizens. But the king, as an authoritative actor, is an office, not a particular personality. An action is deemed authoritative if violators of the penned laws can be *punished* by an official who acts with authority. An action is made a crime by whomever possesses the authority to enforce the crime.[115] A statute or ordinance or judicial decision is

111 *Dialogue*, "Of Soveraign Power," 58-9 (10).

112 *Dialogue*, 85-6 (60-1), 62-3 (17-8).

113 *Dialogue*, "Of Soveraign Power," 96 (80), 61-2 (16); *Leviathan*, chap. 26, 313; 316-17.

114 *Dialogue*, "Of Soveraign Power," 61 (16). When James I had claimed in the *Prohibitions del Roy* that he too was authorized to resolve disputes amongst the citizenry because "the law was founded upon reason, and that he and others had reason, as well as judges," Coke CJ reported his own reply to the King in these words, "... true it was, that God had endowed his Majesty with excellent science, and great endowments of nature; but His Majesty was not learned in the laws of his realm of England, and causes which concern the life, or inheritance, or goods, or fortunes of his subjects, are not to be decided by natural reason but by the artificial reason and judgment of the law, which law is an act *which requires long study and experience*, before a man can attain to the cognizance of it...." (1608), 12 *Co. Rep.* 63, 77 *E.R.* 1342 (K.B.). Emphasis added. Coke's theory of law is examined in William E. Conklin, *In Defence of Fundamental Rights* (Alphen aan den Rijn: Sijtoff & Noordhof, 1979), 13-53.

115 *Dialogue*, "Of Courts," 79 (47).

authoritative if its source can be linked through the patriarchal hierarchy to the supreme office at the pinnacle of the hierarchy. This explains why Hobbes wrote on several occasions that "[f]or the Legislator is he, not by whose authority the Lawes were first made, but by whose authority they now continue to be Lawes."[116]

Civil laws, in sum, are associated with writing. But the writing *per se* does not make a script authoritative. A signed statute or letters patent only provide evidence of authority. The instrument must be duly signed in accord with the procedures posited in texts, which texts in turn are posited by actors under the supreme Representer: "none can make a Law but he that hath the Legislative Power."[117] "A Law is the Command of him, or them that have the Sovereign Power, given to those that be his or their Subjects," Hobbes' Philosopher contends.[118] As such, the moral or subjective content of a rule is immaterial. So too is the political wisdom of the rule's enforcement in any particular circumstances: "[i]t is not Wisdom, but Authority that makes a Law."[119] Nor does legal authority depend upon the power of the individual who occupies the office.[120]

So again, the thoughts signified in the writing are willed by the sovereign. The requisite of writing requires, in turn, that a civil society must first set down formal procedures which identify what writing is authored by the sovereign Representer. These procedures, called 'manner and form' requirements even in Hobbes' day, set down the conditions for the exercise of authority in the name of the sovereign.[121] These procedural requirements posit which actor can speak authoritatively on behalf of the Representer. The supreme Head cannot be perceived. Even the highest institutional actor, including a parliament or king, still gazes towards the "mortal God." Nor can the Leviathan be heard: after all, the Leviathan is an artificial person without a human voice and without the face of a natural person.

Again, we actors have to assume that there is one supreme actor for if there were more than one, potential struggle would remain. One representative must possess dominion over all competing sources of authority. The voices of each subordinate actor must be at one with the monologue of the Representer.[122] Despite the Representer's transparent body and mind, all actors on the patriarchal hierarchy gaze upwards into the heavens as they apply the statutes in the name of the supreme Representer.

---

116 *Leviathan,* chap. 26, 315.

117 *Dialogue,* "Of the Law of Reason," 55 (4).

118 *Dialogue,* "Of Soveraign Power," 71 (32).

119 *Dialogue,* "Of the Law of Reason," 55 (4).

120 *Dialogue,* "Of the law of Reason," 68 (28).

121 They were called such even in Hobbes' day. For a discussion of their import today see William E. Conklin, "*Pickin* and its Applicability to Canada" in *University of Toronto Law Journal* **25** (1975): 193-214.

122 *Leviathan,* chap. 26, 322.

8. Legal Obligation

Why, then, are the multitude of citizens obligated to follow the voice of the Representer if the Representer is believed to speak only to its own actors and not to the original authors themselves? Why must the subservient subjects follow the actors' writing even if the subjects consider substantive content of the writing immoral or unjust?

Hobbes responds in this manner. A citizen is obligated to comply with the actors' laws because the multiple authors, of which the citizen was one such author at the moment of acquiring a language, had willed their authority to their representative and its actors. Legal obligation and liberty are drawn from the authors' tacit or express words "I *Authorize all his Actions*" or "*I Authorize, or take upon me, all his actions.*"[123] Precisely because a civil law is a command by a supreme representative and because all authors have agreed to abide by the voice of such a representative, the unilingual voice of the representative transcends the heterology of voices which had authored the contract. The Representer's voice is now directed towards very different addressees: not the multitude of authors but the actors who speak and write on behalf of the Representer. Although the juridical actors create and enforce the official language of the Representer, the Representer's voice becomes monologic vis-à-vis the actors as well as the citizenry. Its voice is monologic in that the actors passively listen to the Representer and the Representer speaks and writes without finalizing its message. One statute may voice the Representer's intent on one day only to be amended on the next without a response from the addressee. The many citizens and the juridically defined actors may neither renege upon the terms of the contract nor reconsider its terms. Any citizen who disputes the absolute authority of the Representer, Hobbes writes in *De Cive*, is seditious.[124] To renounce the basic contract commits a permanent sin, treason. Put inversely, once the basic contract has been formed, a dissident agrees to abide by the majority will. As an author to the contract, the dissident authorizes the Representer's laws. Not unlike Socrates' 'Speech of the Laws' in the *Crito*, Hobbes argues in *De Cive* that the contract, whereby each is tied to the other to perform absolute and universal obedience to the City, contains all the civil laws within itself to the point that "the subject who shall renounce the generall Covenant of obedience, doth at once renounce all the Lawes."[125]

Is the citizen obligated to follow a statute because the democratically elected legislature has enacted the statute? The key here is that the statute possesses the

123 *Leviathan*, chap. 21, 268. Hobbes' emphasis.

124 *De Cive*, 2.6.13.

125 *De Cive*, 2.14.20.

colour of authority. Juridical actors in the authoritative institutional structure – the legislature, judiciary, police, and other agents – enact and apply signs *as if* the Representer itself had voiced the legal signs. All actors act in the name of the supreme Representer. In order that the signs be "manifest," there must be a time and place when one can identify that the signs have been promulgated. One must be able to trace the signs as if they had been authored by the highest office in the land. If such a trace cannot be made, the sign is not authoritative and the citizen is not obligated to obey the doctrine which the sign signifies. Such a sign lacks authority. The action is *ultra vires* because it no longer signifies the will of the Representer. So, the citizen is not obligated to obey a statute simply because it is published in the public register and ends with the royal seal. Rather, the citizen is obligated because the statute's source can be traced ultimately to the will of the sovereign Representer whose will, in turn, has been authored in the transition from the language-less condition to civil society.

Is the supreme Representer itself bound to its own civil laws? No. Why not? Because in order to be subject to civil laws, the citizen must be subject to the institutional sovereign Representer. But if the Representer were subject to the civil laws, the Representer would be constrained by its own voice. And that would be a contradiction in terms. The Representer may impliedly repeal its earlier statutes. And its generally worded statutes may impliedly repeal specifically worded statutes. If civil laws constrained the Representer, then the civil laws, not the Representer, would constitute sovereignty. But that would postulate the laws as more final than the Representer and that would violate the authors' intent.

If the Representer is so dominant in civil society, may the Representer override the theorems about nature? Hobbes responds clearly in the negative.[126]

May a founding author object to a particular decision or action of the Representer? Here, Hobbes is emphatic. An author creates a product. The authorizing authors exist a-historically. History begins with the Leviathan's commands. An author, once he or she has participated in delegating authority to an agent, is situated external to his or her product, the contract, and the contract's product, the agent or Representer. This view of an author, separate from its product, underlies Hobbes' sense of the relation of the many authors to the Leviathan. If an author refuses to stand by the acts of the Representer or if the author initially consents and then changes her/his mind, that dissenter is an out-law to the Representer's civil laws. Such a dissenter returns to the natural language-less condition where all struggle is resolved in favour of the stronger body.[127] Indeed, mindful of the

126 *Leviathan*, chap. 29, 367.
127 *Leviathan*, chap. 18, 232.

origins of the law of sedition in the previous generation to Hobbes and mindful of Kant's later attribution of treason to those who question the authority of the Head of the civil institutions,[128] one should note Hobbes' caution that "how great a fault it is, to speak evill of the Soveraign Representative ... or to argue or dispute his power, or in any way to use his name irreverently, whereby he may be brought into Contempt with his People, and their Obedience (in which the safety of the Common-wealth consisteth) slackened."[129] If, having explicitly or implicitly agreed to create the Representer, an author refuses to obey the Representer's command, this refusal frustrates the overall purpose for which the original contract was authored: namely, to devolve all legal authority to a supreme representative in order to ensure peace. Even if one verbally dissents from the Representer's commands, the dissenter commits an injustice. For justice originates in the contract which unites the authors to the Representer and all its actors. By voluntarily agreeing to participate in the congregation which contracted to create the Representer, the author agrees that he or she will abide by the majority will. If the author refuses to abide by the majority will after the contract has been formed, the author must either submit to the majority will "or be left in the condition of warre he was in before wherein he might without injustice be destroyed by any man whatsoever." Even if one dissents during the original congregation to the contract, that dissenter must now consent "or else justly be destroyed by the rest."[130] All other contractees may break their covenants with the dissenter.[131] Each citizen in civil society implicitly authors the Representer's commands. Accordingly, if a citizen complains about an act of the Leviathan, one really complains about him- or herself, not about the Leviathan itself.

The supreme Representer, then, is the mind of the civil society; the multitude of citizens is its body. Once the body becomes estranged from the mind (and the estrangement is inevitable, according to Hobbes), the body returns to the natural condition where one body struggles with the next without the mediation of language.[132] For Hobbes, the mind creates signs in order to signify the mind's thoughts. If unable to create signs, creatures lack a mind: they are only driven by the unlimited desires of their bodies. Once the creatures share conventions about signs, the creatures become authors of signs. The signs can be combined to form contracts.

---

128 See Conklin, "The Origins of the Law of Sedition," in *Criminal Law Quarterly* **15** (1972-73): 277-300.

129 *Leviathan,* chap. 30, 381. And again, "for they are bound, every man to every man, to Own, and be reputed Author of all, that he that already is their Soveraigne, shall do, and judge fit to be done: so that any one man dissenting, all the rest should break their Covenant made to that man, which is injustice." *Leviathan,* chap. 18, 229.

130 *Leviathan,* chap. 8, 231.

131 *Leviathan,* chap. 18, 229.

132 *Leviathan,* chap. 21, 272.

Those authors who do not abide by the covenants or, after agreeing to them, refuse to abide by them, are ruled by their bodies and, therefore, are out-laws or outside the supposed civility of language and, therefore, of culture.

9. The Mythology of Legal Authority

Thomas Hobbes elaborates a theory of law which builds upon myth. He does so in order to locate an authorizing origin to the civil laws. Hobbes insists that the mythical and mystical primordial world originates the authority of the Leviathan's laws even though the laws of the civil institutions are autonomous, all-inclusive, and their content in no way dependent upon any particular moral or religious belief system.

Mythology is essential to Hobbes' theory of law. A heterology of voices characterizes the natural condition. Constant flux and movement prevail. One voice brings order to this heterology and flux. Hobbes names the single voice, the Leviathan, a great sea monster with mystical origins, according to medieval legend. The Leviathan is an artificial person. All actors are also artificial persons. They feign or act on behalf of the authors of a grand play. The natural condition and the civil society, the authors and the actors of Hobbes' play, and even the Leviathan itself are metaphors for an imaginary world. So, given the Roman association of legal authority with a source, grounding or *arche*, Hobbes draws from an imaginary world to ensure the authority of the civil laws. The civil laws, he admits, are second-order relations of signs which are retrospectively imposed upon a mythical natural condition which unknown and unknowable creatures inhabit. Even the primordial condition with language-less creatures is itself a second-order sign which supposedly represents a world which we humans have never encountered. The voices of the authors, artificial persons who have acquired linguistic conventions, superimpose their thoughts upon the mythical language-less creatures. Even the monologic voice of the Representer is a second-order chain of signs superimposed over the thoughts of the multitude of authors who, in turn, have superimposed their thoughts upon the beasts. Legal obligation is drawn from a paradise of a sea monster whose actors feign in its name and play in harmony with the sea monster's transcendental will.

Although Hobbes makes the Representer's unilingualism secondary to the primordial condition, the secondary voice of the Representer is transformed into the primary voice of Justice and Authority once the civil institutions are created. The actors, dependent upon the mythical authors and their mythical natural condition for their 'existence,' reconstruct the intent of the authors in the name of the wills of the same authors. Yet that intent, postulated as logically prior to the actors, cannot be retrieved as an immediacy or presence to the actors. Connotative signification dissipates in favour of a higher level of connotative signification.[133] Civil society becomes a juridically constructed paradise, constructed by actors who play in the name of the supreme actor. Even the mythical grounding of the Leviathan's mystical nature is itself invisible in the sense of being inaccessible through language. All juridical actors forget the invisible grounding as they seek out the will of the Leviathan. Indeed, they forget the need for the invisible origin. Without such a loss of memory, the authority of the Representer's civil laws could not be considered separate from the morality of their substantive content.

Hobbes takes the loss of legal memory one stage further, though. The natural condition is inaccessible through the official language of the judges, lawyers, and legislators in civil society. But Hobbes describes God in just such a sense of inaccessibility.[134] The originating grounding of civil laws is lost in the very first act of the Leviathan's actors. All that counts with that first act is writing, and the writing of artificially created actors at that. The authors contract never to return to the natural condition, nor to revise the terms of the contract. The permanent loss of the natural condition, by virtue of conventions about signs, suggests that, even without such a contract, the actors could never return to the heterology of the voices of the original authors: only the common intent of the voices may be retrieved and then only as representations of such commonality. Even the voice of the Leviathan, not being an organism, is inaccessible in that the artificial Leviathan does not really speak. The Leviathan 'speaks' through its actors who act as representatives of the Leviathan, the sovereign Representer. The belief in the sovereignty of the Leviathan encourages the actors to speak a single language. The actors can never access the Leviathan's silent voice: they can only retrospectively reconstruct it. That is, the actors re-present the Leviathan's 'voice.' The actors may never gain an immediacy or presence with that voice nor with the voice of the authors who had created the Leviathan, nor with the unintelligible babble of the language-less creatures in the natural condition. A presence with the Leviathan is impossible.

As Hobbes puts it, the Leviathan is a "*mortall* god" (Hobbes' emphasis). The loss of the natural condition, the language-less creatures, the voice of the authors

---

133 Drawing from a distinction of Roland Barthes, a myth is a second-level semiological system or metalanguage constructed from prior configurations of signs. Roland Barthes, "Myth Today," in *Mythologies* (Paris: Editions du Seuil, 1957), 109-59. Also see Barthes, "From Work to Text," in Josue U. Harari, *Text and Strategies: Perspectives in Post-Structuralist Criticism* (Ithaca: Cornell University Press, 1979), 73-81; "Theory of the Text," in *Untying the Text: A Post-Structuralist Reader*, ed. Robert Young (Boston: Routledge & Kegan Paul, 1981), 31-47.

This view of myth is modernist in that it fails to account for the presentative character of symbols and of rituals in the totemic culture of early Greece, as elaborated in chapters one and three above. This is also discussed in Conklin, "Hegel, the Author and Authority in Sophocles' *Antigone*," in ed. Leslie G. Rubin, *Justice vs. Law in Greek Political Thought* (New York: Rowman & Littlefield, 1997), 129-51.

134 *De Cive*, 3.15.14.

of the Leviathan and the voice of the Leviathan itself: these losses share the very invisible character which Hobbes attributes to the divine Author of the natural condition. For Hobbes understands religion as the "*Feare* of power invisible, feigned by the mind, or imagined from tales publiquely allowed, RELIGION; not allowed, SUPERSTITION. And when the power imagined, is truly such as we imagine, TRUE RELIGION."[135] Hobbes' civil laws, as well as the theorems about nature, carry a religious character to them. The primary figures, the authors, are transparent spirits who travel through the civil laws in the name of the authors' will. Yet, the spirits validate all commands of the actors. Of course, the creatures in the natural condition may be visible in the sense that they look like human beings, as perceived in civil society. But how can we humans signify something that is unsignifiable: namely, an animal which biologically looks like a human but which lacks a language? The creatures in the natural condition are un-human. The best that we actors can do is to *imagine* them in *our* legal language, in the language with which *we* professional knowers are familiar. On Hobbes' own account, human beings are human because they share linguistic conventions to signify their desires. Even the beasts in the natural condition are figments of Hobbes' imagination in that we know now that other species do communicate to themselves through languages, widely defined.

So, the institutional hierarchy of actors becomes self-referential in that all civil laws refer to the supreme source of authority, the Representer or Leviathan which, in turn, commands the subordinate actors in the structure. The need for certainty and clarity in the civil laws requires that there be only one Leviathan. The civil laws cannot allow for a spiritual dominion or religious superstitution for that would raise the possibility that the Leviathan is not sovereign. There would then be two Common-wealths: the one temporal and the other "ghostly."[136] Sovereignty would be divided. Every citizen would be subject to two masters and two kingdoms. When the two kingdoms opposed one another, there would be a risk that the civil society would break into civil war. Civil laws must be all-encompassing without any appeal to some external referent.

And yet, the civil offices of the Leviathan possess a door which opens out to a primordial realm which none of us, even those of us who are mad, has ever experienced or known.[137] Again, like Kafka's parable of the man from the country, the actors, functioning as guardians of the structure, gaze towards a faint imaginary

135 *Leviathan,* chap. 6, 124.
136 *Leviathan,* chap. 29, 370-71.
137 I am drawing here from Jacques Lacan's explanation of the language of the unconscious amongst the mad.

world with imagined creatures. The actors imagine such a world. They cannot retrieve the imagined world because they cannot access a realm which is distinguishable for its want of a language. Fear and dread overcome the actors. Ironically, this very dread permeates the natural condition where creatures are unconstrained in their bodily movements, absent a language through which to deliberate and decide. The very superstition which Hobbes describes of the natural condition permeates the actions of the civil actors. Hobbes could have been describing either the natural condition or civil society when he wrote that

> [f]ear of invisible powers, what is it else in savage people, but the fear of somewhat they think a God? What invisible power does the reason of a savage man suggest unto him, but those phantasms of his sleep, or his distemper, which we frequently call ghosts, and the savages thought gods; so that the fear of a God, though not of a true one, to them was the beginning of religion.... I said superstition was fear without reason.[138]

The civil laws culminate in fantasies about fantasies.

10. The Invisible Origin of the Authority of Hobbes' Civil Laws

The big question now is whether one may properly describe the mysticism about the Leviathan, the authors and the natural condition as divine. That is, do the legal officials conceal the divinity of the authorizing origin as they claim to be authoritative?

To respond to this question, one must return to Hobbes' elaboration of his sense of the divine in the final Part of the *Leviathan*.

Hobbes describes the predicament of the language-less creatures in much the same terms as he does God's situs beyond human language. There are only three ways to access God's will, Hobbes claims in Chapter 31 of the *Leviathan:* first, revelation; secondly, "the voyce of some man (the prophets)"; and thirdly, natural reason. Each medium of God's will either cannot express general laws (such as revelation) or it may do so only through agents (such as prophets) or the medium may be immediately present with God without a mediating language (such as natural 'reason'). Does God speak? How is God's voice signified? Hobbes does describe the First Cause as an author.[139] But how can the First Cause be an author if the First Cause does not speak or write through significations known to human beings?

---

138 "An Answer to a Book published by Dr. Bramhall called the 'Catching of the Leviathan'," in *English Works of Thomas Hobbes (EW)* **4**, p. 292.

139 *Leviathan*, chap. 30, 376.

a) *Revelation*

First, God speaks to a human subject "immediately" through supernatural revelation. But a revelation comes only to the few:[140]

> It is true, that God is the Soveraign of all Soveraigns; and therefore, when he speaks to any Subject, he ought to be obeyed, whatsoever any earthly Potentate command to the contrary. But the question is not obedience to God, but *when* and *what* God hath said; which to Subjects that have no supernaturall revelation, cannot be known, but by that naturall reason, which guided them, for the obtaining of Peace and Justice, to obey the authority of their severall Common-wealths.[141]

Hobbes uses the words "sense supernatural" and "inspiration" as synonymous with "revelation." God reveals a different message to different recipients: "God speaketh not in that manner but to *particular persons*, and to divers men divers things."[142] Since revelation expresses such different messages to different recipients, Hobbes reasons, revelation cannot possibly command universal laws.[143] In chapter 26 ("Of Civil Laws") of the *Leviathan*, in particular, Hobbes explains that a human subject must be assured that, to be supernatural, a command is authored. Indeed, Hobbes writes in chapter 32 that if a human subject pretends that God has spoken to him supernaturally and immediately, "I cannot easily perceive what argument he can produce, to oblige me to believe it." More, revelation cannot be described as 'law' because Hobbes associates 'law' with an author's writing. The revelation is not written down. Hobbes writes in his introduction to a Christian state (chapter 32) that God's revelatory speech to a human subject cannot be transferred nor signified in a language which another subject understands. At best, the recipient can only say that God had spoken to him- or herself in a dream or a "phantasme."[144] The revelation has authority only if the recipient him- or herself had received authority as an agent of God by a supernatural revelation. But that, in turn, is impossible: "No man can infallibly know by naturall reason, that another has had a supernaturall revelation of God's will; but only a beliefe; every one (as the signs thereof shall appear greater, or lesser) a firmer, or a weaker belief."[145]

So, if revelation were the only source of God's will, we would only be left with the civil laws of the Representer as the "authentique" evidence of the divine laws.[146] That is, God's voice, like the voices of the creatures in the natural condition, is

140 *Leviathan*, chap. 32, 410.
141 *Leviathan*, chap. 33, 415.
142 *Leviathan*, chap. 31, 396.
143 *Leviathan*, chap. 31, 396.
144 *Leviathan*, chap. 34, 440.
145 *Leviathan*, chap. 26, 332.
146 *Leviathan*, chap. 26, 333.

unsignified and unsignifiable unless and until actors signify God's will as an authoritative command in civil society. But, at that point, authoritative signification is one step removed from a presence with God. One is *under* the authority of the secular Leviathan, the mortal god, in the re-presentation of God's will.

b) Prophets

Hobbes claims that God may communicate to the language-less creatures of a natural condition in a second manner: through a prophet. Here, unlike revelation, the prophet represents God's will through a language.

But how can God be said to possess a voice to convey thoughts to a prophet if God lacks a language and if God does not even have a tongue with which to begin to make words?[147] When prophets testify to God's will, they testify to the intention of the prophet to honour God, *not to the signification of God's will itself*, according to Hobbes. A language comes into play only when a human agent wishes to re-signify another's claim. But, with revelation, God "speaks" to the prophets immediately: that is, without the mediation of a sign. God is already "present" in the minds of the prophets and so God does not need to signify its will. A human agent cannot enter into a contract directly with God because a contract needs signs to represent its promise and God does not share artificially constructed signs with humans.[148]

Since God does not speak through human constructed names, one must be satisfied with the second best, agents of God's will. Once again, we are taken to civil society where there is writing and artificially constructed juridical persons. The writing must be published and, in addition, express a "manifest intent" of the prophet.[149] Promulgation is very important because "to the nature of laws belongeth a sufficient, and clear promulgation, such as may take away the excuse of ignorance."[150] A writing must be publicly known, Hobbes continues, because "[t]o rule by words, requires that such words be manifestly known; for else they are no laws." The remaining issue to the question of the authority of a religious text, then, is whether the interpreter has gained her/his authority to interpret the text from an office of the Leviathan.[151]

c) Natural reason

"Natural reason" is the third and foremost manner through which God's laws of nature are communicated. Once again, this third source of God's will takes one to

147 *Leviathan*, chap. 36, 459.
148 *Leviathan*, chap. 14, 197.
149 *Leviathan*, chap. 33, 426.
150 *Leviathan*, chap. 31, 396. Also see chap. 26, 319; chap. 32, 409.
151 *Leviathan*, chap. 33, 427.

the Leviathan and its subordinate actors. Theorems about the causes and effects on the movement of bodies concern the causes of causes. The chain of causes is so overwhelming that the individual in a natural condition can never reach the final cause of the movement of bodies. Nor can an individual break the chain of causes. But in order to theorize about the chain of causes, one must infer that there is a first cause: "there must be, (as even the heathen philosophers confessed) one First Mover; that is, a First, and an Eternal Cause of all things; which is that which men mean by the name of God."[152] Hobbes points out in *De Cive* that if there were no First Cause, there would not be a God.[153] Such a First Cause is eternal because it does not possess a further cause. Those who do not believe in the First Cause are the enemies of the First Cause.[154]

Now, when Hobbes speaks of 'natural reason,' he is referring to a reason about this First Cause. Although Hobbes describes the First Cause as a creative author, he explicitly cautions against understanding God as an author: "The right of nature, whereby God reigneth over men, and punisheth those that break his laws, is to be derived, *not from his creating them*, as if he required obedience as of gratitude for his benefits; but from his *irresistible power*."[155] An author creates. But the First Cause of bodily movement is not a creator. After all, how could there be an author of causes if the causes dwell in a condition where there is no script to be authored? The First Cause is an irresistible power which attracts all other causes of bodily movement. When one worships the First Cause, one can only worship the attributes of God, not God's act itself. These attributes are traits which we human interpreters attribute to the First Cause whose nature "we understand nothing of what he is."[156] But, according to Hobbes in *De Cive*, one could not "honour" God if God had no being. Accordingly, God must exist and, therefore, it must possess attributes.[157] To see or to hear are such attributes. The attributes manifest God's great power, not God's voice or language. God exists, "not as Creator, and Gracious; but as Omnipotent." In *De Cive*, Hobbes explains that God's authority to rule emanates from "his sole *irresistible power*."[158] Indeed, like the Leviathan, God is the King by nature.[159] One commits treason against God by recognizing other institutional offices other than those subordinated to the supreme Representer in civil society.

152 *Leviathan*, chap. 11, 167; chap. 12, 170. *Elements of Law*, 1.11.2; *Elements of Philosophy. The First Section, Concerning the Body EW* 1, 26.1, p. 412.

153 *De Cive*, 2.15.14.

154 *Leviathan*, chap. 16, 221-22; chap. 42, 534-37. Cf. *De Cive* 3.15.2.

155 *Leviathan*, chap. 31, 45-46.

156 *Leviathan*, chap. 34, 430.

157 *De Cive*, 3.15.14.

158 *De Cive*, 3.15.5.

159 *De Cive*, 3.16.18.

So, once again, natural reason remains unsignified until one journeys into civil society with its different institutions. Natural reason is revealed in the heart, in the unspoken conscience of the creatures who do not share linguistic conventions. There are no articulate voices in this invisible realm. There are no signs which human beings will recognize. The strange, unrecognizable creatures interpret God on their own, without the aid of signs and without the cognitive objects which such signs can represent. The conscience of the heart cannot intellectualize about the First Cause.[160] Rather, the body, not the mind, intuits. Each creature intuitively interprets the theorems of nature on its own. In doing so, the creature is directly responsible to the First Cause, God, who judges an individual's intention as well as her/his action. The intuited theorems about the natural bodies are only recognized as 'laws' when they are authorized by the Leviathan's civil laws. In addition to representing the will of the authors from a natural condition, the Leviathan represents the First Cause of bodily movement.

The natural reason or consequence of the heart in the natural condition, then, cannot disclose 'laws' properly so-called. Hobbes writes in the *De Cive* that the 'laws' of nature "are not in propriety of speech laws, as they proceed from nature. For the *sacred* Scripture is the speech of God commanding over all things by greatest right."[161] And in the *Leviathan* he writes that

> the laws of nature ... in the condition of mere nature ... *are not properly laws, but qualities* that dispose men to peace and obedience. When a commonwealth is once settled, then are they actually laws, and not before; as being then the commands of the commonwealth; and therefore also civil laws; for it is the sovereign power that obliges men to obey them.... *The law of nature therefore is a part of the civil law* in all commonwealths of the world. Reciprocally also, the civil law is a part of the dictates of nature.[162]

Both Howard Warrender and Michael Oakeshott found this latter passage problematic in their effort to offer a coherent interpretation about Hobbes.[163]

However, Hobbes is coherent when one appreciates his association of 'law' with language. Language marks Hobbes' differentiation of civil society from the natural condition, I have argued above. The Leviathan's laws are written. The civil laws can only be "written" by the Leviathan's actors. The "theorems," which may seem to resemble human 'laws,' concern only bodily movement. God's will,

---

160 Interestingly, Warrender seems to suggest just such an intellectualization. See Warrender *Political Philosophy*, 250.

161 *De Cive*, 1.4.33.

162 *Leviathan*, chap. 26, 314.

163 Warrender, *Political Philosophy*, 166-76; Oakeshott, "The Moral Life in the Writings of Thomas Hobbes," in *Civil Association*, 103-113.

in the sense of the First Cause of all bodily movement, can only be signified in a civil society where there is a language. Theorems are not commands to all residents because the creatures, who look like human beings, do not share a language to understand the theorems. Without signs to author, there can be no author. Civil laws enter the scene when the creatures associate certain sounds and marks with words and sentences. At that point, the words and sentences, according to Hobbes, become signs (of thoughts). Hobbes describes the "natural reason" as synonymous with the divine laws.[164] Can the divine laws be expressed through the signs of human agents? Yes, through the writing of scriptures. But scriptures may only re-present God's will. The addressee of scripture has been transferred from a language-less natural condition to a civil society where human creatures agree as to the cognitive objects which signs represent.

So, the locus of the authorizing origin of Hobbes' civil laws is clear. The originating moment of legal authority in civil society dwells logically and chronologically before the civil laws, in a condition believed to lack a language, a long lost, primordial moment in the cultural progress of human beings.

Indeed, there is a sense in which even the creatures in the natural condition are invisible. Clearly, the invisible realm of a language-less group of creatures cannot provide evidence of the voice of God. Only actors who can speak can do so. Indeed, Hobbes' creatures share the very invisible character which Hobbes attributes to God in *De Cive*: "most men beleeve God to be the invisible Maker of all visible things; whom they also fear, conceiving that they have not a sufficient protection in themselves."[165] A fear of what cannot be accessed through language drives human beings to construct a religion in civil society. Hobbes puts this point in the *Leviathan* in this way: "And this Feare of things invisible, is the naturall Seed of that, which everyone in himself calleth Religion; and in them that worship, or feare that Power otherwise than they do, Superstition."[166] Not surprisingly, Hobbes describes the creatures in the natural condition as possessing the same "power irresistable" as Hobbes describes of God.

We are left, then, with the legal language of the Leviathan's actors as the best evidence of natural reason. But once the Leviathan's actors grant an official version to God's will, the actors are one step removed from the moment when the language-less creatures intuit, if such is possible without signs, the theorems about nature. The source of the authority of civil laws, once again, becomes inaccessible because one cannot gain an insight into the theorems about nature except through a language which one shares in a civil society. Such a language, though, is

164 *Leviathan*, chap. 31, 399.
165 *De Cive*, 3.16.1.
166 *Leviathan*, chap. 11, 168.

absent from the natural condition as Hobbes understands the natural condition. In civil society, one can only re-present the prior will of an author: one cannot be present with such a will – one cannot get inside the will, be at one with it, bond with it, become present with it – because signs mediate between the author's will, as a thought, and the addressee.

Now, originally, God authored the first word, Hobbes suggests early in the *Leviathan*, when God instructed Adam how to name creatures.[167] But Adam's language was lost at the tower of Babel when God struck every man for rebelling against God. The consequence was "the oblivion of his former language." Since God's language was thereby lost, human agents could only enter into a contract with God's "Lieutenant" or agent: namely, the Leviathan. There being no language in the natural condition, God had to appoint an agent in order to communicate on its behalf where creatures shared a language. So, we now observe that the commands of the sovereign Leviathan possess one more gap which opens to the natural condition. Hobbes claims a totality and autonomy to the Leviathan's actors and their commands. But like the natural duties which the Leviathan owes to the originary authors, the Leviathan itself is God's representative in civil society (on earth).

There is a problem once one recognizes the Leviathan as God's representative in civil society. On the one hand, the Leviathan is an artificial person and an actor at that. On the other hand, the Leviathan, despite its character as an 'artificial person,' is said to share a presence or immediacy with God as if God's will were revealed to the Leviathan through its civil laws. But the signs or names of actors do not mediate this presence, according to Hobbes: "[t]he Monarch, or the Sovereign Assembly only hath *immediate* Authority from God, to teach and instruct the people; and no man but the Sovereign, receiveth his power *Dei gratia* simply; that is to say, from the favour of none but God."[168] All other actors – judges, ministers, and other officials – receive their authority from the supreme Leviathan which experienced such an immediacy with God.

Put a different way, Hobbes differentiates between natural laws and civil laws. The Representer possesses a *potentia* or natural power vis-à-vis God who had created the natural condition. In the natural condition, creatures possess the natural right to *summa potestas*. But this is impossible because *summa potestas* only arises from the authoritative civil obligations of the institutional offices. The Representer possesses an artificial *summa potestas* vis-à-vis subjects in civil society. In a sense, the Representer is an artificially created person who represents God's will on earth once creatures have acquired a language. Hobbes tries to

167 *Leviathan*, chap. 4, 101.
168 *Leviathan*, chap. 23, 291. Emphasis added.
169 *Leviathan*, chap. 17, 227. Hobbes' emphasis.

integrate the divine and the secular when he acknowledges the supreme Representer for the first time as "that great Leviathan, or rather (to speak more reverently) of that *Mortall God*, to which we owe under the *Immortall God*, our peace and defence."[169] The Representer is a leviathan because, like the mythical sea monster, its tentacles reach to every part of its proximate environment. The Representer's tentacles institutionalize a totality. The Representer is mortal because human authors have created the monster. When the Representer, the soul of civil society, departs from its body, civil society, there is a risk that the Leviathan will, like a natural subject, die. But the Representer is a mortal god because of the trace of its authority to the immortal irresistible God of the natural condition.

The closest to which a human agent may reach God's unwritten laws of nature, then, is through an interpretation of them. But "a right understanding" of the unwritten laws does not depend upon a mere interpretation of a convention. Rather, a right understanding depends upon "the goodnesse of a mans own naturall Reason, and Meditation."[170]

Who, then, possesses the authority to interpret the unwritten theorems of nature? The judge alone. The judicature belongs to the City.[171] Unwritten laws are obscure. More importantly, though, one cannot understand obscure unwritten laws "without a perfect understanding of the finall causes."[172] But that perfect understanding can only exist in the mind of the one final cause itself, not in the mind of the actors who signify or represent the final cause. The civil judge gives a 'second best' interpretation.[173] Because of the judge's position in the hierarchy of officials who act as agents of the Representer, his interpretation is "authentique": "not because it is his private Sentence; but *because he giveth it by Authority of the Sovereign*, whereby it becomes the Soveraign's Sentence; which is Law for that time, to the parties pleading."[174] So, the civil laws can never be at one with the will of the first Cause of nature.

11. The Forgotten Origin

It is now apparent that the juridical officials, who methodically apply the intent of the Leviathan, forget about the need for an invisible authorizing origin of civil laws. The forgotten origin is this: the authority of the civil laws is grounded in an invisible externality despite the autonomy and totality of the civil structure itself.

170 *Leviathan*, chap. 26, 328.
171 See *De Cive*, 3.15.17.
172 *Leviathan*, chap. 26, 322.
173 *Leviathan*, chap. 26, 323.
174 Ibid.

In addition, the source is invisible to the language of the structure of the civil laws because one may only access the external source through a language and the key differentiating characteristic of the primordial realm is that no such language is shared amongst the creatures of the realm.

Officials, to remain true to the trace of authority of a command to the Leviathan, must forget the invisibility of the authorizing origin of their own reasoning. There is a sense in which the dependence of the civil laws upon the invisible remains a secret amongst the officials. The secret must be maintained because, in order that the Leviathan possess total *de jure* authority over all physical bodies in civil society, its actors must act as if there were no gaps or exceptions to the totality of such control. The actors apply the civil laws as if the gaze of the authors in the natural condition constrained the laws. Of course, the individual authors who create the Leviathan share a language. But they are preoccupied with their experiences in the earlier stage of their condition when there were no shared conventions about signs. The deep desire for peace and for brotherly respect originated in this prior invisible condition. The form of civil society itself is formed from a secret.

Something is forgotten because someone was once cognizant of the forgotten object. If there were no one cognizant of the secret, then it could not be a secret. The Leviathan and its actors alone, especially judges and lawyers, have to possess faith that there was once a natural condition where creatures could not communicate through a language. The authority of the actors is grounded in such a condition. The actors are haunted by the condition. The Leviathan creates an authoritative hierarchy of offices, knowing full well that the hierarchy signifies natural duties drawn from an invisible world. Unless the Leviathan and its actors forget the origins of their authority, the actors would apply the Leviathan's writing as if the Leviathan's commands were not final and binding. But if the supreme Representer's commands were not final, the Representer would not be sovereign or self-legislating. Morality and religion would rush from outside through the acknowledged opening, and this would complicate the actors' simple vision of their reality. That possibility would violate the promise of the originary authors to create a supreme representative and then, to forever divest their authority to the representative. The actors simply must not admit to the possibility of some competing or prior source of legal authority for the decisions of the Leviathan's actors to be authoritative. The authority of laws must be kept separate from their moral content. The content is non-law. The content is drawn from the unwritten realm. The former constitutes legal reality; the latter constitutes an 'ought' realm associated with morality. The authors ensure a forgetfulness of the importance of the invisible to the authority of the civil laws. For the authors agree that the Leviathan's actors may never re-consider the terms of the contract nor retrieve the natural condition which preceded the contract. Hobbes ensures that they will never return to the external world, external to the civil laws, by hypothesizing that there is no language in the external condition and that, therefore, actors will never gain access to the condition except through the public language of civil society.

In the natural condition, the physical body causes the outcome of a dispute. Bodily desires drive the body. The desires are not the sort of desires which might be inculcated after deliberation or reflection, though. After all, the creatures do not think nor understand for they lack a language to think concepts and to understand each other. In the natural condition, they do not share a vocabulary or grammar with which they can reflect about cognitive objects. Once they acquire a language, the creatures become authors of their own expression and the authors desire that all creatures treat each other as each would wish to be treated. A second desire is for peace. What could be more undesirable than the continual strife, fear, anxiety and uncertainty which come hand in hand with a condition where one creature may only communicate through bodily domination? The desires of the unrecognizable creatures in the natural condition express a raw, intuitive moment of the subconscious, without articulation, without reflection, and without consciousness. The desires are naturally embodied – not artificially constructed from the thoughts which words signify. Precisely because they are not artificially created, the desires are carried into civil society. The Leviathan, an artificial person, retains these natural desires. Indeed, the Leviathan is created with the express purpose of protecting these natural desires. In like vein, the Leviathan's actors gaze upwards and beyond their immediate locus towards faceless creatures in a ghostly world. The natural desires are a postulate of the very posit of civil laws.

There is another aspect of the forgetfulness which the Leviathan and its actors must maintain as they enact their civil laws. The natural realm, where these natural duties are located, is characterized by Galilean physio-chemical causes and effects. Only theorems, not laws, govern the relations of the causes and effects: to have a law, one needs a language to signify the object intended by the law. Without a language, it is difficult to speak about there being a mind of an author who intended a certain cognitive object. Language-less creatures may only have theorems *about* the causes of movement. The creatures may desire to abide by the theorems. But they cannot control, create, or author such causes. So the realm of causes and effects is in continual flux. For this flux to stabilize, there would have to be a finality in the movement of the causes. Such a final cause, to be final, must differ from the character of an ordinarily authored law. This first cause is different from the beasts of the natural condition, according to Hobbes, in that the first cause lacks a physical body. The first cause differs from the authors and actors in that it lacks a language to express its will. The first cause is felt immediately through revelation. Hobbes calls the first cause, the Author. And yet, this Author can neither speak nor write except directly through revelation. If the First Cause could speak and write through the language of actors, the First Cause would be a human being in civil society. For civil society alone is characterized by a language.

Thus, the actors must forget a second element of their authority as they posit civil laws. The ultimate external source to the authority of the civil laws is not the Leviathan nor even the authors who create the Leviathan, but the final Author of the material world. First, the Leviathan and its actors forget that externally situated authors, prior in time and space to the self-referential institutional offices, ground the authority of the civil laws. Secondly, the Leviathan's laws must forget that the final grounding of the civil laws is an invisible realm where creatures cannot communicate with each other through a shared language. Thus, a second gap is postulated in the Leviathan's civil laws despite the fact that actors believe that the Leviathan's authority is sovereign.

The officials can never return to the natural condition. Nor may they return to an immediacy with the divine Author of the natural condition. Nor may they even admit to the possibility of an opening to an externality. The civil laws potentially enclose all social behaviour. The officials may not admit to the possibility of an opening to an externality because they have agreed never to return to the prior condition. In addition to their agreement, though, they may never return to the prior world even if they desired to do so. The primordial world exists *before* creatures share conventions about the signs of things. The officials of civil society have acquired such shared conventions. Once acquired, though, the conventions cannot be undone as if they were a winter coat on the first day of spring.

Accordingly, the officials of the Leviathan's "offices" may only *imagine* or *picture* this prior world. They must *imagine* the creatures who cannot speak words or sentences. They must *imagine* that such creatures would desire to treat each other as mirrors of each other. They must imagine that the creatures desire a peace. Dread permeates the actions of all juridical actors. So, the officials must apply the Leviathan's laws *as if* the officials were constrained by a dread of the bodily struggle which had prevailed amongst the imagined faceless, speechless 'beasts' of a natural condition. This imaginary natural condition is an excess to the language of the actors. The language of the officials cannot reach a presence with the condition. The officials, by virtue of their facility to communicate through language, are in a different environing world from that of the creatures. Without language, the creatures are like lions, bears, and other animals, at war with one another, and with limitless desires to conquer all other beasts. The beasts lack an identity. How could one possess an identity if one could not be signified by a name? They are faceless and bodiless. So how could the officials return to the beasts, not being able to recognize their identity nor able to speak nor write *to* them as addressees, nor able to speak or write or think *about* them except as beasts without a shared language?

The natural condition is irretrievable, unrecognizable, and inaccessible. The natural condition is invisible. The officials, agents of the Leviathan, gaze upwards and outwards beyond their offices to such an invisible (and therefore imagined) realm. The actors defer to the natural duties which emanate from such an imagined condition. And they must do so in order to overcome the dread which permeates the imagined mythical realm from which they gain their legal authority to act.

5

Naming the Unnamable: Jean-Jacques Rousseau's General Will

Legal culture during the seventeenth and eighteenth centuries experienced a preoccupation with the will of an author. A very particular sense of the divine came to be associated with an author of nature. The state too came to be described as an autonomous (*auto-nomos*), self-conscious author. The author, situated outside and prior to expression, produces the expression. If any juridical agent could trace violent conduct to the will the state as author, the conduct was transformed from an arbitrary subjective fiat into an objective authoritative act. As I suggested in Chapter Two, Thomas Aquinas had acknowledged the importance of such an author. His author, though, was considered invisible. His was the Author, a divine authorizing origin of all natural and human laws. Hobbes' authors, in contrast, were considered human agents or "artificial persons" in his terms. Human authors, sharing conventions about the signification of words, created a social contract. They delegated their authority to a supra-artificial person, the Leviathan, whose laws guarded the terms of the contract and guided social behaviour. The Leviathan and all offices of the state were "actors" who played with the intent of the contract.

So one can appreciate two senses of an 'author' in late medieval and modern legal thought. First, there are 'historical authors' or what Hobbes called "actors."[1] Such historical authors are locatable in time and space. Generally, they are situated on a pyramidal hierarchy of institutions. Their authority to author statutes and regulations is drawn from such a locus. Offices of the state speak to each other. The enactment of statutes and regulations is historically contingent. And that authority legitimizes their en-*force*ment of the legal doctrines, rules and other standards signified by their texts.

Modern legal positivism, beginning with Hobbes and continuing through Jeremy Bentham and John Austin, focuses upon historical authors. History has a beginning in the positivist project. For Hobbes, history begins after beasts have acquired conventions as to what their particular grunts and noises signify and, in particular, after civil institutions have been created in the name of the wills of the first authors of linguistic expression. At that point, they can produce thoughts by authoring expression. Authors can then speak with each other and make promises

1 Interestingly, Latin (by which Hobbes wrote his first edition of the *Leviathan*) uses *acteurs* and *auteurs* synonymously.

to each other. Even morality and justice begin only when such historical authors can express themselves through a language. Most importantly, for our purposes, historical authors, or "actors," express themselves by positing expression that others recognize as civil law. Legal authority begins with such expression. All else is pre-legal – bodily struggle, morality, political wisdom and theology.

Hobbes is not alone in this regard. John Austin writes that there are "laws properly so called" and these laws, he differentiates from laws "improperly so called." Laws "properly so called" are assignable to distinct authors whose expression is historically contingent. Laws "improperly so called" are not identifiable with authors or, if with authors, then authors who are not distinct nor locateable upon the official pyramidal hierarchy. H.L.A. Hart too differentiates the pre-legal from the language of the legal world. The concept of law begins, Hart claims, when rules are written. But such written rules merely "approximate" a "pre-legal" world that is characterized by unwritten and unspoken judicial practices. Hans Kelsen too distinguishes between a "primitive" legal order and a modern legal system. Historical authors are located in the latter. Historical authors will norms. Without historical authors, there would not be humanly posited norms. We would fall back upon universal transcendental principles, such as Aquinas advocated, for the authorizing origins of civil laws. Even Ronald Dworkin postulates a pre-legal world without historical authors. History begins when human agents, albeit interpreters rather than the 'creators' of texts, create a coherent structure of thoughts in an effort to reach a pre-legal paradise where all rational contradictions have worked themselves pure.

The basic question to be addressed, then, is this: if human agents, or their institutions, author civil laws, how do we know which human agents may author texts authoritatively? What authors count as legal authors? After all, there must be some finality to the trace of historical authors or their rules/norms. We have observed that Plato, Aristotle, Hobbes, Bentham, and Austin each recognized the need for such finality. And each recognized that finality would only arrive on the scene if there were a single externality that grounded the expression of historical authors. One strain of the Tradition of legal positivism, led by Hobbes, postulates that there are *invisible* authors who ground the structure of rules/norms and institutions of the historical authors. Invisible authors, emerging from a language-less condition, are located outside history, for history only begins with the institutional actors who posit civil laws. The invisible authors are absent from the consequential legal structure. As Hobbes remarks, without such a grounding of authority in invisible authors, the enunciations and scripts of a legislature or king are little different from the scripts of a philosopher. Nor are they any more legally weighty than un-authored customs. Precisely because the authors in the natural condition express their thoughts in a world where they have hitherto lacked a language, the historical authors may never return to such a condition. Having gained a language, the historical authors cannot escape from it. Historical authors may only access an object, Hobbes insists, through the signs of the officials in the legal structure. Reality only begins with signs, Hobbes especially emphasizes early in the *Leviathan*. A condition, inaccessible from within the language of the offices of the state, provides Hobbes with the finality needed to ensure that the scripts of human agents are authoritative and, therefore, 'existent' and enforceable. It makes sense, then, that we should call the originary authors, invisible authors.

Today, one is continually reminded of the 'people' in politics and in adjudication, as the judiciary is an unelected institution in a society which claims to be democratically elected by the people. The big question with respect to the problematic of finality, in the context of the referent 'the people,' is whether the habits of the people are, like Hobbes's authors, inaccessible or invisible from within the language of the legal structure. Are the habits of obedience assignable to distinct historical authors? Are the habits quantifiable? Must we signify such habits of obedience through signs? Must the signs be recognizable by judges and lawyers and legislators as legally binding signs? Or, when pressed, are the habits of the people, like the language-less natural condition of Thomas Hobbes, absent from the legal institutions? Indeed, are the peoples really an *in itself*, 'the People,' an invisible author not unlike Hobbes's invisible authors who created the social contract? Do the people, as the ultimate referent of legal positivism, precede history? Do they precede legal existence?

1. The Author as the General Will

a) *The general will*

Jean-Jacques Rousseau (1712–1778) introduces the notion of 'the will of the people' into European legal thought. His theory of the will of the people culminates in his *Social Contract*. Rousseau's final grounding of legal authority shares several characteristics with Hobbes's. The primary legal entities, for example, are admitted to be artificial. Like the civil actors of Hobbes's legal structure, Rousseau's legal officials act in the name of "nothing other than an artificial person whose life consists in the union of its members."[2] Again, as with Hobbes, these artificially created persons, whether legislators or judges, appeal to the terms of a social contract for the source of their legal authority. Rousseau believes that such a contract creates historical authors as artificial persons.

---

2 Jean-Jacques Rousseau, *Social Contract*, ed. Maurice Cranston (London: Penguin, 1968), Bk. 2, chap. 4, p. 74 (hereinafter cited, for example, as 2.4.74).

Most importantly, Rousseau shares with Hobbes the belief that authoritative civil laws are separate from the moral content of such laws. If a juridical official posits his own personal values in the application of a legislative rule, such an official commits an act of violence, Rousseau writes. Violence should "never be exercised except by virtue of authority and law."[3] Put another way, "since the law unites universality of will with universality of the field of legislation, anything that any man, no matter who, *commands on his own authority* is not a law."[4] Because juridical officials may not, in fact, gain an immediacy or presence with the general will, the most that one can say is that such officials ought to gain such an immediacy. The only issue, for Rousseau, is 'what renders the authorizing origins for a civil law?' The rational linkage of a civil law to the transcendental general will transforms the violence of a personal act into the impersonality of an authoritative act. Indeed, the general will, the final grounding of civil laws, provides the archimedean point with which to evaluate the moral content of any one legislated rule or action. Morality, that is, only begins when a society has civil laws. And civil laws depend upon their locus in a system of interconnected civil laws.

But can the general will be accessed through the civil laws? Is the general will knowable to the judges and lawyers who refer to the civil laws of historical authors? Can the general will, at best, be approximated as a *post facto* posit of a civil law whose author claims to be implementing the general will through the civil laws? Is the general will an invisible author much like Hobbes's invisible authors in the natural condition?

Rousseau's legal theory is sometimes associated with natural law theory precisely because of the transcendence of the general will vis-à-vis humanly binding laws. Yet, certain aspects of Rousseau's legal theory suggest a privileging of legal positivism. Rousseau offers us two of the key characteristics of legal positivism.

First, although one may inquire into the moral content of a civil law in order to test whether the law contradicts the general will, this inquiry is not a subjective judgment. Rather, as with Hobbes, the legislated rule is invalid if it exceeds the chain of authoritative rules in civil society. And the chain of authority ends with the general will, "the source and supplement of all laws."[5] If juridical officials apply civil laws unequally, for example, they contravene the general will. Such

---

3 *Social Contract,* 2.11.96.

4 *Social Contract*, 2.6.82. Emphasis added. Rousseau continues that "even what the sovereign itself commands with respect to a particular object is not a law but a decree, not an act of sovereignty but an act of government." A government's act is not a sovereign act because the government is not the author of the laws; the general will is.

5 *A Discourse on the Origin of Inequality*, trans. with intro. by G.D.H. Cole (London/New York: Everyman's Library), 242.

unequally applied laws lack legal authority. So too, legal obligation towards a government is found wanting if the government exploits the citizen. Although Rousseau's analysis entertains a far wider inquiry as to what constitutes an authoritative rule than does Hobbes's, Rousseau phrases the issue of the relation of law and morality in much the same terms of legal authority as does Hobbes. Legal officials act inequitably or wrongly, not because of the Goodness or Rightness of their action independent of the authority of their action, but because they exceed the *vires* allotted to their authoritative action. It just so happens that Rousseau admits that the ultimate author, the general will, transcends the offices on the legal structure, whereas Hobbes insists that the ultimate author, the Leviathan, delegates its authority to actors as agents. That is, Rousseau admits that the general will is located external to the structure of civil institutions and yet, like a spirit, it permeates the minds of historical authors.

Rousseau shares a second characteristic with legal positivism. The scope of authoritative civil laws is comprehensive over all human conduct: "[m]an is born free, and he is everywhere in chains."[6] No particular will, no private thought, no local interest may override the universal laws of the state. Indeed, "no sooner does one man, setting aside the law, claim to subject another to his will, than he departs from the state of civil society, and confronts him face to face in the pure state of nature, in which obedience is prescribed solely by necessity."[7] Naked violence characterizes such a pre-legal realm. The total dominance of the legal structure is compatible with the freedom of the individual.[8] Even the king is subject to the laws. The authority of civil laws is so total that no one governmental office is supreme over the civil laws: "the government be not master of the law."[9] The civil laws work affirmatively to create conditions where the dependence of slave upon master may be terminated.[10] For civil laws express a "celestial voice" and "wonders." Legislators function, then, as guardians of the civil laws.[11] And individual rulers and legislators are less opposed to the general will, as suggested by Dennis Lloyd,[12] than do legislatures manifest one transient moment in the representation of the general will as a civil law.

6 *Social Contract*, 1.1.49.

7 *Political Economy*, 240.

8 Charles Edwyn Vaughan, *Studies in the History of Political Philosophy before and after Rousseau*, ed. A. G. Little (New York: Russell & Russell, 1960), vol. 2, p. 37.

9 *Political Economy*, 241.

10 *Emile*, (Barabar Foxley), p. 49.

11 *Political Economy*, 241: "[b]ut thoyugh the government be not master of the law, it is much to be its guarantor, and to possess a thousand means of inspiring the love of it. In this alone the talent of reigning consists."

12 Dennis Lloyd (1979), *Introduction to Jurisprudence* (London: Stevens; Toronto: Carswell, 1979; 4th edn.), 85.

Yet, despite the separability of authoritative rules from the moral Goodness or Rightness of the content of the rules and despite the total enclosure of human thought and action by authoritative laws, the general will – the authorizing origin of legal reasoning – is inaccessible from the language of the enclosing civil laws. That is, the establishment of civil laws in not itself a legal act. For the general will emanates from a pre-legal condition that judges, lawyers, and legislators can never retrieve. Rousseau admits at the end of the *Discourse on Inequality*, for example, that, once one has grown dependent upon civilization, one may not escape from civilization's hold. Of course, the mark of the first signs of civilization is whether human authors have authored universal rules. The right to private property is such an *indicium*. One is condemned to be a citizen *under* the laws of a constitution even though "there always arise more real calamities than even apparent advantages."[13] One "cannot fail to be struck by the vast distance which separates the two states," Rousseau remarks.[14] Indeed, the road from the state of nature is "lost and forgotten" once the citizen is compelled to live under the civil laws. The officials of civil society forget their own authorizing origin in a state of nature. The origin is "vanished by degrees" to the point that the civil laws lack "any real foundation in nature."[15]

Even if the historical authors of civil society remembered that they had forgotten the authorizing origin of civil laws, they would, like Hobbes, be unable to access the origin through the language of the historical authors and their legal officials. An invisibility encircles the natural condition despite or, perhaps, because of the necessity of the totality of civil laws.

History begins, then, with the human posit of civil laws. Legal existence begins with such civil laws. Civil laws are primary. Morality and justice merely supplement civil laws. Rousseau insists, though, that the general will, a remainder of the forgotten, authorizing natural condition, is part and parcel of the totality of civil laws. That is, though external to the legislated rules, the general will remains present through the civil laws. If the general will is silenced by the rise of particular interests, "everyone, animated by secret motives, ceases to speak as a citizen any more than as if the state had never existed."[16] The civil laws then have private interests as their end. And the state collapses into "an empty and illusory form." The general will remains "always unchanging, incorruptible, and pure," though. The healthy state is the general will. The general will is an *in itself*. As such, *la volonté* is inaccessible from the language of the civil laws. *La volonté* is ever-present, yet invisible. *La volonté* is, perhaps, a holy ghost.

13 *Discourse*, "Appendix," 229.
14 *Discourse on Inequality*, Pt. 2, 219.
15 *Discourse on Inequality*, 220.
16 *Social Contract*, 4.1.149.

b) *Civil society*

As with Hobbes, the critical moment for the trace of the authority of civil laws arises when authority is transposed from the state of nature to a civil society. At that point, one's absolute and natural liberty "is alienated in whole," according to Rousseau.[17] Re-contextualized into civil society, the particular individual recovers whatever he or she lost in the alienation. The individual recovers what he or she has lost through the posit of civil laws.

The individual gains something more, though, as civil laws are posited. The individual acquires greater power than he or she had in the state of nature, because he or she is now "an indivisible part of the whole," the "whole" being the general will. Rousseau considered the participants associated with the general will to be "the people" collectively. Once civil laws are posited, individuals become citizens. The general will speaks through the civil laws. The general will – "an artificial and corporate body" – is sovereign. The people legislate *in the name* of the general will. Likewise, all officials are constrained by the general will. Even the legislature or the government offices are subject to the general will. For example, if a juridical agent imposes disproportionate burdens upon citizens, such action lies "outside the sovereign's competence." Such action lacks authority and becomes a private matter.[18] The agents of the general will are bound to their own covenants.

c) *The invisible origin*

In order to ensure that an action is authoritative, the action must manifest the general will. And this, notwithstanding that the general will is inaccessible within the public language of civil society. The reason why the general will is inaccessible is that the general will speaks through abstract laws. The abstract laws are not posited without a context. They fulfil the instructions of the general will. The specific instructions of the general will are marked by the terms and conditions of the social contract.

And yet, as with Hobbes's Representer, the authorizing origin of all abstract laws – the general will – lacks a determinate identity: "[o]n this analysis, it is immediately clear that we can no longer ask *who* is to make laws, because laws are acts of the general will; we can no longer ask if the prince is above the law, because he is a part of the state."[19] Without an identity, the general will is described as possessing a body (the body politic) and an ego (the will). Like an organism, the body politic is born and inevitably dies, Rousseau writes. The body and will of the general will are indeterminate, Rousseau himself admits.

---

17 *Social Contract*, 1.6.61. This point is discussed in G.D.H. Cole, "Introduction," to *Discourse*, v-xxxviii.
18 *Social Contract*, 2.4.77.
19 *Social Contract*, 3.6.82.

2. The Legislature

Rousseau insists that it is not enough to trace a civil law to some legislature or judge or king or even to the will of the general populace. The general will transcends the particular wills of a legislature, court, government, or populace. And this transcendence alone finalizes the tracing project. If the people transferred their liberty to a legislature or government, for example, such a transference would be "illogical and nugatory."[20] A legislator merely proposes laws to the body politic. The body politic considers whether the general will authorizes such proposed laws. Although I participate through the general will as a citizen, the general will is independent of my legal person, Rousseau insists. The general will is a moral being with a unity, a common ego, a life, and a will of its own.[21] As Rousseau puts it in the *Social Contract*, "[e]ach one of us puts into the community his person and all his powers under the supreme direction of the general will; and as a body, we incorporate every member as an indivisible part of the whole."[22] I am juridically equal with all other juridical persons in the state because the general will rationally transcends the multiplicity of particular differences. Rousseau attributes such a rationality to all juridical persons.

Unlike the Hobbesian situation where intermediaries signify the will of the Leviathan, Rousseau describes a bonding between citizen and general will. The bonding is not unlike the unwritten laws of early Greek tribes, as I have described in Chapter One. Rousseau claims that the citizen shares an immediacy with the general laws. Such a bonding is so tight that "[a]ny law which the people has not ratified in person is void; it is not law at all."[23] Each citizen participates directly in the manifestation of the general will through civil laws. Historically contingent institutions do not authorize posited laws. A representative assembly, for example, cannot posit a general binding law because such a legislature re-presents the general will. An assembly merely submits proposed laws for popular approval. As Rousseau claims, "[l]aws are really nothing other than the conditions on which civil society exists. A people, since it is subject to laws, ought to be the *author* of them."[24] Because particular citizens cannot renounce their individual wills and because a body politic is formed notwithstanding the inalienability of particular wills, a problem remains: "How to find a form of association which will defend the person and goods of each member with the collective force of all, and under

20 *Social Contract*, 1.4.55.

21 *Social Contract*, 1.6.61.

22 *Social Contract*, 1.6.61.

23 *Social Contract*, 3.15.141. Interestingly, the translator, Maurice Cranston has correctly translated Rousseau's notion as a singular 'people.' The People or the General Will is a singular Author. This oneness of the ultimate *arche* is critical to the Tradition.

24 *Social Contract*, 2.6.83. Emphasis added.

which each individual, while uniting himself with the others, *obeys no one but himself*, and remains as free as before."[25] In Book Two, Rousseau offers a pre-existing, rational, universal general will, speaking through abstract laws, as just such an association. Kant later sought to express this universality through the categorical imperative. The general will speaks. The general will speaks through abstract laws alone. This legal voice is "celestial."[26]

Is the general will analogous to Hobbes's authors who emerge from the natural condition? Rousseau responds in the negative. Although Rousseau states in one place that "[a] people ought to be the *author* of [the laws],"[27] he emphasizes towards the end of the *Social Contract* that the citizenry do not necessarily author the general will. Like the Leviathan, the general will is a single unilingual and monologic voice – unilingual because all officials who write in its name write in the same official language, and monologic because the citizens, as addressees, must passively listen to the general will's officials without there being a break for the citizens to interject. A single will, not a multiplicity of wills, constitutes the general will. Further, the general will is "indestructible" in contrast to the contingently situated body politic. The body politic inevitably dies just as does any living organism. Further, the general will is constant. Indeed, rather than arbitrating people's opinions, the minister of censorship speaks on behalf of the rational general will. Particular governments may err in contrast with the general will. Symptomatic of Ronald Dworkin's "law beyond law," the general will can never err. Rousseau puts this point this way in his essay, *Political Economy*:

> But how, I shall be asked, can the general will be known in cases in which it has not expressed itself? Must the whole nation be assembled together at every unforseen event? Certainly not. It ought the less to be assembled, because it is by no means certain that its decision would be the expression of the general will; besides the method would be impracticable in a great people, and is hardly ever necessary where the government is well-intentioned.[28]

In sum, a single, indestructible, constant, infallible rational will transcends the sum of particular wills.[29] Such a general will gives a civil law its authority. The sovereign people alone, not the legislature, judges the common interests of particular individuals.[30] But when the sovereign people treats particular subjects differently (rather than as juridical equals), the populace contravenes the general

25 *Social Contract*, 1.6.60. Emphasis added.
26 *Political Economy* in Cole's edition of *The Social Contract and Discourses*, 240.
27 *Social Contract*, 2.6.83. Emphasis added.
28 *Political Economy*, 242.
29 *Social Contract*, 2.3.72.
30 *Social Contract*, 2.4.74.

will and ceases to possess sovereign authority. In the circumstances of unequal treatment, the public's actions are no longer linked with the transcendent will. For the popular will legislates in the name of or on behalf of the pre-existing transcendental general will. The popular will may never fully and accurately enact the general will. Whereas the popular will is composed from a sum of particular wills, the general will is a universal. The general will transcends particular wills. The general will is general and abstract. As Asher Horowitz puts it, a "doubling of human existence" occurs.[31]

Even a particular, popularly elected government cannot accurately represent the general will. That is, a government cannot gain a presence or immediacy with the general will. A government decrees rules in particular circumstances and thereby discriminates between citizens. As Rousseau says, executive power "is exercised only in particular acts which are outside the province of law and therefore outside the province of the sovereign [legislature] which can act only to make laws."[32] The executive is the brain, whereas the legislature is the heart of the state.[33] Both executive and legislature act as "a particular *ego*, a consciousness common to its members, a force, a will of its own tending to its preservation."[34] The key to Rousseau's analysis of authority, then, is his belief that the general will is a *rational subject* who *presents* or embodies the signs of the *body* politic. As Rousseau explains, "[s]overeignty cannot be represented, for the same reason that it cannot be alienated; its essence is the general will, and the will cannot be represented – either it is the general will or it is something else; there is no intermediate possibility."[35] A citizen may not even renounce his or her own particular will because such a particular will is inalienable: "power can be delegated but the will cannot."[36] Thus, the people's deputies are *agents*, not representatives, of the general will.

As with the invisible beasts in the invisible condition, Rousseau's general will is inaccessible except as re-presented by civil authorities as a secondary language. Elected officials represent particular interests. These particular interests are contingently located in history and in space. The decisions of elected officials cannot be final. Why not? Because the moral content of the decisions must be linked with the general will and only the general will offers finality. Why? Because the general

31 Asher Horowitz, *Rousseau, Nature and History* (Toronto: University of Toronto Press, 1987), 188.

32 *Social Contract*, 3.1.101.

33 *Social Contract*, 3.2.135; 3.7.122; 3.11.137. The body is born, but it inevitably dies because the head always eventually dominates the heart. Rousseau's association of the metaphors of the body with the institutional arms of the "body politic" (his term) is crucial to understanding his refusal to allow civil laws to be entrapped in the representative signs of a semiotic system.

34 *Social Contract*, 3.4.106.

35 *Social Contract*, 3.15.141.

36 *Social Contract*, 3.1.69.

will is a presence or an immediacy with the officials and citizens. There are no signs that can mediate between the general will and the thoughts of the human agents. Rousseau realizes that juridical agents may only *ex post facto* re-present the general will. The public may fail to voice the general will when, for example, the meanest interests of particular wills dominate civil society. In that circumstance, the general will is subordinate to particular interests. Because the general will is permanent, omnipotent, and transcendent, this corruption eventually leads to the death of the body politic. Particular wills, despite their claim to represent the general will, may corrupt the institutionalization of the general will. Although the general will lacks an identity because it lacks particulars, it bears repeating that the general will is said to possess an ego and a body. Moreover, the general will is believed to speak (and thereby to act) in civil society through general laws: "the law is nothing other than a *declaration* of the general will."[37] Accordingly, the government or the popular will may err in their implementation of the general will, although the populace may be misled and although the populace may not discern the public good.[38] The general will is always right. True laws would never be oppressive because, reflecting the "always unchanging, incorruptible and pure"[39] interests of humankind in general, it would not be in the interest of the general will to impose fetters upon the populace or any faction of the populace.

Although the general will articulates the communal interest through laws, the general will stands 'out there' beyond the civil laws. The absence of the authorizing origin drives legislators to continually amend civil laws so as to better approximate the general will. The externality of the general will functions as an archemedean point upon which to ground the authority of the civil laws. The general will, like the "rational and impartial spectator" of Kant's metaphysics of morals and the invisible authors of Hobbes's legal structure, is situated spatially behind and temporally before all posited laws. The general will is an *a priori* concept which does not depend upon some third factor to gain a signification.

3. Civil Laws as the Expression of the General Will

The general will speaks. The general will speaks through general laws. A law is *general* in that it rationally "considers all subjects collectively and all actions in the abstract."[40] According to Rousseau, a law categorizes living subjects. A law "considers all subjects collectively and all actions *in the abstract*; it does not

---

37 *Social Contract*, 3.15.142. Emphasis added.
38 *Social Contract*, 2.3.72.
39 *Social Contract*, 4.1.150.
40 *Social Contract*, 3.6.82.

consider any individual man nor any specific action."[41] Being abstract, a general law is purged of all human inclination and historical contingency. Consequently, the expression of the general will conceals a multiplicity of voices. The general laws recognize a person as universal, rational, abstract, equal, and bodiless, much as Hegel describes the juridical person in the moment of abstract right in *The Philosophy of Right*. All such universal persons are equal *before* the general will, and all such persons are entitled to equal benefit *under* the general will. This formal equality prevents laws from being enacted for particular individuals or a particular set of circumstances.[42]

The general will, as expressed through the legislation of historical authors, *unites* citizens. How so? Purged of the social and historical contingencies of particular wills, the general will transcends particular circumstances and thereby rationally joins them through the transcendent bridge. "According to the fundamental concept," according to Rousseau, "it is only the general will which binds individuals."[43] Civil laws do not bind individuals. This binding unity contrasts with the anthropological or experiential character of social bonding. The unity is artificial, rational, and juridically defined, not an amalgam of particular wills that have been embodied with experienced meanings. The statutes of the people, decrees of a government, and judgments of the judiciary merely approximate the transcendent general will. The authorizing origin of a legislative and adjudicative act is intrinsically valued *in and for itself*. Being an indeterminate transcendental form emptied of particulars, the general will is the first cause of civil laws of a modern state. Even the sovereign state itself is subordinate to such a first cause. The state too is an "artificial person," "a mere fictitious entity (since it is not a man)."[44] The general will is what Judith Shklar describes as "that supreme illusionist."[45] The name of the general will names nothing because it *names the unnameable*.[46]

4. Naming the Unnameable

Despite its formless 'character' as an *a priori* concept, all law-giving is paradoxically enacted in the name of this unnameable source. By associating it with a name, 'the general will,' Rousseau names the unnameable. Perhaps it is best for us henceforth to capitalize the name, as he intends that a proper name be assigned to the "celestial" author.

41 *Social Contract*, 2.6.82.
42 *Social Contract*, 2.4.76.
43 *Social Contract*, 2.7.86.
44 *Social Contract*, 1.8.64.
45 Judith Shklar, *Man and Citizen: A Study of Rousseau's Social Theory* (Cambridge: University of Cambridge Press, 1985), 160.
46 See Samuel Weber, "In the Name of the Law," in *Cardozo Law Review* **11** (1990): 1515-1538, 1537.

Indeed, there is a sense in which the General Will corresponds with Aristotle's unmoved mover of the cosmos. What could be more of an unmoved mover than a single author which is eternal, absolute, transcendent, and unchanging. The General Will gives birth to the civil laws. Rousseau describes the General Will in the *Social Contract* as "the union of origin."[47] In like vein, Rousseau begins his analysis of sovereignty in Book Two with the claim that "the general will alone can direct the forces of the state in accordance with ... the common good."[48] The General Will becomes the name of the unnameable. The General Will rationally causes or grounds all juridical action. Rousseau likens the General Will to the father of a family whose authority rests in nature only insofar as his children are dependent upon him for their preservation. When this is no longer so, the patriarchal natural bond is dissolved and the children, reaching the age of reason, become their own master. "The head of the state bears the image of the father."[49] The General Will possesses "an absolute power over all its members,"[50] "a universal and compelling power to *move* and *dispose* of each part in whatever manner is beneficial to the whole."[51] The General Will is an *a priori* concept in that it is not dependent upon a third proposition. The General Will is an *in itself*. The General Will is located before history, for history only begins with the civil laws of legislatures and courts. The General Will dwells *behind* and *prior* to the enactment of the abstract laws of civil institutions. The authority of the General Will is "wholly absolute, wholly *sacred*, wholly inviolable."[52] The General Will steers all posited laws with "a single body" and "only one will."[53]

Indeed, if the General Will were to err, all civil laws would collapse, according to Rousseau. The General Will cannot err for it is an *a priori*, constant, indestructible, general, pure will. The General Will is an end in itself: there is no other object or goal to which the General Will refers. At least, there simply cannot be a particular other as a referent of the General Will in a modern state. Because the General Will is an intrinsic end whose will cannot be reached within the language of historical authors, its inaccessibility gives it a sacred character.

Once again, as with Hobbes, the juridical agents in a legal structure cannot access the ultimate author of the structure. For Rousseau, an unnameable, rational, unidentifiable *a priori* concept originates the authority of general laws. Yet the General Will itself, drawn from a state of nature, is believed to pre-exist the

---

47 Rousseau, *Social Contract*, 2.10.95.
48 *Social Contract*, 2.1.69.
49 *Social Contract*, 1.2.50.
50 *Social Contract*, 2.4.74.
51 *Social Contract*, 2.4.74. Emphasis added.
52 *Social Contract*, 2.4.77. Emphasis added.
53 *Social Contract*, 3.18.149.

legislatures that enact such general laws. The particular wills of a legislative body are grounded in a formless origin. This unreachable origins is a One rather than the Many, just as Hobbes insisted that all juridical actors defer to a One that stands behind all civil laws. Like a human agent, the One is believed to possess a body and a consciousness. But the One is absent from civil society. The One lacks the public language of civil institutions. The will of the One can only be expressed through general laws. Juridical agents of the General Will can only approximate the thoughts of the One through their posited laws.

In sum, early modern legal thought poses an origin that is absent from the public language of general laws. Rousseau's General Will is one such origin. The General Will is pure in that it lacks any particular identity that would possess the inclinations and particularities associated with historical contingency. Rousseau believes that the citizen is immediately bonded with the absent *arche* of the authority of all human laws, without the significations that Hobbes had considered so important for there to be knowledge. All legislatures and judges act as agents of Rousseau's pure will. Agency governs their actions. It is not a question of civil institutions re-presenting the General Will, but of such institutions acting within the boundaries that the General Will authorizes of its agents. In Hobbes's case, all juridical actors represent a "mortalle God" who, in turn, represents the invisible authors in an inaccessible state of nature. Hobbes's mortal God unifies the multiple wills in this mythical/mystical natural condition. Situated in a pre-history or, more correctly, an a-history, the origin of civil laws cannot be reached through the signs of a legal language. Once again, the authorizing origin of civil laws is pre-legal.

Both Rousseau's General Will and the invisible Author of Hobbes's natural condition possess a purity and presence that we lesser humans in civil society can only approximate through our deliberation and interpretation of civilly posited statutes and other legal documents. Juridical agents can never access such a presence. The King is dead. Only a God can save the King.

6

The Habits of the People: The Origin of John Austin's Laws Properly So Called

Thomas Hobbes grounded civil authority in a 'natural condition' where creatures could not express themselves through a written language. They could only express their feelings and thoughts through bodily behaviour and this, in turn, led to a nasty, short and brutish life. Once such creatures began to share conventions as to what particular sounds and marks signified, they could agree to abide by certain undertakings. A basic contract could provide the terms and conditions under which all civil officials would enact and interpret their posit of scripts. A command was valid if it could be traced to an institutional office located on a patriarchal structure which, in turn, could be traced to authors who had first acquired a language. Such authors contrasted with the beasts who had dominated the natural condition.

Now, with the nineteenth century writers, Jeremy Bentham (1748–1832) and John Austin (1790–1859), an effort is made to excise the natural condition from civil authority in order to ensure that civil laws are unconstrained by an externality, such as Hobbes's invisible authors, the social contract, or natural duties transcribed from a natural condition. Although Bentham and Austin differ in the niceties of their theories, I intend to take Austin's work to exemplify how even a self-legislating sovereign depends upon an externality, outside the institutional structure, for its authority. In particular, Austin grounds legal authority in the habits of the people. But, despite his externalization of the habits of actual people from the legal structure, 'the people' are constructed from the laws "properly so called."

1. The Problematic of Austin's Theory of Law

John Austin faces a problem. On the one hand, he claims that a structure of the civilly posited laws retains an autonomy vis-à-vis the outside world of morals, religion, and politics. This is not to say that the legal officials on the civil structure are not influenced by matters of ethics or religion or politics. To the contrary, Austin admits on several occasions that legal officials are so influenced. It is just that the laws are posited from inside a structure that is separate from moral, religious, or political structures. Autonomy ensures the supremacy of the legal structure vis-à-vis external structures. Ultimately, the rules posited by the institutions on the legal structure may be enforced against all competing moral, religious and political values and structures.

On the other hand, Austin asks 'why is the autonomous legal structure sovereign?' Perhaps put differently, why are the rules posited by the officials and institutions on the legal structure authoritative and enforceable when the rules posited by religious clerics in a church or the edicts of leaders in an organized crime syndicate are not? Why are the scripts authored by a parliament paramount vis-à-vis the scripts authored by judges? Are judges even credited with creating rules or is this characterization left for the legislature? Are the rules of the legal structure authoritative simply by virtue of their being posited? Are the cohesive and self-referring legal institutions themselves authoritative by virtue of the structure having been posited by human agents? Or does Austin go further? Does he justify the sovereignty of the state itself? If so, how is it possible for Austin to do so if, unlike Hobbes's appeal to a natural condition for the authoritative origin of civil laws, Austin's posited laws are apparently authorized by institutional sources independent of the natural condition.

2. Austin's Commentators

Philosophers have offered surprisingly many different interpretations of how Austin tried to resolve this problem.

Their efforts have centred about what they take as the core idea of Austin's view of sovereignty. Joseph Raz has focussed, for example, upon Austin's claim that the bulk of the populace must possess a habit of obedience towards a single sovereign legislature.[1] The habit of obedience is empirically ascertainable, according to Raz. With respect to the habit of obedience, Thomas Broden too has described the sovereign as a single legislature towards which obedience is given.[2] Conversely, H.L.A. Hart complained that Austin associated sovereignty with a single author (such as a legislature). Such a sovereign lacked basic rules for succession. Instead, Hart advocated secondary rules, which allowed for the succession of sovereigns.

Another group of commentators has privileged Austin's focus upon the coercion with which an official enforces a rule. That coercion makes the rule binding, according to these commentators. An unsigned Note in the *Yale Law Journal* isolates the sanction, rather than the habit of obedience, as critical to Austin's

1 Joseph Raz, *The Concept of a Legal System: An Introduction to the Theory of Legal System* (Oxford: Clarendon Press, 1980; 2nd edn.), 43.

2 Thomas Broden, "The Straw Man of Legal Positivism," *Notre Dame Lawyer* **34** (1958-59): 530-55, 534.

theory, for example. Unlike religious and moral systems, according to the Note, the legal system was characterized by the monopolization by a political superior of physical sanctions.[3] Henry Maine had earlier developed this point in his view that Austin's sovereign was the legislature and that "[s]overeignty, for the purposes of Austin's system, has no attribute but force, and consequently the view here taken of 'law,' 'obligation' and 'right' is a view of them exclusively as products of coercive force. The 'sanction' (force) thus becomes the primary and most important member of the series of notions and gives its colour to all the others."[4]

Samuel Stumpf has taken a third tack. Instead of associating sovereignty with the habits of obedience of the people towards a legislature or with physical coercion, Stumpf argues that Austin's laws are "bottomed" in the "necessary" "common nature of man."[5] Sovereignty has a moral basis. After all, Stumpf notes, Austin considers divine laws as laws "properly so called." Why? Because divine laws were posited by an author, God. God is what Austin described as a "remote" source; human agents are the "proximate" source. A moral limitation precedes the very way in which a sovereign legislature is constituted, according to Stumpf. As Austin lectured,

> The law of England, for example, cannot be understood without a knowledge of the constitution of Parliament, and of the various rules by which that sovereign body conducts the business of legislation: although it is manifest that much of the law which determines the constitution of Parliament, and many of the rules which Parliament follows in legislating, are mere law imposed by the opinion of the community, or merely ethical maxims which the body spontaneously observes.[6]

The decisive factor about the sovereign, according to Stumpf's interpretation of Austin, was "not the fact that it [the sovereign legislature] was curbed by no *legal* limitations, but that in fact it was curbed by 'moral' laws."[7] One offers an incomplete picture of Austin's theory, according to Stumpf, if one identifies laws with a self-referential logical system.[8] In sum, commentators have identified four different groundings to legislative sovereignty: the habit of obedience of the bulk of the peoples; coercion; moral laws; and a divine author.

---

3 Note, "Hart, Austin and the Concept of a Legal System," *Yale Law Journal* **84** (1975): 584-617.

4 Henry Maine, *Lectures on the Early History of Institutions* (New York: Holt, 1875; Port Washington, New York: Kennikat, 1966, 7th ed.), 363 (1875 edn.).

5 Samuel Enoch Stumpf, "Austin's Theory and the Separation of Law and Morals," *Vanderbilt Law Review* **14** (1960): 117-49, 123, quoting from John Austin, *The Province of Jurisprudence Determined*, intro. & ed. H.L.A. Hart (London: Weidenfeld and Nicolson, 1832, 1955), 373.

6 John Austin, *Lectures on Jurisprudence* [hereinafter cited as *Lectures*], 3 vols. (New York: Burt Franklin, 1861; reprint New York: Lenox Hill, 1970), vol. 2, lecture 44, 437.

7 Stumpf, "Austin's Theory and the Separation of Law and Morals," 130.

8 Ibid., 135.

As if these did not offer a sufficient spectrum of interpretations, a series of commentators have re-read Austin's theory of law with further diverse, non-legal externalities. Wilfrid Rumble, C.A.W. Manning, and J.W. Harris suggest that the habit of obedience is not an empirically ascertainable phenomenon. Rather, the habit of obedience of the bulk of the populace is grounded in something further: utility in Wilfrid Rumble's view, a notion in Manning's, and a metaphor in Harris's. Wilfrid Rumble takes up the role of morality as the crucial grounding to Austin's theory of posited laws.[9] Rumble privileges the divine as important. The divine law authorizes utility or the greatest happiness of the greatest number, utility being only a partial index or manifestation of the divine will. Positive laws possess a "necessity" that is not capable of empirical proof, according to Rumble. In the absence of a legally unlimited sovereign, the legislature simply may not achieve general happiness amongst the populace. Along a similar vein, Manning emphasizes that a legal system needs a logical correlate to the posited laws.[10] Manning describes the 'habits of obedience' as just such a correlate in that it is a "notion" or "concept" or "abstraction" that is logically prior to particular posited rules. The habits of obedience are pre-legal. The notion of 'the habit of obedience,' as located in a metaphysics external to the legal structure, allows Austin to claim a binding quality to the laws properly so called. The sovereign is located wherever the posited commands, not the people, place ultimate control. Carrying the logical correlate one step further, J.W. Harris writes that the will of the people is merely a "constructive metaphor." The metaphor is logically necessary to ensure a finality to the posited human laws of a complete system of rules "into which all legislative materials and all lawful commands could be forced."[11] The posited rules are so comprehensive as to potentially enclose all social conduct. Harris suggests that, although Bentham and Austin may have accepted Kant's sense of a will as a non-psychological metaphysical entity, it is more fruitful to consider that 'the habits of obedience of the bulk of the people' are a constructive metaphor: the directives of legal institutions and officials are accepted *as if* the people willed each and every binding rule. There needs to be a *single* ruler or body of rulers for such a will. The ruler enacts all the rules of subordinate authorities. The habit of obedience is simply a necessary postulate in order to distinguish the authoritative rules from the non-authoritative, to subsume some rules under other rules on a hierarchy, to reject some rules because they are in conflict, and to confer a duty and a non-duty in the same circumstance.[12]

---

9 Wilfrid Rumble, "Divine Law, Utilitarian Ethics, and Positivist Jurisprudence: A Study of the Legal Philosophy of John Austin," *The American Journal of Jurisprudence* **24** (1979): 139-80.

10 C.A.W. Manning, "Austin To-day: or 'The Province of Jurisprudence' Re-examined," in ed. H. Milford, *Modern Theories of Law* (Oxford: Oxford University Press, 1933): 180-226.

11 J.W. Harris, "The Concept of Sovereign Will," *Acta Juridica* (1977): 1-15, 4.

12 Ibid., 12.

How is it possible that such divergent interpretations of Austin are possible? One common denominator is shared amongst them. The interpretations centre upon Austin's sense of a sovereign. They acknowledge that there is something external to the sovereign and external to the sovereign's civil laws – the habits of obedience of the people, coercion, moral feelings, a notion, a metaphor, a pre-legal postulate, the divine law, utility, or the like. Several of the interpretations make a major effort to reconcile the self-referring posited rules with such external factors. Are the interpretations satisfactory? What is sovereign: the legislature? the electorate? a notion of a make-believe 'people'?

Austin is aware that laws 'properly so called' need a source external to such laws in order to sustain their authority. The habits of the 'people' fulfill such a function. For very special reasons (including Austin's definition of a legal author as a "determinate" body), the habits of the people fail to qualify as "laws properly so called." They dwell outside legal existence since only laws properly so called constitute such an existence. Austin is insistent that such an inaccessible externality cannot possibly legally constrain the legislature, its subordinate bodies, or any other civil institutions. Only commands authored by civil institutions are considered binding. So the officials of the institutional authors must conceal the role of the external 'habit of obedience of the people' in order to ensure the sovereignty of the authors.

3. The Excision of the Natural Condition from Civil Society

Now, with John Austin, an effort is made to expel the natural condition as even relevant to the authority of laws "properly so called." To begin with, Austin argues, an original contract such as Hobbes's, if explicit, must be signified in the language of the contractees. However, the members of an inchoate society without a language, such as Hobbes describes of the natural condition, cannot possibly articulate specific common promises. Of course, Hobbes suggested that citizens may tacitly agree to an original contract. But the position and deportment of a conquered populace could hardly support a tacit contract, according to Austin. The vanquished obey the state from fear of the military sword, not from respect for the terms of some original contract. Historically, Austin adds, Hobbes's original contract never preceded a state's formation. Put simply, Austin states that no one state is legal or illegal, just or unjust. A prior contract cannot make the sovereign state legal or just. Some legal duties bear no resemblance to a convention or contract. Divine and human laws do not enforce a contract because there is a contract per se, but because of the objects and tendencies of the contract. The state just 'is,' according to Austin. It is the role of the jurisprude and official to describe this 'is,' not to evaluate it, according to Austin. All that matters is the civil laws of a *de facto* government.

So Austin aims to describe a legal existence where some institution or aggregate of institutions possess "legally despotic" authority. Such sovereign authority must be incapable of legal constraint. As a consequence, the only laws that count are humanly posited laws: "supreme power limited by positive law is a flat contradiction in terms."[13] The legislature meets Austin's sense of supremacy. Any one legislature may not bind itself into the future. Nor may the general words of a legislature override its specific words. More generally, "a society is not a society political and independent, unless it can maintain its independence, against attacks from without, by its own intrinsic or unaided strength."[14] Its intrinsic autonomy, Austin wants to argue, draws from its authority over all competing substantive moral values.

What does Austin mean by legal authority? Austin associates authority with what he calls a "source" or "fountain." The source that most concerns Austin is "the author." That is his term, although commentators have given insufficient attention to his use of it. The author creates. For Austin, the most important authors are neither Shakespeare, nor Blake, nor Baudelaire, but legal institutions. The authoritative author is located within a system of other authors who refer to each other's work. The institutional authors are linked vertically up a ladder to a supreme head, sometimes to a king or sometimes to a parliament. So a government agency gains its authority by one's tracing its acts or commands to authors in the agency located higher on the ladder. These self-referring institutional authors are sovereign in that their laws properly so called are content independent, because there must be some finality to the trace of legal rules to their institutional sources. And yet, although legal officers and institutions must deliberate and decide as if laws properly so called were content independent, the authority of the institutional authors is dependent upon an external source that the laws properly so called cannot recognize. Even the supreme head of the structure, whether a king or a president or parliament, is dependent upon the habitual obedience of the people to the head.

What is the nature of this necessary, yet legally unrecognizable, externality, according to Austin? The people. To exist, the laws 'properly so called' must be habitually obeyed by the bulk of the people, according to Austin. Why so? What, then, is the role of this externality to the structure, the habit of obedience of the people? Why must there be some external source, the people, to the institutional structure? Why must the legal officials interpret and enact rules as if the people were not a legitimate author of laws properly so called? That is, why must the officials in the

13 Austin, *Province* lecture 6, 254. The first volume of *Lectures* is entitled *Province of Jurisprudence Determined.* The first volume will be cited in the accessible publication of ed. & intro. H.L.A. Hart (London: Weidenfeld and Nicolson, 1955).

14 Austin *Province,* lecture 6, 213

institutional structure trivialize the will of the people by classifying their will as moral sentiment, rather than as the author of laws properly so called?

Austin emphasizes that the people must possess a habit of obedience towards the institutional authors. But this habit of obedience does not constitute a legal constraint upon the authors' legal expression. After all, the written laws may well not even expressly refer to the will of the people. Rather, the statutes, precedents, and other writing may only refer to the signs in other statutes, precedents, and other instruments. Thus, only writing may be considered law properly so called or "strictly legal," according to Austin. In addition, what allows one to describe the institutional structure as sovereign is the very impossibility of an external legal constraint to the structure of laws properly so called. As a consequence, the people, as the authorizing origin of laws properly so called, must be projected as legally non-existent, as non-law, though of fundamental moral and political importance. That is, the will of the people must be credited as non-existent, legally speaking. For the habits of the people are not the written signs that officials can recognize as binding laws properly so called. Only the writing of authors is justicible, for the autonomy of the institutional authors is a 'given.'

The unwritten world *does* enter into the deliberations of the officials, according to Austin. As a psychological or phenomenological matter, the attitudes of the bulk of the people may well influence an official's deliberation about a particular creation of a rule or an official's continued deference to a particular rule, Austin admits. In his *Lectures,* Austin states, for example, that "the case that I am now considering is one of the numerous cases wherein law and morality are so intimately and indissolubly allied that, though they are distinct natures and ought to be carefully distinguished, it is necessary nevertheless to consider them in conjunction."[15] And again, he lectures that sovereignty resides in those persons who are constructed from a "compound of positive morality and positive law, which determines the character of a person, or ... persons..."[16] And again, "[f]or a government may be hindered by *positive morality* from abridging political liberty which it leaves or grants to its subject: and is bound by the *law of God*, as known through the principle of utility, not to load them with legal duties which general utility condemns."[17] And again, "God or nature is not a source of law in the strict sense.... God or nature is ranked among the sources of law, through the same confusion of the source of law with its remoter causes.... But ... [law] is law, strictly so called, by the establishment it receives from the human sovereign.... God or nature is the remote cause of the law, but its source and proximate cause is

15 Austin, *Lectures*, vol. 2, lecture 42, 745-46.

16 Austin, *Province*, lecture 6, 259.

17 Austin, *Province*, lecture 6, 268. His emphasis.

the earthly sovereign by whom it is *positum* or established."[18] In other words, the operative officials of an institutional author are deeply influenced (or content-dependent) by social and moral factors in their decision-making. One such social/moral influence is the official's perception of the will of the people. Austin describes the ultimate authorizing origin of legal institutions – the habits of obedience of the bulk of the populace – as moral sentiment. The behaviour or attitudes of the sovereign's subjects are not a 'law.' Such behaviour, if identified as uniform, is a mere "maxim" or "convention," which Austin associates with "laws improperly so called."

Thus, Austin's posited laws, like Hobbes's, rely upon an inaccessible externality that the officials cannot recognize as a binding law properly so called. Both Hobbes and Austin describe the externality as a creative source or author. Though the externality enters into the intuitions of the officials, it is unrecognizable as law properly so called. The externality remains invisible (in the sense of inaccessible) to the officials.

The externality of the public will or moral/religious beliefs vis-à-vis the laws properly so called ensures the exclusion of emotive beliefs from legal expression. Why are emotive beliefs excluded from what Austin considers laws properly so called? Why does he describe them as moral sentiments? Because Austin considers the habits of the people to be unwritten, vague, uncertain, and indeterminate. In a sense, the habits are legally unconscious. If a legal text incorporated the will of the people, such as through a referendum, into legally recognizable expression, then the people's will would become part of the laws properly so called for the particular purpose posited in the text. But it is the writing and the locus of the writing in the institutional structure that render the habits of the people as an authoritative source of law in that circumstance. Austin asserts that laws properly so called are written in books such as statutes and a judge's reasons for judgment. The habits of the bulk of the people are unsignified in legal expression. Such habits are unrecognized because they lack an identifiable and determinate source of laws properly so called. If a statute incorporates the will of the people (say, through a referendum result), the result is transformed from the unwritten to the written, from the unsignified to the signified, from moral sentiment to legal consequence. Here, Austin's point mimics Hobbes's description of the authors. Hobbes's authors emerge from a "savage" world where there are no conventions as to what certain words signify. The language with which Austin is concerned here, of course, is the legal language whose vocabulary and grammar is located in the written codes of legislators and judges on a hierarchy of institutions.

18 Austin, *Lectures*, vol. 2, lecture 44, 437.

4. The Historical Author

I have just suggested that Austin is quick to affirm that laws properly so called are authorized through the public language of legal institutions. What characterizes a legally binding rule as opposed to a morally or religiously binding rule? What makes a rule a law properly so called as opposed to one that is improperly so called? Let us delve a little deeper into Austin's theory of law in order to respond to these important questions.

Austin's contribution, having excised the natural from civil society, is to concentrate upon the institutions in civil society. Such civil institutions take the form of a cohesive structure in the shape of a pyramidal hierarchy. What Hobbes had attributed as "actors" are now called and considered "authors." The institutional authors originate laws "properly so called." All other rules are "metaphorical or figurative" expressions.[19] But what is a law properly so-called? Why is a rule, posited by an author, a law properly so called when a rule posited by an author on another pyramidal structure, such as that of a religious organization or an organized crime syndicate, is a law improperly so called?

Contrary to the usual interpretation of Austin, more than a rule or command is the material of Austin's theory of laws properly so called. The commands are authored. The authors are not particular authors with personal names: they are *offices* that carry the character of an 'author' whomever occupies the office. The authors are very special offices in that they are located on a special institutional structure that is differentiated from other structures. It is "the position" of the author on the institutional structure that determines the authority of a binding rule. As Austin explains in his important fifth lecture, "[s]trictly speaking, every law properly so called is a *positive* law. For it is *put* or set by its individual or collective author, or it exists by the *position* or institution of its individual or collective author."[20] Austin continually italicizes the word "position" to make this point. As with Hobbes, the substantive content of a rule is not important for the authority of the rule. Rather, the rule is authoritative if it has been authored by the right institutional source in civil society. There are rules that guide and govern such institutions, in turn. They are now called "the pedigree" or the "manner and form" requirements of constitutional law. But these rules are entirely procedural in character. Here too, the substantive content of the procedural constituting rules is unimportant.

The structure of interrelation of institutional authors locates higher and lower, supreme and inferior authors. The institutional structure is what Austin considers

19 Austin, *Province*, lecture 5, 119, 122.
20 Austin, *Province*, lecture 5, 193.

to be sovereign or, using "the inseparably connected expression," an "independent political society." Austin frequently italicizes the latter term. The structure locates authors who are supreme over a person or persons who are "in a state of subjection." The state of subjection is "the correlative expression" of sovereignty. Once again, Austin italicizes the phrase "correlative expression." The position of the authors in a structure of authors distinguishes a human law from a natural law that applies to all human beings at all times and at all places.[21]

Austin diligently emphasizes that the author is not an isolated institution but rather, an institution that is situated inside an "aggregate" of institutions or a "collective whole."[22] The "aggregate" of authors compose a structure with three types of authors: first, a supreme political superior such as a monarch or "other sovereign bodies"; secondly, subordinate political superiors who lie in a state of subjection to the supreme political superior; and thirdly, private persons who carry legal rights.[23] Authors who are not situated on such an institutional structure of authors posit positive moral rules. So too, a political superior or a private subject may posit a positive moral rule if the rule is not authorized as appropriate for an author on the structure. What makes a rule an "imperative" or a "command" is the locus of its source on the structure of authoritative authors.[24] This structure of authors is what Austin describes as an independent political society. Such a structure or "aggregate" of bodies does not depend upon society for its existence. Nor is the collective aggregate subordinate to some other independent political society. Put differently, the civil institutions must not be in the habit of obedience to some other aggregate of institutions. The institutional aggregate is autonomous.

Why does Austin give so much play to the notion of an autonomous author? Because, like Hobbes and, indeed, the Roman deference to an impersonal *auctoritas*, Austin associates the authority of a binding rule with a source or grounding or origin. An author is just such a source of a rule. In his colourful language, a law properly so called "springs and streams" from an author who functions as a "fountain or source."[25] A written script becomes a law by virtue of the position of its author on the pyramidal structure of institutions.

What are the requisites for being an author whose rules and actions count in an independent political society? To begin with, the author must be a distinct and identifiable single body, such as a king, or a composite body, such as a legislature. The author is identifiable in contrast to some indeterminate concept, such as justice

21 Austin, *Province*, lecture 5, 129.
22 See, e.g., Austin, *Province*, lecture 5, 133.
23 Austin, *Province*, lecture 5, 134, 195.
24 "Being *imperative* (and therefore proceeding from *determinate* sources) ..." Austin, *Province*, lecture 5, 139.
25 Austin, *Lectures* vol. 2, lecture 29, 213.

or freedom, or some authorless phenomenon, such as a custom. Once one can identify a distinct author as the institutional source of a rule, the content of the rule is immaterial to the issue, 'is this a binding rule?' Secondly, the author must be identifiable as a source on an institutional hierarchy: a legislature may be designated the author for certain matters despite the fact that the king created the legislature or that the legislature gained its authority from the king, or vice versa. The only important concern is that the right institution author a rule according to the right procedural requirements. The institutional source alleviates any confusion between human laws and divine laws.

Austin suggests a second set of requirements. The statute or judicial decision of a later author – later, that is, in terms of the measurement by a clock – will override the script of an earlier author because the later source best represents the intent of the sovereign. So too, a specifically worded script will override a more generally worded script because a specifically worded statement is clearer evidence of what the institutional author would have intended. The author creates a binding law. The author self-consciously wills the law: a law "springs from the will and intention of an intelligent and rational author."[26]

Now, Austin describes two types of authors. The one, whom he calls an "immediate" author, "directly" and "immediately" expresses its will by signs that the addressee or, at least, representers of the addressee will recognize and then 'understand' as authoritative. A legislature or court exemplifies an immediate author. So too, two immediate authors may will a contract and sign the contract as its authors. An immediate author is a "clear" and "determinate" source.[27]

There is a second type of author: an "oblique" author who is a "remote cause" of a text. The oblique author receives the script of the immediate author and interprets it as a representer of the immediate author. I have emphasized above how Austin focuses upon the structural effect of the linear traces of a text from one immediate author, such as the penultimate Crown, to more oblique authors. Such a linear trace ensures that a rule be considered a law properly so called. A moral sentiment or a custom cannot be traced to such a determinate and originary author. An inability to trace a sentiment or custom to a distinct author arises, for example, when one has to reason by analogy or metaphor. A metaphoric or figurative expression draws from the unwritten law, according to Austin.[28] Even a custom,

26 Austin, *Province*, lecture 5, 174.

27 Bentham makes the same point when he writes that a state is characterized by the disposition to obey "a person or an assemblage of persons, of a known and certain description." *Fragment of Government*, eds. J.H. Burns and H.L.A. Hart.; intro. Ross Harrison (Cambridge: Cambridge University Press, 1977), chap. 1, para. 10. *Limits of Jurisprudence Defined*, intro. Charles Warren Everett (New York: Columbia University Press, 1945), 101.

28 Bentham, *Limits of Jurisprudence Defined*, 119, 120.

though expressed in an imperative style and habitually obeyed, is not a law properly so called because the custom has not been posited by an identifiable and determined institution. Accordingly, a moral sentiment or a custom is a law improperly so called.

Laws properly so called, then, are authored. What is an example of an authored law? A custom? One cannot identify a time and place when a custom takes form. A custom exists 'from time immemorial,' the common law repeats again and again. Austin is so preoccupied with the authorial nature of laws, however, that he even understands unwritten customs in terms of their authorship, albeit "imaginary authors."[29] He distinguishes an imaginary author from an immediate author, an immediate author being a legislature or court for example. What, pray tell, is an imaginary author? How does an imaginary author differ from an immediate author? An immediate author is distinct and identifiable. An immediate author transcends its addressees. Such an author is believed to pre-exist the script in time. The immediate author pre-exists in space by being *external* to the script. A particular legislature is said to be an "immediate" author in that one can associate its script with a particular legislature in terms of time and space. A supreme legislature may be situated at the pinnacle of the pyramidal organization of other legal institutions that gain their authority from the supreme legislature. A custom, in contrast, lacks a time and place when one can say that it has originated. One can also not identify a custom as having originated in a certain institution, such as a legislature. Customs are laws improperly so called: they have the character of moral or political norms, not legal rules. Austin sometimes associates the spirit of a vague indeterminate *Volksgeist* with the origination of customs.

Now, an author writes something – a novel, a letter, a poem, a textbook. For Austin, the writing represents insights or concepts of the author. The author expresses what is in his or her mind through a language. The author is immersed within a language. The most important feature of his theory of law, then, is Austin's understanding of language. The author writes about what is in his or her mind. His or her expression refers to objects, that is. The objects generally are cognitive. For an official, the objects are such cognitive referents as doctrines or rules or principles. The cognitive objects give content to the expression. If writing lies on the page without the referents of concepts, then it is meaningless. For Austin, the cognitive referents are laws. The expression represents a properly so called law if the expression's author is a distinct institution in the aggregate of civil institutions of the independent political society.

Austin's theory of language makes sense when one appreciates the importance that he attributes to the distinct and assignable author. How can an official or an

29 Austin, *Lectures*, vol. 2, lecture 30, 224.

institution be an author if the official or institution does not express ideas in writing? If his or her object is left inarticulated or unconscious or intuitive or gestural, one has to speculate as to what the 'author' intended. The gesture connotes a signification which may well depend upon the addressee's, not the utterer's meaning. The addressee must interpret the gesture.

As with Hobbes, Austin claims that a rule is a law properly so called if the rule is represented in a script that has been authored by an institution or official whose jurisdiction, in turn, has been assigned by a prior author in the collectivity of interrelated institutions. I noted in Chapter Four that Hobbes had called such an institution an 'actor' in that the institution acted as if in a play. The actors in civil society played on behalf of the authors of the play. The authors, not the actors, had created the terms and conditions of the social contract when they had just acquired conventions as to what noises and marks signified.

In Austin's case though, authors are located in civil society. An institution authors a script on behalf of another institutional source placed higher in the civil hierarchy. And that institution, in turn, is authorized to act on behalf of a still higher author. A government official, such as the chief of police of a municipality, may author guidelines or maxims as to when the police officers under the chief ought to spray demonstrators with a chemical. The chief of police may be granted this authority from a higher author, the municipality. The municipality, in turn, may have been granted its authority from a still higher author, such as a cabinet committee or deputy minister of the justice department. That author, in turn, may have been granted its authority from a prior legislature. Even courts of law lie in a direct line from the supreme author, the sovereign, and courts legislate "in subordination to the sovereign" and, as such, are only "reservoirs ... fed from the source of all law, the supreme legislature, and again emitting the borrowed waters which they receive from that Fountain."[30] Each grant of authority has been posited in writing. Together, the network of authorized institutions can be grouped as a self-legislating "body" or structure.

Already, we can appreciate that the rules of the self-legislating structure are laws properly so called in contrast to the rules of the godfather of an organized crime syndicate. The former's rules are expressed in writing and the latter's are expressed in gestures and verbal statements. But the statements of novelists, poets and moralists are also in writing. Again, in the vein of the above questions, what makes the rules of the sovereign legislature 'laws properly so called' and the statements of the novelists, poets, and religious leaders not so? Clearly, one difference is that the sovereign's rules are enforceable by officials on the hierarchic pyramid. That is, some officials on the hierarchy may legitimately coerce

30 Austin, *Lectures*, vol. 2, lecture 29, 213.

addressees who do not follow the rules. Austin clearly sets out this characteristic of coercion as an important difference. In Lecture Five of the *Province*, for example, he defines a positive law as having been directed towards a person "in a state of subjection to its author."[31] A moral rule may well be uttered in an imperative voice. A novelist, such as, say, Charles Dickens or Leo Tolstoy, may have a strident political statement to make. But unless such utterances are accompanied with an enforcement of the narrator's wishes against the persons intended by the novelist's desire, the desire is not a law, simply and strictly so called.

Austin adds a further distinction between the writing of an authoritative institution and the writing of the novelist or poet, or moralist, though. The non-legal author writes for a general audience or, if to a particular audience (such as those who enjoy poetry), as a general proposition. But a law properly so called is issued to a particular group of addressees who will fall 'under' the boundaries of the intended categories in the mind of the legal author. More, although a moral rule may be a universal proposition whose particular author, if it had an author, may have been forgotten, a properly so called laws should have a "determined" and "identifiable" author on the hierarchic pyramid of institutions. A law properly so called need not be directly authored by the supreme legislature. Subordinate institutions or officials, such as judges, situated under the legislature, might author laws. Their utterances might be called ordinances, orders in council, regulations, guidelines, judicial decisions, reasons for judgment or the like. Such subordinate authorities, though, must gain their authority from a logically and chronologically prior legislature. The priority must be in terms of time and logic. The rational linkage ensures that the subordinate authority speaks for the whole network of authors situated above and below the subordinate authority. As Austin put this point, a law properly so called must possess either a "direct" or a "circuitous" nexus with the prior script of some immediate author situated higher on the governmental organization.[32] The structure speaks with one voice. The bodies in the structure consider the structure a totality.

The situs of a distinct and assignable author on an institutional structure of authors, an organization in the shape of a pyramid, then, ensures that a rule is a law properly so called rather than a mere moral, religious or political rule or even a customary rule. The institutional structure is believed to exist before and after an author legislates, before and after the particular personnel adjudicate. The structure continues with the passage of different personalities who occupy the position of author. A law continues long after a particular author created the law. Austin

31 Austin, *Province*, lecture 5, 132

32 Austin, *Province*, lecture 5, 123.

states that posited morality lacks such a determinate author.[33] Morality even lacks a remote author. Moral rules are posited by an indeterminate or uncertain aggregate of persons. Austin suggests that although positive morality may manifest a constitutionalism, such a constitutionalism is separate from laws properly so-called.[34] Even a custom, habitually obeyed, is not law properly so called because it remains un-authored until a distinct and determinate institution later recognises the custom in writing.

Why is the situs of the institutional source or author of a rule so important? Why is an institutional structure of authors so necessary for the rule to be a law properly so called? Because an author is believed to have a mind that *intends* a cognitive object, such as a doctrine or rule or 'command.' A vegetable or "lower animal," Austin advises, may be bound to a law, such as a physio-chemical law, but not to a law properly so called, for a vegetable or lower animal lacks intelligence, Austin states. When a subject lacks intelligence, one can speak of law only in a "metaphorical or figurative" sense. Without intelligence, one cannot possess a will. Austin italicizes the word "*will*" here. A body lacks a will "which law can work on, or which duty can incite or restrain."[35] An individual is said to accept a law when the individual purposively intends an act. One only does so when one has a will, Austin claims. The predictable and regular practice of an individual does not suggest that one follows a law in the strict sense.

What happens to the human subjects who become subservient to the enclosing rules of the institutional authors? May the subjects behave or contemplate thoughts that the institutional authors may not regulate or 'touch'? May the authors even regulate the conduct of the officials who represent the institutional authors? Austin is clear with respect to this issue. All subjects and all officials live in a state of "subjection" or "dependence," according to Austin. Austin remarks about this state of subjection in several places in his lectures.[36] In a sense, although considered in a state of subjection, a human subject is re-defined as a juridical person, according to Austin. Rights and duties define who is a juridical person. The legal officials recognize the person, not by his or her experiences, but by the legal rights and duties that the officials have attributed to the person. The person is a juridical person. The person is cognitively constructed from laws that officials will recognize as authoritative. The enforcement of the rules encloses the subject within the metaphysical boundaries of legal doctrines.

---

33 See generally, Austin, *Province*, lecture 5, 139, 141.

34 Austin, *Province,* lecture 6, 259-59.

35 Austin, *Province,* lecture 1, 12, 17.

36 Austin, *Province,* lecture 6, 193; *Lectures,* vol. 3, lecture 49, 20.

5. Is the Historical Author's Authority Unlimited?

So, who is the sovereign, according to Austin? Is the sovereign a supreme legislature? Is the sovereign the bulk of the people who habitually obey the commands of institutional authors? Is the sovereign the concept of the greatest happiness of the greatest number? Who or what is the sovereign?

We know how Austin characterizes the sovereign. "If a *determinate* human superior, *not* in a habit of obedience to a like superior, receive *habitual* obedience from the bulk of a given society, that determinate superior is sovereign in that society, and the society (including the superior) is a society political and independent."[37] We know what a sovereign may and may not do. We know, for example, that a sovereign lacks any external legal constraint: "[s]overeign or supreme power is incapable of *legal* limitation," whether it resides in an individual, or a number of individuals.[38] Put differently, he continues, "supreme power limited by positive law is a flat contradiction in terms." No foreign official from some other territory may constrain the sovereign. Nor may the sovereign enact laws to constrain some future sovereign. Nor may a human law repeal the sovereignty. For if a human law could do so, the sovereign would not be sovereign. Such a superior command would possess more supreme authority.

That said, the authority of the aggregate rules is unlimited in nature and comprehensive in scope. Or so it seems. No human behaviour or thought is potentially immune from the scope of laws properly so called. The unlimited character of sovereignty is manifested, first, in the *res publicae* or "patrimony of the state," which reserves certain rights (such as the collection of taxes) to itself. Secondly, the sovereign possesses *res private* acts as a trustee as when property escheats to the state. Positive law may not constrain the sovereign itself "from dealing with all things within its territory at its own pleasure or discretion. If it could, it would not be a sovereign government, but a government in a state of subjection to a government truly supreme."[39] Accordingly, Austin continues, the state "has a right to all things within its territory, or is absolutely or without restriction the proprietor or dominus thereof." The sovereign may posit laws "as it may please."

Despite the unlimited character of the sovereign's authority in civil society, Austin realizes that there is something about authoritative commands that discourages one from considering them self-referential. The laws properly so called are not authoritative in and from some self-referring trace. For, like his predecessors, Austin associates authority with the quest for an ultimate authorizing source or ground or origin. There has to be a possibility of an *arche* or origin of origins,

37 Austin, *Province*, lecture 6, 194. His emphasis.

38 Austin, *Province*, lecture 6, 254.

39 Austin, *Lectures*, vol. 1, 55-7.

independent from the institutional authors, in order that the commands be obligatory. This is the point where Austin's focus upon the author of a law properly so called is so important. For we have noted how Austin is preoccupied with the idea that a command can only be considered a law properly so called if it is expressed in writing by an author who is located on the institutional pyramid of government. That pyramidal organization must have a singular voice to bring unity to the whole. The organization reflects this need by postulating a singular rational will at the head of the pyramid.

The origin of the institutional origins, Austin claims, is the people's habit of obedience. He puts the importance of the people to the overall institutional structure in this manner:

> [T]he sovereignty of each of the states, and also of the larger state arising from the federal union, resides in the states' governments *as forming one aggregate body;* [his emphasis] meaning by a state's government, *not its ordinary legislature, but the body of its citizens* [emphasis added] which appoints its ordinary legislature, and which, the union apart, is properly sovereign therein.[40]

Austin is not alone here. As I argued in Chapter Four, Hobbes also postulated that the laws of a civil society gained their authority from many authors who, having recently acquired a language, assigned their authority to a supra-Representer which, in turn, created a cohesive interdependent structure of offices. The offices, including the head of the structure, merely functioned as "actors" on a stage, the play having been authored by persons whose will constrained the actors.

In contrast, though, Austin defers to the historically contingent actors. Hobbes's actors are Austin's authors. Austin still considers an author as an autonomous creator of some later work. The author pre-exists its product, a statute or a court's reasons for judgment. But since Austin incorporates authors into his very legal structure (in contrast to Hobbes, who claims that the legal officials on the civil structure are mere "actors" of the authors' determinative wills at the transition from a natural to a civil society), Austin must allow for some super-author or transcendent source that can finalize the commands of the historical authors. To be final, such a super-author must be radically different from an ordinary institutional author such as a parliament or a court. For Austin, the habits of obedience of the bulk of the populace function as just such a radical other to the historical authors.

Austin's view of sovereignty, and its grounding in the people external to the sovereign legal structure, is shared with Bentham as well as Hobbes. In his early writings, Bentham offered the *a priori* concept of the 'greatest happiness of the greatest number' as such an invisible origin, for example. The ultimate concept of

40 Austin, *Province*, lecture 6, 251.

the 'greatest good' cannot be directly proved, he writes.[41] This final authorizing origin lies beyond the existent phenomenal world.[42] Legislatures can only approximate the transcendent 'greatest good,' according to Bentham. Bentham also acknowledges the inaccessibility of humanly posited laws when he makes the distinction between laws *in principem* and laws *in populum* in *Laws in General*. Laws *in principem* prescribe what the sovereign legislature may or may not do. In contrast, legislatures and courts generally posit laws only *in populum*. But what authorizes the laws *in principem* to constrain the laws *in populum*? Do previous legislatures posit laws *in principem*? If the legislature were constrained by laws *in principem*, then the origin of posited laws would hardly rest with the legislature itself. Accordingly, the laws *in principem* must transcend the sovereign.[43]

The question remains: what authorizes the authority of the laws *in principem*? On the one hand, Bentham writes, the sovereign legislature, through its own will, "enters himself into a covenant" that binds the legislature or, at least, which offers "a recommendatory mandate" to future sovereigns.[44] At another point, Bentham even suggests that judges, as co-sovereign, may enforce the covenants against the sovereign legislature.[45] On the other hand, Bentham suggests that a social contract does not authorize laws *in principem* to bind the sovereign legislature. He writes that covenants control future sovereigns through habit and expediency rather than through legal obligation.[46] Such covenants are unenforceable in a court against the legislature. Social contingencies may be so universally shared and deep-rooted that the sovereign legislature implicitly adopts undertakings of a previous sovereign legislature even though the contemporary legislature desires not to do so.[47] Conversely, contingency prevents laws *in principem* from being enforced.[48]

---

41 *An Introduction to the Principles of Morals and Legislation*, chap. 1, para. 11.

42 The fact that Bentham includes animals as relevant beings in the composition of the 'greatest happiness of the greatest number' reinforces how radically other is the authorizing origin of Bentham's laws.

43 Bentham, *Laws in General*, 64-9.

44 Bentham, *Laws in General*, 65.

45 *Laws in General*, 68-9. Also see *Limits of Jurisprudence Defined*, 101, where Bentham says that a set of persons may be sovereign in some cases.

46 Even in his strongest polemic against natural rights thinking, "Anarchic Fallacies," Bentham suggests that contracts derive their binding force from governments (not vice versa). See esp. *Laws in General*, 65-66.

47 Bentham, *Laws in General*, 66.

48 Bentham, *Laws in General*, 68. Bentham rules out political sanctions by the people because there can be no judge of a sovereign for the sovereign to be a sovereign. However, it seems clear that the *leges in principem* draw upon conditions of law-making *extrinsic* to the posited laws themselves. These conditions of operative power are absorbed through customary rules. As Bentham states, "except where a contract between sovereign and subject explicitly codifies the laws *in principem*, the *authority* [emphasis added] of the sovereign is founded or at least in a great deal influenced by *custom and disposition* [emphasis added]: on the habit of commanding on one side, accompanied by a habit of obeying on the other: and more immediately on the one part in a disposition on the one part to expect obedience, on the other part in the disposition to pay it, according to the course of that custom from whence the disposition takes its rise.

Accordingly, both religious and moral sanctions, not contracts, function to enforce the laws *in principem*. Once again, the authorizing origin of the most basic laws rests upon a non-law in an objectless realm. What could be more alien to Bentham's sense of posited law than to ground such a law in religion or morals?

It is at this point that Bentham introduces a new idea, the "disposition to obey" a law, as the ultimate authorizing source of all humanly posited laws, whether laws *in populum* or laws *in principem*.[49] In *The Limits of Jurisprudence Defined*, for example, Bentham suggests that the psychological "disposition to obey" a particular institution grounds the basic laws of a constitution.[50] He follows up such a view in *First Principles Preparatory to a Constitutional Code*.[51] Civil institutions owe fiduciary duties to an inaccessible source. The source, though, is unrecognizable. In *The Projet d'un Corps Complet de Droit*, Bentham continues that a "state of mind and expectations" ground a sense of obligation towards international law.[52] Bentham calls the "disposition" to obey the law in *Jurisprudence* "the ultimate efficient cause of all power of imperation over persons." Habits and expectations on the part of ruler and ruled alike create such a disposition to obey.[53] The legal structure depends upon the official's "disposition" to obey other officials and this, in turn, necessitates a postulate about an origin that even transcends the historical author as well as the laws *in principem*.[54]

But why is the citizen's psychological disposition binding upon an historical author, as Austin had defined such an author? Is such a disposition really binding? Is it really an issue of justicibility? Bentham's strain of argument, like Austin's, requires that one question the very character of such a disposition as well as the laws *in principem* because they seem to locate their authorizing origin external to what Bentham's judges and lawyers consider 'law.' Why does Bentham find it necessary to incorporate this 'non-legal' factor as the authorizing origin of posited

In such cases the force and efficacy of the law may depend in a considerable degree on the existence, real or supposed, of some customs to which it is or pretends to be conformable. When therefore a law *in principem* is established having custom for its foundation, the appealing to that custom is a sort of step taken towards the ensuring the observance of it." *Laws in General*, chap. 10, 109.

49 Bentham, *Constitutional Code*, vol. 1, 96, 160, 203;

50 Bentham, *Limits of Jurisprudence Defined*, 101, fn. 2.

51 Bentham, *First Principles Preparatory to Constitutional Code*, 289.

52 As discussed in James Steintrager, *Bentham* (Ithaca: Cornell University Press, 1977), 145.

53 Hart acknowledges this departure from the conditions of recognition of valid laws and suggests that one turn to the special form of reasoning that a court employs in its recognition of a constitution. H.L.A. Hart, *Essays on Bentham*, 241.

54 Bentham's later works, *First Principles Preparatory to Constitutional Code* and the *Constitutional Code* confirm the importance of the unwritten as the authorizing origin of humanly posited laws. *First Principles*, 53. Here, in treatises about the best form of government, he shifts his focus from the legislature in the *Fragment* and from conventional limits upon the legislature in *Laws in General* to the People as the ultimate authorizing origin of humanly posited laws.

laws when he also insists that the legislature is sovereign? Here, Bentham makes an important distinction. Historical authors possess a day-to-day operative authority. Constitutive power validates who qualifies as an historical author.[55] Bentham attributes the notion of the greatest happiness of the greatest number to such constitutive authority.[56] Constitutive authority may even justify acts of rebellion.[57] It would seem that the citizenry's disposition to obey the laws underlies the constitutive authority. Such a psychological disposition to obey ultimately constitutes sovereignty, Bentham writes.[58]

Hart quite rightly complains that Bentham's reasoning reaches into the mystical and mysterious at this point. And this, because Bentham's reasoning is circular. On the one hand, officials may hold a statutory enactment invalid because officials recognize that some laws *in principem* limit the legislature's authority. However, the judges hold that the legislature's authority is limited because the judges are disposed to disobey the legislature in the circumstances.[59] Just as I am arguing with respect to Austin's theory of law, Bentham held that the sovereign's posit of a command induces the subject to passively obey the sovereign, and yet, it is that very disposition to obey, a disposition that manifests the greatest happiness of the greatest number, that grounds the authority of all binding laws.[60] Here, once again, one is reminded of Austin's deference to Hobbes's dicta that, once the sovereign has been established in our minds, "the legislator is he, not by whose authority the law was first made, but by whose authority it continues to be a law."[61] The author does not precede the posit of commands, as we might have initially believed in Austin's theory of law. Rather, the author itself is subject to an authorizing origin that Bentham recognizes as located in what officials must consider non-law. What could be more non-legal on Bentham's and Austin's own terms than psychological feelings or a metaphysics of religion?

6. The Inaccessiblity of the Will of the People

The authority of a binding rule rests in its institutional author. But the trace of such a rule to its source and that source to another source higher on the institu-

55 Bentham, *First Principles*, 6.

56 Bentham, *First Principles*, 53, 113. Representatives of the electorate may pursue "the support and encrease" of the happiness of the people as "the only right and proper end to which the texture and conduct of government could have been directed," 127.

57 Bentham, *First Principles*, 113-16. Should a government become "impregnated" with "sinister interests," all citizens must "rise up and endeavour to rid the country of the nuisance." Ibid., 128.

58 Bentham, *Limits of Jurisprudence Defined*, 101, fn 2.

59 H.L.A. Hart, *Essays on Bentham*, 238.

60 Hart, *Concept of Law* 80-1; "Legal Powers," in *Essays on Bentham*: 216-19. I elaborate on this point in Conklin, *The Structuralism of Analytical Jurisprudence* (forthcoming).

61 Austin, *Province* lecture 6, 193.

tional hierarchy still does not explain why Austin considers the voice of the institutional authors binding. Why must a subject be obedient to some supreme historical author, such as a parliament or king or supreme council, according to Austin? Why should the citizen recognize a particular structure of institutions as authoritative? After all, an organized crime syndicate is modelled after a pyramid. A crime syndicate also has immediate and oblique authors. Why ought one not to consider authoritative the commands of a crime syndicate as opposed to the commands of an organization of the state?

The key difference, it would seem, is that Austin realizes that the institutional authors rely upon one final external origin or fount of institutional authority. This quest for a fount of the authority of the legal institutions lifts the possibly subjective evaluation of the content of a rule into an objectivity. Unless there were some such external origin to the trace of authority in such an objectivity, any law properly so called would be temporary – a passing moment in time. Indeed, it would be hard to describe such a transient script even as a binding law. For how could a script be a binding law, indeed how could one even describe the author's rule as a rule, if there were no certainty that it would apply to a similarly situated social circumstance on another occasion? Indeed, the transitoriness or *ad hoc* character of an 'edict' of the head of a criminal organization possesses the very character of transitoriness and ad-hocery for this very reason, for the crime syndicate has no invisible god nor nature nor state of nature with which to claim its authority. Austin realizes that the legal institutions must gain their authority from some fount external to the content of laws and external to their immediate and distinct authors.

There is another reason why an institutional author's authority must be ultimately grounded in an inaccessible externality, in Austin's view. How could a statute or judgment be considered posited or "set down" if there were no final author in the chain of authors? Is not such a text a mere *ad hoc* fragment of writing if there is no finality in the trace of texts? Indeed, would it even be possible to identify any one institution or group of institutions as sovereign? Would there be any limit to the authority of any one author to posit and enforce the object of a script? Is the fragment of writing even binding in that a binding law, as Lon Fuller argued, must apply to two or more persons subject to it. With no finality to the posit of the script, there would be no guarantee that it would be applicable to any one person after its initial posit. How could the object be a law, if there were no certainty that it would be applied to a similarly situated person at another occasion? Indeed, would it be possible to associate any one text with an author? How could one know whether the authority for the text reflected the will of another particular author, by a later rather than an earlier author, or a more specific rather than a generally worded text 'posited' by the same author? How could one say with confidence that a particular object was willed if there were no finality in the willing of any one author? One would not be able to trace one author's will to the jurisdiction posited by another institution because there would be no way to appreciate whether any one author counted as an authoritative institutional source. The trace of a lineage of authors and their texts would be impossible and absurd: "[f]or unless the imagined restraints were ultimately imposed by a sovereign not in a state of subjection to a higher or superior sovereign, a series of sovereigns ascending to infinity would govern the imagined community. Which is impossible and absurd."[62] Why so? Because no one author could be counted as distinct and assignable. No one supreme author could will that another supreme author be constrained without a contradiction in terms.

There just *must* be an authorizing origin, freed from the fetters of humanly authored laws. Such an origin must transcend all the institutional authors. Without such an origin, Austin realizes, coercion would determine why institutional authors are originary. The logic of authority, then, explains why there must be an originary source in the form of a super-legislature. What differentiates an ordinary law properly so called from the ultimate fount of such a law is the situs of the originating ground as external to the laws properly so called.

Jeremy Bentham, from whom Austin drew so heavily, also emphasized the need for an absent authorizing origin. Bentham's unpublished manuscript entitled "What a Law Is" connects authority with the origin of law in just this manner: "[t]he notion of a law is complete when it embraces its *source or origination*, its matter, and its form."[63] So, as with Hobbes, Rousseau, and now Austin, Bentham links authority with an originary moment outside a legal regime. The origin of authored laws addresses two issues: first, the linkage of the origin to the personnel who enact, administer, or enforce the laws; and secondly, the linkage of the origin with the institutional procedure for the enactment of rules. Both issues ignore the

62 Austin, *Province*, lecture 6, 254.

63 University College, London Library, Box lxx, a, pg. 5. As cited in Gerald J. Postema, *Bentham and the Common Law Tradition* (Oxford: Clarendon, 1986), 238. Emphasis added. The "matter" is its contents of ends. Its "form" is its logical structure. Bentham continues to locate the foundation of posited laws beyond the laws themselves in *Laws in General*, edited by H.L.A. Hart, in *Collected Works of Jeremy Bentham*, gen. ed. J Burns (London: University of London Press, 1970), and the *Constitutional Code*, vol. 1, eds. F. Rosen & J.H. Burns (Oxford: Clarendon Press, 1983) from *Collected Works of Jeremy Bentham*. In a footnote to the *Introduction to the Principles of Legislation and Morals*, intro. Charles Warren Everett (Westbrook Conn: Greenwood Press, 1945) and in eds. J.H. Burns and H.L.A. Hart, intro. Ross Harrison *Collected Works of Jeremy Bentham (*Cambridge: Cambridge University Press, 1977), chap. 16, para. 53, fn. 1, Bentham identifies "offences against the Sovereignty." He divides the transfer of sovereignty into two types: by a physical event such as the death of a predecessor king; and by "investiture" where the will of another person or institution invests or divests authority upon the sovereign. In the latter context, the 'sovereign' is not really the sovereign for the new sovereign is invested by a prior, more authoritative source. The distinction between the historical author and the ultimate invisible author clarifies Bentham's analysis. The 'sovereign' is the head of the governmental structure, the traditional source of authority lying external to the pyramidal structure.

substantive moral/social content of the rules *per se*. Of course, this just begs the deeper issue: 'from whence comes the origin of authority to the background manner and form procedures?' As Gerald Postema points out, the issue of authority, for Bentham, is separate from the threat of a sanction.[64] A final grounding may be an ultimate author of an authored law. And this would require that the place and time of the author's situs be linked with the originating situs, which is differentiated from that of authored laws. Bentham puts it this way: "[t]he obedience paid to any particular Law rests ultimately on a circumstance extrinsic to all Laws, a *general habit of obedience*" [his emphasis].[65]

The general habit of obedience raises a serious question as to the nature of sovereignty. Sovereignty connotes several things. One characteristic of sovereignty is that the authority of the authors to enact binding laws is illimitable. And yet, the sovereign legislature depends for its authority upon the obedience of the bulk of the people towards the aggregate of institutional authors. The bulk of the people, which Austin postulates, is situated outside the system of interrelated institutions. The peoples do not possess a legal right to enact or to amend or to repeal or to enforce the commands of the institutional authors. Their rights are not conferred by prior laws properly so called. Their desires are not legally enforceable by the courts. In a sense, the authorizing origin of legal authority is hidden or denied as legally binding and enforceable in a court of law even though the origin is indispensable for institutional authors to be sovereign. Conversely, the head author of the institutional system is free to legislate because it is not subject to any legal duties to the bulk of the people.

The key difference between a law properly so called and a law improperly so called, then, is that, according to Austin, the institutional authors rely upon one final external source or fount of authority, independent and prior to the very existence of the authors. Unless there were some such external source, the rule of the head institutional author would be temporary. Unless the self-legislating authors possess an origin absent from the laws properly so called, their commands would not be authoritative and, therefore, not binding. Arbitrariness and coercion would be 'the rule' of the day.

The inaccessible habits of the people subtly work themselves through adjudication, according to Austin. The rhetoric of the functionaries on Austin's legal structure is authoritative because, like Hobbes's "actors," the legislature is considered the trustee for the people. Judges insist that they do not and cannot question the wisdom of the legislature. The legal officials claim that they act as

64 Postema, *Bentham*, 239.

65 Bentham, UC Box lxix, 204, University College, London Library. As quoted in Postma, *Bentham and the Common Law Tradition*, 240.

trustees, for example, when *res private* or private property escheats to the people as the ultimate origin of laws properly so called. The people, as the authorizing origin of the laws, also reserve certain rights to themselves, rights such as the right to collect taxes, to create an army, or to validate changes to a constitutional text. Such rights constitute the "patrimony" of the final author, Austin insists.[66] Positive laws must leave the institutional authors unconstrained from dealing with all things within its territory at its own pleasure or discretion.[67] But the institutions remain constrained by the habit of obedience of the people. If the people were constrained by the legal structure, the people would not be sovereign. Rather, the people would be in a state of subjection to a legal structure that was truly supreme. So this external author, called the people, "has a right to all things within its territory, or is absolutely or without restriction the proprietor or *dominus* thereof" in the sense that no one posited law may constrain an author on the structure to use its rights "as it pleases."

This appeal to the habits of the bulk of the people raises an irony. On the one hand, the claim that laws are posited by human agents implies that all laws are historically contingent and lack any reference to a transcendental object for their authority. We can locate such authored rules with some predictability and certainty precisely because we can associate them with determinate and certain authors and with the authors' writing. On the other hand, how can there be certainty and predictability of rules if all the bulk of the people remain undifferentiated – if the sources remain self-referential to the point that the will of no one source – no legislature, king, judge or policeman – can be considered final? There just must be one final author, according to Austin, an author that is "free from the fetters of positive law."[68]

The irony is that the officials who enforce the laws properly so called must postulate a non-legal externality in order that the laws be considered humanly posited. The double irony is that the laws properly so called open to an indeterminate source that cannot even be called a 'corporate body' by Austin's own understanding of a civil institution. The ultimate source lacks the intelligibility and rationality that Austin associates with a will. The source is unidentifiable: only justicible rules are recognizable. Only the discrete and assignable offices answer to the description of determinacy and reason, two requirements for a distinct author according to Austin. The institutional authors need an external source, transcendent of the head (say, the legislature) of the institutional structure, in order that the commands of the head author be considered final, that there be commands, that the commands be considered posited, and that the commands be considered laws

66 Austin, *Lectures*, vol. 3, lecture 52, 56-7.
67 Austin, *Lectures*, vol. 3, lecture 52, 55.
68 Austin, *Lectures*, vol. 3, lecture 52, 56-7.

properly so called. The indeterminate and unidentifiable habits of the bulk of the people transcend the institutional authors and thereby bring legitimacy to commands of the authors. Austin describes the irony in this manner. A sovereign authority or perfectly independent source is "perfectly or completely independent of other human power; inasmuch that its acts cannot be annulled by any human will other than its own. But if perfect or complete independence be of the essence of sovereign power, there is not in fact the human power to which the epithet *sovereign* will apply with propriety."[69] There cannot be an authorizing origin to the laws properly so called unless that origin radically differs, in terms of time and space, from the ordinary historical authors. Austin posits the 'general habit of obedience of the bulk of the people' as just such an extra-legal origin of the legal origin of laws properly so called.

7. Austin's Inaccessible *Arche*

Austin makes a precise linkage between the habits of obedience of the bulk of the people on the one hand and the greatest happiness of the greatest number of the people on the other. When Austin makes this connection, the habits of the bulk of the people remain inaccessible from humanly posited laws. The psychological disposition of the people to obey an institutional author is indispensable for the existence of a modern legal order, according to Austin. The importance of a disposition to obey underlies his examination of civil strife.[70] Civil strife arises in two contexts, Austin argues. The first occurs where a society breaks into two sovereign states. The second involves the situation where "the bulk of each of the parties be not in that habit of obedience."[71] Without such a habit of obedience, a society collapses into a state of nature or anarchy, according to Austin. This psychological disposition of subjects to obey the institutional authors ensures the legitimacy or authority of the institutions to author laws properly so called.

But why is the disposition to obey the authors so important? Because the disposition to obey, a psychological or experiential phenomenon, functions to finalize the trace of legal reasoning. The disposition functions accordingly because it is so radically different from the authorial sources that Austin attributes to the grounding of legal authority in civil society. The authorizing origin of the laws properly so called must differ from the ordinary laws in order to finalize the trace of institutional sources in civil society.

But why does the disposition to obey differ so fundamentally from laws properly so called? Why is the disposition a law improperly so called?

69 Austin, *Province,* lecture 6, 214.
70 Austin, *Province,* lecture 6, 198.
71 Austin, *Province,* lecture 6, 198.

Because the disposition of the people, being vague and indeterminate, cannot function as the author of binding laws properly so called. The habits of the people are inaccessible from the laws properly so called. The laws properly so called must be identified with an institutional source in terms of a place and time. But the habits of the people cannot be identified with the precision and determinacy required of the author of a law properly so called. The people are the last authors or, more correctly, the first authors, yet absent from the posited laws properly so called. Precisely because the people are absent from the "operative functionaries" or legal officials who work in the institutions, the officials invariably remain dissatisfied with their enunciations of particular decisions. They are driven to reach the absent will of the people. But the officials can never access such a will. That inaccessibility finalizes the voice of the institutional authors.

A particular sense of legal desire underlies Austin's postulate about the final source in legal reasoning. "[T]he end of my desires," he lectures, is an absent object.[72] Austin differentiates his own view of desire from John Locke's in this respect in that Locke, according to Austin, had claimed that desires "consummate themselves, or ... are followed immediately by their objects."[73] A desire may aim at a determinate object only if the thought is already present in the mind that desires. "Unless the thought desired be present to the mind *already*, there is no determinate object at which the desire aims, and which it can attain *immediately*, or without the intervention of a mean."[74] For Austin, however, a desire cannot attain its object. For he continues, "to desire the absence of a thought is to *conceive* the thought of which the absence is desired, and (by consequence) to perpetuate its presence." The officials never gain a presence or immediacy with the people's will because the people lack the distinct and determinate character that Austin expects of authoritative authors. That being so, the officials can only re-present the will through legally recognizable signs. Legal signs will always mediate the phenomenon of representation. A volition is bodily. Bodily motives physically cause one to will.[75] A desire is cognitive. A wish or desire can never access its desired object, the object being a concept beyond the sign. Consequently, the official must imagine the will of the people.

In sum, Austin succeeds in connecting the habits of the people with the laws properly so called only at the cost of having legal officials *imagine* persons with a singular will. The imagined ultimate source lacks an identity. For only laws properly so called are recognizable and, therefore, legally existent. The image of the

72 Austin, *Lectures*, vol. 2, lecture 18, 86.
73 Austin, *Lectures*, vol. 2, lecture 18, 87, at fn.
74 Austin, *Lectures*, vol. 2, lecture 18, 84. His emphasis.
75 Austin, *Lectures*, vol. 2, lecture 18, 86.

absent origin is represented with the rights and duties that officials recognize. Such rights and duties merely fantasize about the origin. The officials may not quantify nor perceive nor feel the presence of the habits of the people.

The habits of the people are unwritten customs. They are practices that the populace takes for granted. As customs, they cannot be recognized as legally binding for they are un-authored. Austin's officials assume, as does Austin himself, that an author is autonomous in the sense of being self-legislating. The author pre-exists its product (a statute or judicial decision). A custom, though, lacks such a distinct author. A custom lacks a time and place when it was authored. A custom is un-authored and, therefore, it lacks legal authority. The habits of the people are just such customs. The habits lie outside and prior to the institutional authors, which alone create legally binding rules.

So the moral or religious content of the customary practice, including the content of the customs of the people, is irrelevant to the nature of legal authority. The content of the people's habits may be incorporated into a law properly so called. But the content itself is irrelevant to the binding quality of such a law. The habits of the people, as customs, may well be just. The habits may well represent the moral sentiments of the people. The habits may even be identifiable as a social rule. And yet, the habits are not legally binding. Though habitually obeyed, the people's 'will' may not be a binding rule. To be binding, according to Austin, a certain and definable institution must subsequently express the customary rule in writing. But then, the habits of the people have been transformed into a juridically recognizable binding rule, Austin lectures. The habits of the people may well be humanly posited in that human agents gradually create and accept a custom over time. But, unlike a judge or a legislature whose writing can be identified at a particular place and time,[76] a custom cannot be identified in terms of time nor of place. As noted earlier, English common law has it that a custom exists "from time immemorial." The habits of the people are an indeterminate and uncertain aggregate of feelings from the officials' projected world of non-law.

So the habits of the people are excluded from what officials take to be laws properly so called. The authority of binding laws draws from two contexts. The first context goes to the aggregate of governmental offices, such as courts or legislatures or government agencies, which are situated on a pyramid-shaped institutional structure with a head author, such as the king or parliament or president, at its pinnacle. As I noted earlier, a law strictly speaking is "*put* or set by its individual or collective author, or it exists by the *position* or institution of its indi-

76 One should note how a U.K. or other Commonwealth statute ends with the citation of the Clerk of the Privy Council and with the year and session of the particular Parliament.

vidual or collective author."[77] The second context goes to the commands that these offices will. The second context collapses into the first. The commands must be rationally linked with the will of an institutional source and that will in a vertical direction to an institutional head, such as the legislature. That supreme will, in turn, is grounded in an externality: the habit of obedience by the bulk of the people. Any one will must be traced to the jurisdictional boundaries of its institutional author, and that author, in turn, to the jurisdictional boundaries of a higher author on the institutional structure.

The consequence of legal reasoning through authorial sources, then, is that there is a hierarchic structure of commands that correspond with the hierarchic structure of institutional authors. In particular, a statute of a legislature will have a higher authority than a regulation of an administrative functionary. A legislative intent will also have a higher authority than a judicial intent if the legislature rests higher on the institutional structure than a court. The only requirement is that a legislated rule be enacted according to the procedural 'manner and form' conditions that the institutional authors had previously posited.[78] Neither the institutional context nor the consequential rules context considers the substantive moral/social content of the laws properly so called *per se*. Although the officials may well unconsciously or consciously be influenced by non-legal issues, such factors are irrelevant to the issue of whether the trace of posited commands has terminated. Most important of all such non-legal factors are the habits of obedience of the people, the very habits that Austin ironically privileges as the authorizing origin of laws properly so called.

8. Who are 'the people'?

Austin's commentators have sometimes criticized his reliance upon the habits of obedience as naive. Others, that the reliance upon the habits is empirically false. Are 'the people' an empirically identifiable entity? Are the habits of the people measureable with all the analytic skills and tools available to the social scientist? Are 'the People' an empirical entity? What could be more empirical than the habits of the people? Or, for that matter, their psychological disposition to obey? Are the habits of the people a synthesis of a heterology of voices? Is the concept of 'the people' a metaphor? Is it an idea, a concept that functions as an originary object in an intellectualizing play of commands? Is it a single monologic voice that stands for the whole multiplicity of the people's voices? Critics have failed to appreciate that Austin him-

77 Austin, *Province*, lecture 5, 171.

78 As Bentham writes, "[t]he notion of a law is complete when it embraces its source or origination, its matter, and its form." Bentham, *Introduction to Morals and Legislation*, para. 53, fn. 1.

self understood the nature of law in terms of a self-referential institutional structure that defines what are considered subjective values unrecognizable to the offices on the structure. Austin hinges laws "improperly so called" upon such a structure.

Austin, observing the laws properly so called from an external point of view, realized that there must be a rupture in the laws. The rupture must lead to a final source in the trace of authority from one author to another. Austin does not wish such a rupture to return to the natural condition where human creatures could not speak a language. The rupture, though it might well enter into the empirical world, is not a claim of the empirical world. Rather, Austin's is a claim of logic. Austin is putting forth a formal postulate. Austin's central concern is the nature of legal authority. That a psychological habit ultimately grounds the authority of a system of laws properly so called reinforces the logic of the possible total enclosure by the binding laws. Austin's and Bentham's introduction of the habits of obedience towards the institutions is necessary for the sovereign's rules to be binding. The habits are an illimitable source. However, such habits are unenforceable because only signs that represent legal rules are justicible and enforceable. Despite his desire to exclude Hobbes's natural condition from the nature of law, Austin's theory of law takes on Hobbes's concern for the need for a singular originary source in order to ensure that the civil laws are authoritative.

To be sure, Austin wishes to depart from the deontological ethical theory of Kant. The belief that there may be an intrinsically valued end, purified of all contingencies and sentiment, is "nothing but moonshine," in Bentham's words. After all, Austin wishes to support the possibility of a legal order that is posited by human agents. A transcendent 'in itself' would undermine such a possibility and, indeed, would associate Austin's theory of law with a divinity beyond human control. Austin succeeds in secularizing civil laws by insisting that the 'intent of the legislature' or the *ratio decidendi reasoning* blocks an escape to some transcendent founding event. 'The People,' as such, is indeterminate and, if an empirically ascertainable notion, it would be a multiplicity of voices.

Why is 'the people' indeterminate? The key to Austin's sense of an author, that critical source of laws properly so called we have observed, is that the author be a determinable and distinct corporate office on an institutional structure. The legislature is such an office. 'The people' is not a determinate office. If an indeterminate body, one cannot determine and assign all the persons who compose the body. A member of the body is not an empirically identifiable biological body. An indeterminate body is incapable of authorship, of acting as a corporate body. One should be mindful, in this respect, of

Austin's own description of actual human beings at the time as prone to "coarse and sordid pleasures" and of a "stupid indifference about knowledge."[79] By representing 'the people' as the 'intent of the legislature,' Austin is able to ensure that the legal structure remains supreme and yet that it refers to an external authorizing origin for its legitimacy. The origin of the origin ensures finality to legal reasoning. The laws properly so called can now be considered binding. The "habits of the people" are signified as the archimedian source that grounds the authority of all laws properly so called. The people, an indeterminate externality to the legal structure, ensures that reasoning displace force. Or so Austin believes.

It is important to emphasize in all this that the public sentiments of 'the people' are inaccessible from the laws properly so called. As such, the heterology of the voices of many human beings is an illegitimate source of laws properly so called. Referenda do not count. Nor do public opinion polls. Public opinion reflects the values of an indeterminate body of an uncertain and unidentifiable aggregate.[80] Only a determinate author may signify its wish or command to an addressee or subject. The desire of an uncertain body cannot be signified because the intent of the body, as an author, is uncertain just as the body's identity is uncertain.[81] Public sentiment is excluded from being considered a law strictly speaking. Only officials on the institutional structure may duly enact sentiments as laws "properly so called." The laws properly so called and their institutional authors are closed from the external world of public sentiment. The many peoples express moral sentiments and 'oughts' that it is not the role of lawyers and judges to describe as 'law.' The structure defines a legal reality or 'is' world that lawyers and judges are capable of enforcing.

And yet that legal existence depends upon the habit of obedience of the people in order to ensure a finality to the tracing project. The people give finality to the ratiocination project. But the people take form only as an amorphous spirit. Their vague and indeterminate composition adds to their external situs to undermine the possibility that 'the people' are an author of laws "properly so called." At best, a spirit of the heterology of voices in the many peoples may constrain legal officials. Perhaps it is a necessary spirit in order to ensure that the legal structure has a grounding. It is only a spirit because to be more than a spirit, to be embodied with rights and duties as if it were located on the inside of the legal structure, would be tantamount to authorizing moral sentiments as laws properly so called.

79 Austin, *Province,* lecture 3, 66.

80 Austin, *Province,* lecture 5, 154.

81 Austin, *Province,* lecture 5, 156.

9. The Spirit of 'the People'

The habits of the people, then, lie outside and inside the institutional structure of distinct authors.

Unless external to the structure, the habits of the people cannot render finality to the officials' legal reasoning. Since the ultimate ground is external to the laws properly so called, there is a desperate need for officials to be driven to reach a totally enclosed sovereign structure. In their effort to picture the absence that they cannot access, they are haunted by the absent people whose habits remain legally unrecognizable and legally unenforceable in an objectless realm.

And yet, the habits of the people seem to permeate the actions and decisions of legal officials. Like a ghost whose body filters through solid walls and seemingly transparent windows of a law office or court-room, the spirit of the people seems ever-present as the legal officials abstract general rules from the reported social circumstances and from the prior judgments. The judge produces a *ratio* as if the People – the externality that legitimates the closure of the laws properly so called – gaze down upon the judge and other officials from the People's archemedian situs. The judge speculates or supposes what the people, as an outside legally non-existent entity (or, more correctly, non-entity), would have contemplated. The speculation concerns the intent of a no-thing that lacks a juridically recognized body. The judge feels constrained by the intent of his or her image of an outsider. Though foreigners, the people ensure the closure of the whole body of civil institutions. The habits of the people must remain absent from the structure in order for the legal officials to desire commands "properly so called." The officials thereby complete the concealment of any gap to the outside world of non-law. The intent of the people is translated as the will of the founding fathers of the constitution or as the intent of the supreme legislature. Legal officials feel a presence with such an intent: "[u]nless the thought desired be present to the mind already, there is no determinate object at which the desire aims, and which it can attain immediately, or without the intervention of a mean."[82] But the absence of the people ensures that the presence will never be consummated.

Now, what is critical to understanding Austin's theory of law is that he describes just such an immediacy or presence as carrying a divine character when he examines the nature of divine laws. A human source commands a human law through language. But God conveys the divine laws without the mediation of a language, Austin writes.[83] God authors His acts by working through human feel-

82 Austin, *Lectures*, vol. 2, lecture 18, 84.
83 Austin examines this in *Province*, 34-43.

ings "immediately or without an inference of the understanding."[84] The moral sense that Austin excludes from laws properly so called is an "infallible guide" to how one ought to behave. "[T]he 'moral sense' is our index to *some* [of God's] tacit commands, but the principle of utility is our index to *others*."[85] The feelings that reflect this moral sense are "ultimate facts" or "indisputable."[86] The feelings are "written on our hearts, by the finger of their great Author, in broad and indelible character."[87] The Author's unwritten rules increase or decrease the aggregate of happiness.[88] Thus, the greatest happiness is merely an index of God's will, not the source of his will. Although Austin usually talks about the Author as divine, he occasionally slips into describing the 'greatest happiness of the greatest number' as divine. Utility is placed on the same plane as the Deity. Indeed, the general good itself is divine rather than a mere index of the Author's will.[89] God acts through general and inflexible rules such as the greatest happiness.[90] Officials rely upon the universal standard of the 'greatest happiness' because they do not 'know' the Deity's will through reflection and the mediation of legal language. Officials can only *feel* the Deity's will through moral sentiment and that feeling is immediate.[91] Such a moral sentiment drives rational calculation.[92]

So, the legal official must postulate an imaginary person as the source of the final will. That imaginary person is a spirit because it is not a recognizable juridical person. The (non-)entity, 'the people' fulfils the need for a final source of laws. To be final, the habits of the people, as a super-author, must differ from the ordinarily posited scripts of the structure of authors. The finality ensures that the circulation of scripts may be described and closed from the outside world.

Despite Austin's association of the general happiness with divinity, he insists it is "stark nonsense" to claim, as did natural law theorists such as Aquinas, that a humanly authored rule is void if it contradicts the divine law. Human institutions posit the standards of universal justice, according to Austin. Such institutions are guided by general utility. It so happens, though, that divine laws and human laws share the 'general happiness' as the standard of evaluation. A divine law is not good because the divine Author posited it. To claim that a divine law is Good because of its Author would amount to "to talk[ing] absurdly: for every object which is measured, or every object which is brought to a test, is compared with a

84 Austin, *Province*, 36.
85 Austin, *Province*, 100. His emphasis.
86 Austin, *Province*, 95-6, 50-1.
87 Austin, *Province*, 96.
88 Austin, *Province*, 42-3.
89 Austin, *Province*, 43.
90 Austin, *Province*, 48.
91 Austin, *Province*, 51.
92 Austin, *Province*, 52. Emphasis added.

given object other than itself."[93] To be good or bad, a law must agree or differ "with something to which we tacitly refer it as a *measure* or *test*."[94] The 'greatest happiness of the greatest number' functions as just such an external test. Accordingly, the positive and divine laws share the same authorizing origin, Austin admits in Lecture Five. The divine laws of the Author merely embrace a larger circle than that which positive morality entertains, including all voluntary actions, Austin claims. The shared grounding of divine and human laws is the greatest happiness. If the historical authors did not fashion the content of their laws with reference to the greatest happiness, the Author would punish the authors.

We are left to conclude, then, that the very absence of the habits of 'the bulk of the people' from the laws properly so called shares an invisible character with what Austin describes as divine laws. But because the habits of the people, being invisible, cannot be recognized as legally existent, officials forget their dependence upon the invisible origin of legal authority. The laws properly so called, after all, are defined only in terms of the expression of authorial sources. The laws are closed from the realm of non-law unless authors are authorized to deliberate about such non-law. In the latter circumstance, the non-law is explicitly incorporated into laws properly so called. The enclosure is juridically total. No human conduct or thought, no moral sentiment, no social practice, may be considered immune from the scope of the enclosing structure of laws properly so called. Against the background of such a totality, the need and role of the habits of the "bulk of the people" must remain a mysterious, vague externality which, if admitted as legally existent, would rupture the self-referring enclosure. The officials must enact rules, enforce rules, and interpret rules as if the habits of the people did not count as legal sources. Officials must pretend that there is no opening to the external world of morals and social life.

So, ironically, the habits of the people ensure the total enclosure of laws properly so called at the very moment that Austin and Austin's lawyers admit the possibility of a foreign divine grounding of the laws properly so called. Such laws do possess an escape valve to the invisible realm. But from the internal point of view of officials, the officials must forget that possibility as they ratiocinate in their quest for the institutional sources of their laws properly so called. For if officials admitted to a more superior, indeed to an invisible unenforceable source in the habits of the people, the historical institutional authors would no longer remain sovereign. Some further source, other than a parliament or the king or a supreme court, would be self-legislating and, therefore, sovereign. The habits of the people remain a metaphor on the surface and a secret at best.

---

93 Austin, *Province*, 129.

94 Austin, *Province*, 128. Emphasis added.

The habits of the people, as a metaphor, encourage officials to write as if one author wrote all the scripts, as if one language were shared by 'society' and as if the one author gazed down upon every act of the officials. The vague, unwritten habits of the indeterminate people function as a spirit. The spirit of the people completes a picture of the authority of laws properly so called. The spirit makes the picture a totality. The picture portrays an enclosed institutional structure of interconnected bodies that speak and write through a vocabulary and grammar which other institutional authors share. And yet, Austin realizes that the authors too need to gain their authority from some ultimate source. The habits of the bulk of the people function accordingly. But because the people are invisible to the officials, the officials remain haunted by a ghost, an amorphous 'body' that neither speaks nor writes. Austin admits that just such an unmediated presence is divine. The divine presence is not authored by a divine Author. Rather, the divine presence of the habits of the people shares the invisibility of both human and divine laws. Such an invisibility lacks a language that officials will recognize. Only the laws properly so called are recognizable to the officials. Even then, such laws retrospectively constitute the needed invisible origin as authoritative. As the officials constitute the origin, they forget the importance of the divine spirit that dwells behind their laws properly so called.

7

The Invisible Origin of Legal Language: The *Grundnorm*

The dominant strain of the Tradition, so far examined, has associated the authorizing origin of humanly posited laws with an author. The Tradition has offered two senses of an author. The first, associated with Hobbes and Rousseau, considered the author as the invisible creator of the institutional structure of civil society. The second, best manifested in the works of Austin and Bentham, considered the author as historically contingent. During his early and middle period, Bentham believed the legislature to be the sovereign historical author; Austin believed that the people authored the structure of legal institutions. I have emphasized in the previous chapter that, for Bentham and Austin, officials recognize the historical authors to be situated internal to the legal structure.

Hans Kelsen (1881–1973), the most insightful and prolific European legal theorist during the first half of the twentieth century, rejected Austin's focus upon an historical author. What is most important, according to Kelsen, is a later statement, by an official, about the will of such an author. The historical author wills an object. Such a willing occurs in the 'is' world of social behaviour. The judge, as an interpreter, represents an author's object in a statement about how one ought to behave. Such a statement, Kelsen called a norm. What becomes critical is the judge's language. The objects of the judge's statements are rationally joined together into a rationally cohesive structure that transcends the arbitrariness of the historical author's enactment. The authority of a statement must be traced, not to the historical author, but to a previous statement that prescribed how one ought to behave. Such a trace of statements referred to the cognitive referents that the statements signified. The trace, though, required that there be some one final archemedian point that grounded the whole structure of 'ought' statements.

Kelsen calls the final norm, a "*Grundnorm*" or "basic norm." He does so for two reasons. First, all other normative statements presuppose this basic norm and yet, unlike an ordinary norm, the basic norm is inaccessible from the language of legal officials. Second, the basic norm, to be basic, lacks any further referent for its existence. If the final norm possessed the same character as an ordinary norm, an official would be unable to differentiate any one norm as posited, let alone as a law, for a finality is needed to colour a human law. Without a finality, a particular norm would not, with certainty, apply to more than one person and some generality is required to be considered a 'law.' Without a finality, a norm is *ad hoc*, lacking in the permanence needed to be posited. Such a final norm gives rational coherence, autonomy, and a comprehensiveness to what would otherwise remain fragmentary. By virtue of its unsignifiable and referentless character, the *Grundnorm* transcends the structure of cognitive referents (doctrines, rules, and other standards) that statements represent. Kelsen recognizes that this transcendent character of the *Grundnorm* contradicts social reality because it is a mere human thought rather than a human act of will. As a thought, it is abstracted from human acts of will. As a consequence, the ultimate origin "contains contradiction within itself, since it represents the authorisation of a supreme moral or legal authority, and hence it issues from an authority lying beyond that authority, even though the further authority is merely figmentary."[1]

Hobbes's natural condition, Rousseau's general will, Bentham's sense of the disposition to obey, Austin's 'habits of the people,' and Kant's perfectly pure will: each is inaccessible from the language through which officials work. The externality of such authorizing origin of humanly authored laws is not contingent upon their substantive content nor even the pedigree or criteria of authority of the binding human laws. Without an extrinsically located origin, the trace of authored laws would continue *ad infinitum*, leaving any one binding norm a mere textual fragment. And yet, precisely because the origin must be forever absent from the official language of acts of will, the officials cannot know, perceive, or address the origin. The origin is invisible to the officials. Its existence is a mere possibility. The origin is located in the vast objectless realm of non-law, which is unrecognizable to the officials. In order to sustain his theory, Kelsen imports into the pure theory of law the very invisibility that he attributes to the absolutist Author of nature in natural law theory and the absolute state in political theory.

This paradox of the nature of legal authority poses two important issues for the nature of a binding law. First, what is the relationship between the authorizing origin on the one hand and its efficacy in a social context on the other? Secondly, how does the authorizing origin, at least as Kelsen describes it, possess an invisible character? If the origin is invisible, how can one maintain that binding laws are posited by human agents? After all, one shared theme in the tradition of legal positivism is that human agents, not some divine source, posit binding laws. Is not an invisible origin alien to legal positivism? Does Kelsen oppose humanly posited laws to the invisible Author of natural law theory only to recognize that, in order

1 Kelsen, "The Function of a Constitution," in eds. Richard Tur and William Twining, *Essays on Kelsen* (Oxford: Clarendon Press, 1986), 109-19, 117.

sustain the posited character of human norms, the norms need an invisible externality for their authority as binding laws?

1. The Impure Origin of the Structure

Why is a statement by a legal official binding upon others when the same statement by a poet or novelist or leader of organized crime is not? The cognitive referent of a statement is binding, according to Kelsen, if one can locate the statement in a chain of other *'Sollens'* or 'ought' statements that officials accept as binding.[2] The officials make statements *about* the acts of will of earlier legislatures or courts. A statement is not binding because it has been authored by the appropriate historical author, as Hobbes and Austin claimed.[3] The key is that the norms themselves (or what Kelsen defines as statements about acts of will) must be accepted as binding. That 'the people' is defined in terms of the interpreters' statements about acts of will depends, then, upon a basic presupposition: namely, that the referent of a prescriptive statement ought to be binding. So too, officials assume there is a difference between subjective norms and objective norms. But such a differentiation depends upon the postulate that objective norms are carved from an inter-connected structure of cognitive referents that the statements represent. The structure, in turn, is believed to precede the laws.

In the trace of the "chain" (of 'ought' statements) that represents the structure of referents, then, one is left with the question 'what is the character of the presupposition that a chain of statements ought to be binding?' There must be a finality to the trace of statements inside the chain in order to ensure that the objectivity and permanence needed for a norm is binding: "[t]he search for the reason of a norm's validity cannot go on indefinitely like the search for the cause of an effect. It must end with a norm which, as the last and highest, is presupposed."[4] The basic norm, that is, supplements the chain of ordinary norms. The basic norm is an aside, an after-the-fact of legal statements. The basic norm exists only if officials postulate the existence of the structure of cognitive referents of the norms. As Kelsen puts it, the basic norm "is adapted to this coercive order and not the coercive order to the basic norm."[5]

---

2 For Kelsen's sense of a *Sollens*-statement, see Ulises Schmill, "The Dynamic Order of Norms, Empowerment and Related Concepts," in *Law and Philosophy* **19** (2000): 283-310, 284.

3 Kelsen, *Pure Theory of Law*, trans. Max Knight (Berkeley/Los Angeles: University of California Press, 1970; 2d. ed.), 45. *General Theory of Law and State*, trans. Anders Wedberg (New York: Russell & Russell, 1961), 31-2.

4 Kelsen, *Pure Theory*, 194.

5 Kelsen, "Professor Stone and the Pure Theory of Law," in *Stanford Law Review* **17** (1965): 1130-57, 1142. This is a reply to Julius Stone, "Mystery and Mystique in the Basic Norm," *Modern Law Review* **26**: 34-50; and *Legal System and Lawyers' Reasoning* (Stanford: Stanford University Press, 1964).

So, the structure of norms comes first; the authorizing origin of the structure secondarily. The structure presupposes its own existence. The structure defines what is outside (and therefore invalid) as well as inside (and therefore valid). As Kelsen wrote to Renato Treves in 1933, the pure theory is "radically universalistic" in that it "takes as its point of departure the whole of the law, the legal system, in order to comprehend from this standpoint all other phenomena as parts of the whole."[6]

So an ambiguity seems to pervade Kelsen's deliberations. On the one hand, the structure of cognitively produced referents, which the 'ought' statements signify, presupposes the prior existence of the *Grundnorm*. And yet, the content of a *Grundnorm* cannot be identified nor be articulated nor even be assumed apart from the 'ought' statements that join together to represent a coherent structure or prescriptive doctrines and rules. The identity of a norm does not take form with reference to the *Grundnorm*. A norm gains an identity with reference to other statements about acts of will. The chain of statements, internally referring to their own cognitive referents, produce their own history and their own ethical standards. History and ethics remain internal to the interrelated statements about acts of will. In a sense, the normative structure is a-historical and a-moral. The *Grundnorm* supplements and is constructed from the structure even though officials presuppose the *Grundnorm* as the centre of the structure.

And yet, this constructed *Grundnorm* adds an impurity to the self-referential chain of 'ought' statements. For the *Grundnorm*, to be basic or originary, must differ from the statements that represent the cognitive referents. Here, it is important to appreciate that Kelsen's sense of legal language differs from that of his predecessors and successors. For Hobbes and Austin, a language involves oral signs or physical marks that represent cognitive referents. For H.L.A. Hart, a language centres about the essence of a word, there being a penumbra at the circumference of the essence. For Joseph Raz, a language is also highly cognitive. But for Kelsen, a language is constituted from the *meanings* that the interpreter brings *into* the marks and words.[7] A norm is a *statement* about the cognitive referent willed. An ordinary norm is the meaning-content of an act of a will. If the *Grundnorm* were also a statement about an act of will, it would not differ from any other norm for it would refer to a further act of will, and the latter would be (more) basic. Kelsen explains this

---

6 Kelsen, "Letter to Renato Treves," dated 3 August 1933 and reprinted in eds. Stanley L. Paulson and Bonnie Litschewski Paulson, *Normativity and Norms*, trans. Bonnie Litschewski Paulson, Stanley L. Paulson and Michael Sherberg, intro. Stanley L. Paulson (Oxford: Clarendon Press, 1998), 169-75, 172.

7 This is explained in Conklin, *The Structuralism of Analytical Jurisprudence* (forthcoming).

point in "The Pure Theory and Analytical Jurisprudence." The final norm

> ... must be *presupposed*, because it cannot be 'posited,' that is to say: created, by an authority whose competence would have to rest on a still higher norm. This final norm's validity cannot be derived from a higher norm, the reason for its validity cannot be questioned.[8]

Neither its content (as in the case of natural law theory which, according to Kelsen, draws 'oughts' from material facts) nor a derived logical operation produces a *Grundnorm*. Even the founding fathers of any one country presuppose a *Grundnorm* in their historical act of revolt or in their creation of the written constitution. Without the founding fathers' presupposition that officials ought to follow the fathers' own constitutive principles, their claim for authority would collapse into naked coercion. A law, to be law, must be something more than the coercive act of some thugs.

The object (or referent) of a norm is rationally connected to the object of another norm until the official reaches a first cause in the trace of authority. Even if a norm referred to an object external to other referents already signified in the chain of authoritative statements, its empirical content would dissipate as the retracing enterprise gathered momentum. For the enterprise retraces ought *statements*, not the original acts of will of authors. Once signified in a statement, the former non-legal sign would now be recognized as legally binding, according to Kelsen. Of course, an official may never gain access to the *Grundnorm* because, if the *Grundnorm* were articulated as a statement in legal language, it would become a norm like all the others, and there would have to be another statementless *Grundnorm* for that last *Grundnorm* to be signified as a statement. The *Grundnorm* is not legislated by the founding fathers of a constitution. The *Grundnorm* is silent, without a corresponding statement to represent it. It is a "genuine fiction" that metaphysically transcends the authority of the referents' structure itself.[9] A silent fictional unrepresentable prescriptive 'thought' authorizes the constitution of the structure of cognitive referents. Such a thought underlies an otherwise interminable retrace of 'ought' statements.

2. An Hypothetical or a Categorical Origin?

A serious issue now comes to the fore. Is the *Grundnorm* an 'hypothetical imperative,' to use a term from Kant's *Grounding of the Metaphysics of Morals*? That is, is the *Grundnorm* conditional upon historically contingent facts? Such a conditional context would suggest that the official be able actually to identify and

---

8 Kelsen, *Pure Theory*, 195.

9 Kelsen, "The Function of a Constitution," 116.

to name the condition in a time/space spectrum of the empirical world. For example, 'if a society accepts the authority of the monarch, then all norms must derive from the monarch's delegates'; or, 'if a norm or "ought" statement is willed according to certain procedures, then the creation of any "ought" statement in accord with the procedures will be valid.' Once a society is enclosed within the boundaries of such a condition, the authority of humanly posited norms is assured: 'if..., then....' The authoritativeness of any particular norm, then, would be socially and ethically contingent.[10] The 'oughts' would depend upon the 'is' world of knowledge, after all. Further, the content of the condition would be an arbitrary choice. And the official would ultimately have to be familiar with social history in order to be able to ascertain the hypothetical in any particular time and place. The *Grundnorm* would take on an ideological character because the content of the social relativism would be transformed into an objective universal claim.

On the other hand, is the *Grundnorm* a categorical imperative? That is, is it unconditioned by any empirical contingency? If so, does it dwell entirely in a noumenal realm of pure thought? And is this categorical imperative, being categorical, inaccessible to the officials in that the condition draws from a transcendent categorical condition, unconditioned by the social or cultural context?

a) Efficacy

Kelsen's works have long been plagued with an ambiguity. The ambiguity is manifested in this way.

On the one hand, Kelsen maintains the radical separation of the 'is' from the 'ought.' Efficacy is usually understood as part and parcel of this 'is' reality. Efficacy is, he writes in "God and State" (1922/23), a "psycho-physical force."[11]

Binding laws, though, must be understood as part of the 'ought' world. The authority of a norm is estranged from the efficacy of a norm in the 'is' reality. So too, the *Grundnorm*, rooted in the trace of 'ought' statements about acts of will, is also divorced from the social context, Kelsen claims. The only way in which Kelsen can reconcile this is/ought separation and his understanding of law as grounded in the ideal or 'ought' world, on the one hand, with an inefficacious chain of norms, on the other, is to claim that a revolution takes place when the ideal chain of norms becomes inefficacious. The revolution is a legal revolution. In such a revolution, the authoritative norms are so inefficacious in the 'is' world that a radical shift of the *Grundnorm* is necessary in order to bring it in tune with the 'is.'

So, despite his insistence that norms are located in the 'ought' part of the is/ought boundary, Kelsen admits that the authority of a chain of norms may collapse

---

10 Kelsen, "The Function of a Constitution," 217-18.

11 Kelsen, "God and the State," in *Essays in Legal and Moral Philosophy* (Dordrecht: Reidel, 1973), 61-82, 71.

once the chain is no longer efficacious. In the first edition of the *Pure Theory*, for example, Kelsen describes the *Grundnorm* at one point as dependent upon "a certain material fact."[12] Here, Kelsen emphasizes that the efficacy of a structure, drawn from a brute facticity, is so important that, if efficacy is not joined with norms, the authority of the norms dissolves. For example, Kelsen writes that an addressee might refuse to follow a judge's norm due to the judge's insanity. So long as the presupposition of sanity is efficacious in the sense of being followed by addressees, the *Grundnorm*, presupposed in the judge's posit of norms, remains objective. The basic norm is not questioned if the referents of the chain of 'ought' statements are not questioned.[13]

Ultimately, Kelsen states again and again, the referents that prescribe certain conduct are coercive. The statements about acts of will must be coercively imposed upon others. As he ends the second edition of the *Pure Theory*, "[f]rom the point of view of a consistent legal positivism, law, like the state, cannot be comprehended otherwise than as a coercive order of human behaviour."[14] Legal norms are binding because they are presupposed to be binding and, if pressed, officials must impose that 'binding' character upon all addressees who fall within the cognitive boundaries of a norm: "if we ask for the reason of the validity of the historical first constitution, then the answer can only be (if we leave aside God or 'nature') the validity of this constitution – the assumption that it is a binding norm – must be *presupposed*."[15] So Kelsen does, indeed, have a role, however unclear, for efficacy to play in the authority of a normative structure. Kelsen describes efficacy as a condition, though not the grounds, for the authority of a system of norms: "[t]he effectiveness of the legal order [structure] – it must be stressed – is only the condition of the validity, not the validity itself."[16] Indeed, in his later work, the *General Theory of Norms* (1979), he claims that the authority of an institutional structure completely dissipates when the statement loses its efficacy.[17]

Despite the important, if ambiguous, relation of efficacy to the authority of a norm, Kelsen cautions in the *General Theory of Law and State* and in the *Pure Theory*, efficacy is not synonymous with legal authority. Efficacy does not authorize the norm. Efficacy and authority remain in separate realms: "[t]he norms of a

12 Kelsen, *Introduction to the Problems of Legal Theory* [hereinafter cited as *Introduction*] (Oxford: Clarendon Press, 1992), 59. This was first published as the first edition of the *Reine Rechtslehre* [*Pure Theory of Law*] (Vienna: Franz Deuticke, 1934).

13 See generally, Kelsen, *Introduction*, 203.

14 Kelsen, *Pure Theory*, 319. Kelsen emphasizes the coercive character of the imputation of a norm in the "Foreword" to *Main Problems in the Theory of Public Law* (1st edn., 2d printing, *Pure Theory*) in *Normativity and Norms*, 3-22, 9-10.

15 Kelsen, *Pure Theory*, 200, 202.

16 Kelsen, *Pure Theory*, 78.

17 Kelsen, *General Theory of Norms*, trans. Michael Hartney (Oxford: Clarendon Press, 1991; 1979), 140.

positive legal order are valid *because* the fundamental rule regulating their creation, that is, the basic norm, is presupposed to be valid, not because they are effective; but they are valid only *as long as* this legal order is effective."[18]

Kelsen distinguishes norms from efficacy in several ways. First, as I have already noted, for Kelsen, effectiveness is an "is-fact" that goes to the issue of whether a system of norms is actually applied and enforced. Authority (Kelsen frequently uses the term 'validates'), in contrast, asks whether the norm ought to be obeyed. A norm may be authoritative even though it is ineffective. Moreover, its authority is established logically *before* the norm is considered (in)effective. Efficacy is only "a necessary condition for the validity of every single norm of the [legal] order."[19]

This leads to a second reason why efficacy is separate from the authority of a norm, according to Kelsen. This second factor draws from Kelsen's theory of meaning. The authority of a norm encompasses the trace of the meaning of a statement about an act of will. Officials bring meaning into the trace. The trace reconstitutes legal meaning from whatever the legislature may have intended in its act of will. An official's meaning is directed towards a reconstituted referent intended in a statement. The trace of statements postulates that the statements represent a chain of cognitive referents, intellectually joined the one to the other into a coherent, self-referring structure. Because the meaning has a "real" act of will as its referent, the reconstructed meaning idealizes what the official takes as a natural or social reality.[20] The meaning idealizes the historically contingent event surrounding the legislated will. Without the original legislative (or judicial) authorship that expresses the act of will, Kelsen suggests, there could be neither an act of will nor a sign to stand for the act of will. As a consequence, the 'is' world of legislated acts of will conditions the reconstitution of that will as officials make statements about it.[21] Efficacy provides the context for such a nexus of the initial act of will and the reconstructed meaning of the statement attributed to the historical author.

This nexus encourages us to return to the ambiguous relation of the authority of an 'ought' statement with its efficacy.

b) *Efficacy as a discursive phenomenon*

When one returns to Kelsen's explanation of the relation of an historical author's act of will and the judicial (re-)statement of the act of will, Kelsen makes a move

18 Kelsen, *General Theory of Norms*, 212.

19 Kelsen, *General Theory of Law and State*, 119.

20 Kelsen, *General Theory of Norms*, 211. Kelsen does not explain what he means by "the reality of being."

21 Kelsen, *General Theory of Norms*, 212.

that undermines his claim that efficacy is the condition for the authority of a norm. Allow me to return to Kelsen's explanation.

Commentators have often understood Kelsen's sense of a norm as an historical author's act of will. One can glean such a view from his later essay, "The Foundation of the Theory of Natural Law" (1964), for example.[22] However, during his 'classical period' when he wrote the first (1934) and second (1970) editions of the *Pure Theory of Law* as well as *The General Theory of Law and State* (1945), Kelsen explains that a norm is the *statement* about the historical author's act of will. A statement represents or signifies how one ought to behave. A legal act, he writes, is the statement about the meaning of the authors act of will, not the authorial act itself nor, for that matter, the author's originally intended referent.[23] Kelsen urges that one focus upon the *language* of prescriptive claims rather than the abstract thoughts that may be attributed to an historical author, as if the author could express its mind through a transparent language.

Now, against this background, the will about which officials make statements is a rational, not an experiential, will. A rational will is purged of all emotion and inclination that one experiences as one desires an object. This abstracted will renders efficacy problematic. For the core to efficacy, Kelsen holds out, is the very experiential phenomena that he excludes from the will. Despite this purging of the will of its empirical content, though, Kelsen still describes the act of will as embedded in an 'is' world. This abstracted or rational will, Kelsen claims, joins the legal act to the natural and social reality. And yet, the act of will, which is the centre of a norm, is not an 'is' element of social behaviour for it is purged of all empirical content.

What, then, does Kelsen mean when he suggests that efficacy is the condition for the authority of a norm? How can efficacy relate to the social 'reality' if a norm is not the actual act of will of the historical author but rather, later statements about the act of will? Perhaps, our initial focus upon such a social-empirical context of an historical author's is misdirected once one understands a norm in the context of a language.

Kelsen's works are preoccupied with an interpreter's conferral or imputation of meaning (of a referent) into a statement.[24] But an interpreter does not confer meaning as an isolated human being. The statement itself is immersed in a "chain" of other statements, Kelsen emphasizes. Kelsen especially urges one to consider efficacy in this context of the constitution of meaning when he restates his pure

---

22 Kelsen, "The Foundation of the Theory of Natural Law" (1964), in *Essays in Legal and Moral Philosophy*, 114-53, especially 115.

23 Kelsen, *Pure Theory*, 10.

24 This is substantiated in Conklin, *The Structuralism of Analytical Jurisprudence* (forthcoming).

theory of law in the *Law Quarterly Review*:

> That which makes the process into a legal (or illegal) act is not its factuality, not its natural, causal existence, but the objective significance which is bound up with its meaning. Its characteristically legal meaning it receives from a norm whose content refers to it. The norm functions as a schema of meaning. It itself is born of a legal act which in its turn receives its meaning from another norm.[25]

In addition, the statement commands, authorizes, or permits an addressee to behave according to the referent intended in the 'ought' statement.

If the meaning of one norm depends upon the meaning in another norm, one should think that there must be an addressee of each 'ought' statement. Accordingly, when Kelsen writes that efficacy is the condition of authority, he may really have in mind the Husserlian idea that the meaning must be fulfilled by an addressee for a statement to make sense. That is, a will may be efficacious if an addressee recognizes the sentence. The addressee recognizes the statement as signifying the historical author's act of will. Put differently, if the legal officials and the addressee, whether another official or the citizen, do not recognize a statement about what the addressee ought to do, then the statement is 'meaningless.' If the statement lacks meaning for an addressee, then it can hardly be said to be efficacious.

'Efficacy' may take on this special discursive sense for Kelsen once one appreciates, first, that a norm represents the meaning of a rational act of will, not the original psychological motive of the historical author; and secondly, that that representation gains its signification from a pre-existing chain of statements that signify a cohesive structure of cognitive referents. 'Efficacy,' then, is not the efficacy of brute social 'facts' that are posited as beyond the control of the official. Efficacy is contextualized in a theory of signification that lifts reconstructed meanings from the psychological desires of historical authors. The critical point in Kelsen's theory of legal meaning is not 'what did the legislature intend by its expression?' but 'how do other expert knowers of the prescriptive statements interpret the legislature's expression of its will?' If no other official recognizes a legislative or judicial statement as "authentic" or authoritative, then the statement is no longer efficacious.

What becomes important in the efficaciousness of a system of norms, then, is the hidden structure of cognitive referents in which the norm is located. In "Law, State and Justice in the Pure Theory of Law" (1948), Kelsen writes "[b]ut it cannot be denied that a legal order [structure] is considered to be valid only if the human behav-

---

25 Kelsen, "The Pure Theory of Law. Its Method and Fundamental Concepts: Pt. 1," trans. with intro. Charles H. Wilson, in *Law Quarterly Review* (1934) **50** (1934): 474-98, 479. The second part of the essay is in *Law Quarterly Review* **51** (1935): 517-35.

iour to which this order refers is, by and large, in conformity with the order [structure]."[26] If the behaviour is not in conformity with the structure as a whole, an official's statements about acts of will can no longer be fulfilled by other officials, let alone by the individuals whose conduct is authorized, prescribed or permitted.

If 'efficacy' goes to the fulfilment of meaning rather than to the social-historical context of the act of will of an historical author, Kelsen may be right in his insistence that the condiiton of a norm is that it be efficacious or fulfilled. An official's statement comes first. The official's very utterance of the statement claims authority. What is authorized? The cognitive referent of the statement. The referent is what Kelsen considers the meaning of the statement. But the statement is meaningless except to the utterer, isolated from others, if the addressee does not recognize the statement as binding. The statement cannot be binding if it is a mere fragment of writing, discontinuous with the writing and utterances of officials. Rather, the statement takes its meaning from a structure of objects signified by the statements. That is, the 'ought' statement is meaningless if the statement (and its hidden structure of referents) is not fulfilled by the addressee(s). The condition of authority is, first, that addressees recognize the statement as authoritative in the chain of other statements and, second, that the addressee recognizes the overall structure of cognitive objects that the statements signify. One official's acceptance of the referent of a statement reinforces the hidden structure of referents that other binding statements signify. As soon as the officials and, perhaps, the non-officials no longer recognize the statements conferring the structure as a whole, the legal structure and every legal norm lose their authority.[27] So, efficacy in the sense of the fulfilment of a signified object is, indeed, a condition for the authority of a norm. Ultimately, this sense of efficacy (or the fulfilment of the meant object) depends upon the efficacy or recognition/fulfilment of the structure of referents as a whole.

So, when Kelsen writes about a system of norms that lose their authority when the system no longer "agrees" with reality, the reality to which Kelsen refers may be a discursive reality rather than the more usual understanding of reality as posited natural or social facts as so many commentators have assumed.[28] Rather, it may be the interpretive context with which Kelsen is preoccupied. Interpreters of statements must share a presupposition in order

---

26 Kelsen, "Law, State and Justice in the Pure Theory of Law," in *What is Justice? Justice, Law, and Politics in the Mirror of Science* (Berkeley/Los Angeles: University of California Press, 1971), 288-302, 290.

27 Kelsen, *Pure Theory*, 212. Also see *General Theory of Law and State*, 119.

28 Precisely because efficacy has been understood in such a positive sense, commentators have found Kelsen inconsistent in his claim that efficacy is merely a condition of authority, though authority becomes non-existent when efficacy dissipates. As an example, see Julius Stone, *Legal System and Lawyers' Reasoning* (Palo Alto: Stanford University Press, 1964), 102-21.

for their statements to be fulfilled amongst discussants.[29] This shared meaning (that is, the shared referent) lifts the subjectivity of the solipsistic conferral of meaning into an objectivity of shared meanings. Kelsen thereby remains within the realm of what he considers an objectivity (namely, the cognitive referents of statements) even when he examines efficacy.

Of course, there is a risk that one will understand efficacy as a posited brute fact because statements may continually refer to the acts of will as if the acts were uncontrollable. In such a circumstance, the official/citizen must either accept the *Grundnorm* or reject it. The acceptance of the *Grundnorm* may be an 'all-or-nothing' affair. No one individual may challenge the singularity of the *Grundnorm* without questioning the intended structure as a whole. The only option left to one who does not accept the *Grundnorm* is revolution in the sense of a radical displacement of the *Grundnorm* in the legal discourse. Against the background of the given, posited facticity of the social 'real,' the addressee remains passive until the revolutionary moment. If the addressee fails to fulfil the referent of such a positivist view of reality (that is, if the addressee fails to accept such a view of reality as facticity), the addressee must explode into a revolutionary rejection of the total structure. It may well be that Kelsen understands 'efficacy' in terms of such a discursive reality, even though the discourse entertains the 'real' as posited brute facts.

Although Kelsen's theory of the legal act suggests such a discursive theory of the social, and although he does attempt to incorporate Edmund Husserl's theory of meaning into his own theory of the norm,[30] Kelsen fails to carry his theory through to an analysis of the relation of the legal act to efficacy. Instead, his works are overcome by a preoccupation with the Kantian division of knowledge into the *phenomenal* and the *noumenal*. Kant's works, in turn, are bereft with a theory of discourse. Working within Kant's paradigm, Kelsen fails to push his own theory of meaning to its full completion in terms of the fulfilment of meaning. As a consequence, Kelsen returns to Kant's notion of the perfectly pure will as the categorical condition for the normative structure to exist.

c) A categorical imperative?

The key to Kelsen's analysis of efficacy is his view that the *Grundnorm* functions epistemologically in an *ideell* realm. The *Grundnorm* is an epistemological presupposition as judges interpret prescriptive statements. Kelsen puts the epistemological character of the *Grundnorm* in this way:

---

29 Kelsen, *Pure Theory*, 205.

30 Kelsen, "Note 6," in *General Theory of Norms*, 276-78, 172. Also see Kelsen, "On the Concept of Norm" (1965), in *Essays in Legal and Moral Philosophy*, 223-24, fn. 8.

> the validity of a norm, created according to another norm, rests on that other norm, whose creation in turn, is determined by a third one. This is a regression that ultimately ends up in the presupposed basic norm. This basic norm, therefore, is the highest reason for the validity of the norms, one created in conformity with another, thus forming a legal order in its hierarchical structure.[31]

An epistemological presupposition makes interpretation possible, Kelsen argues: the *Grundnorm* makes it possible "to interpret the subjective meaning of the constitution-creating act (as well as of the acts established according to the constitution) as their objective meaning, that is, as objectively valid legal norms."[32]

The epistemological function of a norm erases the socially and historically contingent context from the trace of norms. As Kelsen puts it, the *Grundnorm* is not freely chosen or invented.[33] A sense of necessity surrounds the *Grundnorm*. There is a sense in which legal officials involuntarily accept the *Grundnorm*.

And yet, being an 'ought,' the *Grundnorm* is humanly constructed. Without a presupposed *Grundnorm*, how could one know what counts as a valid ordinary norm? Why would the official even be capable of tracing norms?

What is the quality or character of the *Grundnorm*? Kelsen tells us that, in order to be basic, the *Grundnorm* differs from the statements that signify a structure of interconnected cognitive referents. But how does it differ? Is the *Grundnorm* a superfluous and misleading supplement to the structure or is the *Grundnorm* an hypothesis or postulate of the legal act? Is it a social-empirical conditional hypothesis, to use Kant's intended use of the term, or is it a "metaphysical hypothesis," to use Kelsen's term?

In the context of issues of legal authority, a norm functions as the reason or ground for a juridical agent to act. The juridical agent justifies a statement in terms of a prior statement. The referent of the second statement functions as the epistemological justification of the referent of the first statement. The official situates the two statements in a chain of *Sollens*-sentences. The *Grundnorm* functions as the originary prescription for all the statements in the chain. But the *Grundnorm* is not a statement: it is a mere "figmentary" thought that cannot be stated if it is to be basic.

The non-signifiable character of the *Grundnorm* distinguishes the *Grundnorm* from ordinary norms. The *Grundnorm* functions much as does Kant's perfectly good will. Even Kant hinged the pursuit of a grounding of morality upon the possibility of one perfectly good will or what he sometimes referred to synony-

31 Kelsen, *General Theory of Norms*, 222.
32 Kelsen, *General Theory of Norms*, 202.
33 Kelsen, *General Theory of Norms*, 201.

mously as the "pure will." There no longer are duties owed if one gains access to the pure will because duties only arise if one's action is influenced by inclinations or subjective emotive values. Since 'oughts' only occur if one is plagued with inclinations and personal preferences, there would be no 'oughts' if, lifted entirely into the noumenal realm where there are no inclinations, there is a pure will.[34] Kant describes such a pure will as a "holy will." Much like Kelsen's later description of the *Grundnorm*, the pure will is a pure thought, rather than a will, since a pure will, to be a will, would have to act towards some further referent. If the pure will had to so act, it would no longer be pure: the further referent would be the pure will. So it does not make sense to say that the pure will is an act. Similarly, if one wished to have a legal structure, then one had to presuppose that there is one ultimate 'ought' unencumbered with the inclinations, felt experiences, and subjective values. Such a pure norm functions as the ultimate referent of all other 'ought' statements in a *noumenal* realm. Though he aspires to elaborate an anti-metaphysical theory of law, Kelsen's theory succumbs to such a metaphysics.

Kelsen's focus upon the metaphysics of the *Grundnorm* is best manifested in his writings about the authorizing origin of a written Constitution.[35]

On the one hand, preoccupied with the efficacy of the legal structure, it would make sense that one would accept the historically first constitutional text as the *Grundnorm*: "it is the fundamental presupposition of our recognition of the legal order founded on this constitution that which the original authors declared to be their will should be regarded as a valid norm."[36] Tony Honore has described this as "the Big Bang theory."[37]

On the other hand, Kelsen argues, a basic constitutional text cannot finalize the trace of 'ought' statements. More generally, no historically contingent institution can posit a *Grundnorm*.[38] If it did so, the will of the founding fathers of the text would be more final than the constitutional text. More specifically, the appeal to the will of the founding fathers would presuppose that the text, even if described as 'the Constitution,' would represent an objective norm rather than a subjectively imposed norm. In addition, the appeal to the constitutional text would presuppose that certain interpreters act authoritatively.

---

34 Kant, *A Grounding of the Metaphysics of Morals*, trans. James W. Ellington (Indianapolis: Hackett, 1981; 2d ed.), 440.

35 Kelsen, "On the Concept of Norm," in *Essays in Legal and Moral Philosophy*, 200-02.

36 Kelsen, "The Pure Theory of Law. Its Method and Fundamental Concepts: Pt 2," 518.

37 Tony Honore, "The Basic Norm of a Society" in eds. Stanley L. Paulson and Bonnie Litschewski Paulson, *Normativity and Norms*, 89-112, 101.

38 See esp Iain Stewart, "Kelsen and the Exegetical Tradition" in eds. Tur and Twining, *Essays on Kelsen* (Oxford: Clarendon, 1986), 123-47, at 132-33.

Accordingly, it is irrelevant whether a *Grundnorm* has ever actually occurred in an historically contingent context. The *Grundnorm* is an 'ought.' In contrast, an historical context involves sociological events. The basic norm is shared by those who make and interpret 'ought' statements about the meanings of other 'ought' statements. So the basic norm emerges from the cognitively produced structure that the 'ought' statements represent. The basic norm does not pre-exist the structure as a thought. If it did so, then logic, not arbitrary acts of will, would resolve social conflict. Logic, again, is the tool to reflect about the thoughts. The *Grundnorm* exists *after* the structure has taken form. The structure of norms creates and regulates the structure's own institutional agents.[39] The trace of the authority of one referent from another requires a final referent or, more correctly, a presupposition about such a final referent. Such a presupposition terminates the trace of referents that the 'ought' statements signify, according to Kelsen. The ending (or origin) unifies all cognitive referents.

And yet, the origin does not pre-exist the structure. Officials retrospectively 'create' the *Grundnorm* as they represent their cognitive referents through 'ought' statements. Other officials recognize the referents as legally binding. As a consequence, efficacy merely conditions legal analysis *after* juridical agents presuppose that they ought to obey certain 'ought' statements. That is, the empirical context of a legal order enters legal analysis after the *Grundnorm* is presupposed. So, although the *Grundnorm* manifests, rather than causes, the normative structure, the language presupposes that the *Grundnorm* pre-exists the empirical realm of natural facts.[40]

The *Grundnorm* 'exists.' But, presupposed as the origin of a chain of 'ought' statements, the *Grundnorm* exists a-historically and a-socially. The *Grundnorm* also exists independent of language (that is, the 'ought' statements or norms). This strange silent 'existence' of the *Grundnorm* can be gleaned from Kelsen's distinction between an act of will and an act of thought.[41] An act of will is an author's expressed intent directed towards an object. We have observed that the object of an act of will is categorical rather than natural. But when we examine his comments about legal interpretation closely, we uncover that a norm may continue to exist after the historical author of the act of will has dissipated. Indeed, he says, "the norm does not become valid until the act of will whose meaning the norm is has been accomplished and hence has ceased to exist."[42] That is, the meaning of the official's statement about the act of will displaces the generating legis-

---

39 Kelsen, *Pure Theory*, 209.

40 Kelsen, *Introduction to the Problems of Legal Theory*, 13.

41 See esp. Kelsen, *General Theory of Norms*, 256.

42 Kelsen, *Pure Theory*, 10.

lated or judicially created act of will. A norm is valid only *after* the official has situated the norm in the chain of other authoritative norms and after the official has gleaned a signification of the object intended in the act of will in such a context of *Sollens*-sentences.

Kelsen divides knowledge into acts of will and acts of thought. A *Grundnorm* is a mere thought and an unconscious thought at that. A mere thought lacks a will. A thought also lacks an object that an author *means* or embodies with his or her *prejudice*, to use Gadamer's sense of the latter term. A *Grundnorm*, according to Kelsen, is a thought in that, being a presupposition of acts of cognition, it is an unwitting and unconscious reflection about the interconnected structure of referents that legal language signifies. One must not forget that the legal act involves the conferral of meaning. One must also not forget that the conferral of meaning is a cognitive project: "[t]he science of law remains a merely cognitive discipline even in its epistemological statement that the basic norm is the condition" under which subjective values take on an objective meaning.[43] Being a presupposition, the *Grundnorm* does not and cannot represent a referent. If the *Grundnorm* were an act of will, it would refer to a further object: such a '*Grundnorm*' would be one more act of cognition that officials could consider an authoritative norm. The referent of the will, not the *Grundnorm*, would be basic. Accordingly, "the basic norm, the ultimate reason for the validity of these norms, is not created by a real will at all, but is presupposed in legal thinking."[44] The *Grundnorm* exists, to the extent that it exists, only as an implicit unsignified and unsignifiable pure thought about no-thing.

The *Grundnorm* is unnameable. The *Grundnorm* is an "imaginary will,"[45] "a genuine fiction"[46] or what Kant would describe as a "mere phantom of the brain."[47] Since the *Grundnorm* is neither perceptible nor verbalizable nor signifiable in a statement, it remains inaccessible to language. Indeed, if the *Grundnorm* were recognized as a sign, it would no longer be presupposed. Some deeper *Grundnorm* would have to be presupposed as the authorizing origin of the language of the structure.

Being unsignifiable, the *Grundnorm* is invisible. That being so, the *Grundnorm* contradicts the very empirical reality that Kelsen claims as the "condition" for the authority of a norm. The *Grundnorm* also contradicts the authoritative legal structure "since it represents the authorisation of a supreme moral or legal authority,

43 Kelsen, *Pure Theory*, 204.

44 Ibid., 23. Again, in his essay "On the Basic Norm," he asserts that "it cannot be a norm created by the act of will of a definite individual." *California Law Review* 47 (1959): 107-10, 108-09.

45 Kelsen, *Pure Theory*, 9.

46 Kelsen, "The Function of a Constitution," 117.

47 Kant, *Grounding of the Metaphysics of Morals*, 462.

and hence it issues from an authority lying beyond that authority, even though the further authority is merely figmentary."[48] The *Grundnorm* is "an independent legal norm."[49]

The *Grundnorm* functions as an optical illusion to the officials. Inaccessible from within their language, the invisible *Grundnorm* remains the centre of the language. The officials take it for granted that they ought to obey the hierarchy of cognitive referents signified by the legal statements. What is taken for granted is a final 'ought' of such a hierarchy. The *Grundnorm* remains unsignified until an official brings the presupposition to consciousness in language. At that moment, such as when a society recognizes a constitutional text as basic to the language of the structure, the *Grundnorm* becomes a statement. Its silent presence as an *a priori* thought becomes, at best, another representation in chains of *Sollens*-sentences. The *Grundnorm* is no longer basic. It has become an ordinary norm undifferentiated from the others.

The purity of the interpretive act of cognition necessitates that a oneness should characterize the normative structure, according to Kelsen. If a further syllogism were possible, then the 'final' norm could not be a *Grundnorm* because the major proposition of the new syllogism would finalize the trace. The *Grundnorm* ultimately constitutes "the common source for the validity of all norms that belong to the same [normative] order."[50] The one ultimate reason or ground for any particular norm is shared as a presupposition of all officials in their justification of norms. The tracing project links one norm to another to another and, implicitly, to the silent Oneness at the pinnacle. As an 'ought' thought that cannot be signified, the *Grundnorm* is content-independent. The presupposition of a presuppositionless basic norm unifies the trace just as it finalizes the analytic project. There can only be one *Grundnorm* that a juridical agent presupposes as basic: if there were more than one, then contradictoriness would characterize the trace of authority. There would no longer be a *Grundnorm*. As I pointed out in Chapter Two, Kant similarly insisted in his legal writings that one head must occupy the pinnacle of law (*Recht*). Kant also suggested that if there were a pure will, then there would only be one such pure will.

3. The Origin as an *a priori* Concept

Kant's analysis of the invisible origin of law (*Recht*) sheds insight into the invisible grounding of Kelsen's 'pure' theory of law. This is, at first, incongruous for, after all, Kelsen describes Kant as a 'natural law theorist' and Kelsen defines his own

48 Kelsen, "The Function of a Constitution," 117.
49 Kelsen, *Pure Theory*, 57.
50 Ibid., 195.

position in juxtaposition to 'natural law theory.' Moreover, Kelsen insists that his positivism has no place for a transcendent metaphysical Absolute, such as the perfectly pure will in Kant's metaphysics of morals. Kelsen contrasts his own pure theory to Kant's by associating the pure will with an Absolute Author. This is so because Kelsen understands the divine in the sense of a Creator/Author of the natural universe.

But Kant offers a sense of the divine that is very different from an Author. Rather, he describes, as divine, an authorless *a priori* concept. In the *Critique of Judgment* and *The Critique of Pure Practical Reason*, for example, Kant describes this *a priori* concept as divine and, on occasion, as holy.[51] Along similar lines, for his part, Kelsen associates the divine with just such an *a priori* concept. In the *General Theory of Norms*, for example, he describes God as "a specific *ideell* Being, rather than a *real* Being," the latter as a "Being of natural, sensibly perceptible, reality."[52] Again, in the *Pure Theory*, he describes the *Grundnorm* as absent from the trace of humanly posited norms. Offering a finality to legal reasoning, the *Grundnorm* is presuppositionless and referentless. While signifying nothing, the *Grundnorm* still magnetically attracts, invites, and seduces all legal reasoning to the *Grundnorm*. The *Grundnorm* is an excess beyond the language of humanly posited norms. Because it is presuppositionless and possesses no particulars, the *Grundnorm* cannot be said to represent or signify any particular norm.

Accordingly, unlike posited norms, the *Grundnorm* cannot be named. The *Grundnorm* is inarticulatable, unpronounceable, and unwritten within the familiar norms (or 'ought' statements about acts of will). Kelsen goes one step further than Rousseau: the unnameable remains unnamed.

A finality may characterize a chain of norms only if the originary norm differs from all other norms. Kelsen emphasizes that the *Grundnorm* differs from an ordinary norm in that a norm is a statement about an intended will directed towards an absent object, such as a doctrine, whereas a *Grundnorm* cannot be stated nor, if it could, could it refer to any further object. For the *Grundnorm* lacks an object or referent.

Again, the *Grundnorm* is intrinsically valued in that it lacks any further referent. The *Grundnorm* is not an instrumental means to some further referent or object. Kelsen puts this point in the *Pure Theory* in this way: "if one does not presuppose an a-priori, that is, absolute, moral value, one is unable to determine what must be considered good and evil, just and unjust, under all circumstances."[53]

---

51 See, e.g., Kant, *Grounding of the Metaphysics of Morals*, 439.
52 Kelsen, "Note 103," in *General Theory of Norms*, 342.
53 Kelsen, *Pure Theory*, 65.

One cannot infer a judicially authored norm from the will of a legislator. This is so because a norm is an official's statement about the meaning or constituted referent of the earlier legislature's or court's will. The norm reconstructs the legislature's act of will. The final norm, the *Grundnorm*, is an *a priori* concept or thought that, as a final grounds, includes all ordinary norms. Kelsen puts this point this way in his later essay, "Law and Logic": "[b]ut even in the relationship between a general norm and the corresponding individual norm posited by the law-applying organ, a logical relation exists, insofar as the state-of affairs established *in concreto* by the court can be subsumed under the state-of affairs defined *in abstracto* in the general norm."[54] Any one norm is "justified by" "grounded in" or "founded in" the authority of another norm.

The *a priori* character of the *Grundnorm* situates the *Grundnorm* as inaccessible from the language of the legal structure. Here, Kelsen follows the path of Hobbes, Rousseau, Bentham, and Austin. Indeed, the *Grundnorm* cannot be authored by a human will in that an author directs his or her will towards an object, Kelsen claims. The *Grundnorm* is intellectually contentless. Lacking an object to which it may refer, the *Grundnorm* is just a thought – not even an act of thought since such would contradict the silent passivity of the *Grundnorm*. Its lack of a referent and, therefore, of an author associated with the will places the situs of the *Grundnorm* as radically other to the 'ought' statements, as external to the language of the structure. This otherness of the *Grundnorm* continues the tradition of legal positivism, initiated with Hobbes's and Rousseau's state of nature and furthered with Bentham's concept of the 'greatest happiness of the greatest number' and Austin's 'habits of the people,' of associating the grounding of humanly willed laws with an invisible authorizing origin. Unlike the externality of Hobbes's invisible authors or Austin's habits of the people, though, Kelsen wants the *Grundnorm* to emanate from *within* the structure. Without the structure, there is not a *Grundnorm*.

What, then, does Kelsen mean by the *Grundnorm* being a presupposition whose authority evaporates when the structure of norms is inefficacious? One way to understand the invisibility of the *Grundnorm* vis-à-vis the language of the structure is to draw from Kant's hypothesis at the end of the *Grounding of the Metaphysics of Morals*. Here, Kant claims that morality ultimately hinges upon a perfectly pure will in a noumenal kingdom of pure thought. At the end of the first edition of the *Grounding of the Metaphysics of Morals,* Kant admits,

---

54 Kelsen, "Law and Logic" (1965), in Kelsen, *Essays in Legal and Moral Philosophy*, ed. Ota Weinberger, trans. Peter Heath (Dordrecht/Boston: D. Reidel, 1973), 228-53, 246.

though, that morality hinges upon an 'as if' condition:

> The satisfaction of reason is only further and further postponed by the continual inquiry after the condition. Reason, therefore, restlessly seeks the unconditionally necessary and sees itself compelled to assume this without having any means of making such necessity conceivable ... reason cannot render conceivable the absolute necessity of an unconditioned practical law (such as the categorical imperative must be).[55]

That is, the grounding of morality depends upon the condition that people desire to be moral. Without a similar 'as if' 'ought' (that is, that people desire to have a legal structure), the structure of cognitively produced doctrines would no longer be binding. Nor would the structure exist as a structure. We would return to a stateless, lawless 'natural' condition without 'oughts.' For, the ultimate reason for the authority of a binding norm is presupposed in the figmentary imagination of the officials of the structure alone.[56] Though a perfectly pure thought in that it is not representable as a statement, the *Grundnorm* remains an 'ought.' Kelsen maintains the is/ought distinction here. The *Grundnorm* is drawn from a realm of 'oughts,' not from the 'is' world of acts of will. That being so, the 'as if' condition cannot possibly be contingent upon an empirically ascertainable desire on the part of the people to possess a legal structure. Kelsen's theory of law does not permit Raz's claim that legal obligation rests with an attitude of respect towards the institutions.[57] The *Grundnorm* is an *a priori*.

The unsignifiable character of the *Grundnorm* vis-à-vis norms renders the *Grundnorm* 'inaccessible' from the officials' norms. But Kant described just such a pre-linguistic external *a priori* concept as divine. Kant considered the possibility of a perfectly good will, so necessary for moral meaning, as divine in that no human agent, conditioned by inclinations, could ever know or experience such a pure will. The perfectly pure will was a mere possibility. Just such an unknowability also led Hobbes to describe the invisible authors as having constructed a "mortale God." And on at least one occasion, John Austin too described the concept of the 'greatest happiness of the greatest number' as divine. Public officials may well signify the *Grundnorm* with a configuration of statements. But no official may gain access to the *Grundnorm* by playing with the norms: the *Grundnorm*, being an analytic *a priori* thought, lies logically prior and external to the language of ordinary norms, the latter being *acts* of will signified in synthetic statements that depend upon third terms for their authority.

---

55 Kant, *Grounding of the Metaphysics of Morals*, 463.

56 Kelsen, *Pure Theory*, 23.

57 Raz's view will be examined in Chapter Nine.

Nor can an agent of the *Grundnorm* gain access to the *Grundnorm* because, although a posited norm is the statement about an act of will and, as such, a cultural construct, the *Grundnorm* itself is a thought. Nor may the *Grundnorm* even be signified as a statement because Kelsen insists that it is presupposed. Thus, it is irrelevant that there be an invisible author – a God or the founding fathers of a civil constitution – who has posited the *Grundnorm*. The importance of the *Grundnorm* lies in its presupposed absence from the trace of norms. The *Grundnorm* transcends; it is logically necessary; and it is a presupposition. The *Grundnorm* is a "transcendental-logical presupposition." The *Grundnorm* is the situs of a presupposition necessary for the logical unification of the multiplicity of norms. Such a unity is needed for officials to be able to recognize a norm as authoritative. Indeed, without such a unity, a norm would be unrecognizable as binding and as posited. The juridical officials, who trace norms, do so in the name of a nameless and contentless origin.

Now, notwithstanding the invisible character of the *a priori* authorizing origin of norms, Kelsen fails to recognize its invisibility because he associates the invisible only with a divine Author. Kelsen holds out, for example, that Aquinas had connected Nature with a divine Author/Creator. Kelsen also interprets Aquinas as claiming that God creates moral requirements. More precisely, according to Kelsen, natural law theory claims that God moves everything. God is the first cause of movement: the unmoved mover. Kelsen differentiates such a first cause from the *Grundnorm* in that the first cause is believed to author or create. But the *Grundnorm* is merely a passive thought, not an active author. Moreover, the *Grundnorm* is presupposed. That is, it is unnameable in the language of the officials. Because God has created and designed the world, God's identity is immanent within the material world. Implanted in nature, the Author's inclinations are exhibited in Nature. The natural world is then represented as manifesting moral requirements.

I elaborated a very different sense of the divine in Chapter Two, however. Drawing from Kant's works on ethics and law, I suggested that this alternative view associates the divine with an analytic *a priori* concept. Such a concept is unauthored. The *a priori* concept subsumes reasoning under it. According to this alternative view, an unauthored authoritative norm displaces the author whose act of will creates an object. Hans Kelsen adopted such a view of the displacement of meaning.[58] He also adopted Kant's sense of an *a priori* concept as the *Grundnorm*.

The big question remains 'why did Kelsen attribute the authorizing origin of "ought" statements to a concept rather than to an author?' Kelsen explains that if God had created such a *Grundnorm* as 'One ought to obey the commands of God,'

58 See generally, Conklin, *The Structuralism of Analytical Jurisprudence* (forthcoming).

such a norm would be a God-created norm and the *Grundnorm*, in turn, could not possibly be the final norm: a divine Author would still remain more supreme than the *Grundnorm*. Thus, all authors must be subordinate and instrumental to the basic concept or *Grundnorm*. The concept at the origin of legal authority is an end in and for itself. The *a priori* concept is an intrinsic rather than an instrumental end. The *Grundnorm*, unlike all ordinary norms, does not need a third factor to produce a predicate: all predicates, all ordinary norms, subsume under the *a priori* concept itself. The *Grundnorm* is a lack in that, because it is unsignifiable and unsignified, it precedes the officials' language. The *Grundnorm* lacks particulars (it is contentless) because it remains unsignified and unsignifiable as an 'ought' statement.

In *What is Justice?* (1952), Kelsen acknowledges that the problematic of the pure theory lies precisely in the inaccessible character of the *Grundnorm* from within the language of the officials.[59] For if all behaviour were justified in terms of a presupposed originary moment, that behaviour would, in turn, be justified only "conditionally": that is, under the condition that the presupposed end was justifiable. But the final norm cannot be justified by reference to a further referent, for such a referent would displace what had hitherto been considered final. Thus, the *Grundnorm* is intrinsically valued in and for itself because it needs no prior cognitive nor physical object nor any subsequent object as a particular or a referent. Intrinsic values, Kelsen insists, transcend human reason and human language. The consequence, he suggests, is that "that absolute justice is transferred from this world into the transcendental world." The authorizing origin of all humanly willed norms is unconditional. The authorizing origin is a transcendental object.

This returns us to the important question, 'why did Kelsen attribute the authorizing origin to a concept rather than to an author?' Again and again, Kelsen insists that his pure theory is anti-metaphysical. A transcendental object encourages rational beings to appeal to the very religion, absolute truth, or a political saviour that natural law theory offers for comfort, Kelsen surmises.[60] Some superhuman being must be believed to author the absolute justice without conditions if one accepts such a transcendental object. One can only gain access to humanly posited norms for such norms are historically contingent statements about the meaning (the objects) of historically contingent acts of the legislated will. One cannot gain access to a transcendental justice. To justify the finality of authored laws, one must fall back upon a God and a faith in that God in natural law theory. Without such a God, one would be "deceived" into believing that human reason could gain access to the transcendental realm when, in fact, reason cannot do so.[61]

59 Kelsen, "What is Justice?" in *What is Justice?*, 1-24, 9.
60 Kelsen, "What is Justice?" 10.
61 Kelsen, "What is Justice?" 21.

Torstein Eckhoff and Nils Kristian Sundby best describe this element of Kelsen's theory in that Kelsen is said to depersonalize the power of the state.[62] That is, Kelsen continues the practice, initiated with the Romans, which associates *auctoritas* with impersonality. That Tradition institutionalizes impersonality with one supreme source or grounding. Here, Kelsen shares the quest for an *arche* with his version of natural law theory.[63] Kelsen rejects Austin's appeal to the will of an historical commander/author only to replace the latter with an impersonal surrogate. He has rejected the Aristotelian notion of an end embedded within the movement of socio-cultural customs, only to replace such an end with one that transcends the norms of a normative structure. Without such an authorizing origin, any normative structure would collapse, Kelsen admits. The origin unifies precisely by transcending the interrelation of contingent posited norms. The origin is invisible in the sense that it cannot be reached within the language of the structure. Being inaccessible through signs, the *Grundnorm* is unknowable.

The *Grundnorm* is an originary moment that takes on the very mystical traits of the postulated Creator of the material and moral world. However, the *Grundnorm* would not exist without the language it presupposes. And yet, the *Grundnorm* remains inaccessible to that language, Kelsen claims. Although the *Grundnorm* is a thought, the *Grundnorm* magnetically attracts all legal desires of officials who work through the language. In effect, the *Grundnorm* is inside and outside the language of the officials. In this respect, despite Kelsen's effort to differentiate the pure theory from the impure natural law theory, the *Grundnorm* functions much like the Author/Creator associated with Aquinas's interpretation of Aristotle. Without a will and therefore without an author, the *Grundnorm* acts as the first cause or source of all other norms. Both the Author/Creator and the *Grundnorm* transcend phenomenal experience. Both transcend the ideal realm of legal language.

4. The Invisible Origin of the Authority of Norms

Let me be more precise. Three factors work to give the *Grundnorm* an invisible character in the sense of being a linguistically unknowable first cause of pure practical reasoning.

First, whereas change and movement characterize the normative structure in that the retrospective search for an *arche* does not end with the acts of will of historical authors, Kelsen realizes that this process of interminable movement would continue

62 "The Notion of Basic Norms(s) in Jurisprudence," in *Scandanavian Studies in Law*, ed. Folke Schmidt, **19** (1975): 121-51, 136.

63 See generally, Ebenstein, *'The' Pure Theory 'of' Law* (New York: Augustus M. Kelley, 1945; Rothman reprint, 1969), 83.

unless there existed a basic norm that transcended the language of the officials. This basic norm, in contrast with ordinary legal norms, must remain fixed in order to function as an ultimate grounding of the whole structure of referents of the officials' statements. Otherwise, the syllogistic movement would not have an ending and, without an ending, the (re)production of one norm for a major and another for a minor premise would be incoherent. After all, the *Grundnorm* brings unity to the normative order. Rational coherence and unity necessitate only one *Grundnorm*, Kelsen adds. There must be one *Grundnorm*, situated external to the language of historical authors, in order to function as the engine of synthetic *a priori* reasoning.

The point bears repeating. If there were two or more basic norms, one would have to transcend them in order to find the one authorizing origin of the norms as a whole. A multiplicity of basic norms, which the legal expert would claim to 'know,' would lack the fixed singularity needed for a commonly shared norm.

Secondly, logical syllogistic reasoning works only if the general norm possesses a signification. That signification is drawn from the norm's relation to other general norms within the normative structure. But one cannot differentiate a *Grundnorm* from the familiar, differentiated norms. Indeed, there is a sense in which it lacks signification, first, in that it is silent vis-à-vis the differentiated norms that do have signification and, secondly, in that there is only *one Grundnorm*.

Why does it matter that a oneness characterizes the *Grundnorm*? An object, such as a legal doctrine, can be signified only if it is differentiated from another sign or group of signs. Being a single basic norm, it cannot be signified. If it were differentiated from another statement, it would no longer be basic because one becomes self-conscious through statements. The *Grundnorm* lacks signification until its agents begin to become self-conscious *about* the *Grundnorm*. At that moment, the *Grundnorm* becomes an ordinary norm. The signless *Grundnorm* also lacks an object to which it can refer. That very lack of a referent ensures that the *Grundnorm* finalizes the trace of norms.

Signless and referentless, the *Grundnorm* is invisible to the officials who work through the familiar signs of legal language. The *Grundnorm* is a thought norm, Kelsen reminds us again and again. A thought norm is not an *act* of thought. Thought norms "do not have a place in reality, but are thought or imagined as one can think or imagine anything possible which is not existent in the real," as Kelsen puts it in "On the Concept of Norm" (1965).[64] In a sense, considered as a single thought, the *Grundnorm* cannot be a norm in that a norm is a *Sollens*-sentence or 'ought' statement. The *Grundnorm* is an 'ought' thought abstracted from a chain of 'ought' sentences, rather than a *Sollens*-sentence itself, to use Kelsen's own terms.

64 Kelsen, "On the Concept of Norm," in *Essays*, 220.

Indeed, thirdly, Kelsen suggests that the final movement from the most fundamental constitutional norm to the *Grundnorm* is an act of faith. It is commonplace that a syllogism works only if the general norm in the first proposition is known. Until one reaches the justification of the final constitutional principle of the network of norms, an official works through a chain of 'ought' statements and their syllogisms. But the *Grundnorm* dwells external to statements in order to be a *Grundnorm*. As Kelsen writes in the *General Theory of Law and State*, "positive norms are valid only on one assertion: that there is a basic norm which establishes the supreme law-making authority. The validity of this basic norm is improved and must remain so within the sphere of positive law itself."[65] Indeed, I have drawn from Kelsen that the *Grundnorm* has to be formless and nameless. Accordingly, an abyss or untranslatable gap dwells between the inter-relations of ordinary norms and the *Grundnorm*. It would seem to be impossible for an official rationally to link the primary constitutional norms to the *Grundnorm* without a jump from the one to the other, from language to a thought without a language. A void lies between the two. The official must jump from ordinary norms to the *Grundnorm* as he or she proceeds to justify the *auctoritas* of norms. The jump must be taken as an article of faith. The article of faith rests upon the official's ability to reach a conclusion from a major premise (the *Grundnorm*), which is formless and nameless. That major premise, given on an act of faith, is applied to a minor premise (the constitutional norm).

Such an act of faith conditions the trace of authority by which the state is defined. Kelsen is not alone in this respect. In the same manner, for example, Aquinas describes the laws of nature as "indemonstrable." He says that they are intuitively known. Kelsen claims in like vein that the pure theory of positive law must ultimately rest upon an indemonstrable *Grundnorm*. Similarly, just as Aquinas privileges faith in his derivation of natural laws from divine laws, so too Kelsen relies upon faith in his claim that the final ordinary norms may be justified in terms of the formless, particularless and nameless *Grundnorm*. Language cannot fully express the identity of the *Grundnorm*: signs can only approximate or represent the *Grundnorm* and when the signs do so, they become ordinary norms for norms are statements in a language. Once expressed, the statement about the *Grundnorm* becomes one more ordinary norm which, in turn, presupposes a further *Grundnorm* in order that the interpretive enterprise be coherent. A norm-positing institution must act and an official must interpret as if a *Grundnorm* pre-existed legal language.

---

65 Kelsen, *General Theory of Law and State*, 395.

And yet, the origin of the 'pure' theory is invisible through legal language, through, that is, the chains of 'ought' statements. And, as such, the 'pure' theory is plagued by the very metaphysics that Kelsen attributes to natural law theory. The *Grundnorm* is inaccessible in that it is absent from the language of 'ought' statements. The inaccessibility of the *Grundnorm* renders it invisible. All juridical organs act in the name of the *Grundnorm,* although, in a sense, the *Grundnorm* is unnameable. With this unreachable *Grundnorm*, we have reached the end of the *Pure Theory*, both literally and figuratively. If Kelsen is correct, as I believe he is, that the *Pure Theory* represents the purest moment of analytical positivism, we have also reached the end (that is, the origin) of legal positivism.

The divinity of the *Grundnorm* stems from its mere possibility, dwelling on the other side of legal existence. Although Kant did not elaborate as sophisticated theory of language as Kelsen, Kant too described the pure will as such a mere possibility. In Kant's case, the pure will is absent from the phenomenal realm and even from the kingdom of ends, where human beings, acting with inclinations, possess duties or 'oughts' towards others. The *Grundnorm* transcends all contingent acts of the founding authors of a particular constitution. Moreover, constituting an origin to legal reasoning, the *Grundnorm* itself does not refer to any further referent. Further, the *Grundnorm* lacks any third term to connect the author of a statement about the *Grundnorm* to the predicate in the statement. Lacking a third term, the *Grundnorm* is just a thought or form without particulars and without a sign to signify the thought. The invisible boundaries of the thought enclose all norms as predicates without any intervention to a further particular. Since the *Grundnorm* is a form without particulars or signs to represent the particulars, the *Grundnorm* lacks an identity or content. In addition, Kelsen notes, the presupposition of a basic norm contradicts legal reality to the extent that that reality is drawn from acts of cognition about an object expressed through statements about an act of will.[66] Such a presupposed basic norm does not function epistemologically in terms of the signification about a prior act of will. Moreover, the *Grundnorm* contradicts itself since it must issue from an authority beyond "a supreme moral or legal authority": "it represents the authorization of a supreme moral or legal authority, and hence it issues from an authority lying beyond that authority, even though the further authority is merely figmentary."

Kelsen admits to the transcendental character of the *Grundnorm*. Kelsen admits too that the *Grundnorm* must, to all intents and purposes, be accepted as an act of faith. Without the faith in the possibility of some final grounding that transcends the language of posited norms, officials cannot retrospectively situate a norm in *Sollens*-sentences as if the latter were the only matter that existed. Indeed, Kelsen

66 Kelsen, "The Function of a Constitution," 117.

describes as a "legal miracle" the view that an absolute state can create a legal structure and then be bound by the created legal structure. Kelsen too has his own "legal miracle." Kelsen builds into his own pure theory a legally unintelligible source that makes legal norms intelligible. One requires a faith that there is an origin on the other side of legal language.

In sum, the absence of the *Grundnorm* from the norms or "ought" statements, the unsignified and unsignifiable character of the *Grundnorm*, the relation of the *Grundnorm* as an inaccessible first cause of legal reasoning, and the act of faith which makes the *Grundnorm* a possibility, but not a part of legal existence. These four factors suggest that authoritative norms presuppose an invisible origin after all.

When he presses his argument, Kelsen admits to the possibility of an invisiblity of the *Grundnorm*. At one point in *General Theory of Law and State*, for example, Kelsen describes the trace of norms to one ultimate norm that cannot be humanly posited. Such an ultimate norm may only be presupposed.[67] Here, he likens the *Grundnorm* of a chain of norms to the presupposed belief in God and in the authorities that He institutes in a religious structure. In another example, in the *Pure Theory*, Kelsen traces the authority of a norm to the point that "[i]t looks as if one could give as a reason for the validity of a norm the circumstance that it was established by an authority, human or divine."[68] When he asks himself a few pages later whether the inaccessibility of the *Grundnorm* renders Kelsen's theory a natural law theory, he infers that God possesses a similar character: "if we ask for the reason of the historically first constitution, then the answer can only be (if we leave aside God or 'nature') that the validity of this constitution – the assumption that it is a binding norm – must be *presupposed*."[69] A few pages later, Kelsen compares the reasoning that necessitates the presupposition of a *Grundnorm* in legal reasoning to the syllogistic reasoning of a religious command: "one ought to obey God's commands. God has commanded to obey the commands of the parents. Hence, one ought to obey the commands of the parents."[70]

Kelsen is at a loss to differentiate the invisible origin of a religious theory from the invisible origin of legal positivist theory. He can only insist that "but the difference between the two [positivist and natural law theory] is large enough to exclude the view (which ignores this difference) that the positivistic theory of a basic norm, as advanced by the pure Theory of Law, is a theory of natural law."[71] Kelsen's theory of a *Grundnorm* cannot explain what it is about a *Grundnorm* that

---

67 Kelsen, *General Theory of Law and State*, 115-16.
68 Kelsen, *Pure Theory*, 193.
69 Kelsen, *Pure Theory*, 200.
70 Kelsen, *Pure Theory*, 202.
71 Kelsen, *Pure Theory*, 219.

differentiates a legal from a religious structure. Indeed, he describes the religious structure on various occasions as "normative."

Kelsen cannot differentiate the two because the *Grundnorm* of a legal structure shares the same invisibility as the *Grundnorm* of a religious structure. First, the *Grundnorm* of both the legal and the religious structure shares an invisibility, the very invisibility that Kelsen attributes to the divinity of the Judaeo-Christian Author. Secondly, the *Grundnorm* is the concealed centre of the self-referring chain of "ought" statements. The structure, legal or religious, precedes the *Grundnorm*. Without the coercive binding structure, there would be no *Grundnorm*. When Kelsen follows his line of reasoning about the presupposed *Grundnorm* in the *Pure Theory*, he finds it necessary to conclude that "one might describe the difference between a positivistic theory of law and a theory of natural law as relative rather than absolute."[72] For both legal positivism and natural law theory, he admits, have faith in the possibility of the *Grundnorm*. The *Grundnorm* is not posited as existing in either legal positivist or natural law theory. Kelsen describes his theory of law as positivist in that laws begin with the human being's conferral of meaning into the authored acts of will of an historically contingent institution (or "organ"). And yet, Kelsen claims in the *Pure Theory* that norms are authoritative if they can be rationally traced to an authorizing origin or *arche* point that is particularless (and therefore, lacks content) and unsignifiable through a language.[73]

The *Grundnorm* is a figment of the *imagination* of legal officials, Kelsen suggests. Despite its emptiness and its very alien character to a chain of norms, the *Grundnorm* just must 'exist' as an 'ought,' as a fiction in isolation from language. Without a foreign and contentless *Grundnorm*, humanly willed norms could not possess an *auctoritas*. Legal officials must imagine the *Grundnorm* when they reconstruct the structure of norms. Kelsen describes the *Grundnorm* as imaginary: the *Grundnorm* is "an imaginary authority whose (figmentary) act of will has the basic norm as its meaning."[74] He continues, the *Grundnorm* is "a genuine fiction." But the fictive character of such a crucial component of a legal structure, it would seem, contradicts the 'existence' of norms. The authorizing origin contradicts reality "since no such norm exists as the meaning of an actual act of will." Moreover, the fiction contains a contradiction within itself. How so? The idea of a *Grundnorm* contradicts itself because, as explained in the previous section, the *Grundnorm* functions as the authorizing origin of the sovereign structure of norms (that is, the hidden structure of cognitive referents or doctrines signified by the "ought" statements) even though it remains external to the structure and

72 Ibid., 219.
73 See Kelsen, "The Function of a Constitution" (1964).
74 Ibid., 117.

"figmentary" at that. Though the authorizing origin of the trace of norms, the *Grundnorm* is an intellectually constructed phantom without a sign with which it can be represented and without particulars with which it can possess an identity. The *Grundnorm* is a radical other to legal existence.

The invisiblity of the 'pure theory of law,' then, adds an alien, yet necessary, character to humanly willed norms.[75] Kelsen admits that such an alien element may make any legal theory impure in the sense that a pure theory should preclude all foreign elements to the cognition of willed norms.[76] As he writes on the first page of the *Pure Theory*, the 'pure theory' aims "to free the science of law from alien elements."[77] Yet, the *Grundnorm* is precisely just such an alien element and it must remain alien for the structure of norms to remain rationally cohesive, unified, and a totality. Unlike ordinary norms, the *Grundnorm* is a thought. So long as one does not question the origin of a legal norm, the origin is presupposed and the structure of cognitive objects remains intact and cohesive. The *Grundnorm* lacks a referent, a third element, a will, or even a further presupposition. If the *Grundnorm* were not presupposed, the interconnection of norms would lack finality. Flux would replace the fixity of a posited norm. Norms derive their validity from an origin that transcends all acts of will. The origin dwells external to the structure of norms. Thus, the 'pure' theory of law hangs upon an impurity for its own *auctoritas*.

Though signifying no further object, the *Grundnorm* still magnetically attracts, invites, and seduces all legal reasoning to the *Grundnorm*. The *Grundnorm* is an excess of the structure. The *Grundnorm* cannot be accessed through language. It cannot even be thought in the sense that thought involves a self-consciousness. The *Grundnorm* cannot even be represented in legal discourse because it is presupposed. Once an official becomes conscious of the *Grundnorm* by articulating a sign to represent it as an 'ought' statement, what has been presupposed as a *Grundnorm* is no longer a *Grundnorm*, but a representation of an unrecognizable or signless no-thing. This helps to explain why Kelsen does not need a founding Author/Creator as the further grounding of the *Grundnorm*. Yet, posited laws meet their limit in a *Grundnorm,* which itself is not posited law. In this, the *Grundnorm* approximates the invisible hand of the invisible Author of natural law theory.

Embedded in a grand Tradition of an impersonal *actoritas* which, in Chapter Two, I attributed to the Romans, the 'pure' theory of law takes for granted the

75 Roberto Vernengo points out in this regard that Joseph Raz errs in his re-reading of Kelsen. Raz interprets Keslen so as to support Raz's theory of the historically contingent character of the grounding of legal authority. Vernengo rightly emphasizes the *transcendental* character of the *Grundnorm*. See Vernengo, "Kelsen's *Rechtssatze* as Detached Statements," in *Essays on Kelsen*, 99-108, 103-05.

76 "The Pure Theory and Analytical Jurisprudence," in *What is Justice?*, 266-87, 266.

77 Kelsen, *Pure Theory*, 1.

association of *auctoritas* with some originary moment when legal history begins. That originary moment, Kelsen writes, is presupposed in any structure. Though presupposed, the authorizing origins is invisible from within the language of 'ought' statements. Indeed, the legal structure lacks any one sign to signify the *Grundnorm*. Without a sign, the *Grundnorm* cannot be represented as can an ordinary norm.

The point bears repreating: the 'pure' theory of law is plagued by the same metaphysics and religious mysticism that Kelsen had attributed to his strawperson, natural law theory. Only, in Kelsen's case, the mysticism is paradoxical because of Kelsen's claim that authoritative laws are the consequence of a human constitution of meaning and that the *Grundnorm* is presupposed as emanating from within the 'ought' statements rather than from some one originary source. Four factors make for the divinity of the *Grundnorm*: the absence of the *Grundnorm* from humanly willed norms; the inaccessibility of the *Grundnorm* to the representations of 'ought' statements; the transcendental character of the *Grundnorm* as the first cause of legal reasoning; and the leap of faith that is necessary to jump from the most basic constitutional norms to the *Grundnorm*. The *Grundnorm* is believed to be present, yet its presence is always beyond the significatory grasp of the legal official. All officials interpret as if the *Grundnorm* existed. Yet, the officials can never regain a presence with the *Grundnorm*. For the authorizing origin of the modern legal structure remains invisible. And with the invisible *Grundnorm*, one finally reaches the end of the purest moment of the tradition of legal positivism.

8

The Forgotten Origin: H.L.A. Hart's Sense of the Pre-Legal

The classic canons of the tradition of legal positivism suggest that officials forget that the authorizing origin of humanly posited laws is inaccessible to the language of humanly posited laws. The problematic of this tradition, then, has been to postulate an authorizing origin to humanly posited norms/rules, but the origin, to be an origin, must differ from the character of humanly authored laws. The origin must be external to what officials take as legal existence. Hart was more open than his predecessors were about the externality of the origin. He certainly was more conscious of the importance of the externality of the origin than are his supporters today. Indeed, there is a sense in which his commentators have unknowingly worked to conceal the externality of the origin. The objective of this chapter is to elaborate the nature of the forgotten origin and, as a consequence, to question the viability of important claims attributed to legal positivism.

Hart elaborates two types of rules: primary and secondary rules. Previous legal theory had been marked by its failure to take account of the importance of rules, according to Hart. Legal theory had focussed upon orders, obedience, habits, and threats. His introduction of primary and secondary rules, he believed, overcame problems that earlier theories of law had faced.

Primary rules require human beings to act or to abstain from acting in a certain manner. These primary rules impose duties. Both criminal law and civil liability arise from primary rules. Secondary rules provide conditions under which certain institutions and officials possess the authority to enact, adjudicate, administer, or enforce the primary rules. The secondary rules depend upon the primary rules in that the secondary rules articulate what had hitherto been the unwritten practices that primary rules assumed. Foremost among the secondary rules, according to Hart, are the rules of recognition. As an example, special rules of recognition define 'what is a *parliament*' and 'what is an *enactment* of a parliament' Other secondary rules are "rules of adjudication" and "rules of change." These constitutional rules must be taken for granted or consciously addressed before primary rules can be considered authorized. The primary rules recognize the secondary rules as authoritative. The "union" of primary and secondary rules is at the "centre" of a modern legal structure.

When commentators have examined the authorizing origin of primary laws, according to Hart, they have focussed upon the nature of secondary rules. Rules of recognition provide authoritative criteria for identifying primary rules of obligation. A law exists if one can trace the grounds of one primary rule to another primary rule and, ultimately, to a rule of recognition. A rule of recognition identifies what primary rules are authoritative and what primary rules are not. Hart's commentators believe that Hart intended to consider the rule of recognition as an issue of descriptive sociology. At one point, Hart writes that the rule of recognition or the network of rules of recognition constitute the sovereign of a state. Here, he believes that he has departed from traditional analytic legal theory or, at least, from the theory of John Austin and Jeremy Bentham in that they had associated sovereignty with the commands of an historically identifiable author, such as parliament, which the bulk of the people habitually obeyed.

1. The Rule of Recognition

Now, the key to the recent commentaries about Hart is the claim that, in seeking an *arche*-point for the authority of a modern legal structure, the origin of the legal structure lies with a rule, the rule of recognition. Accepting the rule of recognition as the starting point of authority, they have only asked whether the rule includes or excludes non-legal considerations.

One of Hart's early critics, Ronald Dworkin, asked whether the rule of recognition was a social rule. Dworkin defined a social rule as the "reporting" of a rule of social behaviour.[1] What is critical to appreciate at this point is Dworkin's interpretation of Hart's theory of law as privileging an originating *rule* that justifies all primary rules. Social rules can be empirically observed, according to Dworkin. The social rules arrive in the legal enterprise first; the primary rules after the social rules. The social rules are "facts" that Hart accepts as 'givens,' according to Dworkin. Argument is unnecessary to validate such social facts. The givenness of rules of social behaviour can be "reported." The social rules suggest to one that he or she 'ought' to follow a practice or behaviour. Further, according to Dworkin's interpretation of Hart, there is no legal phenomenon prior to the 'givenness' of the social fact. It is this behaviouralism and the accompanying positivism of social rules that Dworkin finds most objectionable about Hart's theory of law. For Dworkin,[2] the issue in his early essays – the essays that most poignantly

1 Ronald Dworkin, "Model of Rules 1" and "Model of Rules 11," in *Taking Rights Seriously* (London: Harvard University Press, 1977), 14-45, 46-80.

2 Ronald Dworkin, "Is Law a System of Rules?" in ed. Ronald Dworkin, *The Philosophy of Law* (Oxford: Oxford University Press, 1977), 38-65, at 64-5; *Law's Empire* (Cambridge: Harvard University Press, 1986).

address Hart – is whether moral-political principles, which argue in a direction, should be considered the authorizing origins of the rule of recognition. Dworkin contrasts such principles with rules that apply in an all-or-nothing fashion. Principles are justificatory arguments, and they contrast with the social facticity that Dworkin claims of Hart's concept of law. The important point, for our purposes, is that Dworkin reads Hart as grounding legal authority in the rule of recognition and that Dworkin then categorizes Hart's theory as exemplifying a positivism that accepts a rule about an empirically verifiable social behaviour as the rule of recognition.

Joseph Raz and Jules Coleman continue this inquiry. Joseph Raz has supported social facticity in the form of given legal institutions as the authorizing origin of a legal structure.[3] Both Raz and Coleman have insisted that the rule of recognition incorporates moral or non-legal arguments about right conduct.[4] Coleman has asked whether the rule of recognition, of necessity, incorporates a judicial practice of appealing to reasons for judicial decisions and reasons for criticizing judges for not doing so.[5] Like Coleman, Neil MacCormick, has suggested that the rule of recognition incorporates moral or prescriptive claims.[6]

Other commentators have also centred their analyses of Hart's work about the rule of recognition.[7] The legal structure is said to begin and end with primary and secondary rules which, Hart himself admits, constitute the heart of the concept of law. Having ascertained that the rule of recognition founds a legal system,

3 See, e.g., Joseph Raz, "Legal Principles and the Limits of Law," *Yale Law Journal* **81** (1972): 823-54.

4 Jules Coleman, "Authority and Reason," in ed. Robert George, *The Authority of Law: Essays on Legal Positivism* (Oxford: Clarendon,) 287-319, 294; Coleman, "Rules and Social Facts," *Harvard Journal of Law and Public Policy* **14** (1991): 703-25; and Jeffrie G. Murphy and Coleman, *Philosophy of Law: An Introduction to Jurisprudence* (Boulder: Westview, 1990), 22-5. Murphy and Coleman go so far as to suggest that even the non-legal or pre-legal world contains primary rules. Ibid., 28. Coleman's essays are preoccupied with the rule of recognition and whether it includes or excludes morality. That the rule of recognition is the authorizing origins of the legal structure, albeit as a rule rationally constructed from "convergent social practices," there is no doubt for Coleman. The rule of recognition is a social rule, which Coleman defines as "a convergent social practice and a shared critical or reflective attitude towards the practice."

5 Jules Coleman, "Authority and Reason" in ed. Robert P. George, *The Autonomy of Law*, 287-319. Also see my comments about Coleman's essays in the Introduction.

6 Neil MacCormick, "Natural Law and the Separation of Law and Morals," in ed. Robert P. George, *Natural Law Theory: Contemporary Essays* (Oxford: Oxford University Press, 1992), 105-33.

7 For earlier essays accepting the rule of recognition as the authorizing origin of the concept of law, see, e.g., Robert S. Summers, "Professor H.L.A. Hart's Concept of Law," *Duke Law Journal* (1963): 629-60, at 632-45, and Norman E. Bowie, "The 'War' between Natural Law Philosophy and Legal Positivism," *Idealistic Studies*, 145-55. For a more recent series of essays which examine the nature of the rule of recognition and whether a constitution is grounded in a rule of recognition, see Michelman, "Constitutional Authorship," in ed. Larry Alexander, *Constitutionalism: Philosophical Foundations* (Cambridge: Cambridge University Press, 1998), 64-98; Michael Perry, "What is 'the Constitution'? (and Other Fundamental Questions)," in *Constitutionalism*, 99-151; and Jeremy Waldron, "precommitment and Disagreement" in *Constitutionalism*, 271-99.

commentators have asked questions like the following: How do we identify what is an authoritative rule?, What is the content of the rule?, Does the rule include principles as well as rules? Social conventions?, Does the rule include morality?, Can a primary rule be logically derived from a rule of recognition?, Can the rule of recognition be actually applied to particular circumstances? One critical issue, for example, has been whether there is one rule of recognition, several rules, several rules with one master rule, or several master rules?[8] Joseph Raz has suggested, for example, that several rules of recognition are connected to the legal structure. Another series of theorists have claimed that the rule of recognition need not be authored in a basic text, but rather, as Kent Greenawalt and Neil MacCormick claim, that it is grounded in custom and that custom includes more than rules.

Despite their differences, though, these legal theorists and others[9] have shared several claims that take the locus of the grounding of modern legal theory in humanly authored rules – whether primary rules or secondary rules – for granted. In particular, first, they claim that the authorizing origin of humanly posited rules/norms must pre-exist the primary rules. I have argued in earlier chapters that Hobbes, Rousseau, Bentham, Austin, and Kelsen make this claim. If the origin does not pre-exist the primary rules, how may one claim that the primary rules are authorized by the origin? If the ultimate justificatory origin does not pre-exist the primary rules, how may one say that the primary rules are even grounded? Indeed, how may one say that they are posited? Sometimes, this claim about the prior existence of an origin is identified with the concept of the 'rule of law.' Indeed, Hart's commentators have been preoccupied with the rule of recognition precisely because of its importance in granting authority to enact and enforce primary rules or, conversely, because officials derive the authority of a primary rule from the logically prior criterion of authority represented by the rule of recognition.[10]

---

8 Kent Greenawalt, "Hart's Rule of Recognition and the United States," *Ratio Juris* 1 (1988): 40-57; Joseph Raz, *The Authority of Law* (Oxford: Oxford University Press, 1979), and *The Morality of Freedom* (Oxford: Oxford University Press, 1986). Also see Jules Coleman, "Second Thoughts and Other First Impressions," in ed. Brian Bix, *Analyzing Law* (Oxford: Clarendon, 1998): 257-322, 261.

9 See, e.g., Roger A. Shiner, *Norm and Nature: The Movements of Legal Thought* (Oxford: Oxford University Press, 1992).

10 See, e.g., Neil MacCormick and Ota Weinberger, *An Institutional Theory of Law: New Approaches to Legal Positivism* (Dordrecht: D. Reidel, 1986), 132, where they argue that there must be some values that ground emotive preferences. Even preferences need to be grounded in a theory of law. In his *H.L.A. Hart* (London: Edward Arnold, 1981), 119, MacCormick argues that one can bring in customary rules as part of the rule of recognition or constitutive of it "provided we avoid the view that judges *cannot* pre-exist a power-conferring rule of adjudication, provided we accept that the judicial role depends on the concept of "duty" not on that of "power."

The tradition of legal positivism – again, what I have called *the* Tradition – has shared a second claim: namely, that the origin is postulated by the officials.[11] As a postulate, the officials construct the origin. The origin, that is, is not a self-mover, as it was with Aristotle, Augustine and Aquinas. Hart shares this theme of legal positivism.[12] Each of Hart's commentators insists that if one accepted that the authorizing origin of posited rules/norms ultimately rested in an inaccessible source that proscribed the content of the rules/norms, then such a view should properly be considered a natural law theory, not a theory of legal positivism. Natural law theory claims a transcendental source or *arche* to authoritative humanly posited rules. To be authoritative, humanly authored rules must conform with the universal standards that transcend the humanly authored rules. Natural law theory failed to appreciate the importance of the distinction between an exteriority and interiority to binding laws, according to Hart.

Hart and Hart's interpreters have made a third claim: namely, that officials signify the authorizing origin through a written language and that the written language excludes the experiential meanings (what interpreters have described as "preferences," "anthropological," "emotive," and the like) which the official brings *into* the written language. John Austin was preoccupied with justicible rules. Only written rules were justicible. The rules had to be posited by distinct institutional authors who could be located on a pyramid of official authors. Bentham and Austin understood the historical author as the authorizing origin of such a language. A legislature or a court posited rules in a particular time and place. The rule was promulgated in an official act. Here, Hart falls back upon Austin's privileging of the historical author: a legal obligation only arises in a statement that has been consciously *authored*. That is, only writing is legally binding. For Hart, customs are unauthored and, as such, they cannot be considered rules of legal obligation when an official works through primary rules.[13]

But Hart also relies upon Kelsen. What is important here is not the author's will but the statements within which that will is immersed and from which the will is signified. The signification of the will is more important than the act of will itself. So, a legislative or judicial author's expression of its will does not end one's analysis of legal language. Even when one of Hart's sympathetic commentators, such as Kent Greenawalt, has described the rules of recognition as conventional, he has embarked upon the project of identifying the nature and situs

11 See, e.g., MacCormick and Weinberger, *Institutional Theory* 4, 129. Kent Greenawalt, "Too Thin and Too Rich: Distinguishing Features of Legal Positivism," in ed. Robert P. George, *The Autonomy of Law: Essays on Legal Positivism* (Oxford: Oxford University Press, 1996): 1-29, 2.

12 H.L.A. Hart, *The Concept of Law* (Oxford: Clarendon Press, 1961; 1994, 2nd ed.), 185-86.

13 Ibid., 230.

of the rules of recognition in writing.[14] As Hart puts it, "the enactment of a law, like the giving of an order, *is* a deliberative *datable* act."[15] The commentators have presupposed that the origin of humanly posited rules/norms is *accessible* to the legal officials through a written language. They have understood the origin to be the rule of recognition.[16] They have addressed whether the rule of recognition is a mere procedural or 'pedigree' requirement or whether it includes the substantive moral-political values. But such theorists have been more or less satisfied with the claim that a rule of recognition can, without difficulty, recognize an unwritten convention or behaviour or 'social fact' as a rule, a point elaborated below. Associating 'understanding' with the assimilation of pure categories, it is not surprising that contemporary analytical jurisprudence would postulate the possibility of such a rational recognition.

But once one appreciates that signs represent or signify such cognitive objects as doctrines, rules, principles, and other standards, the conventionality thesis is problematic. Hart himself privileged such founding social conventions as "unspoken." A rule of recognition, however, is expressed in what he earlier called "thought statements."[17] And the rule of recognition, not the unspoken and unwritten conventions, is said to ground the authority of the primary rules. The rule of recognition seals the legal structure so as to make the trace of the authority of one rule from another rationally cohesive. Legal writing, in the form of primary and secondary rules, constitutes the concept of law. The authority of a legal rule may only be traced to the writing of institutional authors. The ultimate written rule takes the form of a rule of recognition.

As Jules Coleman remarks, it is the legal community's 'understanding' *of a rule*, not the originating social behaviour that the rule recognizes, that determines the scope and content of justicible laws.[18] A critical reflection, or what Coleman calls 'understanding,' crystallizes into writing. Only writing, not the behaviour that the writing signifies, is justicible. After all, how could officials speak and write about the unspoken except through their familiar signs, which represent posited rules/norms? As Hart himself wrote, the legal language, signified in a rule of recognition, may only "approximate" the unspoken social conventions. The unspoken remains *outside* the justiciable rules. The unspoken is "pre-legal." The event of writing itself, in this context, connotes a modern civil society. Written rules – primary and secondary – constitute legal existence. So, Jules Coleman,

---

14 See Greenawalt, "The Rule of Recognition and the Constitution," *Columbia Law Review* **85** (1987): 621-71.

15 Hart, *The Concept of Law*, 44. Emphasis added.

16 For Raz, there may be several rules of recognition.

17 See, e.g., Hart, "Signs and Words" (reviewing J. Holloway, *Language and Intelligence*), *Philosophical Quarterly* **2** (1952): 59-62.

18 Coleman, "Truth and Objectivity in Law," *Legal Theory* **1** (1995): 33-68, 65.

Neil MacCormick, and others rightly acknowledge that an official cannot help but incorporate substantive moral-political 'oughts' into the content of a rule that officials recognize as legally binding. These 'oughts' go to the 'manner and form' requirements that define 'what is a parliament' and 'what is an enactment of parliament.' Or they may go to the substantive content of the primary rules, such as the primary rule that 'all rules will respect free speech.' In either case, the 'oughts' establish minimal procedures and substantive content for the creation, modification, and annulment of primary rules. But once such a criterion of membership in legal existence includes unspoken conventions, legal positivism still claims that there must be at least one logically possible legal structure where moral value or moral worth is not a condition of legal authority.[19] That is, there must be a logically possible series of posited norms/rules that is not grounded in non-law.

Once one begins legal analysis with the articulated rule of recognition, rather than with an unexpressed convention that the rule signifies, it is possible to speculate that there is an objectively determinate answer to any particular legal issue and that such an answer is grounded in a system of rules independent of morality. In this manner, a system of cognitively produced rules/norms is self-referring. A judge and lawyer must remain content that all legal analysis begins with written texts. A "critical reflective reason" may characterize the legal analysis of the rules/norms. The conventions, being *pre*-scriptive, are "pre-legal," to use Hart's term, or "primitive," to use Kelsen's and Raz's, or "savage" to use Hobbes's. The pre-legal, inaccessible through the language of the justicible rules, can be easily forgotten. After all, the pre-legal is non-existent since it is located in a world of non-law. The pre-legal is untrue since truth begins with (legal) existence (that is, with inscribed rules/norms). Being untrue, the authorizing origin of the rule of recognition may be invisible. Faith alone permits us to believe that the origin exists as a social convention despite the fact that the content of rules/norms may include non-law. The identity of the members of legal existence is a separate issue from 'why is a rule authoritative?' Once we differentiate legal doctrines from some realm that lacks familiar signs, the latter realm is inaccessible to the legal language and the conventionality thesis becomes problematic.

I wish to argue that Hart postulates that when one appreciates his theory of legal language, there is an origin of the origins: that is, there is an authorizing origin of the rule of recognition itself. The rule of recognition is only what Hart describes as an "external *statement*" which re-presents the origin of the origins. The origin of the origins is the immediacy or presence or bonding which an official experiences vis-à-vis a habit or practice. Hart excludes such an origin of the

19 Coleman, "Second Thoughts and Other First Impressions," in ed. Brian Bix, *Analyzing Law* (Oxford: Clarendon Press, 1998), 257-322, 266.

origins from the legal. The modern legal structure begins and ends with a written language and, Hart claims, excludes the immediacy by which the official bonds with a social practice. In the project of forgetting the authorizing origin of the concept of law, Hart undermines the three claims that his commentators (and, on occasion, he himself) have made about legal positivism. Indeed, juridical officials, for Hart, forget that they had forgotten the originary moment of bonding from which officials had elaborated secondary and primary rules. Indeed, to the extent that they recognize the importance of the originary moment, they reject it as pre-legal. The officials proceed to assume that the written language of statutes, precedents, regulations, and the like constitute the whole of legal language and exclude the experiential meanings that the officials bring into writing. All that matters are the written statements about primary and secondary rules. And statements are written if they have been authored by a distinct and assignable author. As a consequence, the unwritten origin remains forgotten in the concept of law of a modern state.

2. The Immediacy and the Statement

Let there be no mistake. The officials who ground the primary and secondary rules, according to Hart, forget about the logically, chronologically, and phenomenologically prior moment of immediacy or bonding that they experience as they signify primary rules in statements. The officials experience the immediacy. They experience the immediacy through their bodies, not their minds. Is such a felt experience of immediacy what Hart calls an "internal statement"? No. An internal statement is a statement. Hart excludes a felt experience from statements. A moment of immediacy differs from an internal point of view when one's statement manifests an internal sense of obligation towards a primary rule. The moment of immediacy is "unstated." The feeling of bonding lacks reflection and deliberation. An official intuits when he or she feels a bonding with an object or with another official. Hart excludes such a felt experience from what he considers language. Language re-presents (or represents) the felt experience. Language takes on a *written* character. Writing recognizes the signified felt experience. A metaphysical barrier demarcates the felt experience from the legal writing. The subject and object are fused in the moment of immediacy: "[v]ery often when a person accepts a rule as binding and as something he and others are not free to change, he may see what it requires ... quite *intuitively*, and do that *without first thinking* of the rule and what it requires."[20] The moment of immediacy involves "a *direct* response to the situation" before one speaks or writes. Such a direct response is

20 Ibid., 140. Emphasis added.

"*unmediated* by calculation in terms of rules." A signification or statement retrospectively intellectualizes *about* the moment of bonding, according to Hart. In a sense, the moment of immediacy is pure, raw, perhaps natural. It is uncontaminated with the legal officials' signifying representations and their reflection and deliberation about such representations.

Legal obligation arrives on the scene, according to Hart, when the immediate experience is signified with "a characteristic vocabulary."[21] Such a signification "manifest[s]" one's own "acceptance of them as guiding rules" from an "internal point of view." The signification re-presents "an attitude."As Hart put it at an early point of his argument in the *Concept of Law*, this signification in a characteristic vocabulary "is not itself the crucial step: what is crucial is the acknowledgement of reference to the writing or inscription as *authoritative*, i.e., as the *proper* way of disposing of doubts as to the existence of the rule."[22] The acknowledgement comes when an official recognizes the writing as binding from an "external point of view." With that external recognition through "marks," a criterion of authority take hold. A legal obligation is said to exist. The recognition from an external point of view allows for the possibility of a unifying coherence to the fragmentary internal statements.

3. Examples of Hart's Distinction between Immediacy and Legal Statements

a) *The pre-legal and the legal*

Hart writes that the moment of immediacy, before being signified in speech and writing, characterizes "primitive" or "pre-legal" communities.[23] Here, a small community is bonded together by "kinship, common sentiment, and belief" in a stable environment of "unofficial rules."[24] Such a pre-legal bond lacks a "system," according to Hart. Yet, members of the pre-legal community, like Antigone or members of the early Greek or Amerindian tribes, feel compelled to follow the un-authored customs with which they are at one. Precisely because the writing about primary and secondary rules is authored, Hart claims in his chapter on "Laws and Morals," one "voluntarily" accepts legal rules in a modern legal structure. Such a voluntariness marks legal positivism, natural laws being unwritten in the conscience or heart of human beings. The voluntariness suggests a conscious posit

21 Ibid., 102-3.
22 Ibid., 95.
23 Ibid., 92.
24 Ibid., 92.

of a rule by a human official. The official consciously and voluntarily writes down the primary rule in the medium of a statute or judicial precedent.

In contrast, in a "pre-legal" community, one "involuntarily" accepts customs as un-authored.[25] The customs are not consciously and voluntarily posited. They are not the subject of deliberation unless they are explicitly incorporated into a written rule in which case they are posited in a conscious and voluntary manner. This involuntary bonding moment, according to Hart, pre-exists the later moment of signification when an official authors an authoritative rule/norm through official writing. The authors of the writing posit primary and secondary rules.

Throughout his formidable classic, *The Concept of Law*, Hart consciously distinguishes between the moment of immediacy or the "pre-legal" on the one hand and the signification moment or the 'legal' on the other. This distinction between the pre-legal and the legal is crucial for an understanding of Hart's arguments.

In a simple legal system, he says, both moral and legal rules join together into the moment of bondedness. In a modern legal structure, though, such a primitive sense of authority manifests a "pre-legal" set of practices.[26] In the later chapter entitled "Justice and Morality," Hart states that legal rules harden into rules of obligation when they are "identifie[d] through the official system" so as to mark "the step from the pre-legal into the legal world."[27] At that moment of transition, many socially and morally accepted rules are rejected as external to the structure of primary and secondary rules. Such social and moral rules are absent from the legal. Pre-legal, social/moral rules may be phrased with similar vocabulary. They may partially overlap with legal rules. But only the legal rules that officials recognize through a written language, count as law, according to Hart. The demarcation of the authoritative from the origin, an absent, external moment of immediacy, is arbitrary.

Signification is the critical characteristic of a modern legal structure, one which natural law theory fails to appreciate according to Hart.[28] For the separation of the pre-legal from the legal differentiates authoritative rules (both primary and secondary) from an origin that never existed until the primary and secondary rules were authored by officials in writing, and then only in terms of a very special

25 Ibid., 201.

26 Hart distinguishes between Rex I, the absolute monarch, and Rex II, the son of Rex I. As for Rex II, "there is nothing to make him sovereign from the start. Only after we know that his orders have been obeyed for some time shall we be able to say that a habit of obedience has been established. Then, but not till then, we shall be able to say of any further order that it is already law as soon as it is issued and before it is obeyed. Till this stage is reached, there will be an *interregnum* in which no law can be made." Hart, *Concept of Law*, 53. Emphasis added.

27 Ibid., 170.

28 Ibid., 186.

understanding of writing that excised the moment of bonding as external to the language. The official can never retrieve or return to the presence that characterized the bonding. The statements can only signify or re-present the moment of immediacy through writing. Legal writing is a second order or meta-language. This second-order character of legal language, not unlike the act of representation, which Kelsen attributed to "the legal act," explains why Hart expels the moment of immediacy as simply "pre-legal." All primary and secondary rules, believed to be impure in that they can merely approximate or re-present or mediate the authorizing origin embedded in the unwritten moment of immediacy, ironically recognize the pure origin as only 'existing' at the very moment that the origin is signified. The impure (the written signification) supplements what the official takes as the former moment of purity, the immediate felt experience of bonding. But because the impure recognizes the pure through writing, the supplement supplements the supplement. The officials, on Hart's analysis, construct the authorizing origin of the system of primary and secondary rules. The writing supplements the pre-language (or pre-written felt-experience). Yet the officials take the supplementary as the primary: namely, the primary and secondary rules inscribed in statements. The officials thereby internalize their own conditions of authority. In effect, to Austin's, Kelsen's, and Hart's question 'what is legal existence?' there is no pre-legal moment of immediacy. The structure of primary and secondary rules excludes the felt experience of bonding as legally binding. Tribal communities had once incorporated such a bonding into the law of a tribal community. Legal officials admittedly share such felt experiences. But such experiences of bonding are a radical other to binding primary and secondary rules. Yet, despite the exclusion of the felt experience from legal existence, this radical other is necessary for the very authority of the secondary and primary rules. This pre-legal, the radical other to the primary and secondary rules, is necessary for the rules to acquire an identity.

b) Hart and Kelsen

In this respect, Hart reads Kelsen's theory of law as inadequate in that Kelsen, he says, incorporated the experiential (what Hart calls "the psychological") element into the meaning of an 'ought' statement or norm. Hart excises the psychological as a motive or belief, which he assigns to the pre-legal. Hart interprets Kelsen's theory as a psychological theory[29] rather than as a theory of meaning.[30] Having so interpreted Kelsen, Hart excludes Kelsen's theory of the conferral of meaning as a psychological element and, therefore, associated with the pre-legal. Hart seems

29 Hart, "Kelsen Visited," in *Essays in Jurisprudence and Philosophy*, 286-308, at 304-05.
30 Ibid., 290.

to miss that Kelsen is really offering a phenomenological description of the constitution or conferral of meaning into an 'ought' statement by an interpreter. Categorizing Kelsen's theory as a psychological theory, Hart is "puzzled" that Kelsen would describe the pure theory as a descriptive account of 'ought' statements.

Directing his attention to Kelsen's theory as "a psychology," Hart also misses the cognitive experience in Kelsen's theory of meaning. In Kelsen's view, legal meaning is an *act* whereby the interpreter reads a *cognitive* object into an 'ought' statement. This conferral of meaning, not the legislative posit of a rule, is the legal act, according to Kelsen. What is important for Kelsen is the conferral of a cognitive signification, not the felt experience, into an act of will. Kelsen does offer a theory of meaning as indispensable in understanding what a legal act is. For Hart, meaning goes to the use, not to "the mention," of statements.[31]

Of course, Kelsen advocates a theory of meaning that can hardly be described as the mere mention of words. What is important, for Hart, is that a listener recognize the utterer's statement. Without such a recognition of a signification, a statement deteriorates into "a meaningless emission of a noise."[32] The listener recognizes the author's mark. Hart calls the recognition a "social rule." Until the recognition of the noise as a signification takes place, one can only speak of habits or practices or feelings of bonding with those habits. The noises become binding only when recognized as writing. Because Hart assumes that the intuitive or immediate experience of bonding occurs before and independent of language, Hart excludes such a felt experience from the legal act. Hart fails to appreciate that Kelsen considered the experience of conferring meaning, albeit a cognitive experience, as critical to the legal act. Hart also misses the point that Kelsen describes an experience as a legal act. This is a far different enterprise than a psychological inquiry into the unconscious as a scientific object, as Hart considers of Kelsen's theory. Hart is mystified that Kelsen would claim that legal meaning produces "a clarity, consistency, and order not present in the original [words expressed in an act of will]."[33] It is not surprising, then, that Hart considers Kelsen's theory of meaning as "surprising" and "puzzling,"[34] "difficult" and possibly "alarming."[35] It is also not surprising that Hart would consider as "idiosyncratic," Kelsen's theory about the relations of 'ought' statements to each other.[36] Hart projects, as the

31 Hart, "Kelsen Visited," 292.
32 Hart, "Signs and Words," *Philosophical Quarterly* **2** (1952): 59-62.
33 Hart, "Signs and Words," 292.
34 Hart, "Signs and Words," 292.
35 Hart, "Signs and Words," 292.
36 Hart, "Signs and Words," 292.

enemy of the functional use of signs, the method of defining *per genus et differentia*: 'what is law?' or 'what is a right?' Hart advocates that we understand marks in terms of their functional utility vis-à-vis the essence of a concept. Hart wrongly categorizes Kelsen as supporting such an essentialist theory of language. Instead, Kelsen too counters the essentialist approach. But he does so with a phenomenological theory of language, albeit a theory that understands experience as exclusively cognitive. Accordingly, Hart's critique of Kelsen's theory of language is misdirected.

Hart seems to miss more than the phenomenological character of Kelsen's theory of legal meaning. Like Hart, Kelsen too excludes the bodily experience from the legal act. The legal act is a cognitive act, Kelsen insists again and again. Even the act of will, according to Kelsen, is a common rational will independent of the multiplicity of individual wills that initiate a statute or precedent. If the bodily experiences were included in the legal act, the is/ought dichotomy, so indispensable to understanding the modern view of science and of law, would collapse, according to Kelsen. Kelsen documents how, in the early tribal sense of law, for example, morals do fuse with binding laws. In a tribal legal culture, the 'is' of felt experiences does fuse with the prescriptive 'oughts.'[37] But the modern legal system radically differs from such a tribal sense of 'law,' according to Kelsen, because the modern sense of 'law' coincides with the separation of scientifically observable brute facts and a prescriptive set of norms. Kelsen is preoccupied with the *cognitive* conferral of meaning into statements of such prescriptions. To incorporate bodily experiences would conflate the 'ought' into the 'is' and thereby undermine Kelsen's basic tenet.

In this respect, Hart's concept of law is not so different from Kelsen's 'pure' theory, for both excise the bodily experience from the legal act. The felt experience is precisely what Hart postulates as the pre-legal element of the legal psyche. The bodily experience constitutes the 'is' world and law involves prescriptive 'oughts.' Such an experience, according to Hart, is non-legal precisely because it is not, as yet, articulated in language. Hart criticizes Kelsen's *Grundnorm* because the *Grundnorm*, being a presupposition, fails to offer an articulated criterion in order to distinguish the members of the legal structure from non-members. For Hart, a criterion of validity must be articulated in a language. With such a

37 See, e.g., Kelsen, "Causality and Accounting" (1960), in *Essays in Moral and Legal Philosophy* (Ota Weinberger Intro.; Peter Heath trans.; Dordrecht: D. Reidel, 1973), 154-64, at 157-61; "Causality and Imputation" (1950) in *What is Justice?* (Berkeley: University of California Press, 1971), 324-49, at 327-30; "The Natural-Law Doctrine before the Tribunal of Science" (1949) in *What is Justice?*, 137-73, at 137-38; "Causality and Retribution" (1941), in *What is Justice?*, 303-23, at 304-14; "The Emergence of the Causal Law from the Principle of Retribution" (1939), in *Essays on Moral and Legal Philosophy*, 165-215, at 166-84.

signification, one cannot recognize what is authoritative and un-authoritative. "When we have laws that explicitly or implicitly refer to other laws, or their existence or validity," Hart writes, "we cannot determine from these relationships alone whether they belong to the same or different systems."[38] The *Grundnorm* is presupposed and, as such, it does not offer a written criterion of authority.

So Hart too privileges language as the critical medium of a modern legal structure, though Hart and Kelsen have very different theories of language and meaning. For Kelsen, language involves the cognitive conferral of meaning into a statement. For Hart, language involves statements that one *uses* to represent an essence of a concept. In both cases, the pre-language is excluded as non-law. *Bodily*, rather than cognitive, experiences are considered as such phenomena of pre-language. Yet Hart locates the authorizing origin of statements about posited primary and secondary rules in just such a realm of pre-language. Law begins with language, according to Hart, and a written language at that. So the origin of the origins of authorized rules is legally non-existent, external to legal existence, inaccessible from the written statements that constitute legal language. The authorizing origin of the language of the structure is a possibility in that it rests beyond the familiar signs of legal language. The origin rests in an objectless void, a legal non-existence, an unknown.

c) *The pre-legal as the legal unconscious*

Hart's theory of legal positivism manifests the distinction between the fused immediacy and the second-order moment of signification in more than his distinction between the pre-legal and the legal. Hart also relies upon the immediacy/ signification distinction in his analysis of legal obligation. Hart makes it clear that the felt experience of immediacy is not peculiar to the totemic legal culture. Even officials in a modern state share such a pre-legal felt experience of immediacy or, to use Hart's term "bonding." Rules may manifest such an immediacy. Hart calls such manifestations "social rules." But, like the felt experiences of bonding in a tribe, the social rules are excluded as binding laws. A social rule is "the normal, *though unstated*, background or proper context" when a juridical official states that one is legally obligated.[39] Such an unstated background, Hart asserts, characterizes "the figure of a *bond* binding the person obligated, which is buried in the word 'obligation.'"[40] This bonding moment, an experience before the juridical official speaks and writes through a special vocabulary, "*haunts* much legal thought," Hart continues. The moment of bonding offers the background to an

38 Hart, "Kelsen's Doctrine of the Unity of Law," 313.
39 Hart, *Concept of Law*, 83.
40 Hart, *Concept of Law*, 87.

obligation, like "a chain binding those who have obligations so that they are not free to do what they want."[41] The moment of immediacy is an experience, Hart writes. The unstated experience is a feeling of being obliged, rather than the thought of being obligated, to follow a practice.

Hart continuously excludes such a bonding experience from legal reasoning. The "internal point of view," which an official's statement manifests, is "misrepresented" as a "feeling," he claims.[42] The psychological feelings, though they may be shared amongst officials, "are neither necessary nor sufficient for the existence of 'binding' rules." Rather, what is important for a rule to be binding is an "internal point of view." The "internal point of view" involves "an acceptance" of a certain rule without necessarily involving the experience of feeling compelled to follow a rule. One accepts "being obliged" even though one may not personally feel compelled to follow a certain conduct, he argues. The acceptance is represented by an internal statement. The internal statement chronologically follows or comes after the feeling of bonding with a rule. The feeling of bonding is social. The official's internal acceptance of the bonding, as manifested in an internal statement, is legal. By privileging the "acceptance" in a manner that excludes what he considers the "psychological" experience of feeling bonded towards a rule, Hart also rejects Kelsen's theory of the norm as the linguistic re-presentation of an act of will.[43] Hart's error is to understand Kelsen as offering a psychological, rather than a phenomenological, theory of meaning.

d) Internal statements, external statements and bodily experience

Hart distinguishes the official's internal acceptance of a rule from more than the psychological feeling of bonding with the rule. Hart makes a further distinction in his theory of language.[44] The internal acceptance of a rule differs from the official's external recognition of the acceptance. An official's external recognition retrospectively recognizes that many officials accept a particular rule. The acceptance is evidenced through their internal statements. Legal obligation pertains to such an external recognition, according to Hart. In the second signification – that of the recognition of an acceptance of the rule as evidenced by internal statements – the official is two stages removed from the original experience of bonding. The legal language of duties (and rights) exists in such a second level.

This distinction between the official's internal acceptance of a rule and an official's external recognition of the rule plays an important role in Hart's analysis

41 Hart, *Concept of Law*, 88.
42 Hart, *Concept of Law*, 57.
43 See Hart's criticism of this element of Kelsen's pure theory in "Kelsen Visited," 305.
44 See, e.g., Hart, *Concept of Law*, 57-61.

of the rule of recognition. Hart claims that officials 'accept' a practice in an internal statement and they recognize the practice as legally binding in an external statement. The practice transforms into a social *rule* when the practice is recognized. The social rule is transformed into a legally binding rule when external statements recognize the internal acceptance as binding. At this point, Hart's analysis plays with the three elements of reaching a legal obligation: the immediate experience of feeling bound; the internal statement that accepts and manifests the practice experienced; and the external statement that recognizes the acceptance. Hart excludes the first element, the experience, as a pre-legal element of the legal intentionality. The concept of law, according to Hart, begins with written language, not with the experience that, Hart believes, precedes language. Language begins after such an experience. Signification through a language of internal and external statements characterizes the legal reasoning of a modern legal system.

A secondary rule is unstated, for example, in that, when applied, the rule is not articulated in a statement until *after* its application. A social practice is articulated in an "internal" statement. Such a social practice is an immediately felt connection. The shared convention does not exist as a rule of recognition until *after* a primary rule is accepted and then applied as an internal statement. The internal acceptance of the unstated social practice – the forgotten centre of the primary and secondary rules – is signified in an internal statement. The internal statement "manifests" being obliged. But a later juridical official, situated from an external point of view, recognizes the acceptance of being obliged. With that recognition, one is obligated. The statement, which accepts being obliged, is transferred into an external statement of obligation. With the external statement, according to Hart, the acceptance becomes recognized as a signification *about* the hidden intuitive experience of immediacy manifested in the officials' internal statements. The external statement "supplements"or is secondary to the internal statement. The internal statement is primary. Legal authority goes to the official's later external recognition of the earlier acceptance by other officials of an internal point of view. With the external statement, a secondary rule is articulated and, with that articulation, there arises the criterion of authority that Hart believes was missing in Kelsen's *Grundnorm*. The secondary rule identifies what social practices have been accepted by officials as legally binding. The secondary rule recognizes only internal statements as the end of that acceptance. Values, feelings, and beliefs are excluded from the inquiry of acceptance *unless* they have been signified in (internal) statements. But then, they have entered into legal language, according to Hart. Thus, the external statement looks backward in the direction of the internal statements' lost experience of bonding, though only an internal statement that manifests such bondedness can count as part of the legal. In contrast, the internal statement is uttered towards the future.[45]

Permit me to be more specific. The modern legal structure, in contrast to the experience of immediacy in a "primitive" legal order or in the unstated bodily experience of officials in a modern state, is instituted through "statements." Statements may be of two kinds: internal and external.[46] Internal statements are "signs" that manifest that one is obliged to follow a certain rule. The utterer – whether a judge or a lawyer or police official or other official – "manifests" that he or she accepts a practice "as [a] guiding rule." But the acceptance takes the form of an *ex post facto* statement. The acceptance is a question of an internalized experience that one accepts without question in the form of a statement. Hart then writes that "with this attitude there goes a characteristic vocabulary different from the natural expressions of the external point of view."[47] The internal statement about an official's disposition to follow a practice is inadequate to render the internal statement authoritative or legally binding, according to Hart. The official's recognition of the practice must also be "accepted and employed" by other officials as they interpret and apply primary and secondary rules.[48] So, the external statements are "signs" that an official makes about the "observable regularities of behaviour" of other officials in the institutional structure. The external statements recognize the regularities of the internal statements. The external statements "approximate" or "very nearly [but not perfectly] reproduce" the manner in which the internal statements function.

So Hart analyzes the concept of law in terms of more than just the "internal" and "external" point of view. Hart associates the concept of law, more generally, with a written or verbal language that, he believes, is radically separate from the bodily experiences or feelings that one may confer *into* statements. And this, despite Hart's description of his own theory as a phenomenological account of the concept of law.

In particular, when an official "accepts" a rule, he or she recognizes it in writing: that is, he or she accepts it as a practice that is signified or represented through "marks" or "signs," terms that Hart uses interchangeably. An internal rule, as signified, still comes *after* the still earlier moment when other officials have experienced the unsignified practice as a *feeling* of being obliged or bonded with a

45 Ibid., 105. Hart indicates in "Problems of the Philosophy of Law," in P. Edwards ed., *Encyclopedia of Philosophy*, vol. 6 (New York: Macmillan and Free Press, 1967), 264-76, that he is drawing from Richard Wasserstrom, who made much of the distinction in *The Judicial Decision* (Stanford: Stanford University Press, 1961).

46 Hart, *Concept of Law*, 89-90.

47 Hart, *Concept of Law*, 102.

48 Hart, *Concept of Law*, 108.

social practice. When inscribed as an "internal statement," the former feeling of bonding may evaporate, Hart writes.[49] Indeed, Hart cautions that one often misrepresents the internal aspect of rules as a "feeling." "But such feelings are neither necessary nor sufficient for the existence of 'binding' rules." One may "accept" a binding rule and yet "experience no such feelings of compulsion." The inscription abstracts from the feeling of intentionality and transforms the feeling into a primary rule about which an official may critically reflect. One becomes bound to the rule in that one gains an obligation that overtakes the feeling of being obliged. The feeling of compulsion involves "psychological experiences" and is quite independent of the more rational sense of "feeling bound." Hart is clear on this point: "No doubt ... individuals may have psychological experiences analogous to those of restriction or compulsion. When they say they 'feel bound' to behave in certain ways, they may indeed refer to these experiences. But such feelings are neither necessary nor sufficient for the existence of 'binding' rules. There is no contradiction in saying that people accept certain rules but experience no such feelings of compulsion. What is necessary is that there be a critical reflective attitude to certain patterns of behaviour as a common standard."[50] That critical reflective attitude enters into the scene through statements and, in particular, through external statements about the internally accepted statements.

Hart's biographer, Neil MacCormick, remarks about this disjunction between feelings and the volitional.[51] Issues of 'ought,' 'must,' 'should,' 'right,' and 'wrong' take one to the later moment of signification in a language. And the moment of "recognition," from an externalized point of view, still arrives on the scene even after an internal statement has manifested an "acceptance" of a practice. So, Hart situates the psychological experience of bonding with the pre-legal. Hart's analytic distinctions – the felt experience of feeling fused with a practice, the acceptance by an official of such a feeling in an internal statement (being obliged), and the later official's recognition of the acceptance (being obligated) – are critically important to one's understanding of Hart's concept of law. These distinctions reinforce Hart's exclusion of the felt experience of bonding from the authority of binding rules in a modern state. And they reinforce his distinctions between the pre-legal and the legal, the legal unconscious and the legal consciousness.

e) *Feelings of intolerance, indignation and disgust*

This distinction between the bodily experience of an immediate bonding with a practice, on the one hand, and its signification in a statement, on the other, helps to explain why

49 Hart, *Concept of Law*, 57.
50 Hart, *Concept of Law*, 56.
51 MacCormick, *H.L.A. Hart*, 34.

Hart was so critical of Lord Devlin's claim that posited laws should not be considered separate from morals. As with Kelsen, 'morality,' for Hart, does not take on what one might consider the preserve of philosophy, of the search for the good or right conduct, that is. Rather, morality is the feeling of immediacy that phenomenologically precedes internal and external statements. Such an immediacy is subjective or personal and, as such, foreign to the language of legal obligation.

Lord Devlin had claimed that just such immediately felt experiences (of "intolerance, indignation and disgust") should be included as legally binding.[52] For Hart, only the 'after the fact' moment of *intellectualization* through an external statement could provide the basis of legal authority in a modern legal structure. Such "thought" and "critical reflection" distinguish the legal from the unsignified feelings of the pre-legal. Critical reflection, not some unstated feeling of disgust, recognizes an internal statement as manifesting a legal obligation. Critical reflection is manifested through three forms of analysis: analytic criticism, expectations of conformity to certain social practices, and statements that acknowledge that such criticism and expectations are justified. We are now familiar with how Hart can be expected to treat Devlin's claim. Before the signification of a concept, one experiences a feeling of disgust not unlike the feeling of bonding. Such a feeling is located in the moral realm, Hart has insisted. Indeed, in the pre-legal experiences of pre-modern legal regimes, customs fused with feelings of bonding (morality). So too, Hart stresses that sexual mores, unregulated by primary rules or even moral language, are a part of 'morality.'[53] Hart adds that writing must signify even pure speculative ideals before a legal official may consider the latter authoritative. The legal only begins *after* an official signifies a feeling of disgust as an internal statement and only *after* an external statement recognizes the language manifested in the internal statements. It is just Devlin's appeal to the inarticulated experiences that Hart rejects as pre-legal because, according to Hart, they phenomenologically precede the feeling of being obliged.

Thus, the inscription of a rule in a written language (the external statement) demarcates law from morals. The authority of a rule encourages the official, as an impartial external observer, to recognize 'oughts' in the sense of obligation that an internal statement manifests. Once recognized in an external statement, the originary feeling is expelled as moral even though 'oughts' accompany such feelings. Not surprisingly, then, Hart insists in "Positivism and the Separation of Law and Morals" that the 'ought' of legal authority "need have nothing to do with

52 Hart, "Immorality and Treason," in Richard Wasserstrom, ed., *Morality and the Law* (Belmont, CA: Wadsworth, 1971): 49-54, 51.

53 Hart, *The Concept of Law*, 174-75.

morals."[54] After all, Hart's 'ought' is not an anthropological feeling of disgust. We have observed that, according to Hart, judges abstract rules from internal statements that reflect other officials' acceptance of an unwritten and unspoken practice. The ultimate rule of recognition is then recognized from the judiciary's external statements about such internal statements. The pre-legal world of a felt experience is inaccessible to the rule of recognition. The extrinsic and distanced situs of the judge, as observer of unstated judicial practices, reinforces the inaccessibility of the originary feelings of bonding.

The judge's statements about binding rules, then, are several experiential stages after the initial experience of bonding. Judges, through external statements, recognize "internal statements" that are believed, in turn, to "accept" the experiences of bonding. The external observer need not personally accept the rule of recognition, nor need the external observer use it as a guide to legal action.[55] The juridical official observes or recognizes the regularities, predictions, probabilities and signs of conduct shared amongst other officials who interpret humanly imposed primary rules. The official does not and should not pry "before" or "behind" the internal statements in order to account for the manner in which members of a group accept the rules. The external observer is a scientist who is supposed to recognize the internal statements as 'givens' and who then writes about his or her recognition of the 'givens' through external statements.

Hart distinguishes "statements," then, in terms of internal (or primary) and external (or secondary) statements. Neither type of statement is equivalent to the felt experience of immediacy because Hart excludes just such an experience from language. The primary statements exemplify an immediacy without reflection. External statements are written *about* the internal statements. The latter are secondary to the primary internal statements. The external statements are external to the internal statements. The external statements are 'after the fact' of the primary statements and the primary statements are 'after the fact' of the felt experience of bonding.

Now, Hart is clear that what the external statements cannot reproduce "is the way in which the rules function as rules in the lives of those who normally are the majority of society."[56] The latter would involve an issue of prediction, which would assess the direction and intensity of the moment of immediacy. But both internal and external statements, according to Hart, go to the *reasons* or *grounds* of the rules. With the internal statement, the official states that 'it is the law that....' With

54 Hart, "Positivism and the Separation of Law and Morals," *Harvard Law Review* **71** (1958): 593-629, 629; and as reprinted in Frederick A. Olafson, ed., *Society, Law and Morality* (Englewood Cliffs, NJ: Prentice-Hall, 1961), 439-70, 469.

55 Hart, *The Concept of Law*, 89.

56 Hart, *Concept of Law*, 90.

the external statement, the official states that 'in England they recognize the law that....' The latter external statement signifies or represents the former internal statement. And the internal statement, in turn, signifies the unsignified or unstated feeling of immediacy that an official possesses towards an unstated practice. Hart has emphasized that the immediacy is unsignifiable. Signification re-presents the immediacy. Hart emphasizes that when one immediately identifies or bonds with a practice, "obeying a rule (or order) *need* [his emphasis] involve *no thought* [my emphasis] on the part of the person obeying" that he or she ought to act according to the rule![57] Indeed, the addressee may not even believe that the rule is morally right. But Hart is emphatic that the concept of law takes hold *after* officials have intuitively or immediately accepted a rule. In the later moment of signification in statements, the decision "for the most part" is reached "either by genuine effort to conform to rules *consciously taken* as guiding standards of decision or, if intuitively reached, are *justified* by rules which the judge was *antecedently* disposed to observe" [emphasis added].

Whether internal or external, though, a "statement" can only approximate the moment of experience before an official inscribes his or her intentional experience in writing and speech. The approximation takes the form of a re-presentation. The mark-statement re-presents the intentionality. Thus, the moment of immediacy should not be confused with what Hart calls the psychological. The latter goes to the process of thought that one experiences in reaching a judgement. The statement that the rule of recognition exists can only be an external statement about an empirical fact as manifested in internal statements. Like Kelsen, the legal structure is coercively binding. For Kelsen, the *Grundnorm*, as the authorizing origin of a legal language, is divorced from the empirical world, the *Grundnorm* being a mere thought without particulars. For Hart, however, the ultimate *arche* of authority is embedded in a raw social experience as recognized as a rule in an external statement. Like Kelsen's *Grundnorm*, the rule of recognition is neither valid nor invalid.[58]

The official transforms the authorizing genesis of binding rules from the unwritten experiential character into writing where statements secondarily represent the experiential. Hart thereby revises Kelsen's explanation of the idealized source of the *Grundnorm* at the presupposed origin of synthetic *a priori* reasoning. Hart adds that the act of thought, which Kelsen had attributed to the *Grundnorm*, is indeed signified in a statement. The authorizing origin cannot be presupposed, for legal officials need to recognize criteria of validity in order to identify what primary rules are included as authoritatively binding. And as with Kelsen, Hart accepts

57 Hart, *Concept of Law*, 113.
58 Hart, *Concept of Law*, 83.

that if one claims that a rule is authoritative, the rule is recognized *in a language*, albeit a cognitively constituted language.[59] The phenomenal is transformed into the justificatory. The modern legal structure begins with the latter. The location of a proposed rule depends upon the ultimate justificatory grounds of rules vis-à-vis the criterion of authority in secondary rules. A criterion is an independent test of recognition, independent of the primary rules themselves and independent of the experienced immediacy shared in the application of the primary rules.[60] Without an independent test, one could not differentiate objective from subjective acts of fiat. The external *ex post facto* character of the act of recognition allows the official to derive the authority of one rule from the grounds of another rule.

One might better appreciate Hart's concept of law if one recalls the importance of the author in modern legal positivism. In the old-fashioned view of an author, some author produces a statement as a product. The feelings of that author are external and phenomenologically prior to the scope of the legal act. Authoritative rules begin with the statements about the rules, not with the phenomenologically primordial experience of feeling obliged. All that matters are *the statements* themselves. The statements alone characterize a modern legal structure. To situate the experience of immediacy in language itself just does not make sense, Hart believes.

Both primary and secondary rules are authored. The primary rules reflect the *author*'s intended object. The secondary rules are authored in that the judges, as externally situated readers of the prior author's internal statements, recognize that the author accepted a certain practice as his or her intended object. According to Hart, the rule of recognition *recognizes* that officials *intend* the acceptance of a certain practice as a recognized obligation. But the obligation only takes form when the official recognizes the practice as a rule in writing. Both the intentionality of the author of the primary rule and the signification that recognizes the author's intended object occur *after* the moment of immediacy when officials did not consciously intend any object.[61] Like the customs of early Greek and Amerindian tribes, such officials involuntarily accept a practice before they begin to signify it in a binding statement. The primary and secondary objects are postulated to come after the 'authorizing origin' of the statements about the rules. As a consequence, the authorizing origin in the moment of immediacy is forgotten in the language of primary (internal) and secondary (external) statements.

59 Hart, "Kelsen Visited," 307.

60 Hart, "Kelsen's Doctrine of the Unity of Law," 338.

61 Bernard Jackson, *Making Sense of Jurisprudence* (Liverpool: Deborah Charles, 1996), 89.

4. Does the Authorizing Origin Pre-exist Primary Rules?

The critical question is now posed: is the moment of immediacy really the authorizing origin of a legal structure in a modern state, according to Hart?

The key to understanding Hart's sense of the authorizing origin, I wish to emphasize, hangs upon his distinction between the official's felt experience of immediate identification or bonding with a judicial practice on the one hand and the signification of that bonding in what Hart considers a language. The distinction is crucial in order to appreciate Hart's influential text. Unfortunately, it is a distinction that contemporary commentators of Hart and of legal positivism have missed.

a) The retrospective production of rules

The crucial point here is that, upon a close reading of Hart, the search for the locus of authority in some ultimate grounding or source, a project that has been with officials since the Roman times, carries a *retrospective* character to it. Contrary to Kelsen's critique of Austin, Hart and his commentators identify the *arche* of legal rules as resting inside a legal language. Institutional authors express such a language. A legislature or court is such an institution. Officials deliberate, reflect, enact, and then adjudicate their own rules. This helps to explain the importance of a centrally organized set of institutions for legally binding rules on a modern state. Linked with one another in pyramidal fashion, authority, granting institutions authorize a *potential totality* over all social conduct and thought.[62] This pyramidal institutional structure creates the "legal" structure as opposed to the "pre-legal" (non-)structure.

One can identify a time and place when a legislature or a judge inscribed a rule in statements. After such an inscription, a judge or scholar *retrospectively* abstracts secondary rules from previous statements. The secondary rules make statements *about* the primary rules. A secondary rule is considered authoritative, depending upon whether, in retrospectively studying the primary or internal statements, an official can identify whether such statements consistently assume unstated practices, standards, or reasons for the structure as a whole.

The latter unstated reasons, when articulated as secondary to the internal statements, thereby function *ex post facto* as justificatory criteria with which to recognize the authoritativeness of other internal statements of acceptance. That is, the secondary rules are signified *after* the primary rules have been inscribed. The justificatory standards are secondary in that they supplement the prior (or primary) rules. Without the primary rules, there could not possibly be standards that recognize the unstated practices manifested in the internal (primary) statements.

62 Hart, *The Concept of Law*, 202.

Hart calls the latter 'rules of recognition' in that officials recognize the shared unstated practices embedded in the statements about primary rules. Hart describes the phenomenological moment of the recognition of both primary and secondary rules, then, as an 'after the fact' moment. The secondary statement about the unstated practice, hidden in a series of primary rules, comes *after* the primary rules have been accepted and applied. Hart makes the same point in the *Concept of Law* on a later occasion: "[t]he truth may be that, when courts settle previously un-envisaged questions concerning the most fundamental constitutional rules, they *get* [his emphasis] their authority to decide them accepted *after* [my emphasis] the questions have arisen and the decision has been given. Here all that succeeds is success."[63]

In the Postscript to the second edition of the *Concept of Law*, Hart carefully describes the nature of secondary rules so as to differentiate the later moment of their signification from the earlier moment when internal statements manifest or exemplify a sense of acceptance of a hitherto unstated practice. The rule of recognition "is in effect a form of judicial customary rule existing only if it is accepted and practised in the law-identifying and law-applying operations of the courts."[64] Of course, primary rules authorize the main element of such law-identifying and law-applying operations. Primary rules exist as legal rules "from the moment of their enactment before any occasion for their practice has arisen and the practice theory is not applicable to them." That is, primary rules exist only when they have been inscribed in writing.

There is an interesting twist to primary rules, though. Hart continues the above analysis with the condition that inscribed primary rules are "identifiable as valid rules by the criteria provided by the rule of recognition."

In this manner, the primary rules, though they exist from the moment of being authored, are justified as authoritative only in terms of the *ex post facto* higher grounding in a rule of recognition. But Hart emphasizes that the "marks" of criteria of validity are inscribed *after* primary rules have been authored in internal statements. This post-primary rule phenomenon renders a secondary character to the rule of recognition. Hart writes that the secondary rule "supplements" the primary rule.

Hart describes the supplemental "existence" of a secondary rule as retrospective even when he examines the legal regime of an absolute monarch. Hart calls the monarch, Rex I. Rex reigns with the aid of general orders backed by coercion. The habit of obedience is a personal relationship with Rex I. When Rex I dies and his son, Rex II, begins to issue general orders, the latter commands will not be law because the general habit of obedience had been owed to Rex I personally. At

63 Hart, *Concept of Law*, 153.
64 Hart, *Concept of Law*, 256.

best, there is an interregnum until one can retrospectively recognize a habit of obedience towards Rex II:

> There is nothing to make him [Rex II] sovereign from the start. Only *after* we know that his orders have been obeyed for some time shall we be able to say that a habit of obedience has been established. Then, but not till then, we shall be able to say of any further order that it is already law as soon as it is issued and before it is obeyed.[65]

In order to follow an uninterrupted continuity of legal authority, there must be secondary rules of succession that identify what commands of future monarchs will be considered binding.

And again, when Hart describes the "manipulation" by English courts of the binding force of precedents, Hart makes the same point. The judicial manipulation of precedent exemplifies that "power acquires authority *ex post facto* from success."[66]

b) The loss of the origin

It is not surprising, then, that Hart would be so concerned that Ronald Dworkin would characterize Hart's own theory of law as a "plain fact positivism."[67] Dworkin's label misses the post-primary-rule phenomenon: that is, that the rule of recognition, which sets out the criteria of authority, is articulated in the legal discourse *after* the primary rules have been inscribed. Dworkin also misses that the rule of recognition only exists in a statement: that is, in the writing that officials alone recognize as authoritative. More, because a primary or authored rule is authoritative only if it can be justified in terms of the criteria of identification in the rule of recognition, the moment of the judicial practice is fixed once it is transformed into an epistemological criterion of justification. This contrasts with the flux of a social practice. Finally, Dworkin misses that what Hart calls a "social practice" (though it is really only a judicial practice) is concealed inside the internal and external statements. Hart intends that the most important element of the social practice is the bonding through which officials feel at one with a practice. Such an experience is hardly a "plain fact," as Dworkin claims.

Indeed, Dworkin (and with him, the commentators of both Hart and Dworkin) arguably reads his own positivism into Hart's theory. Hart excludes the experiential as pre-legal and, in doing so, he excludes what Dworkin himself erroneously takes as "plain facts." Legal history begins with language, not with the "plain facts" of social experience, according to Hart. And that language loses the social

---

65 Hart, *Concept of Law*, 53.
66 Hart, *Concept of Law*, 154.
67 Hart, *Concept of Law*, 247.

experience, according to Hart, at the very moment that internal statements accept the practice. The statements are considered constitutive of the legal as opposed to the pre-legal. For Hart, what is most important is the *rule* of recognition, not the prior experienced feeling of bonding. That rule of recognition contrasts with the continual flux of intuitive experiences. Thus, to describe Hart's theory of law as rooted in 'plain facts' is misdirected indeed. For the ultimate grounding of the authoritative primary rules, according to Hart, does not lie in some prior externally posited social facts.

The rule of recognition is a retrospective reconstruction of the originary immediacy of bondedness. The retrospectivity can be best appreciated in terms of Hart's distinction between a psychological experience on the one hand and the 'existence' of written signification on the other. When a primary rule is applied, the rule leaves the secondary rule unstated.[68] As unstated, the rule is not really yet a rule but an unsignified judicial practice. When signified as an external statement, the practice becomes a rule with the status of law. The secondary rule need not resemble a codifying act of legislation. Once recognized from an external viewpoint, the judicial practice is no longer an unwritten judicial practice: the practice is signified in a statement. The external statement recognizes the practice.

Thus, the context of the primary rule shifts from a statement in which a judge internally accepts the conditions of his or her authority to a statement which a later, externally situated official/observer makes *about* such acceptance.[69] Hart's originary grounding of primary and secondary rules, the unstated judicial practices, is dependent, first, upon the emergence of authored primary rules in internal statements and then, secondly, upon the recognition in external statements of practices manifested in such internal statements. That is, the referent, the unstated judicial practices, is 'rediscovered' in later statements *about* the originary moment of a bonded immediacy between agent and practice. The latter is lost and then forgotten in the 'rediscovery' in the form of a representation.

The evidentiary proof for the authority of a primary rule, then, lies "external" to the existence of the primary rule itself. The proof is an issue of what Hart calls descriptive sociology. The secondary rules are empirically verifiable by the 'sociologist' who, without making any moral judgment as to its merits, assesses whether a particular practice has been followed.[70] The proof refers to a moment of bondedness as a referent. But that referent is lost as a prescriptive experience

68 Hart, *Concept of Law*, 108.

69 Hart, *Concept of Law*, 109.

70 See esp. "Postscript," in Hart, *Concept of Law*, 242, where he writes of a "non-participant external observer" who describes the manner in which participants view the law. The descriptive legal theorist must "understand" without endorsing the morality of the internal point of view accepted by the legal participant.

when legal language – or, at least, Hart's understanding of legal language – takes over. For the moment of immediacy is excluded as external to that language and, therefore, as "pre-law." At the least, a proof is avoided as juridical officials trace the authority for their acts of inscription through the chains of statements *about* the lost referent.

c) Mis-recognition

Thus, rules of recognition become signified *after* internal statements of acceptance have authored primary rules. The 'social' – the very unstated judicial practices that had encouraged Hart to describe his theory as "sociological" – is constructed *after* institutions have posited primary rules, even though the secondary rules are framed as "recognizing" the "acceptance" of a social rule through a prior internal statement. What is being sought as the authorizing origin of a legal structure has to be assumed to exist. The origin is merely a possibility for only statements, not unstated practices, constitute legal existence, for, the origin's identity can only be re-presented as a statement about primary rules.

The authorizing origin itself is inaccessible through legal language. The origin is invisible. The rules of recognition, in a sense, become rules of mis-recognition because the bonding or immediacy of official with social practice – what Hart considers social experience – cannot be recognized except *after* the moment of immediacy and then only *after* external statements have reflected about the internal statements that have manifested an acceptance of bonding. Only primary rules and their principles, inscribed in writing – not the unwritten felt experiences – can be recognized. For Hart, the rules of recognition recognize a *statement*, not the pre-legal experience of immediacy that the statement signifies. Legal officials recognize statements by other officials as they author or state primary rules. But the origin of those rules, the unspoken and unwritten judicial practices, are excluded, and then forgotten as officials search for statements that recognize an acceptance of the primary statements. The revised signified 'origin,' the rule of recognition, becomes the secondary external statement. Authority is claimed for the writing, not for the experience that the writing represents at a second level. Moreover, the rule of recognition mis-recognizes the referent. The origin is mis-recognized as an inscribed rule rather than as a primordial feeling of bonding with a practice. More importantly, the referent, the unstated judicial practice, takes form after, rather than before, the act of recognition. And, finally, the revised 'origin' is thereby mis-recognized as a statement instead of a felt experience. The felt experience is considered "pre-legal" and the statement alone is considered "legal." The origin is mis-recognized through written/verbalized statements rather than through some interpersonal social nexus that Hart believes does exist independent and prior to legal language. As a consequence of these factors, the juridical officials forget about the absent origin as they carry on their enterprise of constructing the origin through external statements about internal statements.

Accordingly, Hart also mis-describes his own theory as a "descriptive sociology." For, what Hart takes as the social (the moment of immediate bonding of official to a practice) dissipates (in Hart's analysis) as judges make statements about the 'social,' the unstated judicial practices. Hart distinguishes the social origin in a pre-linguistic phenomenal realm from the reflective justification that abstracts a rule from the pre-linguistic experience. This intellectualization takes place through language or, to use Hart's continual reference, to internal and external "statements." The phenomenal concerns are exemplified when one addresses why individuals and groups feel obliged toward the rule[71] or whether juridical agents in point of fact feel obliged towards one another.[72] Hart is preoccupied with the epistemological question of what makes a rule authoritative once the rule is signified as a statement. The emotive feeling of being bound is unnecessary for the existence of a binding rule.

d) Existence

Like Kelsen, Hart gives what the non-lawyer might take to be a very peculiar meaning to the word 'existence' in this respect. A rule "exists" when an official recovers it from the unstated and the unwritten and when the official intellectualizes *about* the unstated/unwritten. The intellectualization is inscribed as a representation of the unstated and unwritten. Other officials accept and then recognize their acceptance of the inscribed intellectualization. Here, Hart acknowledges his debt to Richard Wasserstrom, who distinguished between the discovery and the justification of rules.[73] Hart holds that a judge justifies rules. Why a judge is induced to obey rules is a 'discovery' issue of "descriptive psychology." A motive for action is not the same as a justificatory reason for action. Authority draws from the standards that judges respect as they make statements about the reasons justifying the law, however empirically reached and however deeply felt.[74] These standards connote a precept.

Authority, then, dwells in the metaphysics that arrives on the scene, Hart believes, after a judge discovers the rule through a statement. Even with Wasserstrom, though, the felt experience of immediacy is forgotten as one tries to discover whether officials feel obliged. For the legal sociologist, like the constitutional lawyer, makes external statements about the internal statements, not about the phenomenal experience that the internal statements accept.

71 Hart, *Concept of Law*, 193-94.
72 Hart, *Concept of Law*, 109.
73 See esp. Hart, "Problems of the Philosophy of Law," 268-69, and Richard Wasserstrom, *The Judicial Decision*.
74 See especially Hart, "Problems of Philosophy of Law."

External statements *about* internal primary statements do not bring one into the moral world, despite the prescriptive character of the justificatory statements. Hart distinguishes the legal obligation from the psychological commitment to make a moral judgment. Hart makes the point in this manner:

> [t]hose who accept the authority of a legal system look upon it from the internal point of view, and express their sense of requirements in internal statements couched in the normative language which is common to both law and morals: 'I (you) ought,' 'I (he) must,' 'I (they) have an obligation.' Yet they are not thereby committed to a *moral* judgment that it is morally right to do what the law requires.[75]

Secondary rules, again, do not inquire into the anthropological genesis of a judicial practice: such would take one along the path of Lord Devlin. Nor do secondary rules necessarily institutionalize what is morally right conduct. A judge or other juridical official internally accepts a primary rule as an 'ought' without necessarily recognizing the rule as a moral 'ought.' The judge analyzes the 'oughts' of other internal statements from the 'outside,' as it were, *after* judges have authored their internal statements about rules, according to Hart. The judge does so in order to predict certain regularities of behaviour.[76] The judge makes a prediction, then, by studying the grounds of internal statements of primary rules. This is a far cry from basing the prediction upon a sociological analysis of the class, gender or race assumptions or the personality traits of the earlier judges. The latter inquiries would take the judge into the pre-legal realm of affectation and intuition. The judge is confined to the legal realm of language, especially a language that other judges, not sociologists nor psychologists, would recognize.

e) The idealization of the social

Thus, the official traces statements about primary rules to an ultimate statement that recognizes an unstated and unwritten judicial practice as manifested in internal statements. Internal statements, uttered through the legal language, do not necessarily ensure obedience by others. Why groups obey the statements about rules may differ from self-interest to inherited beliefs to a justification of what is right conduct. The crucial issue, for Hart, is that groups possess an internal sense of obligation towards the rules as stated. Hart's lawyer identifies and predicts – that is, recognizes – that internal sense of obligation. Hart's official only recognizes "signs" or "critical marks" or "statements." Situated as an impartial observer, the judge recognizes hidden practices embedded in such statements. The recognition of the hidden practices takes the form of an external statement. Such an external

75 Hart, *Concept of Law*, 203.

76 Hart, "Introduction," in *Essays in Jurisprudence and Philosophy*, 1-18, 14. Also see Hart, "Scandinavian Realism," in *Essays*, 161-69, 165.

statement recognizes a secondary rule of recognition. Prior to the inscription of the rule of recognition, the judges internally accept the rule as an unstated and unwritten practice.[77] Perhaps this unwritten hidden practice was what Kelsen considered as the presupposition that constitutes the *Grundnorm*. The judge envisions or pictures the rule of recognition about the primary rules, from the outside, *after* the primary rules have been articulated through writing.

And yet, the authority for the primary rules, Hart claims, rests upon the justificatory grounding of primary rules in the prior rule of recognition. The rule of recognition offers a criterion of validity. The juridical officials can only trace the authority of primary rules and legal institutions if they accept primary and secondary rules and their enactment by legal institutions in a manner that demarcates their legality from their absent external forgotten origin: the pre-linguistic *unstated* experience. To retrieve the originary moment of immediacy would return the legal official to what Hart calls a "primitive" legal system and that would contradict the modern intellectualizing project of tracing the justificatory grounds of one primary rule to a secondary rule. The concept of law thereby becomes an idealized reading of social experience.

Part of this idealization takes place because the experiential moments of immediacy are believed, according to Hart, to involve the passions of the body. But the misrecognition of the transformed 'origin' as secondary rules in external statements excises the experiential body as "pre-legal," "anthropological," or "social/moral." As officials reflect, deliberate, or, more generally, intellectualize about bodily practices through external statements, they transform the originary experience into a secondary rule and that rule, in turn, becomes the referent for the authority of primary rules.

Hart is clear, for example, that one must distinguish between the human subject with an experiential body on the one hand and the faceless juridical person without a body on the other. Even international law falls under his understanding of law, according to Hart, because states are juridical persons that legal writing, in the form of treaties, have recognized.[78] The state does not need a body. The state only needs to be recognized as a juridical person. Hart realizes that his analysis, when considered as explaining a sophisticated legal structure, "brings with it a new application of the word 'exist.'"[79] The existence of a primary rule means little more than that it is "valid given the system's criteria of validity." The system's criterion of validity exists, in turn, in writing. A primary rule "exists" if it is authoritative. And authority rests in the tracing of the justification of a primary rule to a rule of

77 Hart, "Scandinavian Realism," 167.
78 Hart, *Concept of Law*, 223.
79 Hart, *Concept of Law*, 110.

recognition. But the rule of recognition is only recognized *after* the inscription of primary rules. A primary rule is authoritative if, after a rule has been authored, one can recognize the rule as consistent with external statements about the unstated practices implicit in that and other internal statements of primary rules.

Hart's analysis offers one an interesting twist. The criterion of authority, as manifested in a secondary rule, is written *after* the primary rules have been authored, although the authority for the primary rule postulates the prior existence of the criteria of authority in secondary rules. Hart can privilege the justificatory project vis-à-vis the prior rule of recognition only by expelling the authorizing origin from legal language, as pre-legal.

5. Is the Authorizing Origin Internal to the Primary and Secondary Rules?

a) Claims of legal positivism

So, Hart makes an important claim about legal positivism: namely, that the revisionist or second-order 'origin' of authoritative rules (that is, the rule of recognition) is retrospectively posited over an invisible moment of presence or bonding between an official and a social practice. Hart's insight into the retrospectivity of the posited binding rule is consistent with the tradition of legal positivism.

Now, Hart's insight into the retrospectiveity of a binding rule makes a second claim about legal positivism. Indeed, several commentators have insisted that this is the one crucial factor that distinguishes legal positivism from natural law theory. The claim is that all authoritative laws must be authored by a human agent. In contrast, natural law theory is said to postulate a non-human, transcendent source as the authorizing origin of human laws. Such a transcedndent source authorizes the *content* of human laws. Hans Kelsen especially distinguishes positive from natural laws along these lines. Even when Neil MacCormick and Kent Greenawalt claim that the authorizing origin of posited laws rests upon convention, they accept that conventions are accessible through a legal language as Hart has described such; that is, as inscribed in writing.[80] They too thereby forget about the felt experiences that embody inscription. That is, they too excise the phenomenological experience from the external statements that recognize unwritten conventions.

---

80 See, e.g., MacCormick, "*The Concept of Law* and the Concept of Law," in ed. Robert P. George, *The Autonomy of Law*, 163-93, 181: "It [the rule of recognition] is a custom that sees the overall unity of authorization and hammers out priority as between rival authorizations, that alone can finally underpin an abstract constitution and make it constitutive of a going legal order." Kent Greenawalt assumes the viability of the identity of "conventions" by seeking out the many different recognizable conventions at the state level in the United States. See Greenawalt, "The Rule of Recognition and the Constitution."

b) Recognition through language

To what extent does legal positivism postulate that all authoritative rules must be inscribed by human agents? The judge, situated from an external vantage point, recognizes the 'social' origin, a judicial practice, in the inscriptions of texts. "What is crucial" in the shift from the pre-legal to the legal moment of deliberation and justification, Hart insists, is that the referent for law is a "statement," not a social experience. The statement manifests a practice in "writing or inscription."[81] Hart describes the social practice variously as "latent" and "hidden" in statements. Authoritative rules can only be located in writing. Hart continues that writing alone constitutes "the *proper* way of disposing of doubts as to the existence of the rule." The writing acknowledges the practice as legal. An "external" statement is the "natural language" of an observer, according to Hart. An observer records *ab extra* the fact that a group of lawyers and judges has accepted or intended certain rules. The observer need not personally accept them. The observer's record is written; it is an inscription. The observer provides "an authoritative mark" that signifies that there is a "system" to otherwise "discrete, unconnected" rules. That is, a written language constructs a systematic structure of interconnected rules. The external "mark" or "inscription" or "statement" recognizes the unwritten judicial practice. The mark of recognition constitutes "the germ of the idea of legal validity."

c) A pre-existence (of language)

Accordingly, the authorizing origin of the legal structure is believed to pre-exist language. The origin is external and admittedly inaccessible through what Hart takes as the language of the structure. The originary experience of immediacy remains unretrievable except through secondary rules which re-present the experience as an *ex post facto* new beginning of the legal structure. The writing, after the judges have immediately shared the acceptance of certain primary rules, re-presents the authorizing origin as writing. The originary experience – the unstated judicial practice – is forgotten once the legal project of writing begins. That is, lawyers and judges must be satisfied with a second-order reproduction of a first-order, pre-linguistic experience which must be forever excluded as non-legal and moral. The origin is absent from the primary and secondary rules for binding rules can only be expressed through language, according to Hart. Agents of the origin can only recognize the origin through written signs.

Interestingly, contemporary commentators of Hart have been preoccupied with recognizing the 'foundation' of a legal structure in the articulated statements *about*

81 Hart, *Concept of Law*, 95.

rules, themselves objects of inscription, rather than with the forgotten originary moment of immediacy (if the latter moment were ever recognizable other than through writing). The origin of the rule of recognition is discarded as pre-legal or primitive, as exterior to the trace of authoritative rules. The origin is displaced in favour of a new, revised, transformed origin. Morality is rejected as pre-legal. But once language re-presents the pre-legal as a secondary rule, law becomes separated from this anthropological origin. Morality takes on a very special meaning as any object that is external to the authoritative language of the legal structure. Indeed, Hart raises the possibility that morality is any "non-legal" object which the legal structure, unified under the rule of recognition, excludes from the statements of primary and secondary rules.[82]

More specifically, Hart writes that the authorizing origin of the rule of recognition is "generally not stated." Nor is the origin signified at the moment of being internalized amongst juridical experts. The rule of recognition takes on an 'existence' when legal officials retrospectively *envision* or *picture* the internalized acceptance as a rule of recognition. The internal statements offer the raw material with which to recognize the acceptance. The picture of the internalized acceptance is represented as an externalized signification about the acceptance. Hart calls the signification here an external statement. Primary rules can now be justified in terms of the criterion or criteria (per Raz) articulated in the external statement. The existence of the rule of recognition is "shown" as the juridical officers trace one rule backwards to another in a never-ending quest to ensure that primary rules are consistent with the criteria of validity inscribed in external statements.[83] The "internal standpoint" is "unstated" in contrast with the external standpoint of an impartial observer who states, as an issue of fact, that juridical officials accept the rule. The "unstated" constitutes the background or context for the statements about judicial practices. But the unstated convention, like the postulate of Bentham's and Austin's theories of law, is essential to render a finality to the otherwise infinite ratiocination of primary rules. Without such a finality, there would be no ultimate sovereign.[84] Nor would there be posited rules: flux and fragments of writing hardly make for the fixity associated with a posited rule.

d) The separation of language from experience

Hart goes to great pains to dissociate the external statement about a rule of recognition from the anthropologically experienced practices that internal statements manifest (and statements can only manifest such practices). The

82 Hart, *Concept of Law*, 170.
83 Hart, *Concept of Law*, 101.
84 See discussion in Hart, *Concept of Law*, 66-67.

practices are experienced by legal officials. An external statement intellectualizes a oneness from a multiplicity of experiences so as to produce a social rule. Again, the excluded experience precedes such a social rule, according to Hart. When he confronts the position of Lord Devlin, again, Hart differentiates the feelings of "intolerance, indignation and disgust" with his revisionist authorizing origin of a legal structure. Feelings offer "multiple criteria, not a single criterion" with which to authorize the limitation of a liberty.[85] "Thought" or "critical reflection" transforms popular morality into a singular authoritative action.

So too, Hart dissociates the authorizing origin from "any psychological or physical fact" when he analyzes a right. A right exists by virtue of a sentence that states that the right exists, according to Hart. Such a statement signifies a right, he adds. The signification justifies the right. Justification inheres to a statement 'I have a right to....'[86] Once again, whether a group follows a practice of respecting each other's dignity does not go to the authority of that practice. Rather, authority draws from *statements about* the practice. Whatever the members of the interpretive community mean by their practice as they intuitively experience the practice is irrelevant to the retrospective legal signification. The latter, Hart believes, lifts the experience into a language that other legal officials will recognize.

e) Incorporation of non-law into law

Against this background, one can appreciate why Hart would insist that laws are separate from morals. As Hart puts his claim, legal positivism means "the simple contention that it is in no sense a necessary truth that laws reproduce or satisfy certain demands of morality, though in fact they have often done so."[87] With respect to the latter caveat, Hart does admit that judges so incorporate non-legal factors into their justificatory analysis of primary rules. All human beings universally share certain physical, psychological, and economic conditions, according to Hart. Hart identifies five such "elementary truths concerning human beings": human vulnerability, approximate equality, limited altruism, limited resources, and limited understanding and strength of will.[88] In his important essay "Positivism and the Separation of Law and Morals," Hart describes these empirically contingent conditions as so universally shared that, absent the conditions, one would not have social rules. That is, there would not be social practices that writing could recognize. Indeed, certain legal rules are "so fundamental" that one

85 Hart, "Immorality and Treason," 51.
86 See esp. Hart, "Are There Any Natural Rights?" in A.I. Melden, ed., *Human Rights* (Belmont, CA: Wadsworth, 1971), 49-54, 51.
87 Hart, *Concept of Law*, 185-86.
88 Hart, *Concept of Law*, 193-200.

would not have any other legal rules without them. Hart offers the examples of proscriptions against violence to the person or to private property. "All legal systems in fact coincide with morality at the intersection of such conditions and primary legal rules," he writes.[89]

Accordingly, the shared conditions of peace and property constitute a "minimum content of natural law." It is these empirical conditions that induce the internal point of view that one 'ought' to obey certain primary and secondary rules. Hart admits that such rules incorporate these internal social conditions. "No 'positivist' could deny that these are facts, or that the stability of legal systems depends in part upon such types of correspondence with morals. If this is what is meant by the necessary connection of law and morals, its existence should be conceded," Hart writes in the *Concept of Law*.[90] A rule of recognition recognizes the social bonding experience as a stated rule.

f) Two origins

Thus, Hart postulates two origins to a modern legal structure. The one, the pre-legal, is excluded and then forgotten in internal and external statements. The second, alone recognized as authoritative in legal language, is signified in external statements about the forgotten origin.

Hart considers the signified rule of recognition (the second-level origin) as a 'given,' beyond the judiciary's control, even though the judiciary retrospectively constructs the rule of recognition as it makes statements about the first origin. Notwithstanding the 'givenness' of the signified origin as the major premise of the logical relation, the official creates the first origin (the unstated origin), first, in that legal officials "voluntarily" accept the unstated and unwritten judicial practices; secondly, in that they utter statements *about* the practices; and thirdly, in that they identify what primary rules should be included in the legal structure by justifying them in terms of the *ex post facto* revisionist origin or criteria of validity. The criteria are inscribed as rules of recognition.

g) Critical reflection

The project of linking rules to such criteria is the project of "critical reflection." One critiques the primary and secondary rules by accepting the rules of recognition and then intellectually analyzing the consistency of the primary rules with the rules of recognition. Hart considers the concept of law as confined to the relations between primary and secondary rules. The unsignified is excluded as pre-legal.

89 Hart, "Positivism and the Separation of Law and Morals," at 623, *Harvard Law Review* and 464 of Olafson, *Society, Law and Morality*.

90 Hart, *Concept of Law*, 204.

The unsignified is the realm of feeling, and legal criticism only begins with the acceptance or recognition of certain signs as binding. As Hart explains:

> But such feelings are neither necessary nor sufficient for the existence of 'binding' rules. There is no contradiction in saying that people accept certain rules but experience no such feelings of compulsion. What is necessary is that they should have a critical reflective attitude to certain patterns of behaviour as a common standard, and that this should display itself in criticism (including self criticism), demands for conformity, and in acknowledgements that such criticism and demands are justified, all of which find their characteristic expression in the normative terminology of 'ought,' 'must,' and 'should,' 'right' and 'wrong.'[91]

Accordingly, the rule of recognition is really a rule of mis-recognition because the authorizing origin – the felt experience before language – is mis-recognized as a rule of recognition instead of the unstated bonding experience that, Hart claims, precedes and grounds the inscribed rule of recognition. Hart does allow that all laws in a modern legal structure are the consequence of human will.

h) The lost referent

But, at the same moment that officials make statements about primary or secondary rules and thereby inscribe criteria of validity, the referent – the unstated judicial practices – is excluded and even forgotten in the legal analysis. The authorizing origin of the primary and secondary rules, then, becomes unknowable through the authoritative language. The referent of the concept of law becomes an inscription about the unstated origins. Legal authority depends upon an invisible source or grounding – invisible through the statements of primary and secondary rules – as the referent for what is authoritative. The authorizing origin, that is, cannot be considered 'legal' nor can it be recognized except 'after the fact' in legal language, according to Hart. The judiciary can, at best, "approximate" the authorizing origin through a statement. As he puts it, the official, because he or she externally recognizes the origin, can, at best, "very nearly reproduce" the origin.[92] Not all customs are legally binding. Only those customs are binding if officials recognize "statements" about customs, Hart writes about Rex I at an early stage in the *Concept of Law*.[93]

Again, the recognition of a custom in a "statement" takes one from the "pre-legal into the legal world."[94] The unstated origin, by itself, is not part of the legal

91 Hart, *Concept of Law*, 57.

92 Hart, *Concept of Law*, 90.

93 Hart, *Concept of Law*, 53. Hart writes that, until the moment when a custom is inscribed, "there will be an interregnum in which no law can be made."

94 Hart explains that a small community "closely knit by ties of kinship, common sentiment, and belief, and placed in a stable environment" needs to supplement "unofficial rules" because, first, such unofficial rules do not provide "a system" or structure; secondly, the rules are static; and thirdly, there is an inadequate institutional means to resolve private disputes (*Concept of Law*, 92-93). The remedy for

structure: a habit of obedience is not enough to account for the right of an official to rule.[95] The habit, a custom, is inscribed in writing. The custom is promulgated in a quantifiable time and space in the form of a statute or regulation or judicial precedent. Once inscribed, though, the custom is no longer a custom. The bonding experience, by itself, does not confer authority upon an official. Nor is the experience a referent for the authority of primary rules, according to Hart. The authorizing origin of the concept of law, though indispensable to the authority and construction of primary and secondary rules, must be excluded as pre-law, as moral, as a radical other to the authoritative primary and secondary rules. This is the ultimate irony of a great text that claims to offer a positivist theory of law.

6. Is the Authorizing Origin Accessible to Legal Officials?

The lost originary referent takes me to the final claim that Hart and his commentators have accepted without question. Hart makes it clear that whether a custom is authoritative hangs upon its "origin."[96] Some customs do not posses the authority of law, for example, if they have gone unrecognized in a particular legal system. A custom is recognized, Hart writes, if juridical officials inscribe the custom as a "statement." Commentators on Hart's *Concept of Law* have not questioned whether it is, indeed, possible to recognize the origin if they exclude the origin as pre-legal. Even Hart assumes that the origin is accessible to legal language, despite "the jump" of faith from the legal to the pre-legal.

Let us return to what Hart says about the accessibility of the authorizing origin of humanly posited primary and secondary rules. For if the origin is inaccessible through the authoritative language, even by Hart's own admission, it would be difficult for Hart and his commentators to maintain that their positivist theories entirely leave it to human agents to posit laws.

Rules of recognition are external statements, inscribed from the outside, *about* the unwritten and the unspoken assumptions that authors of primary rules accept. The referent of the external statements are the internal statements. The external statements themselves supplement the referent, the internal statements. As noted, Hart describes the external statements as supplements.[97] Once the juridical officials recognize the hidden practices through their external statements, the officials can continue with their justification of primary rules in terms of the inscribed

these defects, according to Hart, "consists in supplementing the *primary* rules of obligation with *secondary* rules which are of a different kind" (94). Such a remedy "might, in itself, be considered a step from the pre-legal to the legal," he continues.

95 Hart, *Concept of Law*, 59.

96 Hart, *Concept of Law*, 44-9.

97 See, by way of example and only as an example, Hart, *Concept of Law*, 91-9.

supplementary rules. Accordingly, although the secondary rules supplement their own authoritative origin in the unstated and unwritten, the authority for the primary rules arrives on the scene of the legal enterprise after internal statements have been inscribed in writing. So too, the authority for the secondary rules is recognized after internal statements have been inscribed in writing. Permit me to emphasize: legal officials revise the authorizing origin as a statement from the unspoken human experiences of bonding that the primary rules are supposed to re-present. The rule of recognition is thereby a rule of mis-recognition. In the process of mis-recognition, the unstated judicial practices of the moment of immediacy, though everything is done in an effort to articulate them, are forgotten in the search for authority.

a) The loss of memory

Let us focus more closely on the excluded moment of the felt experience. The forgetting occurs at the moment when the official recognizes a secondary rule through an external *statement* and then justifies a primary rule in terms of that statement. Thus, a judge traces the reason for a primary rule to a "footing" that an external observer would recognize after the primary rule has been written. At the moment of application, though, the authorizing origin of the footing is unrecognized as a signification in legal language.[98] Hart attributes recognition as the moment when a practice is signified by legal signs. That is, the authorizing origin, when applied, is left unrecognized until later signified in an external statement about internal statements. The authorizing origin precedes legal language. The preceding experience is excised from legal analysis because no external observer can yet signify the experience as a referent in a written statement until other internal statements have been inscribed. The "footing" for a primary rule – the 'stuff' of a modern legal structure – becomes a retrospectively imposed act of writing. The authorizing origin is signified *after* it has been internalized as an experience shared amongst juridical officials. The authorizing origin is also signified only *after* juridical officials have tacitly accepted the footing in their internal statements.

If one accepts for the moment that a statement is expressed by some preceding author or creator, the expert who studies the statement searches for the referent that the authored statement signifies. The referent is absent from the statement. Hart calls the referent, a rule. A rule categorizes or typifies a social event or person. A trial judge, for example, includes and excludes evidence with reference to an authoritative primary rule that inscribes categorical boundaries for a typified social event. A precedent abstracts such cognitive boundaries from a prior internal statement. So too, legal analysis begins with another rule, the rule of recognition,

98 Hart, *Concept of Law*, 103.

as the criterion of validity for primary rules. The rule of recognition is the referent for the justification or "grounds" of the primary rule even though Hart describes how primary rules manifest the rule of recognition. The referent for the rule of recognition is another statement, an internal statement, which presupposes a hidden and forgotten unstated and unwritten experience. The rule of recognition can only approximate that experience as Hart limits legal analysis to the justificatory grounds that officials implicitly accept through internal statements.[99] The ultimate referent, the unwritten experience, is absent from the language of primary and secondary rules. As such, the experience cannot be a referent since it cannot be signified, according to Hart, except as a statement. Hart admits to the externality of the experience by excluding it as pre-legal. How Hart's works manifest such an exclusion is exemplified in Section Two above. The authorizing origin of posited rules is lost in that legal analysis is believed to begin only with the external statements that recognize a rule of recognition.

Unlike the primary and secondary rules, the origin of the rule of recognition – the unstated bonding experience of judicial practices – lacks a referent. If the unstated practices did refer to a still further referent such as, say, a divine Author, then the practices would not originate the concept of law. A still further object, before the practices, would found the primary and secondary rules. The unstated judicial practices would be merely intermediate moments between the signified rules on the one hand and the unsignified practices on the other. Hart acknowledges the importance of this point in several contexts. He thereby continues the problematic of the tradition of legal positivism. Only Hart takes a different tack from his predecessors. Hobbes had resolved the problematic by grounding the authorizing origin in authors who had just escaped from the invisible condition. Austin finalized the trace of commands in the non-justicible habits of the people. Kelsen finalized the trace of 'ought' statements in one final "phantom of the brain," as Kant put it.[100] Hart now tries to resolve the problematic of legal positivism by postulating an exterior, pre-linguistic experience as a radical other to the legally binding primary and secondary rules. Hart postulates the pre-legal judicial practices as existing before legal officials recognize them through writing.

b) *The picture of the origin*

The best that Hart's lawyers and judges can do – and perhaps that any human agent can do – is to picture or envision the lost origin. A picture delineates boundaries. The boundaries *form* a shape. The shape is transparent because Hart postulates that it lacks an identity since an identity can only be formed in a legal

99 Hart, *Concept of Law*, 107.
100 Kant, *Grounding of the Metaphysics of Morals*, 462.

existence; that is, in a signifying writing. The shape lacks a body and mind associated with biological beings. Only forms that are signified in external and internal statements can take on a legal existence, he insists. Though the shape is transparent, Hart says, legal agents are "haunted" by the faceless shape of bonding.[101] The bonding experience is primordial. As later judges and lawyers fill the shape with the particulars of internal and external statements, the shape takes on an identity. The rule of recognition especially gives particulars to that identity.

And yet, the identity is imagined as the origin of the rule of recognition remains a spirit-like shape on the other side of the radical void between the legal and the pre-legal. Because Hart associates authors with statements, the new-found identity of the origin – the rule of recognition – is sometimes believed to have been authored by founding fathers. External statements give 'body' to the author, although the body lacks the face of a human body. The body of the founding author(s) lacks the shape of a biological body. Indeed, the founding author lacks the possibility of having had a bodily experience. The haunting spectre, which grounds all primary and secondary rules, floats through the corridors of the courthouses, the libraries of the law offices, and the analyses of law students exam answers. The originary source can be neither perceived nor experienced in that juridical officials must exclude the origin as pre-legal. Again, the haunting source can only be "approximated" in statements. Hart has the judges and lawyers reach closer to the shapeless originating moment as they rigorously analyze internal and external statements about rights and duties and the like. But they can never access this authorizing origin because it is set up as the radical other to the authoritative primary and secondary rules. All that legal officials can do is to play with the statements that the officials themselves write in the name of the nameless origin.

c) *Faith in a possibility*

Thus, there remains an act of faith in the possibility that there is even a pre-legal experience before legal existence. The official must "leap," to use Hart's term, from the one to the other. How does the judge envision the authorizing origin, according to Hart? The judge envisions the origin by representing it in a statement. According to Hart, though, the origin, the referent, of legal authority never is a statement. For if the origin were a statement, it would be a rule. But the rule of recognition refers to an immediately unsignified origin as manifested in internal statements. Primary authoritative rules are "shown" and "derived" from prior statements that judges retro-

101 Hart puts the point this way: "The figure of a *bond* binding the person obligated ... is buried in the word 'obligation,' and the similar notion of a debt laden in the word 'duty.'... in this figure, which *haunts* [emphasis added] much legal thought, the social pressure appears as a chain binding those who have obligations so that they are not free to do what they want" (*Concept of Law*, 87).

spectively situate within a secondary statement about the primary rules. The latter secondary statement is what Hart calls a "supplement" to the primary rules.

Thus, the authorizing origin of a legal structure is transformed from the hidden, 'unwritten' practices that legal officials accept through their primary rules into the rule of recognition, which the judge *ex post facto* states *about* the unwritten, tacitly accepted practices. Hart appreciates this point. In Section Three above, I offered examples from his works where his own concern is manifested. Like Kelsen, Hart believes that the moment before speech and before writing can never be accessed through the language of a modern legal structure. This helps us to understand why Hart must excise this originary moment as "pre-legal."

The retrospective signification of the unwritten experience transforms the unwritten into an inaccessible authorizing origin for posited rules. Because the rule of recognition is written *after* a judge applies a primary rule, the judicial practices, as the authorizing origin of the primary rule, can never be reached through the internal and external statements, Hart postulates. Moreover, because the rule of recognition, an act of signification after the moment of immediacy, becomes the revisionist "foundation" for the authority of all primary rules after the latter are posited and after the rule of recognition is recognized from a configuration of internal statements, even the second-level rule of recognition too is inaccessible through the language of the structure. Neither the judicial practice as the referent of all secondary rules nor the secondary rules themselves are accessible through the language of internal statements. The secondary rules merely supplement the primary rules, and the latter are held out as pre-existing the secondary rules. The unstated judicial practices cannot be reached until the practices are recognized in legal language – the "statements" – and that moment occurs after the unstated experience and even after the primary rules have been "applied." The statements arrive on the legal scene first. What Hart considers the supplement – the language – becomes primary.

Contrary to the view that the rule of recognition constitutes the authorizing origin of a modern legal structure, a view which many of Hart commentators accept,[102] the authorizing origin of the posited rules associated with a modern state cannot be recognized. The origin cannot be recognized as a moment in the time of a clock because time can be quantifiably identified only if time is represented as a sign in a language. That is, the signs of a language signify the time when a legislature or judicial or administrative agent has promulgated the signs. Nor can the authorizing origin be identified with a particular place, such as a particular parliament or court, because a place must also be signified through language. Once Hart postulates a pre-legal where, once upon a time not unlike the

102 See the references cited above, fns. 1-4, 6-7.

Greek totemic legal culture described in Chapter One, morals had fused with law, human actors cannot promulgate nor even author the origin without contradicting the exclusion of the origin from the legal. Though laws are "capable of creation or change by deliberate act," the moral feelings, rules, principles, and standards external to the language of primary and secondary rules cannot be considered as deliberative of authoritative rules.[103] For how could one say that an origin has been authored when in fact the origin is unsignified until after the fact, after the experience of immediacy with a practice? The authorizing origin 'exists' as an inaccessible source, absent from the language of juridical officials.

7. The Forgotten Origin

H.L.A. Hart's insights into the concept of law encourage one to pose the big questions. How can an experiential moment be accessed when Hart excludes such an experiential moment from what he considers legal language? For Hart, posited binding rules begin only with language and a written language at that. That said, the experiential is excluded as moral. Though the legal inevitably includes such moral or pre-legal considerations, the legal is lifted above the pre-legal into a language of primary and secondary rules. Accordingly, the legal official must possess an act of faith that the secondary rules do indeed accurately re-present the bonding experiences that, according to Hart, remain only a possibility. The authority of primary and secondary rules depends upon the hypothesis that a primordial experience, once upon a time, did fuse the moral (bodily experience) with law. And yet, the experience can never be retrieved, having been excluded from the start as absent from existence. Judicial officials can only write *about* the experience as a possibility. Officials believe the writing arrives *after* the experience 'existed,' in Hart's view. But legal existence is constituted from the writing that signifies primary and secondary rules, according to Hart. The writing only re-presents the presence that the legal officials experience.

Consistent with Hobbes, Austin and Kelsen, then, Hart takes the authoritative origin of humanly posited rules as absent legal existence. Human beings can only approximate the origin. The unwritten becomes the raw material for the written all the while that the unwritten must be excluded as non-legal. The claim that binding laws may only be posited by human authors collapses, for Hart postulates an authorizing source that transcends such binding laws. Human agents "voluntarily" accept an unwritten practice. They do not voluntarily accept the experience. When one consciously posits a rule, then only the rule is authored by a human being. The bonding experience of the practice is postulated as inaccessible

103 Hart, *Concept of Law*, 176.

precisely because Hart excludes experience from language. Humanly authored laws exist by virtue of an authority. But the authority is associated with the later Greek sense and the Romal legal practice of an *arche* and that *arche*, to be an origin, is invisible to the language of the primary and secondary rules.

a) The problem

Hart's legal officials, then, have a problem. The boundaries of their analytic enterprise is confined to internal statements about primary rules and external statements about secondary rules. The primary and secondary rules are of the "*essence* of law."[104] Yet the authority for these rules is believed to pre-exist the statements. Yet, despite its preceding existence, the officials retrospectively recognize the origin as a statement. The statement re-presents the origin as a revisionist 'origin' because legal existence excludes the pre-scriptive or pre-writing.

This problematic is not peculiar to Hart. Since the period of Roman lawyers, perhaps even since Plato's *Laws*, the authority of laws has been associated with an *arche* or final source or ground which, to be a final ground, must remain an exteriority from the humanly posited laws. To be final, the origin must lack a referent. To be an *arche*, the origin must be unlike any legal standard recognized as a primary or secondary rule. The origin is a moment of purity. The origin is silent, unspoken, unwritten, and without particulars. Internal and external statements cannot retrieve a presence with such a pre-linguistic experience. Statements can only "approximate" the presence as a "supplement."

b) The loss of memory

As a consequence, the presence is forgotten inside the language of primary and secondary rules. In the quest for authoritative legal rules, the agents of the lost origin are "indifferent" to the "motives, intentions, or other 'internal' accompaniments of conduct" that go to the immediacy of bonding.[105] Without the particulars that come with a language, legal officials just cannot access the origin through what Hart considers a language. Since Hart demarcates and then excludes human experience from language and since he privileges language alone as expressive of the true/real of legal authority, the originary moment of experience is inaccessible from within the language of the legal structure. Even though Hart believes that legal officials are unable to experience or even to know the forgotten origin through legal language, Hart privileges such officials with the monopoly of interpreting the statements about the origin by virtue of his admission that the language of the structure is self-binding. Indeed, officials organize themselves into law 'societies,'

104 Hart, *Concept of Law*, 154.
105 Hart, *Concept of Law*, 172.

which include and exclude persons as members who may authoritatively profess the language. Those persons admitted to the society claim to know which rules are authoritative and which are not. The rule of recognition, not the moment of immediacy, becomes the "ultimate rule."[106] And at that point, a modern legal system can be said to have taken form.

Accordingly, the language of primary rules and secondary rules, by excluding the immediacy of an experience as the "pre-legal" or as 'moral,' legitimizes or authorizes its own self-referentiality. In order to maintain the officials' claim to know which rules are authoritative, then, the inaccessibility of the authorizing origin is forgotten by officials. Something is forgotten if one was conscious that it earlier existed. The forgotten authorizing origin, though recognized as important to the authority of primary and secondary rules, remains a dark, lost moment because the concept of law or, at least, the concept of a modern legal system, necessitates that the forgotten origin remains concealed inside what Hart takes to be legal language. Legal officials must maintain that, at some point in time, deep within the recesses of the felt experience, there was an experiential moment when the subject and official experienced a shared bonding with their practice. The experience was raw, unmediated through a language. The experience was not intellectualized through reflection. The experience was anathema to a critical reflective mind. The experience is a radical other to legal statements. This radical other offers what the legal structure is not: an experience that is considered legitimate, yet lacking a sign with which to represent the experience. Between the two worlds of the pre-legal of experience and the legal of language, there dwells an "interregnum."[107] History, Hart believes, begins with what he understands as language. The pre-legal is an a-history. Morality, properly so called, is believed to begin with the non-experiential language, as a "critical reflective morality." The pre-legal is an amorality. The primary and secondary rules are "not only the heart of a legal system but a most powerful tool for the analysis of much which has puzzled both the jurist and the political theorist."[108]

c) The double loss of memory

There is a double forgetting, though. For juridical officials, as they continue to ground their primary rules, secondary rules, and power-granting institutions in the rule of recognition, forget that they have forgotten something. As a consequence, the official's quest for an authorizing grounding or justification of a primary rule is self-referential and self-binding. The official encloses himself or herself within

106 Hart, *Concept of Law*, 105.
107 Hart, *Concept of Law*, 53.
108 Hart, *Concept of Law*, 98.

a metaphysical world that excises the felt experiences of social life of lawyer and non-lawyer alike. For Hart, both the internal and external point of view are internal to language. The language conceals the moment of immediacy. Hart himself writes again and again that the body experiences an immediacy of bondedness before the body makes an internal statement. It becomes very difficult for judge and jurist to expose the moment of the forgetting of an origin. Such a double concealment is critical to the claim of the tradition of legal positivism that all laws are humanly posited.

With the concealment maintained, it is a subtle shift for the officials to maintain that they feel constrained by what is forgotten. Kent Greenawalt especially emphasizes that whatever is said about the indeterminacy of rules, officials at the appellate level act as if they are seriously constrained by unwritten conventions.[109] The legal officials even give the constraining factor a name: they call it the 'rule of law.' The judges and lawyers construct the necessity of the absent origin and yet they believe that they are constrained by the absence, as if it were independent of their acts. The image of the absent origin drives the legal officials to complete their picture of a totality. But the authorizing origin is a remainder to the totality. The officials desire the origin precisely because it is absent from the officials' cognitive grasp.

We know from Thomas Hobbes and John Austin and Jeremy Bentham and Hans Kelsen and, now, H.L.A. Hart that the origin of *auctoritas* must differ from ordinarily authored rules. The difference is needed in order to resolve the problematic of finality. Hart admits that, without such a finality to rules, a legal structure would lack sovereignty.[110] Moreover, a rule could not be said to be posited for it would merely mark a transient trace of unconnected statements.

But can an unspoken practice offer a finality to the trace of authority from primary rules to secondary rules if the practice is pre-scriptive; that is, if it is postulated as dwelling in the experience of the body before officials intellectualize about that experience through language? The origin is supposed to pre-exist the ordinary primary and secondary rules. But I have shown how Hart emphasized that the rule of recognition, and even the "unstated" origin that that rule recognizes, enter legal language *after* the human posit of primary rules and *after* the felt experience of bonding with something hidden behind such primary rules. How can any object that is taken as an origin finalize a trace of humanly constructed rules if the origin is signified *after* the trace has taken place?

---

109 See, e.g., Greenawalt, "Too Thin and Too Rich: Distinguishing Features of Legal Positivism" in ed. Robert P. George, *The Autonomy of Law*, 1-29, 24; "Hart's Rule of Recognition and the United States, 53-55; and "The Rule of Recognition and the Constitution."

110 Hart, *The Concept of Law*, 66-7.

Hart's theory of the experiential origin of the modern foundation of posited laws raises one final set of critical issues. If the origin is, indeed, unstated, as Hart says, then why can one not compare the authorizing origin of humanly posited laws with Dante's own description of Paradise (and of Beatrice) as "unspeakable"? Had we best describe the authorizing origin as invisible? Is the origin divine in the sense of being unknowable as Kant claimed for the perfectly pure will in the *Grounding of the Metaphysics of Morals* and of being a pure *a priori* thought, as Kelsen claimed for the *Grundnorm*? Does Hart, not unlike Kelsen, admit that legal officials must take a leap of faith as they ground the rule of recognition in the unknowable? Is the moment of immediacy a mere possibility? After all, only rules exist in a modern legal structure, according to Hart. And does the authorizing origin of primary rules not become a mere excess or a supplement, just as Hart describes, to the primary and secondary rules, even though all legal authority is traceable to the supplement as the authorizing origin of the structure? Indeed, is the originating moment of legal authority merely imagined or, in Kelsen's words, "fictive" in order to make sense of otherwise disparate fragments of internal statements? These questions come to the fore once one remembers the forgotten origin of H.L.A. Hart's concept of law.

9

Forgetting the Act of Forgetting: Raz's Inaccessible Origin of Legal Reasoning

The tradition of legal positivism, we have now observed, has consistently expelled the authorizing origin of posited norms/rules from what officials consider legal existence. Hobbes required, in the form of a social contract of autonomous authors, that the officials never return to the origin of their civil laws in a natural condition. Jean-Jacques Rousseau acknowledged the importance of legislated laws only to supplement a General Will which, I argued from his works, was divine. John Austin took up the notion of 'the habits of the people' only to expel them as laws improperly so called because the people were not a distinct and assignable author on the institutional hierarchy that officials consider the 'real' and the 'practical.' Kelsen realized the importance of a pure concept as the presupposition of the trace of authority through the language of officials, but he understood the concept in such a manner that it was unsignified and unsignifiable and, as such, invisible to the language of the officials. H.L.A. Hart shifted the authorizing origin to the immediacy of bonding that an official experiences with a judicial practice only to exclude such an immediacy as pre-legal. The legal, for Hart – as for Hobbes, Rousseau, Austin, and Kelsen – was written in scripts that distinct and assignable officials, situated on a pyramidal hierarchy, authored. With each great thinker, the most important source or *arche* of authorizing posited laws was inaccessible from the language of legal norms/rules.

Now, unlike his recent predecessors, Joseph Raz acknowledges the importance of the pre-legal for a theory of legal obligation. Further, legal existence – as represented by the civil institutions that author legal writing – could not 'exist' without the deep experiential attitudes of respect that officials share towards legal institutions. Raz analyzes the pre-legal in a manner in which the tradition of legal positivism has not noted since Thomas Hobbes. And yet, like his predecessors, Raz excludes this very pre-legal realm, acknowledged by Raz to be so important for legal obligation, from (legal) existence. A legal official, immersed in the concepts and values that institutions posit, begins and ends his or her reasoning by excluding the pre-legal from legal analysis. As legal officials address texts and events from the legal point of view inside the structure, their exclusionary project forgets the importance of the pre-legal attitudes that Raz has recognized and privileged in his theory of law. The "ultimate" authorizing origin of posited rules, Raz claims, is located *inside* a coherent structure of norms that the institutions posit. The experiential attitudes, what Raz acknowledges as the origin of legal obligation, are forgotten in the quest for authoritative rules. Raz's version of legal positivism requires that officials forget that they had even forgotten the authorizing origin of their posited norms and values.

1. Experiential Bonding as the Origin of the Legal Structure

Raz's argument in support of positivism, on its own terms, manifests how legal officials forget the authorizing origin of humanly posited norms. I intend to reconstruct the several stages in his argument. The initial stage claims that the authorizing origin of legally binding norms rests with the experiential attitude of respect towards a society's legal institutions in general. Legal officials, Raz points out, exclude such an inaccessible origin from legal reasoning. The experiential meanings go to what is non-law. So, allow me to address how Raz privileges the experiential in his theory of the nature of law.

First, Raz privileges the experiential body in his theory of the common good. The common good is more important to the individual than is the enjoyment of a right.[1] Rights involve the politics of conflicting interests of individuals. But the common good transcends such a balancing of individual interests/values, according to Raz. How does the common good transcend the balancing of values? What is the common good? Is it located in a speculative metaphysics, such as Thomas Aquinas suggests? Or is it grounded in a social context where the values are added and subtracted from each other in order to gain the greatest good? Or, is the common good drawn from a social unity and social stability built upon a consensus of the whole populace?

Raz takes up the latter alternative. The common good is produced from the bodily meanings of officials and/or the populace.[2] Such meanings manifest a bonding of the individual with the common good. As he ends his essay, "Facing Diversity" (1990), the common good is characterized by an immediacy between individual and the common good. Here, an individual *means* the common good as he or she draws from what Gadamer calls his or her past forestructures of meaning

1 Raz, "Rights and Individual Well-Being" (1992), in *Ethics in the Public Domain: Essays in the Morality of Law and Politics* (Oxford: Clarendon Press, 1995): 44-59, 53-5.

2 For the importance of the experiential body in legal interpretation, see generally, Conklin, *The Phenomenology of Modern Legal Discourse* (Aldershot/Brookfield: Dartmouth/Ashgate, 1998).

and expectations into the future.[3] The bonding is an unquantifiable experience. Raz explains that, over time, an official or citizen slowly becomes attached to

> national symbols, cultural and conventional as well as legal (language, literature, foods, flag, and anthem). These evoke emotion, and create common bonds among those who state these attitudes. The bonds are important elements in shaping one's imagination, and in defining one's historical horizon. People share a common pride in a shared historical experience. Such identification normally includes attachment to certain values.[4]

Symbolic and affective elements cement a society into a social unity. The non-cognitive characterizes the bonds, though they may be expressed in terms of very abstract concepts such as liberty, fraternity, and equality. Such concepts "overlap" with the shared experiences in order to produce "a very firm foundation for social unity and stability." Even principled arguments "feed expectations and breed a common understanding of the legal culture of the country to which they in turn are responsive and responsible," as Raz puts it in his final chapter in *Ethics in the Public Domain*.[5] The individual emotionally identifies or bonds with the symbols. Symbols, such as a flag or anthem, manifest the common good.

Which is more important: the overlapping categories or the experiential meanings conferred into the statements representing the categories?

Here, Raz is ambiguous. On the one hand, Raz associates the obligation to obey the law with the pre-legal affective bonding experiences with the institutional sources of particular laws. On the other hand, Raz clearly emphasizes that an affective belief cannot be the believer's reason for thinking that a legal proposition is true: there must be some external cognitive standard to which an *impersonal* appeal can be made.[6] Truth is a reason for action, not the fact that one holds a belief, according to Raz. Indeed, one can have a belief only if one is capable of distinguishing between the belief in a proposition and the truth of the proposition. The reason for action (which Raz considers truth) of the proposition contributes to the common good.

Raz privileges the phenomenal body when he argues that the legal official must experience a belief that his or her action is justified in terms of the shared bonding with legal institutions.[7] The belief goes to the likelihood that an action's substantive content will be sound or true. The belief, an experiential meaning,

---

3 As explained in Conklin, *Phenomenology of Modern Legal Discourse*, 21-4.

4 Raz, "Facing Diversity: the Case of Epistemic Abstinence," (1990) in Raz, *Ethics in the Public Domain*, 60-96, 83.

5 Raz, "The Politics of the Rule of Law" (1990), in *Ethics in the Public Domain*, 370-78, 374.

6 Raz, "Facing Diversity," 89.

7 Raz, "Liberalism, Scepticism and Democracy" (1989), in *Ethics in the Public Domain*, 97-124, 115.

precedes the rational justification of any particular action.[8] The belief that one's action can be justified goes to the individual's well-being and, in turn, to the common good of society even though one's particular action is wrong or unjust.[9] That is, the independent justification of a decision in terms of argument is not determinative of the authority of an action. The belief that one's action is justified connects with the common good because, as an experience, it may be accessed by all and it may be a benefit to all without a justification of a particular action. What is critical to a good legal judgment, then, is not the balancing of moral arguments regarding a particular judgment but the rational linkage of such a judgment to an institutional source and that, in turn, with "the common values and shared practices of the legal culture."[10] Raz suggests that such a legal culture is constituted from the "social conventions and cultural precepts" of legal officials.[11] In a good judgement, a judge "mix[es] the fruits of long-established traditions with the urgencies of short-term exigencies" so as to integrate the legal unconscious with legal doctrine.[12] The official's personality fuses immediately with the doctrine. The fusion of self and doctrine brings the feeling that one *belongs with* the society. With such a feeling, one will be loyal to the society's institutions. Such a mutual loyalty, not unlike the feeling of friendship, gives rise to "expressive reasons" in support of the common good.[13] The individual "feels that it [society] is his and that he belongs to it."

Raz privileges the pre-legal experiential body in a second context. Heretofore, according to Raz, philosophers had addressed the issue of legal obligation in terms of whether a citizen was morally obligated to obey a particular law. Raz argues, however, that any one law should be read in the context of the hierarchy of institutions from which the law is posited. The attitude of respect varies from person to person. The moral duty to obey a rule logically depends upon whether one possesses a prior attitude of respect towards the institutions generally. If one possesses such an attitude, one is morally obligated to obey the norms that the institutions posited. One accepts the likelihood that the institution, in more cases than not, will reach the correct judgment and posit the value that best resolves a conflict of values. The institution's posit of a value will be accepted over any individual posit of a value.

What is the nature of such an attitude? Is it a subjective attitude that an official projects towards the institution? Is it an objective attitude that an academic, as an

8 Raz, "Liberalism," 116.

9 Raz (with Avishi Margalit), "National Self-determination" (1990), in *Ethics in the Public Domain*, 125-45, 139.

10 Raz, "The Politics of the Rule of Law," 375.

11 Raz, *The Authority of Law* (Oxford: Clarendon Press, 1979), 259.

12 Raz, "The Politics of the Rule of Law," 376.

13 Raz, *The Authority of Law*, 259.

observer, might possess? Or is it comparable to a scientific point of view that an official, despite his or her personal attitudes, takes from the viewpoint of the structure as a whole? Is this attitude a cognitive phenomenon? Or is it constituted from the official's bodily experiences? Is Raz addressing the prejudgments that one brings *into* one's meaning of a text or social event?[14]

The "attitude of respect" towards an institution is manifested in terms of the experiential bonding of an individual with the institutional hierarchy. "Respect for law is an aspect of *identification* with society (the reverse of alienation)."[15] If one possesses an attitude of respect towards the institutional structure, one must, to be morally consistent, follow a particular law posited by an institution. Perhaps, Raz suggests, at least government officials possess a moral duty to obey the law for, if this were not so, one would doubt whether there would be a government (and institutions) with the authority to posit decisions.[16] But there is no moral argument that ensures that one owes an attitude of respect towards an institutional structure. Such an attitude precedes moral argument, the attitude drawing from the pre-legal and pre-moral realm of experience. The pre-legal works to produce "a culture of legality, of respect for the law, and a willingness to abide by it even when one loses by it," as Raz ends *Ethics in the Public Domain*.[17]

Like friendship, the immediacy between citizen and institution evolves over time. One takes on obligations towards a friend as the social relationship evolves over time. One takes on a duty of loyalty towards the friend. The duty is semi-voluntary in that one participates in the creation of the friendship. This bonding overrides any particular action of a friend, no matter how intensely one disagrees with the friend. That is, the friendship excludes one from questioning the moral content of any particular decision by the friend. One is not morally obligated to be a friend. A friendship evolves and, with it, moral obligations to the friend arise. The friendship does not serve an instrumental purpose: the friendship is intrinsically valued.

Raz privileges the pre-legal in a third aspect of his legal theory. Here, Raz addresses whether the implied or explicit consent of the governed to the legal order binds a citizen. In "Government by Consent,"[18] in particular, Raz argues that what is more important than the consent of the governed is the deep feeling of belongingness that a citizen possesses towards legal institutions. Such a feeling of belonging is intrinsically valued in and for itself. A consent, in contrast, is instrumentally valued as a means to fulfil individual desires.

---

14 See Conklin, *The Phenomenology of Modern Legal Discourse*, 136-65.

15 Raz, *The Authority of Law*, 259. Emphasis added.

16 Raz, "The Obligation to Obey: Revision and Tradition" (1987), in *Ethics in the Public Domain*, 341-54, 346.

17 Raz, "The Politics of the Rule of Law," 378.

18 Raz, "Government by Consent" (1987), in *Ethics in the Public Domain*, 355-69, esp. 366-69.

Raz likens such a feeling of belonging with the trust between friends. One's actions manifest such a trust when an institution deserves the trust of the individual. An express or implied consent to the government cements such an attitude of trust.[19] The sense of belonging is distinguished from the consent of the governed, secondly, in that the governed deliberately author consent in a particular time and place, such as in an election or a referendum. Such a formal consent represents the deliberate and formal end of the spectrum of trust. But the sense of belonging shared amongst the citizenry or the officials is not authored at a deliberate time and place. "Such attitudes of trust and respect are normally formed, not through deliberate decisions, let alone formal acts of consent, but through the normal habit-forming processes of education and habituation." A precise time and place when the habits originated cannot be identified. Nor are the *indicia* of the habits – unwritten symbols, rituals, and ceremonies – necessarily the consequence of reflection. The individual identifies immediately with the symbol without the intercession of cognitive objects. Consent is auxiliary and marginal to the immediacy that characterizes the feeling of belonging with society's institutions. Indeed, the indispensable "processes of education," so important to the sense of belonging with the institutions, may be "blind" to the moral deliberation that characterizes consent. Unreason may characterize the ultimate origins of a legal order. Yet, the unreason may still be "responsive to right reason." "Right reason" differentiates moral arguments in support of particular values. A legal order may be characterized by an experiential unreason that defers to moral argument.

This takes us to the fourth context where Raz privileges experiential meanings as the authorizing origin of a legal order. Here, Raz argues that the affective experiences of the citizenry and of officials are so important that they are considered intrinsic goods, valued in and of themselves, in contrast, say, to a referendum or individual rights.

Now, the big question with each stage of Raz's theory of law is whether the official's or citizen's attitude of respect towards institutions (that is, their sense of belonging) is a cognitive or an experiential phenomenon. Raz addresses this issue in *The Authority of Law*.[20] The attitude of respect possesses two integrally related elements: the attitude involves a "complex attitude comprising emotional, cognitive, and normative elements."[21] The one element, the cognitive, concerns the moral value of law. Here, one appeals to cognitively produced standards independent of one's experiential beliefs. This cognitive aspect does include

19 This trust draws from what H.L.A. Hart described as a bonding of individual with institution in internal statements. Raz admits as much in "Government by Consent," 368, fn. 10.

20 Raz, *The Authority of Law*, 250-53.

21 Raz, "The Obligation to Obey," 354.

"affective and practical inclinations and dispositions" in the sense that one may be reluctant to support proposals to reform the institutional structure because one cognitively respects the structure. Or one may possess an affective desire to persuade others to share such a cognitively produced attitude of respect. The non-cognitive element of the cognitive attitude includes pride, satisfaction, admiration and beliefs, all of which have as their referent the cognitively produced, external reasons for action.[22]

As I pointed out above, Raz claims an obligation to obey a particular law if the law has been posited by an institution for which one possesses an attitude of respect. One does not owe an obligation independent of such an attitude.[23] The obligation cannot be derived cognitively, even from a cognitive attitude that includes non-cognitive elements, according to Raz. Although one may have prudentially important reasons to obey a particular law, these do not give rise to a moral obligation to obey the law. Even the duty to support and uphold legal institutions does not establish an obligation to obey a law. What is important, according to Raz, is to begin with the "practical" experiential meanings which one brings *into* a reading of an institution's actions. Here, one possesses a "disposition" of hostility towards law breakers or a "disposition" to approve law-abiding behaviour, or shame or guilt if one has broken a law, and the like. The experiential respect is directed towards the symbols that manifest the bonding with the social. The symbols, unlike the transparent language of the cognitively produced moral arguments, manifest "an attitude to certain institutionalized aspects of the community."[24] One may believe that, however unjust or unsound a particular law, one's mutual loyalty to legal institutions and their symbols brings with the loyalty a duty to obey the institution's particular laws.

A social realism, understood in terms of bodily experiences, grounds what Raz takes as the attitude of respect towards legal institutions. With this realism as a background, one's attitude of respect may vary from person to person and from one society to another. Although the cognitive and the "practical" attitudes are intertwined in "actual life," one may possess a cognitive disrespect for the law and yet manifest a practical respect towards it, according to Raz. If one does not possess a cognitive respect towards the law, it is "morally unjustified" and "morally intolerable" for legal institutions to inculcate a practical feeling of respect.[25]

---

22 Raz raises a problem here, though. One may identify with society without respecting its legal institutions. An identity with society may require an active opposition or, conversely, an active respect for the law. And this problem takes one to the moral issues of the common good. Raz, *The Authority of Law*, 261.

23 Raz, *The Authority of Law*, 233-49; "The Obligation to Obey," 343, 347, 350.

24 Raz, *The Authority of Law*, 261.

25 Raz, *The Authority of Law*, 252.

But such a morality of the cognitively produced respect is a separate issue from one's obligation to (dis-)obey a law, given such an experiential attitude of respect.

When Raz addresses the ultimate grounding for posited norms, what matters are the "practical" or experiential meanings, not the cognitively produced reasons that justify actions of the legal institutions. Such an experiential attitude lacks any comparative moral foundation, according to Raz. There is no universal obligation to obey a law. But those who do possess such an experiential attitude of respect are, indeed, under a moral obligation to obey the laws. That is, the experiential attitude must come first in the logic of legal obligation. The attitude constitutes one's meanings and, when meanings are so conferred, one may possess a moral obligation in terms of a moral consistency with the meanings. For this reason, legal officials are most likely to possess a moral obligation to obey the law for, without such an experiential attitude of respect towards legal institutions, it is unlikely that the institutions could exist efficaciously. The experiential attitude of respect becomes a reason to obey a law. The experiential attitude becomes what Raz calls an "expressive reason," as opposed to the "natural reasoning" that balances moral arguments in favour of some posited value. The natural reasoning exists independently of the judge's or lawyer's personal posit of value (an expressive reason). The natural reason offers a reason to obey a norm. But the natural reason does not necessarily offer a general moral obligation to obey all particular norms.

What is important here is that Raz acknowledges that the obligation to obey a norm is not posited by a legal institution, nor does the obligation emanate from some implicit consent to be governed, nor from some reasoned inference of a transcendental norm. Rather, the obligation is self-originating in that the obligation is tied to one's bonding experience, independent of any speculative argument about rights or the good life. Both the loyalty of friendship and the experiential attitude of respect for legal institutions "grow, develop and cement over time."[26] If a friendship or attitude of respect have cemented, neither a friend nor an official may escape from the relationship as if it did not exist.

In sum, Raz introduces an element of legal theory that has for too long been excluded as "savage" (Hobbes), "wild" (Locke), "improperly so called" (Austin), "primitive" (Kelsen), "pre-legal" (Hart), or "non-law" (Dworkin). Perhaps for the first time in the tradition of legal positivism, we have a philosopher who privileges this forgotten element. The "feeling that one belongs" induces a moral obligation to accept a norm, its substantive content come what may. The ultimate source for belongingness presupposes an immediacy or presence between self and society. One experiences a "belief," not a cognitive object, that "the law is one's [own] law." The issue of moral obligation enters the fray at this point:

26 Raz, *The Authority of Law*, 257.

> One *feels* that one betrays the community if one breaks the law to gain advantage, or out of convenience, or thoughtlessness, and this regardless of whether the violation actually harms anyone, just as one can be disloyal to a friend without harming him or any of his interests, without even offending him.[27]

The feeling of belonging with one's environing world, according to Raz, is intrinsically valued in and for itself. Such an experiential attitude, if it exists in a community, brings with it an obligation to obey the laws of the institutions, whatever the content of those laws.

2. The Official's Forgetting of the Experiential Origin

At this point, Raz introduces a paradox in his legal theory. Raz has privileged the experiential attitude as critical to the very existence of a legal structure. Without such an attitude on the part of legal officials, there would not be an efficacious bureaucratic structure and without such a structure there would be no authoritative laws. Nor would there be a legal obligation on the part of the official or a resident to obey a particular law. The paradox is that, despite Raz's retrieval of the bonding experiences as the ultimate condition precedent of a legal structure (and therefore of a binding norm), he excludes such an experience from what he considers a binding norm. Indeed, working within the structure of institutions, an official rationally traces one institutional source to another as if there were no authorizing origin external to the structure, according to Raz. The official's point of view is that of the structure as a whole. And that structure is autonomous of all social, moral, and anthropological experiences. The experiential attitude of respect is inaccessible from the legal point of view.

The consequence of the official's disassociation of the legal structure from the non-legal realm of experiential meaning is a *differend* or untranslatable void between the legal structure within which the official works on the one hand and the experiential meanings that constitute the authorizing origin of the structure on the other.[28] The void is constructed as officials forget the importance of the authorizing origin and then forget the inaccessibility of the origin to what the officials (and Raz) consider the nature of a binding norm. The act of forgetting is manifested in each stage of Raz's exposition of the nature of legal reasoning: his view of morality, moral argument, moral and legal positivism, exclusion, and the nature of law.

27 Raz, "Duty to Obey," 354.

28 I describe how this gap arises in an important case in Conklin, "The Transformation of Meaning: Legal Discourse and Canadian Internment Camps," *The International Journal for the Semiotics of Law* 9 (1996): 227-56.

a) Morality

First, Raz makes a point of emphasizing that officials incorporate moral values as they deliberate about what ought to be included as 'law.' But like H.L.A. Hart, Raz understands morality in a very special sense. According to his view of morality, morality does not incorporate the experiential meanings that Raz privileges as the ultimate authorizing origin of a legal structure.

Like most of us, Raz is a product of the Enlightenment. For Raz, a reflective self-consciousness characterizes morality. The project of morality addresses a "cognitive" attitude rather than the "practical" attitude that Raz associated with the experiential bonding with legal institutions. The cognitive seeks ideal-directed arguments about what is intrinsically valued as a good. Raz distinguishes such a speculative project from the "brute facts" of bodily desires, which Raz associates with the feeling of loyalty and trust towards legal institutions.

Indeed, Raz re-reads 'desire' through the lens of the cognitive. Though all human beings may lack the ability of self-reflection, an enlightened self-awareness is "logically possible" all humans, according to Raz.[29] Desires are "intelligible." Desires, like beliefs, are guided by reasons. Further, rights and duties entertain cognitively produced reasons. The duty to respect self-regarding conduct is one such moral duty. The intellectual world of argument is far different from the experiential meanings that ground the structure of legal institutions.

Having privileged the shared common beliefs as the indispensable condition of a legal order, Raz, like Hart, dissociates morality from such beliefs.[30] Morality, Raz claims, involves

> a system of reasoning or a network of intelligible connections between interconnected ideas. Moral theory is not committed to reproducing or vindicating common moral beliefs. Moral reasoning aims at displaying connections between moral ideas and principles in ways which manifest their intelligibility.[31]

Morality, for Raz, refers to cognitive referents, despite the fact that Raz claims to be offering a "phenomenological" argument about morality.[32] Hart also understood morality with the justifications of cognitive, as opposed to anthropological, objects, and he described his legal theory as sociological. Both Raz and Hart appeal to argument and evidence, rather than to the constitutive meanings that dwell deep in the anthropological beliefs of an official's constituted meanings. Indeed, when Raz re-reads Dworkin's sense of the term 'morality,' Raz understands

29 Raz, "Liberating Duties" (1989), in *Ethics in the Public Domain*, 29-43, 36-7.
30 Raz, "Rights and Individual Well-Being," 47.
31 Raz, "Rights and Individual Well-Being," 47.
32 Raz, "Rights and Individual Well-Being," 44.

Dworkin's sense in terms of the very pursuit of ideal-directed arguments that Raz himself adopts as 'moral reasoning.' Raz fails to appreciate that Dworkin conditions such arguments as only those which are morally acceptable inside the narrative structure of a genre: Dworkin's "best moral justification," Raz erroneously asserts, is "close to an ideal, correct or true morality."[33] Raz errs in his reading of Dworkin because Dworkin locates the best justification *inside* a genre with its own assumptions, style, vocabulary and grammar.[34]

b) Moral argument

Against a background of a special sense of morality that appeals to cognitively produced referents, Raz describes moral reasoning in a manner whereby legal officials forget the experiential bonding that originates a legal order. Moral reasoning, in Raz's strict sense of the word 'moral', involves a deliberation about the justifications for one's action. Raz calls such a deliberation, "natural reason."[35] Justifications address the substantive merit of an action. Here, one may disagree with another as to which value judgments ought to be privileged in society. This deliberation involves a reflection about the relation of individual well-being to the common good as well as a contemplation about the best means to fulfil a good life. But a rights-based morality fails to address the common good.[36] Reasonable disagreement goes hand in hand with such deliberation. So too does the quest for cognitive referents.[37]

---

33 Raz, "Authority, Law and Morality" (1985), in *Ethics in the Public Domain*, 210-37, 222. Raz is erroneous because Dworkin stresses that the "best moral justification" is conditioned by the unwritten assumptions and style of writing of the genre in which the official finds himself or herself. Like Aristotle's sense of a good constitution in the *Politics*, Dworkin himself distinguishes the best moral justification from the ideal, the interpretive community from an ideal community.

34 This is explained in Conklin, *The Structuralism of Analytical Jurisprudence* (forthcoming).

35 Raz, "On the Autonomy of Reasoning" (1993), in *Ethics in the Public Domain*, 326-40, 339.

36 A common good transcends any rights-based morality. Raz, "The Nature of Law" (1983), in *Ethics in the Public Domain*, 195-209, 209. Rights should be appreciated in the context of the quest for such a common good. First, conflicts between individuals' rights do not monopolize the types of social conflict in society. Raz, "Liberating Duties" (1989), in *Ethics in the Pulbic Domain*, 29-43, 34. Common goods may be enjoyed in a non-competitive way. One does not possess a right to such goods because others are not held to a duty to respect one's individual interests in the right. Nevertheless, public institutions may possess duties to provide and preserve such common goods, independent of any support for individual rights. Secondly, rights-based morality diminishes the status of rights by virtue of their confrontational context between individuals. In contrast, Raz claims that a common good originates individual rights. Thirdly, a right functions to protect one's interests but not all moral interests. A rights-based morality is narrow, as a consequence, because it misses the balancing of interests that inevitably enters into the deliberation as to whether a duty exists.

37 The balancing of values draws from "the middle level of morality." The middle level of morality refers to cognitive objects rather than to the meant objects of an experiential constitution of meaning. Raz, "Liberating Duties," 35-6. For the distinction between meant and posited objects as well as examples of meant objects, see Conklin, *The Phenomenology of Modern Legal Discourse*, 130-68. For examples of posited objects, see Conklin, *Phenomenology of Modern Legal Discourse*, 69-101, 234-35.

Such a deliberation about moral arguments characterizes legal reasoning. Such a deliberation may arise, for example, because the content is unsettled. In such a circumstance, a court is a law-maker. The court deliberates about the substantive content of a law. The social features that identify law "entail" that the posited norms possesses moral values. Such an entailment differs from saying that the posited norms "endorses" certain moral values.[38] To say that the structure entails certain moral values goes to the identity of the question 'what is law?' Raz emphasizes that this identity question has been mistakenly associated with 'what is the nature of the authoritative?' The important point, for now, is to appreciate that moral reasoning often dominates the deliberative stage of a decision or rule.

Many different considerations enter into one's arguments about the substantive merit of a particular practice or rule. Reasons "of a moral character" (that is, ideal-directed arguments about the good life) will often dominate, Raz claims.[39] Raz likens this deliberative stage to the legislative stage of a liberal political system. Courts are also "law-makers" in this deliberative sense. In particular, a judge incorporates moral considerations when the judge endorses as efficacious what had hitherto been "extra-legal" factors. Aside from the identity of 'what is law,' a judge incorporates what had hitherto been considered non-legal factors of weight.[40] Raz uses a special term, "entailment," to describe the incorporation of non-law into the deliberative act of adjudication.

Extra-legal factors are incorporated into the law in a series of circumstances. First, a rule may be so imprecise or ambiguous that reasoning will not identify what specific rules are binding. Second, a series of rules may project gaps between the rules and, at that point, the courts must legislate extra-legal considerations to fill the gaps.[41] Third, even if there were a duty of the court to apply a certain rule, the rule would not be authoritative until a higher court issued a writ of mandamus or an injunction requiring respect for the rule. Fourth, even if precise, a rule may direct that judges incorporate certain extra-legal considerations.[42] Such a direc-

---

38 Raz, "Authority, Law and Morality," 229.

39 Raz, "The Nature of Law," 207.

40 Raz, "The Nature of Law," 209.

41 See, e.g., Raz, *The Authority of Law*, 72-5.

42 Raz, "The Inner Logic of Law" (1984), 238-53, at 241-50. Also see "On the Autonomy of Legal Reasoning" (1993), 326-40, 333; *The Authority of Law*, 31. In "Legal Rights," Raz adds three specific circumstances where a law may grant moral rights: that is, where legal rights become legally recognized moral rights. First, the law may change one's legal interests, thereby changing his or her moral rights, and may then proceed to recognize the latter moral rights. Such occurs, for example, when a legislature changes one's property interests by enacting a property law. The latter changes a social practice into a moral entitlement: one may be entitled to the privacy of a certain level of residential building without the influx of factories in the neighbourhood. And that changed legal interest, in turn, is recognized 'by the law.' Secondly, a legal interest, such as, say, of a tenant, may exist only with the consent of another, such as, say, of a landlord. Third, although one may initially disagree with the substantive content of a law (such as, say, a law that proscribes the use of contraceptives), one may have a moral obligation to agree with a legislature's proscription because one already shares a deep respect for the legislature's authority.

tion takes place, for example, with a constitutional bill of rights. That is, one legally authoritative rule indirectly entails another extra-legal consideration. The court is directed to take the law in one direction rather than another. Fifth, a court may reserve an authoritative rule and replace it with another. In each case, what makes the rule authoritative is its enforcement by the court. And in each case, the court is directed to incorporate extra-legal considerations into the judgment – extra-legal, that is, until the moment when they become authoritatively enacted by the court, at which point they become legal.

The exclusion of the bodily experience continues when judges, deliberating about arguments, endorse the arguments into a rationally coherent whole. The coherence lies in terms of the inter-connected *concepts*, not in terms of the relation of such concepts to the individual's beliefs.[43] Raz lops off or, better, dis-embodies such beliefs from binding law in that they are inadequate reasons for action. By so excluding beliefs from the enterprise of legal coherence, the judge's experiential bonding with legal institutions is also excluded. An adjudicative coherence unifies into a single normative structure of concepts, whatever the diversity of personal beliefs in the society. Because of this need for a rational unity of concepts, the coherence must draw from a base of doctrines and rules. The base of rules provides the "starting-point" for legal analysis. The base must be the same for all believers in the structure. The base is not the experiential attitude that bonds officials together. The base is constituted from cognitive objects.

The starting point of deliberative analysis, then, accepts a "base" that intellectualizes about cognitive objects that institutions endorse. The base also includes, though, the institutional sources that endorse the rules, principles, and other cognitive standards of the base. Ronald Dworkin's error, and the error of the coherence project as a whole, according to Raz, is to accept the base as if the institutional sources did not matter.[44] Even when authoritative rules do not offer a definite answer or when there is no authoritative rule in the circumstance, the court still searches for a narrative coherence, according to Dworkin. Such a narrow view sacrifices a search for the good life in favour of an epistemic coherence that becomes an end in itself. Instead, the judge strives to connect the adjudicative coherence to an overall structure of norms and to evaluate the norms in the light of a theory of the good life. Raz considers that the base offers "contact with the concrete reality of the law."[45] But because the official begins legal analysis with cognitive objects (such as doctrines, rules, and principles) as the base, judges forget the importance of the immediacy of bonding that is said to originate the

43 Raz, "The Relevance of Coherence" (1992), in *Ethics in the Public Domain*, 277-325, 287-88.
44 Raz, "The Relevance of Coherence," 301.
45 Raz, "The Relevance of Coherence," 289.

legal order. By virtue of the enclosure of social differences within the invisible boundaries of categories, the oneness of narrative coherence conceals the "subjective" beliefs of each individual official and citizen.

c) Moral and legal positivism

This takes one to the third factor that contributes to the official's act of forgetting the experiential bonding that grounds the legal order as he or she reasons about humanly posited norms.

In the deliberation about moral well-being, according to Raz, reasoning, at some point, runs out.[46] One balances one moral argument against another until one reaches a unified, single coherent normative structure. But the coherent structure presupposes the importance of one value or interests over another and that conflict cannot be resolved by reasoning, according to Raz. When moral reasoning terminates, one posits a value choice. The posit of the value, or what Raz sometimes calls an "interest," grounds the stream of argument. Any arguments that contradict the posited value should be excluded from the coherence project. This explains why Raz considers value pluralism so important in a realistic account of liberalism. Moral deliberation ends when one chooses one value over another. With the posit of the value, one makes a decision. The decision is effectively a 'political' decision by virtue of the termination of the moral reasoning.[47]

The value, which an official posits at the termination of moral arguments, resembles the experiential attitude that Raz attributes to the immediacy that characterizes the bonding with a legal institution. The belief is "evaluative" in that it identifies which values ought to be pursued, what reasons for action ought to guide social behaviour, and what norms ought to be binding.[48] The evaluation is "inescapable." The fact that the belief has been posited transforms the belief into a "moral fact." The moral content of the belief is immaterial to the existence of such a moral fact. The fact that a belief has been posited raises the importance of the source, not the content of the belief. So, an institution's posit of a value also guides action. Institutional procedures that lead to such a posit of values become "facts". Once again, what is taken as a fact is the posit of a value, not the justice or morality of the content of the value. Raz insists that there is no transcendent intellectual criterion to favour one value over another.

Raz saves the posited value, though, from any colour of naked violence – or so he believes. The posit of a value at the end of the deliberative act does not leave one with an arbitrary subjective value. The critical issue becomes 'who posited

46 Raz, "On the Autonomy of Legal Reasoning," 335, 338-39.

47 Raz, "On the Autonomy of Legal Reasoning," 339.

48 Raz distinguishes between evaluation and moral reasoning. "Authority, Law and Morality," 237.

the value?' 'Was the value posited by an official who had been assigned the role to posit the value in such circumstances?' 'Did the official exceed his or her jurisdiction?' 'Did the wrong institution posit the value in such circumstances?' The latter considerations take one to the role of the decision-maker in a complex bureaucratic structure of institutions.

This inquiry into institutional roles raises two issues: first, what institutional source in a bureaucratic hierarchy of institutions is entitled to posit the value; and secondly, what reasons count for an institutional action. Raz calls such institutional issues, normative theory.[49] The subjectivity of the posit of an individual value at the end of moral reasoning is abstracted and then transferred into another context, that of the inter-relation of institutional sources that posit values. Like the individual posit of a value, the institutional posit of a value is a "moral fact" that begins and ends legal analysis. Whether this or that institution ought to posit such a value is not an issue for moral analysis. Once again, it is the fact that a value is posited, not its substantive content, that terminates moral reasoning even when one considers the institutional source of the posited value. The otherwise subjective posit of a value is 'law' if an institution has posited the value.

Raz argues that the (that is, his) theory of authority transforms the personal posit of a value, which otherwise characterizes the termination of moral argument, into an objectivity. The institutional context introduces an "artificial reasoning."[50] But does the artificial reasoning, which shifts from the balancing of arguments to the institutional source of the norm, also run out? Must an institution ultimately posit a choice of one value over another? "Surely morality and reason never run out in matters which can be adjudicated before the courts," Raz inquires. "Here I beg to differ," he responds.[51] First, previous binding rules may direct one particular answer. Second, individuals may have formed expectations about such rules and acted accordingly. Third, any one political issue may offer several alternatives from which an institution may choose. Accordingly, a "value pluralism" confronts the institutional decision-maker. The institution decides. By choosing one value over another, the institutional source seems to objectify what would otherwise appear to be an arbitrary subjective value.

---

49 Raz, *Practical Reason and Norms* (Princeton: Princeton University Press, 1990, 2d edn.; London: Hutchinson, 1979), 12.

50 Raz, "On the Autonomy of Legal Reasoning," 339, 340. Raz also describes this institutional context of resolving the values to be posited in terms of "naturalistic" description as opposed to a moral description. Raz, "Authority, Law and Morality," 235. The social facts (about institutions) can be described without resort to the moral justifications of the content of particular decisions that side with one value over another.

51 Raz, "On the Autonomy of Legal Reasoning," 338.

The posit ends any debate about justice in a particular circumstance. Perhaps issues of justice may be reconsidered if it is alleged that the evidence was not fully examined or that a procedure was improperly followed or that the judge was bribed or intimidated. Short of these circumstances, the institution's decision about the choice of values is accepted as a 'given.' Issues of justice are redirected from the content of the value posited to the appropriateness of the institution to posit the value.

In the same manner that one invariably posits an incommensurate value at the end of moral reasoning, so too "what takes over [with an institutional decision] is choice, a determination of the will not itself determined by reason."[52] The institution need not even offer an "expressive rationality" about the particular value posited. The key issue is that the value has been posited by the proper institution assigned the role to posit a value in such circumstances. The decision takes its flavour from "the fact that they [the values] are decisions taken by bureaucratic institutions, by people not acting for themselves but fulfilling a role of trust." Such an issue excludes "doctrinal reasons, reasons of system, local simplicity and local coherence." In "The Relevance of Coherence" (1992), Raz insists that "[w]hen we ask about the nature of law we aim to discover how things are independently of us." He continues that "I do not mean that the law as it is is independently of human beings and their activities, only that what it is independent of my, or anyone else's, inquiry into its nature. Therefore, our preferences or value judgements are immaterial."[53] Legal reasoning "takes on a life of its own," independent of the substantive content of the values posited at the termination of deliberation. The posit of the value by an institution displaces the posit of the value by an individual. Posited values begin and end legal analysis. Such a positivism by human institutions distinguishes legal positivism from natural law theory, according to Raz.[54]

d) Exclusion

Raz raises a fourth element in the official's legal reasoning whereby the official forgets the experiential basis of legal authority. One might claim that the legal official does, indeed, incorporate the experiential attitudes of respect, so indispensable for the very existence of a modern legal structure according to Raz. Raz, I have pointed out, rejects such a possibility first, because he associates morality with the quest for cognitive referents and second, because the individual's choice of values (which might arguably include the experiential attitude of respect) is displaced in

52 Raz, "On the Autonomy of Legal Reasoning," 339.

53 Raz, "The Relevance or Coherence," 287.

54 Raz, *The Authority of Law*, 44-5, 134; *Practical Reason and Norms*, 162-63, 165-66. As Raz defines legal positivism, a law is posited if "it is made law by human beings." *The Authority of Law*, 38.

favour of the institutional endorsement of values. However, even if I have misjudged Raz's intent here, Raz explicitly excludes the experiential (including any attitudes of respect towards the institutions) from a legally binding norm.

The institutional posit of a value excludes any consideration of issues that go to the arguments in support of the individual choice of one value over another in the deliberative stage of moral reasoning.[55] Even if the individual choice of a value reflects the individual's experiential meanings, legal reasoning excludes such experiential meanings by virtue of the institutional displacement of the private posit of a value. Raz reinforces this exclusionary character by distinguishing, in *Practical Reason and Norms*, between first- and second-order reasons.[56] A first order reason goes to the merit of an action. The ordinary deliberation about moral reasons, such as a deliberation that terminates in the posit of a rule, constitutes, for example, a first-order reason. The declaration of an emergency by a cabinet on the basis of the evidence is one such first-order reason.

A second-order reason excludes such a first-order reason. The 'supremacy of the legislature' is often given as the second-order reason why a judge ought not to question the 'wisdom [or content] of an enactment.' The second-order reason leaves it to the executive, as an institution, to decide whether there is an emergency even if the evidence for the *de facto* emergency is questionable and even if the political theory that justifies such a declaration is debatable. The rule, which specifies what institution should make the decision, *excludes* the first-order reason as a reason for action, despite the fact that the first-order reason may be sound or meritorious on the evidence. The idea behind the exclusionary reason is the belief that, more often than not, the second-order exclusionary reason will result in the soundest decision even though, in the particular circumstances, the decision may not be sound.

In summary, the first-order decision, where one value is posited at the end of moral reasoning, goes to the content of the decision: that is, to the merits of the substance of the decision. Here, one balances the values and interests in a deliberative act. The

55 Raz, *The Authority of Law*, 22-5; 234-37; *Practical Reason and Norms*, 141-46; and "Reasons for Action, Decisions and Norms" (1975), in ed. Joseph Raz, *Practical Reasoning* (Oxford: Oxford University Press, 1978), 128-43. Raz is not alone in his privileging of the institutional source of a posited norm. Ota Weinberger and Neil MacCormick have independently elaborated institutional theories of posited law. See generally, Ota Weinberger, "Neo-Institutionalism: My Views on the Philosophy of Law," in ed. Luc J. Wintgens, *The Law in Philosophical Perspectives* (Dordrecht: Kluwer, 1999), 253-72; *Law, Institution and Legal Politics* (Dordrecht: Kluwer, 1991). Neil MacCormick and Ota Weinberger, *An Institutional Theory of Law: New Approaches to Legal Positivism* (Dordrecht: Reidel, 1986). MacCormick, "My Philosophy of Law," in Wintgens, *The Law in Philosophical Perspectives*, 120-45; MacCormick and Zenon Bankowski, "Speech Acts, Legal Institutions and Real Laws," in MacCormick and Peter Birks, *The Legal Mind: Essays for Tony Honore* (Oxford: Clarendon Press, 1986), 121-33.

56 Raz, *Practical Reason and Norms*, 36-45.

exclusionary decision addresses the role of a particular institution to decide this type of decision. That is, the exclusionary reason addresses "whose judgement regarding the balance of reasons to trust."[57] Here, the fact that a particular institution makes a decision itself is the reason for action, the substantive content of the decision, come what may. A decision puts an end to deliberation. The decision terminates the legitimacy to consider the experiential meanings that an official may have brought into a judgment. The decision may even terminate an enquiry into the experiential attitude of respect that a judge possesses towards the institution.

Raz compares the exclusionary character of legal authority to a promise.[58] Once made, one may not re-evaluate the merits of going against the promise. A promise is a promise. The promise excludes a consideration of the merits of a promisee's action in a particular circumstance. A legal decision, like a promise, is content-independent.[59]

An exclusionary rule is also analogous to a decision in practical reasoning, according to Raz. A decision is a mandatory norm.[60] The decision becomes a reason for action for the future. When a similar circumstance arises in the future, one's mind has already crystallized, however strong the substantive arguments about the rule at issue, pro or con. The exclusionary reason is a second-order reason because it excludes other morally compelling reasons as reasons for action. The rule excludes first-order reasons, and the latter may well argue against the substantive content of the rule.

Raz characterizes the exclusionary character of a judicial decision by virtue of several features. First, the decision is a reason for officials – police, sheriffs, lawyers, persons affected – to act. Such a reason for action contrasts with a belief. A belief draws from the affective, experiential factors that enter into deliberation. A reason for action assumes the posit of such factors as a 'given,' lifts their subjectivity into an objective institutional context, and defers to the institution's posit of such values. The decision of the official, not his or her belief, is binding. Only the deliberative stage of adjudication arguably scrutinizes beliefs and even here,

---

57 Raz, *Practical Reason and Norms*, 64.

58 Raz, *Practical Reason and Norms*, 69-71.

59 In a sense, Raz is advocating a rule utilitarianism: one ought to follow a certain institutional rule even though, in a particular circumstance, the balance of values and reasons would lead to a different rule in the particular circumstances. The *reference to the institutional rule* is for the greater good. The institutional rule excludes a consideration of the substantive merits of the problem for the good of the structure as a whole. An exclusionary reason manifests such a rule utilitarianism because one takes the exclusionary rule, not the merits of the particular rule, as a reason for action. *Practical Reason and Norms* 194. 195-96. If one re-examined the justificatory arguments of the particular rule on each occasion when it possibly applied, then there would no longer be a rule. Each circumstance would lead to a different resolution, depending upon the posit of the value.

60 Raz, *Practical Reason and Norms*, 72-3.

we have noted, the scrutiny goes to the cognitive justifications of the belief. The expectation that the decision will be a reason for action allows the citizen to plan ahead as if the decision will be made. Such an exclusionary reason manifests a reluctance to re-open the deliberative stage of adjudication and thereby to permit an official to posit a new value. The decision is a decision that other institutions will enforce. The officials consider the institution as a social fact. If the institution posits a decision, the addressee, whether an official or a citizen, is not normally allowed to question the authority of the institution that made the decision, whatever the injustice or lack of merit of the content of the decision. More about this in a minute.

A second factor colours the exclusionary character of an adjudicative decision, according to Raz. The decision displaces the personal opinions that the decision entails. Raz calls such a displacement, a "pre-emptive reason."[61] The decision also displaces the framers' intent of a rule, even if the decision strays from the framers' *de facto* intent. The incorporated reasons of the deliberative stage "merge" with the decision to render a re-opening of the pre-emptive reason *res judiciata*.

e) The nature of law

I have finally arrived at Raz's full theory of the nature of legal authority, the one consistent concern throughout his writings. With it, one retrieves how the legal official finally buries the experiential realm that Raz privileged as the originary "attitudes of respect" towards legal institutions.

Despite his privileging of such an experiential world, Raz excludes the experiential or what Hart, his mentor, called the anthropological, from an authoritative law. I have already showed how such an exclusion is manifested in Raz's understanding of morality, deliberation, the posit of values in moral reasoning, and the "intelligible" and "artificial" analysis of institutional roles. The experiential is inaccessible to legal reasoning even if one accepts that the value posited at the end of moral reasoning reflects the experiential respect of an individual towards legal institutions. Raz completes the exclusion of the experiential with his analysis of the nature of law.

The nature of law raises the question 'why is a rule binding?' Raz makes an important conceptual distinction with respect to this question: the entailment and the endorsement of a law. A deliberation about competing arguments in support of an individual posit of a value "entails" or identifies different values. But we have now read Raz to show that the subjective posit of a value is objectified once one focuses upon the institutional source of the posit of the value. The institution "endorses" the value that moral deliberation "entailed." The endorsement authorizes

61 Raz, "Authority, Law and Morality," 213.

or validates the choice of value. Raz describes the entailment of the value as the incorporation thesis: laws incorporate moral values. The incorporation of values occurs at an individual judge's deliberative stage of moral/legal reasoning. Raz describes the endorsement as raising the separation thesis: the authority of a law is separate from the moral values entailed or incorporated into the content of a rule. The authoritative nature of binding rule comes into play when the individual judgment is contextualized in terms of its institutional source on a hierarchy of institutions. An individual judge does not posit a value in isolation of such an institutional structure. Institutional sources "endorse" what meritorious factors a judge may "entail" in his or her deliberative act. Raz concludes that "in fact the incorporation thesis is incompatible with the authoritative nature of law."[62] The incorporation thesis addresses the issue of 'how a legal rule is identified' and the separation thesis addresses the question, 'why is a legal rule binding?' Dworkin focussed upon the first issue, but merged that issue into the second issue regarding the authority of a law, according to Raz.[63]

That a judge incorporates non-legal values into the substantive content of a rule does not render a rule legal. In order to erase the subjectivity of the posit of a value from legal reasoning, Raz asks 'did the bureaucratic structure authorize the particular institution to posit the value?' Even here, though, the institution's "artificial" reasoning runs out at some point and the institution must posit a value. This is the moment when the institution *decides*. Raz describes the institutional character of sources much as common law courts have distinguished a judicial from an administrative function. A third party appeals to a body of rules in order to adjudicate a dispute between two parties (a *lis inter partes*).[64] The decision is 'the law,' independent of the moral values "entailed" in the deliberation leading to the decision. The entailed moral considerations become *res judicata*. Once decided, the citizen and official are committed to following the decision "blindly."[65] The very decision excludes a scrutiny of all moral values entailed in the deliberation leading to the decision.

62 Raz, "Authority, Law and Morality," 227.

63 Raz, *Practical Reason and Norms*, 64; "Authority, Law and Morality," 216-17, 225-26 . A third issue is 'how is legal authority acquired?' The identity of a rule goes to its content. 'What extra-legal considerations does a judge incorporate into his or her judgment?' Dworkin asks. Dworkin merges the identity problem with Raz's authority issue by holding that authority addresses the morally best justification of a decision, given the narrative structure of a particular society. The morally best justification, Raz points out, presumes that an institutional source has posited the rule. Thus, even Dworkin accepts such an institutional structure as a given, according to Raz. Ibid., 224. Yet Dworkin fails to appreciate that such an institutional structure, as the ultimate source of authority, logically precedes the deliberative stage of moral-political argument.

64 Raz, "Legal Rights" (1984), in *Ethics in the Public Domain*, 254-76, 256.

65 Raz, *The Authority of Law*, 24.

In contrast, natural law theory requires that the judge evaluate the substantive content of a norm or the content of the institutional source of the norm.[66] The content and institutional context are evaluated with reference to principles that transcend the norm and the institution. Such a content-based view of law, according to Raz, distorts the nature of law because "the most fundamental feature of legal systems" is that a social institution posits a choice of values and the institutional source is located in an interlocking relationship with other institutions in a bureaucratic hierarchy. It is the locus of the decision in such an institutional hierarchy that renders the binding quality to a rule. The structure of legal institutions, not some unifying transcendental principle, endorses a norm as legal. Even the goodness of the structure is precluded from an inquiry as to 'what is law?' As a consequence, Raz believes, his theory of law makes for a "socially oriented" approach to law.

The nature of law postulates an institutional structure. Such a structure logically precedes the deliberation about the arguments and values in moral reasoning. Without a hierarchic, bureaucratic structure of institutions, we would not possess a law as we know it, according to Raz. In effect, the authority of a rule depends upon the postulate that we ought to organize our social relations according to the finality of a modern sovereign state. Raz makes this point in "Legal Rights,"

> [m]odern law is not just an institutional normative system, it is also a bureaucratic system. Its institutions are manned, for the most part, by professionals. Its proper functioning depends upon full-time judges, barristers, solicitors, and other legal officials, their professional associations, law schools and the like. Though legal systems have preceded their bureaucratization, contemporary law relies heavily on bureaucratic processes, many of which are designed, at least in part, to give conscious, explicit, and complete articulation of law. This makes it a particularly clear instance of an institutional normative system.[67]

Such a bureaucratization hardly describes what the tradition of legal positivism considers 'pre-legal' cultures.[68]

Why is a norm authoritative? A norm is authoritative if it is binding. Why is it binding? Because a second-order rule about an institutional role excludes the addressee or any official from raising new or more compelling reasons about the content of the rule posited by the institution. That is, because the institutional principle, such as the principle of legislative supremacy, requires that an addressee

66 Raz, *Practical Reason*, 162-65. *The Authority of Law*, 134.
67 Raz, "Legal Rights," 255.
68 The role of a legal profession in a bureaucracy is frist examined in Max Weber, "Bureaucracy," in *From Max Weber: Four Essays in Sociology*, trans. H.H. Gerth and C. Wright Mills (London: Routledge & Kegan Paul, 1970): 196-244; *The Social Interpretation of Reality*, ed. J.E.T. Eldridge (New York: Charles Scribner's Sons, 1971), esp. Pt. 1 & 3.

ought to abide by the decision of the institution without consideration of the substantive arguments or individual values entailed by the decision.

With the binding decision of a judge, the exclusion of the experiential is complete. A norm is binding irrespective of its substantive moral content. At some point, Raz argues, the deliberation about moral (and other) arguments ends. An official of an institution sides with one line of argument over another by positing some value as the grounding of the argument. When the "natural" moral reasoning and the "artificial" legal reasoning run out, the judge then takes the detached legal point of view of the structure as a whole in order purge the subjectivity entailed by the posit of the value. The "strength" of the judge's artificial reasons is considered a logical strength. Raz distinguishes such a de-personalized logical strength from a "phenomenological strength." Even the latter, though, excludes the experiential meanings that constitute an official's decision: the phenomenological is measured "by the degree to which the thought of the reason preoccupies a person and dominates his consciousness."[69] At a minimum, Raz claims, the binding decision excludes the recipient's desires.[70]

Several specific factors about a legal norm contribute to its binding character.

First, according to Raz, the directive is capable of being authoritative if it addresses how a citizen or official ought to behave into the future. This directive does not describe how persons in fact behave. Nor need the directive be just or wise.

Secondly, in order for the 'ought' directive to be binding, the time and place of the institutional authorship of the directive must be identifiable. Such a linkage of the decision to the time and place of its institutional source displaces any moral argument in support of the merits of the decision: "[a]ll one need do is establish that the enactment took place, and what it says."[71]

Thirdly, the binding quality of a decision excludes its author or any addressee from revisiting the merits of the decision. If one could revisit the merits of the decision, it would not be a decision, let alone an authoritative decision. If one could question the merits of the decision independent of its linkage with an institutional source, the questioning would, as Socrates suggested in the *Crito*, implicitly challenge the institutional authority to posit the rule as binding.

Fourth, it is not just any institutional author whose decision is binding. The author must be located in a pre-existing bureaucratic hierarchy. Such an institutional structure must allocate the role to make different decisions to different institutions on the hierarchy. The 'givenness' of the structure forecloses any further

---

69 Raz, *Practical Reason and Norms*, 25.
70 Raz, *The Authority of Law*, 23-4.
71 Raz, "Authority, Law and Morality," 221.

inquiry into some transcendent or shared common good. If there were a transcendent authorizing Good vis-à-vis the structure, then any one decision of an institution on the structure would not be final nor, therefore, a decision. One would continue to deliberate when a decision was demanded. Ultimately, the institutional structure terminates legal reasoning, irrespective of the content of a legislative, administrative, or judicial decision. Even the trace of institutional sources – the trace that displaces the otherwise arbitrary substantive posit of a value – must end with a value: namely, that the institutional structure itself is a good in itself. That is, the sovereign state represented by the institutional structure is a logical and moral (in Raz's particular sense of the moral as the Good life) 'given' and, as such, the origin of moral/legal reasoning. The state, represented by interlocking institutions, has displaced the experiential attitudes of respect as the authorizing origin of humanly posited laws. And with that displacement, the concealment of the authorizing origin of binding norms is complete.

3. The Legal Point of View

Joseph Raz's writings, it is fair to say, are preoccupied with the question 'why do officials consider a humanly posited norm binding or authoritative?' In his effort to respond to this issue, Raz explains why an official excludes the very experiential attitudes and beliefs that he, Raz, attributes to the authorizing origin of the binding norm. Now, Raz adds one further critical mark that detaches the experiential meanings from legal reasoning: the legal point of view. An artificial reason overcomes the natural reasoning of the deliberation about a particular norm. Yet, here too, according to Raz, the legal official purges a binding norm of all experiential meanings and then forgets what he or she has expelled from reasoning.

Raz draws from both Hart and Kelsen in his elaboration of the legal point of view. Hart distinguished an internal from an external point of view. An internal point of view is a statement that manifests an individual's personal point of view or what Raz calls a "committed statement."[72] Here, a legal official, working through legal statements, is committed or internally bonded with the standards that the statements recognize. The official regards the norms as valid for himself or herself as an official. Hart distinguishes two types of statements: first, those from the committed point of view and, second, those of an observer who, from an external vantage point, observes a social practice as existing despite the fact that the observer may personally object to the practice. From the external point of view, one may make a series of statements that describe social practices. One makes a statement

72 Raz, *The Authority of Law*, 137-39.

without the observer personally adopting the rules or without taking the internal viewpoint.[73]

Contrary to Hart, Raz does not believe that the legal official takes an internal point of view towards a law. If the official did take such an internal viewpoint, he or she would allow for the experiential to implicitly enter reasoning through the back door. Instead, Raz adds a third type of statement. Drawing from Hans Kelsen, Raz privileges a scientific point of view that is neither internal nor external to the rules. From the internal or committed viewpoint, the official would subscribe to the norm as just or reject it as unjust. But the justice of a norm is immaterial to the scientific or legal point of view. The scientist does not immediately identify with the objects of scientific observation. In the context of legal reasoning, the official may not immediately identify with the norm that the official considers authoritative. Raz quotes Kelsen as noting that "even an anarchist, if he were a professor of law, could describe positive law as a system of valid norms, without having to approve of this law."[74]

Raz re-reads Hart's sense of an internal statement so as to expunge the official's experiential commitment to a particular norm or institution. In Raz's view, an official's statement takes a scientific point of view towards a norm. The official's statement "endorses" its normative content, even though the official's personal commitment towards the norm may entail a very different attitude towards its content. The official endorses a rule without necessarily approving its content. The endorsement is often manifested by the official's repetition of the norm in his or her judgment or legal opinion. The experiential or committed meanings that the official brings into a statement are "detached" from the legal statement. An official makes a "detached" statement that describes the normative situation without being experientially committed to the substantive content of the statement. Indeed, the official may make a detached statement while morally condemning the norm. The passion of the experiential body is exhumed from the official's language.

What is the vantage point of the official if the official takes neither an internal committed point of view nor the external viewpoint of an observer? The official takes the vantage point of the legal structure as a whole. That is, much like the interpreter of Dworkin's legal genre, the official immerses himself or herself into

---

73 The authority or morally binding character of a legal rule does not depend upon the personal belief that a rule is a good one on the balance of interests and values. Further, the fact that a particular rule is practised and the subject of emotive values of a community does not make the rule legal. A legal rule must possess a normative or ought character. The fact that a rule is practised may explain the conventionality of rules. But to state that 'such and such' is a legal rule is not to state that it is a practice. Rather, it is to state that one ought to behave in a certain manner. For these two reasons, and others, Raz rejects H.L.A. Hart's practice theory of rules. Raz, *Practical Reason and Norms*, 56-8.

74 Kelsen, *Pure Theory of Law*, trans. Max Knight (Berkeley: University of California Press, 1967; 1970) 218 at fn. 82 as quoted in Raz, *The Authority of Law*, 140.

the institutional structure as a whole without personally endorsing the moral content of the rules of the structure. That the official's personal or professional experiences contradict the content of the norms is immaterial. So too, the justice of the norm is immaterial. In order to sustain the legal point of view, so critical to the analysis of exclusionary reasons, institutions need to develop "distancing devices" to ensure that judgments are made independent of personal tastes and independent of the personal choices of incommensurate interpretations.[75] Ultimately, the legal point of view hangs upon a faith or "trust" that the institutions will make the best decisions, whatever the moral considerations that an individual may consider important in deliberating about the decision.

The effect of the legal point of view is that the experiential bonding with the legal institutions is forgotten as officials "artificially" reason from the viewpoint of the institutional structure as a whole. The official must put his or her biases to the side. One must detach one's judgments from one's own views about right and wrong. One must detach the legal statement from the evaluative opinions of others as to what values ought to be chosen. Wisdom, an understanding of human nature, moral sensibility, an enlightened approach: these do not manifest the legal point of view, according to Raz.[76] Instead, the judge must investigate and describe the authoritative rules in a value-neutral manner, as if he or she possessed no conscious or unconscious opinion or prejudgment about what values ought to be posited when moral reasoning runs out in the deliberative stage of legal reasoning.[77] One's "knowledge of the law" and "skills in interpreting laws" are what count for the legal point of view. The legal point of view encourages the official to lift a legal category above his or her personal values and yet, to remain an indispensable link to the legal structure; and to remain a part of the structure without extraditing the official to the exterior viewpoint of a scientific observer.

More particularly, the official has no choice but to take the viewpoint of the institutional structure as a whole. Returning to Raz's view of morality, morality runs out at some point. The legal point of view, immersed within the institutional structure, fills the vacuum at the termination of moral reasoning and thereby objectifies what would otherwise be inevitably subjective. The legal point of view does not represent any particular attitude of the populace. The legal point of view represents "the legal man," to use Raz's term. And that viewpoint does not commit oneself to some transcendental moral value nor to the prejudgments that one

75 Raz, "On The Authority and Interpretation of Constitutions," in ed. Larry Alexander, *Constitutionalism: Philosophical Foundations* (Cambridge: Cambridge University Press, 1988), 152-93, 190.

76 Raz, *The Authority of Law*, 48.

77 See esp. Raz, *The Authority of Law*, 42, 140.

might have gained from one's personal or professional experiences. The legal official "adopts" the legal point of view in a "professional and uncommitted way."[78]

Perhaps surprisingly, the legal point of view emulates a "practical critical attitude," Raz argues in *Practical Reason and Norms*.[79] A practical critical attitude is manifested by a 'there is a reason' statement. What is the referent of such a justificatory statement? An object external to the interpreter. And why is the justificatory statement practical? Because the premises of an argument require that one share a belief in an inferred conclusion. One need not morally approve or disapprove the conclusion. One must believe in the rationality of justificatory argument. Raz calls any inferred consequence of a practical critical attitude, an "operative reason."[80] One may desire the conclusion. But this desire is a cognitively produced or "reason-based desire" rather than a bodily or experienced desire. Once again, the experiential attitudes that ground the legal structure are forgotten.

The legal point of view, so indispensable in understanding the rule of law, is consistent with slavery, widespread poverty, and racism, Raz admits. Since the justice of the content of a norm has been excluded from a binding law, this exclusion does not have the effect of a legal structure that endorses slavery. "For the lawyer, anything is the law if it meets the conditions of validity laid down in the system's rule of recognition" or other authority-conferring rules.[81] Raz admits that

> a non-democratic legal system, based on the denial of human rights, on extensive poverty, or racial segregation, sexual inequalities, and religious persecution may, in principle, conform to the requirements of the rule of law better than any of the legal systems of the more enlightened Western democracies.[82]

Raz goes further: "[t]he law may, for example, institute slavery without violating the rule of law."[83] Or, put differently, "[e]ven a bad law, as the inevitable official doctrine, should be obeyed for as long as it is in force."[84] Whether morally good or evil, the objectives of a legal rule ought to be effected. The artificial reasoning of the legal point of view "endorses" what would otherwise be a subjective posit of a value.

Despite his empathy for belief-based theories of norms,[85] Raz considers Hart's explanation of statements from the "internal" or "committed" attitude towards a practice as misdirected when one addresses the issue of 'what is a legally binding

78 Raz, *The Authority of Law*, 142-43.
79 Raz, *Practical Reason and Norms*, 32.
80 Raz, *Practical Reason and Norms*, 33.
81 Raz, *The Authority of Law*, 213.
82 Raz, *The Authority of Law*, 211.
83 Raz, *The Authority of Law*, 221.
84 Raz, *Practical Reason and Norms*, 216.
85 Raz, *Practical Reason and Norms*, 171-75.

norm?' Instead, what makes a practice legal is the official's detached point of view from the institutional structure as a whole. The legal point of view is like a statement "made on the assumption that something is the case, for example, that a certain scientific theory is valid."[86] A scientific statement does not presuppose, for example, that the scientific theory is true nor does it presuppose that the scientific theory must be true for the statement to be considered scientifically valid. So too, a legal statement does not presuppose that the institutional or normative structure is morally good. The legal statement is made from the point of view of the structure *as if* the structure were morally good. The goodness of the structure itself is a logical and chronological 'given' for Raz's officials.

In effect, then, the legal point of view privileges an 'as if' condition. A legal statement is 'true' if, from the legal point of view, an authorized norm directs that an individual follow a certain conduct. The 'ought' or normative character of the directive draws from the detached point of the view of the structure as a whole, not from the authority or substantive merit of the particular norm. The legal point of view does not postulate an empirically ascertainable social fact. And this, despite Raz's own claim that his theory of authority is a social theory. Further, the legal point of view does not postulate that any particular legal structure ought to exist as an issue of speculative moral argument. The legal person assumes that the legal institutions are a premise from which 'practical' conclusions may be inferred with deep consequences for the moral content of any one norm. The legal point of view postulates the existence of an institutional structure as if that socially contingent institutional structure were an intrinsically valued good from which inferences may be drawn.

4. The Unwritten Experiential Beliefs

What has happened with the attitudes of respect that Raz associated with the ultimate authorizing origin of the primary institutions?

Raz has not forgotten the non-cognitive character of such an origin. It is just that the official works from the legal point of view. The legal point of view recognizes that the origin is unrecognizable as binding. The origin is simply an 'as if' possibility: if there is an experiential attitude of bonding amongst the officials, then the institutions exist and the institutions, in turn, may authoritatively posit values and norms. Legal reasoning begins with the existence of the institution. In the act of reasoning, the official forgets that he or she had forgotten the origin of the institution in the quest for the authority of a posited norm in its institutional source.

86 Raz, *Practical Reason and Norms*, 175.

The important point in this context is that Raz considers reasons for action (that is, the "artificial reasons" of "right reason"), rather than the experiential attitudes for the reasons, as fact.[87] Attitudes, emotions, and beliefs are reasons for facts, not the facts themselves, Raz remarks.[88] Reasons become facts when one transfers the "natural" reasoning of balancing arguments in the deliberative stage of reasoning into the institutional context of addressing 'which institution has been endorsed to posit binding values?' Norms direct one as to how one ought to act, not what one believes is the right action. Only a reason for action, not a reason for belief (even the belief that one ought to follow the institutional structure), is a norm. An institution creates a norm. What is a norm? A norm prescribes how one ought to act. The prescribed action is an action, not a mere experienced belief. Once again, then, Raz severs the legal from the pre-legal experience. A reason for action, not a reason for belief, renders a norm binding.

Further, an ultimate justification for the reasons for an official's action is not needed. The ultimate justification may well be the experiential attitudes of respect that officials owe to the institutions. For Raz aims to explain the role of norms in the practical reasoning of officials who already believe in the authority of the norms. The latter belief logically precedes the authority of the rules and, therefore, the authority of the institutional structure that transforms a belief into a right reason. And yet, despite its importance, the belief that an institution makes a reason for action is excluded from legal existence, just as are the beliefs that the officials may have towards the substantive content of the particular norms that the institutions posit.

More specifically, according to Raz, an action is justified by virtue of its posit by an institution on the bureaucratic hierarchy, whatever the actual justification of the particular action. Why is something a norm? Because, Raz explains in *Practical Reason and Norms*, one *believes* that a law directs individuals to act in a certain manner.[89] An institution's decisions are authoritative because of a "reasoned trust" that there are "adequate reasons" to abide by the decisions' directives.[90] One believes, he continues, that the decisions will "yield the benefits they are meant to bring only if we rely on them rather than on our own independent judgement of the merits of each case to which they apply. This is the whole point of admitting that the decision-making power should be with the authority." What is especially important is that the officials who use normative language *believe* that norms are authoritative reasons for action, Raz insists. The officials, especially judges, believe that norms are authoritative reasons for action to such a point that

87 Raz, *Practical Reason and Norms*, 15-20.
88 Raz, *Practical Reason and Norms*, 198.
89 Raz, *Practical Reason and Norms*, 170.
90 Raz, *Practical Reason and Norms*, 193.

the norms exclude the judge's personal preferences or the judge's view of the majority's non-legal values as relevant to the legal character of a norm unless the norm requires the judge to include such non-legal values. In a double-take, the official's legal point of view rejects just such a belief in the givenness of an institution as legally recognizable, justicible, and efficacious.

The distinction between the experiential belief and the reason for action, the latter appealing to a cognitive referent, thereby reinforces the institutional source as the key determinant of a legal norm. Taking a legal point of view, officials need not personally believe that a norm is morally or prudentially correct. But the official must believe that he or she is justified in following the norm. Perhaps the norm should not have been made. Perhaps the norm should be changed. But the norm is authored by an institution. Any norm must be linked to an institution that officials recognize as authoritative in civil society. Such an institution is part of an interconnected structure of institutions that Raz takes as representative, if not constitutive, of the sovereign state. The official must *believe* in the analytic (and moral and legal) given-ness of that structure in order to take the legal point of view. As Raz puts it in the recent essay "On the Authority and Interpretation of Constitutions," 'givenness' includes a claimed moral authority.[91] "Once the moral justification of those ultimate legal rules (i.e., those whose legal validity does not presuppose that of any other law) is established, *or assumed*, the moral justification of the rest of the law is – up to a point – established by technical legal argumentation."[92]

The consequence, then, is that Raz assumes what his theory of authority aims to explain. The officials believe in the authority of their institutions. The institutions claim an authority for their decisions. In "On the Authority and Interpretation of Constitutions," Raz suggests that "the authority of constitutions cannot derive from that [the authority] of their makers, standing at the birth of their states, cannot have authority themselves. All authority derives from the constitution that they themselves made *without prior authority to do so*."[93] The institutional structure is "self-legitimizing."[94] The *belief* in the authority of the institutional structure – a belief which, as a belief, must remain unrecognized as legally binding – ensures the authority of a particular decision. The legal analysis of exclusionary reasons excises beliefs, especially the belief in the authority of the institutions, from membership in the legal, let alone from the authority of such members. Raz restates this point: "[it is important for institutions acting for the public not to take

91 See esp. Raz, "On the Authority and Interpretation of Constitutions," 159.

92 Raz, "Authority and Interpretation of Constitutions," emphasis added. One should note Raz's caveat "up to a point," although the caveat is not critical to my argument here.

93 Raz, "Authority and Interpretation of Constitutions," 158. Emphasis added.

94 Raz, "Authority and Interpretation of Constitutions," 175.

decisions the explanations for which are the non-rational dispositions or tastes of the people who hold office in them."[95] An official must assume the belief in the moral goodness and the logical premise of the structure because to make such a belief an issue of legality would render accessible the phenomenology of the experiential bodies of the officials.

The above exposition of Raz's claims and argument suggests that we return to the question, 'does the institutional structure possess an authorizing origin?' On the one hand, officials do possess an affective belief that their decisions are authoritative. Affective feelings of trust and loyalty towards the institutions are indispensable for a modern legal order. Without such a belief in the authority of the structure, Raz suggests, it is unlikely that a bureaucratic structure and the state would exist.

On the other hand, an institution defines its own authority in that officials, without argument, claim an authority for the institutional sources to which the officials appeal in their reasoning:

> The law's claim to authority is manifested by the fact that legal institutions are officially designated as 'authorities,' by the fact that they regard themselves as having the right to impose obligations on their subjects, by their claims that their subjects owe them allegiance, and that their subjects ought to obey the law as it requires to be obeyed (that is, in all cases except those in which some legal doctrine justifies breach of duty).[96]

The official excludes the experiential as non-law. The experiential, though foundational, is absent from the legal structure and absent from the legal point of view. The experiential is pre-legal. The official excludes the pre-legal from law, though the pre-legal may admittedly enter into the posit of one's value at the end of deliberative reasoning if the law directs that one include the pre-legal. The affective feelings of loyalty, being for the most part unwritten and unconscious, remain unrecognizable. Legal recognition, despite Raz's occasional deference to unwritten customs, is constituted as officials bring their experiential meanings *into* the officials' writing. The experiential body is forgotten. And, as officials take the legal point of view, the officials forget that they had forgotten the authorizing origin. The origin is irretrievable from legal memory. The origin is non-existent and, therefore, a non-truth.

95 Raz, "Authority and Interpretation of Constitutions," 190.
96 Raz, "Authority, Law and Morality," 216.

5. The Language of the Legal Point of View

I have now identified several factors in Raz's moral/legal thought. Raz admits, as do Austin and Hart, that officials may incorporate non-legal factors into their deliberative stage of legal reasoning. But once a decision is rendered, the decision, to be a decision, excludes the non-legal from the authority of the decision. The decision or rule may direct future officials to incorporate what has hitherto been considered morality. A constitutional bill of rights, I suppose, would be the best example of this. But such an incorporation must be authorized by an institution located in the hierarchic pyramid. The authority of a decision or binding norm does not lie with the substantive content of what the decision/rule incorporates but with the linkage of the decision/rule with an institutional source recognized as authoritative in civil society. Raz distinguishes, then, the incorporation of directed moral factors into a decision/norm from the authority of the rule/norm. The authority of the rule/norm is separate from the directed moral content of the rule/norm.

The thrust of Raz's arguments addresses the latter issue of the nature of an authoritative rule/norm. Raz has been consistently concerned with practical reasoning and how binding decisions exclude the moral considerations that a rule/norm may direct an official to include. What a rule/norm cannot include, to be a norm/rule in a modern legal structure, according to Raz, is the very experiential attitude of respect towards a legal institution, the attitude that Raz considers critical to legal obligation and to the very existence of a legal system. Such experiential attitudes are independent of the moral values that binding norms/rules may direct an official to include. The attitudes cannot be linked with a distinct and assignable institutional author. The attitudes are external to the civil institutions. The attitudes are not part of legal existence, even a legal existence where binding rules/norms direct officials to include morality. Morality, for Raz, has a very special sense that appeals to arguments about the intrinsically valued Good life and right and wrong conduct. Ultimately, such moral reasoning runs out, just as does legal reasoning, and, after moral reasoning, an official must posit a prescriptive value. The posit of such a value, even if directed by a binding rule/norm, ends moral/legal analysis, according to Raz. But does it?

The official's exclusion of a consideration of the experiential in practical reasoning raises important issues. Despite an institution's apparent posit of a value, is it not possible that the official interprets the directed expression of the value in a manner that brings the interpreter's experiential meanings *into* the expression? Does Raz acknowledge that an official may read the official's prejudgments into the posited value, as expressed? Is the institutional structure really a "moral fact" without an examination of the constitution of meaning of the norms posited by the institution? Is it that easy to accept the posit of a value as a 'fact' without understanding the meaning that one brings *into* the value? Can one shift from the termination of moral or "natural" reasoning to the institutional source of the posit of a value (or "artificial" reasoning) without examining how one constitutes meaning as one 'reads' what is the role of different institutions in the institutional structure? Does an institutional source really lift the subjective choice of a value into a realm of objectivity without the official, as interpreter, reading in his or her professional, if not personal, experiences *into* the linkage of the norm to the institutional source?

Raz does not address these important issues about the phenomenology of language. Instead, he reinforces his claim about the inaccessible character of the experiential from legal reasoning by elaborating a consistent, rigorous analysis of "the legal point of view." Raz's notion of the legal point of view solidifies his claim that officials must exclude the experiential world as an illegitimate factor in the deliberative and the decisional stages of legal reasoning. The notion of the legal point of view aids one in understanding Raz's theory of morality and law.

Legal statements, according to Raz, are "detached," "value-free" and taken from the viewpoint of the institutional structure as a whole. For Raz, language is constituted from such "statements" and the statements express cognitive, not meant objects.[97] The experiential body is purged from language. A legal statement may be true or false if the referent of the statement is a fact, according to Raz. Statements express the relation of a cognitive object to such a fact. A given institution is an "intelligible fact." In expressing the relation of a cognitive object to an "intelligible fact," the statement is considered "pure." Raz claims that legal statements can even be "pure." A statement is "pure" in that, being value-free and immune from social/historical contingencies, the statement's referent is another endorsed norm, not an empirically observable fact nor a non-legal experience. A statement merely expresses what was in the mind of the institution in choosing one value over another. Language supplements such a mind.

Concepts are the core material of law, according to Raz. Indeed, for Raz, concepts can be formed without language. For language enters the scene *after* the concepts are formed, according to Raz. When Raz addresses the institutional source that objectifies the subjective posit of a value, ideal-directed concepts interpose between the institutional source and the language by which the institution expresses the value.[98] The concept is willed and the official expresses his or her will through statements. A statement is an "operator" or "indicator": "it is the law that...," "one has the legal right to...."[99] A statement is a means to an end, the end

97 The distinction between a cognitive and meant object is elaborated in Conklin, *The Phenomenology of Modern Legal Discourse*, 103-107, 125-31.

98 Raz, *The Authority of Law*, 62.

99 Raz, *The Authority of Law*, 63.

being a concept (or cognitive object, to use my earlier term). The statement expresses the concept; the statement does not (re)produce an event.[100] Even a reason, such as friendship, is expressed as a concept.[101]

Since a concept can be formed without a language to express the concept, logic controls the language when language enters legal analysis, according to Raz.[102] One may even "logically stratify" different types of legal statements. Reasons for action form the most elementary stratum of legal language, according to Raz. Above the reasons for action, there are permissions, duties, and powers. The referent for a permission, duty, or power is the more 'solid,' reason for action. The reason for action, that is, provides the conceptual basis or grounding for the legal duty. The permissions, duties, and powers, in turn, ground or provide the referent for individual rights. Rights and powers provide the grounding for contracts. Each type of statement is logically analyzed as immune from a socially or historically contingent context.

Raz even describes his own theory of the nature of law as a conceptual theory.

A rule is not a justified statement, let alone a statement.[103] A rule is a "thing" or object. The rule, as an object, is cognitive. Language functions as the medium to express the content of the object. Language does not imprint the content of the cognitive object with a particular choice of value. Language comes *after* the rules, as concepts, have taken form. The truth of a legal statement is ascertained if the rule, which the statement describes, is legally authoritative. The objects (rules) simply do not 'exist' if they are invalid or lacking in authority. Just as a non-existent stone is not a stone, an invalid (and therefore, non-existent) rule is not a rule. A rule exists if it is recognized in an interlocking structure of categories.

Even with the narrow understanding of language as constituted from statements, truth lies in the world of concepts independent of language and independent of any conferral of meaning as one reads or hears statements. Truth, for Raz, lies in the trace of one concept from another in the quest for some one ultimate concept. Raz recognizes that such a quest will never be satisfied and that the quest would continue *ad infinitum* unless the human subject intervened with the posit of a value. Moral reasoning even ends with the trace of authority to some one institutional source. The institution ends the trace with the posit of a value. So the posit of a personal value is lifted into the intelligible "facts" surrounding the institutional context. The institutional posit of a value functions as the referent for legal truth. Legal

100 The distinction is made in Conklin, *Phenomenology of Modern Legal Discourse*, 130-68.
101 Raz, *The Authority of Law*, 255.
102 Raz, *The Authority of Law*, 63.
103 Raz, *The Authority of Law*, 148.

analysis takes place through a transparent language, purified of the very experiential attitudes of respect with which Raz grounds the modern legal order.

The big question is whether one really makes a sharp demarcation between the deliberative and exclusionary stages of moral reasoning. Raz isolates the deliberative and the executive as the two phenomenological stages of legal reasoning. Raz also differentiates between the individual's choice of a value at the end of deliberation on the one hand and the institution's choice of a value on the other. The latter, to be binding, excludes the content of the former. But is such a demarcation so clear? May one even make the demarcation between deliberation and execution, between individual choices and institutional choices, if the interpreter plays even a minimal role in the interpretive act? If language is opaque rather than transparent? If legal meaning is constituted as the interpreter reads a statement?

Raz exemplifies his postulate about the transparency of language in "Authority, Law and Morality." An income tax statute decides the fair distribution of public funds, according to Raz. Raz claims that one need not evaluate the content of the statute in order to reach a conclusion about its legal authority. The content addresses an issue such as 'what is the fair distribution?' The tools of legal analysis need "little more than knowledge of English (including technical legal English), and of the events which took place in Parliament on a few occasions."[104] Raz assumes, that is, that the judge, as the interpreter of the statute, may accept the words of the statute as if they existed 'out there' in some objective realm, as if the events in Parliament might be interpreted as given objective facts that could be impartially observed as facts, and as if the text and the parliamentary events could be objectively observed without the observer/interpreter incorporating his or her own prejudgments about the role of parliament, as one of several institutions, or without incorporating the substantive content of the tax rule into his or her interpretive act. The problem is that, if the official is to the trace of the institutional source of the tax rule and thereby to exclude the substantive content of the tax rule, the official must know what is the excluded part (the content) as well as the included part (the institutional source) in order to make the exclusion. And that can hardly be understood without reading both the tax rule and the 'intelligible' fact of the deliberations of parliament in a socially contingent context. The consequence of Raz's theory of language is that the statements that express legal rules are contextless. Raz's theory of language offers an extreme form of legal meaning. The second-order exclusionary rules exclude the very conferral of meaning whose importance he recognized as the ultimate authorizing origin of a modern legal order. That is, in addition to affirmatively postulating that one may legally understand a text or political event to the exclusion of its social/cultural context, Raz understands a language as a series of

104 Raz, "Authority, Law and Morality," 221.

"statements" to the exclusion of the very bodily experiences that the official may well bring *into* the institution's statements as the official reads them.[105]

Of course, I have noted that Raz himself is conscious of the experienced prejudgments of the legal officials and the citizenry. He describes them as "attitudes" and "beliefs." Indeed, a citizen or an official is legally obligated to abide by a particular rule, whatever its content, if he or she possesses a "feeling" or "attitude" of respect towards the institutions that posit the rule. Raz explains that such an attitude is formed by habits over many decades or centuries. But Raz is insistent that the official, immersed inside an institutional structure, excludes such prejudgments. The official does so when he or she refers to cognitive objects in morality, when his or her choice of a value is displaced in favour of "artificial" reasoning (institutional), when the binding decision, to be binding, excludes the substantive content that Raz describes of the deliberative moment of reasoning, and when the official expresses the binding norm from the legal point of view of the institutional structure as a whole.

Language, for Raz, is a tool to be used, an operative object, an instrumental means. Like an individual's choice of an individual value or an institution's choice of a collective value or the posit of a social fact, legal sentences – and, again, Raz considers a sentence to be the core element of a language – are posited as 'givens.' The statements, as detached, value-free, objective conduits of cognitive objects, may be scientifically observed. Statements are used to express invisible concepts. The important element of the concept of a legal rule is its normative character, normative in the sense of directing one as to how he or she ought to behave in the future. A statement about such a norm *describes* the norm, according to Raz. The utility of the statement to describe the normative concept does not establish that the statement is law: "Everyone can use normative language to describe a legal system. People who live on the other side of the world or who live thousands of years after the period during which the legal system was in force can use normative language to describe the law," Raz states.[106] What makes a statement normative, according to Raz, is the cognitive referent of the statement. The referent is contextless in time and place. What matters for the referent to exist is not its substantive content but its trace to its institutional source from the legal point of view. And the legal point of view is expressed in (not 'through') detached, as opposed to committed (internal) and external statements.

Though loyal to the central claim of the separation of law from morals, as described in Chapter Three, Raz misses, unfortunately, that language involves

105 This distinction is elaborated more generally in William E. Conklin, *The Phenomenology of Modern Legal Discourse*, 135-68.

106 Raz, *Practical Reason and Norms*, 170-71

more than simply statements and more than statements that represent cognitive objects. And he misses that concepts, however logical, do not pre-exist language. Language includes the experiential meanings that a reader or 'observer' confers *into* the statements.[107] Raz misses the phenomenology of language because he takes language as a formalistic conduit for an official's concepts as if the official could even think from the legal point of view without the embodied meanings which he or she brought into the differentiation of one concept from another. Raz claims that what makes a rule 'legal' is the very expunging of the experiential meanings from the nature of norms. In the act of reading such a claim and in describing how a legal official does do so through "natural" reasoning, "artificial" reasoning, the institutional posit of values, exclusionary reasons, the binding quality of a norm, and the legal point of view, Raz idealizes what is 'law.' His description of his theory of legal positivism as grounded in the social is an optical illusion.

6. Violence and the Constitution of the Institutions

At this point, we run into a series of issues that bring Raz's legal positivism into question. If the authority of a humanly posited rule rests, ultimately, with a structure of interrelated institutions, such as a parliament, courts, police, government agencies, and all the other offices that constitute the modern state, there remains the question 'what authorizes a particular institution to legislate, adjudicate, or enforce its norms as binding?' How do we determine whether an institution has made a decision according to the proper role assigned to that institution? When does an institution exceed its authority? How does one determine when one sovereign has succeeded another? These issues suggest that, in addition to the structure of interrelated institutions, there must be basic rules that grant authority to the institutions. These are generally called 'power-conferring' or 'authority conferring' rules. If a structure of institutions does not possess authority-granting rules, how may one be certain that any one official or group of officials represents the institution?

So, along these lines, the authority of a posited law may not lie with an institutional author that pre-exists the rule. Rather, certain rules recognize what institution and what officials are authorized to posit the rule. Raz acknowledges the importance of such authority-granting rules. But which comes first: the institutions or the authority-granting rules that create and limit the institutions? If the authority-granting rules, what gives the authority-granting rules their authority? If the institutions precede (logically and chronologically) the authority-granting rules, what authorizes the authority of the institutions to posit authority-granting rules? Social conventions? An attitude of respect towards the institutions? Violence?

107 Raz, "The Nature of Law," 195-98.

Must the attitude of respect towards the institutions be shared only amongst the officials and, if so, do authorized posited laws possess a violent character against all those non-officials who may not share such an attitude of respect? If social conventions authorize the authority of institutions to posit authority-granting authority, are the conventions also a disguised form of violence?

Instead of social conventions authorizing the institutions to act, however, authority-granting rules may precede the authority of institutional sources. If so, what makes the authorizing rules authorizing? And how does one find such authority-granting rules? Are they authored in codes? If so, are not those codes constitutive of the sovereign state? Or do social conventions authorize the institutions to author the rules? Must the conventions be shared amongst officials alike? Must the conventions manifest the *behaviour* of officials? How relevant is the behaviour of non-officials, the electors? Must the behaviour be signified in writing at some point? Does the rule, as writing, merely "approximate" the unwritten convention, as Hart suggests? What authorizes the institutional source: the unwritten conventions or the inscribed rules that recognize the conventions? Does the institutional context really transform a subjective value into an objective one? Does not subjectivity remain if the authority-granting rules precede the authoritative existence of the institutional structure?

If authority-granting rules are superimposed over the laws of, say, another state, does an act of violence constitute the institutional structure that, in turn, authorizes the human posit of all rules and other legal standards? What authorizes the authority of authority-granting rules if the territory lacks the recognizable institutions of a modern sovereign state? Must the system of institutions, for example, possess a singular head? Must the institutions be vertically connected in the model of a pyramidal hierarchy? Is the sources thesis applicable to a monarchical or autocratic constitution, with no bureaucracy of advisors? These issues are particularly relevant to the analysis of the relationship of indigenous legal cultures and the given bureaucratic institutions of a modern state. Are authority-granting rules authorized to posit institutions and rules over indigenous customs and institutions, for example? Is violence the ultimate authorizing 'grounding' of either the authority-granting rules or the institutions that posit such rules? Is the initial constituting moment of a sovereign state ultimately illegal? Whether it is a break-away republic or some multi-ethnic state that claims statehood over all indigenous ethnic groups, what arguably determines the validity or authority of either the new set of institutions or their authority-granting rules? May legal officials even ask the above questions if the institutional thesis is to be taken seriously? Is the trace of the rule to some institutional source a logical premise for legal reasoning? Does legal existence begin from such a 'given.' Does legal reasoning begin with such a 'given.' Are the personal views and values of the officials irrelevant to the binding character of an institution's decision? Is the justice of the content of a particular rule irrelevant? Does the institutional thesis suggest that the justice of the substantive content of posited rules is non-law, as outside the law? As Socrates considered in *The Crito*, any challenge to the wisdom or morality of the substantive content of an institution's rules would seem to challenge the authority of the institution itself.

But if the coercive posit of a rule by an institution constitutes the authority of rules, how can one consider such a violent act legal? How can one consider the interstitial interpretation of a particular technical rule legally binding? Is even the constitutional law of a modern state legal? Is law – even posited law – distinguishable from violent acts?

7. The Idealism of Raz's Legal Reasoning

Now, one might claim that Raz himself has considered the experiential character of language and that he has protected his theory from the above reading of his works. After all, Raz strongly criticizes H.L.A. Hart's "linguistic" or essentialist approach to the nature of law.[108] One might criticize the above reading on two accounts. First, my focus upon the role of the experiential body in the second-order decisional stage of legal reasoning may unduly privilege the individual norms that Raz emphasizes, again and again, must be displaced in favour of the artificial reasoning of the institutional source of the particular norm. Secondly, my reading of the formalism of Raz's theory of authority may be misdirected in that Raz's "legal man" excludes experiential meanings precisely because authority rests with the second-order exclusionary reasons in an institutional context. That is, even if a judge in fact reads experiential meanings into a text or event, that phenomenon is irrelevant because it addresses the norms's substantive content rather than the institutional source of the norm and only the latter renders an experience authoritative. Permit me to address both possible criticisms of my re-reading of Raz's works in turn.

Raz's first claim, again, is that what characterizes an authoritative rule/norm is an exclusionary artificial reasoning of institutional sources. This artificial reasoning differs from a "natural" reasoning where an official balances one value against another with respect to the substantive content of a particular norm. Despite Raz's effort to ground his theory of legal reasoning in a social realism of "intelligible facts", a navïeté permeates Raz's demarcation of the first-order deliberative reasoning from the second-order executive stage of reasoning. Deliberation concerns the cognitive, we have observed of Raz's argument. Raz's elucidation of the deliberative stage of legal reasoning explicitly excludes the experiential body from the

108 See text supra section 2(e) between pp. 253-7, notes 61-72.

arguments and justifications of a rule. In the process, Raz idealizes even the first deliberative stage of legal reasoning.

Further, one just cannot make Raz's distinctions so easily. Raz distinguishes, we will recall, the first-order reasons from second-order reasons, the content of a norm from the trace of the rule to some institutional source, the incorporation thesis from the separation thesis. But, in order for one to make each differentiation, one must be conscious of the referent on both sides of the boundary. To understand the nature of a binding norm, the content of the norm – whatever moral values are incorporated – is excluded. One must know what is categorized as a first-order reason or the content of the norm. To distinguish the second-order reason from the first-order reason, the inside (the legal decision) from the outside (the deliberation about the content), one must know what is on the outside as well as the inside.

Further still, Raz himself admits that law includes unwritten principles and rules in addition to a statute or regulation. How can one differentiate the unwritten rules from their institutional sources without initially appreciating the content of the unwritten rules on the other side of the boundary between written and unwritten rules? After all, one cannot locate a quantifiable time and place when an unwritten norm has taken form: if one could, it would be 'written.' And even if an unwritten norm possessed an institutional source (again, something which is difficult to contemplate for it to be unwritten), how could one locate such an institutional source without also studying the substantive content of the unwritten norm? And could one situate the institution within an interdependent institutional structure without also reading the content of the unwritten norm in the context of the social-cultural content of the evolution of the institutions of the society?

This takes me to the second possible concern in my reading of Raz's works. Even though officials may incorporate experiential meaning into the deliberation about norms, Raz might claim, a consciousness of such an incorporation is misdirected because it addresses a particular norm's substantive content, not its institutional source and only the latter renders an experience authoritative. The critical point of Raz's theory of law is his postulate that 'law' begins with the 'givenness' of the sovereign state. I have noted his association of the second-order exclusionary, institutional reasons with the sovereign state.[109] Raz associates the institutional sources – so indispensable to the binding character of 'law' – with the institutional bureaucracy of a sovereign state. He distinguishes such an institutional structure from a "primitive" society.[110] Indeed, in "On the Authority and Interpretation of Constitutions," Raz suggests that his argument is confined to 'originating' constitutions that accept the institutional structure associated with the colonial states

109 Raz, *The Authority of Law*, 87.
110 Raz, "On the Authority and Interpretation of Constitutions," 158-60, 184-85.

of Europe.[111] In a modern sovereign state, "[e]very state – by which is meant a form of political system and not a juristic person – has one legal system that constitutes the law of that state and every municipal legal system is the law of one state."[112] The structure, or what Raz calls "the system," is constituted from interdependent institutions modelled on a pyramid. The institutions are "centralized bodies concentrating in their hands the authority to make binding applicative determinations."[113] A norm is authoritative "if and only if it is valid because it belongs to a legal system in force in a certain country or is enforceable in it. i.e. if it is systematically valid."[114] The givenness of the bureaucratic institutional structure, as the referent of all legal analysis, assures the existence of authoritative norms: "since laws exist only in legal systems, to ask whether a law exists is to ask whether it is part of the legal system concerned."[115] This 'givenness' of the bureaucratic institutional structure of a modern sovereign state functions to objectify what Raz considers an arbitrary subjective value in moral reasoning.

But how can one make such a postulate without considering other legal orders that were not socially contingent upon the postulate of the modern European sovereign state? Are there not other ways to organize social relations than the sovereign state? Is one not naive to postulate the centrality of the sovereign state in an economically interdependent world where the state competes for the support of international legal units far wealthier than many states themselves? Is it not important to include an analysis of how the sovereign state assimilated radically different ways of organizing social relations such as those experienced by the pre-conquest Amerindian tribes? Indeed, does the totality of the institutional structure, postulated by the sovereign state, privilege the very cognitive world that Raz also privileges to the exclusion of an inaccessible origin in the experiential body? Does not the sovereign institutional structure, as a postulate, bring into question the very autonomy of the structure?

This takes me to a further problematic with Raz's theory of law. The institutional sources thesis assumes that there is one institutional source for each legal statement. The thesis also assumes that the time and place of the institutional promulgation of the statement is sufficient to assure the authority of a norm. Such an assumption reinforces the very essentialism that Raz rejects in his critique of Hart's linguistic approach to the nature of law. For Raz conceives that a norm (which he defines as a concept or cognitive object) can possess an essence and

111 Raz, *The Authority of Law*, 98-99.
112 Raz, *The Authority of Law*, 110.
113 Raz, *The Authority of Law*, 19, 116-18.
114 Raz, *The Authority of Law*, 85.
115 Raz, *The Authority of Law*, 72.

that there may be gaps between such norms.[116] The institutional source is a-historical. The structure itself is believed to lack a social-cultural content. When an institution posits a clear norm in a formally promulgated instrument, is the trace of the norm to some institutional context really that straightforward without the official's examination of the opaqueness of the statements of the state's institutions? Not unlike his predecessors, Raz is determined to objectify the apparently inevitable choice of a value at the termination of moral (that is, "natural") reasoning. Does Raz's postulate of the 'givenness' of the institutional exclusionary norms idealize the grounding of a binding norm?

At first glance, Raz's focus upon the referent of an institutional source seems to bear fruition when one considers the constitutionality of a statute in a federal state, for example. Here, common law courts have been preoccupied with whether the proper legislature, or subordinate agency, enacted the statute or regulation. The courts have been loath to admit that they were examining the "wisdom of the enactment" (that is, its content). And they have framed their judgments in terms of the "framer's intent," rather than their own personal values about the content of the legislation. Even the introduction of constitutional bill of rights has reinforced Raz's claim, to an important extent, that the authority of a constitutional norms rests with the issue of 'which institution possesses the authority in the institutional structure to choose constitutional values?' rather than 'what is the appropriateness or justice of the choice of the substantive values by the institution that posited the values?' The rhetoric of constitutional adjudication reinforces Raz's theory of the nature of law.

When one closely examines the judgments interpreting the basic constitutional text of a common law country, however, it becomes very difficult to understand how a legal official can follow a rule in the basic constitutional text or a constitutional judge-made rule endorsed by a prior court without the judge implicitly, if not explicitly, evaluating the substantive content of the constitutional rule or even the goodness of the institutional structure as a whole.[117] All judgments presuppose a general theory of 'what is law' and what could be more of a substantive content than the deepest question of all, 'what is law?' Even a judgment that claims to be exclusively based upon the institutional source of the norm presupposes a theory about the content of the norm: namely, the theory that the substantive content of a norm is immaterial to the authority of law. Even the detached observer, that Raz

---

116 See generally, William E. Conklin, *Images of a Constitution* (Toronto: University of Toronto Press, 1989) and Conklin, *In Defence of Fundamental Rights* (Alphen aan den Rijn: Sijtoff & Noordhoff, 1979).

117 *Local Prohibition Reference* [1896] AC 348 (PC). For Pigeon's and Beetz' theory of the autonomy of the provinces, see Conklin, "The Constitutional Prism of Louis-Philippe Pigeon and Jean Beetz," 30 *Les Cahiers de Droit* **30** (1989): 113-36.

privileges, implicitly asserts particular theories about the substantive content of a norm: first, a theory about the functions and features of a norm that are worth isolating and excluding from non-law; second, a further theory about the role of the official as an interpreter in the detached observation of 'facts' and 'law'; and third, a still further theory about the success of official's objectification of a subjective posit of a value as the official refers the judgment to the institutional source instead of the subjective posit of the value. Further, an official who excludes the substantive content of a norm altogether – or who believes that he or she does – presupposes a criterion of the value for legal authority (that authority rests in an intellectual grounding or, ultimately, an *arche*), and further, the official manifests a general view of law – that the content fails to meet the criterion of 'what is law?' In sum, Raz offers a theory of legal reasoning that asks that the official uncritically adopt a theory of law – the positivist theory of law. That is, Raz asks that the official forget the important issues that trigger an inquiry into the invisible origin of binding posited norms.

Further, independent of the foreclosure of a critical evaluation of the theory of law presupposed in the exclusion of the substantive content of a law, it also becomes difficult to understand how a legal official can trace the statutory or common law norm to an institutional source (either the national or the provincial legislature in a federal system, for example) without interpreting the content of the norm. Indeed, the trace of a chosen value to the institutional source requires an interpretation of the centre of gravity of the statutory rule and that requires an identification of its implicit objectives, its social and economic consequences, its social premises and the like. That is, the shift from the individual's choice of a value to the institutional context does not terminate nor exclude moral arguments about the content of the statutory enactment nor about the content of the constitutional source from the legal point of view.

How is it possible to trace the statements in sections 91 or 92 of the *Constitutional Act* (*British North America Act*), *1867-present*, for example, without accounting for any one judge's 'committed' meanings as a citizen or a professional lawyer as he or she has experienced expectations and forestructures of meaning in the past? Is it possible to read sections 91 or 92 without reading in prejudgments about the autonomy of the provinces (Lord Watson, Justice Pigeon and Justice Beetz),[118] the supremacy of the sovereign (Dicey),[119] a "social compact" (Lord Sankey),[120] unrestrained free enterprise (Idington),[121] a "living organ-

118 *The Law of the Constitution* (London: Macmillan, 1885).

119 *Reference re Regulation and Control of Aeronautics in Canada* [1932] AC 54; [1932] 1 DLR 58 (PC).

120 *Reference re Board of Commerce* (1920), 60 SCR 456; 54 DLR 354.

121 *Edwards v. AG Canada* [1930] AC 123; [1930] 1 DLR 98 (PC); *Francis Pulp and Paper v. Manitoba Free Press* [1923] AC 695; [1923] 3 DLR 629 (PC).

ism" (Lord Sankey, Viscount Haldane and many others),[122] or a centralized state (Laskin)[123] of Canada? Armed with different metaphors and images of 'what is a constitution' the legal official interprets the content of both the challenged statutory rule and the constitutional rule in a manner that manifests the particular judge's image of what is a constitution.[124] Here, the detached specialized vocabulary and grammar of legal language will not help. Indeed, to identify any institutional source to the exclusion of the substantive content of the norm which the institution supposedly posited and to the exclusion of the 'content' of the social/cultural context of an institution role, again, idealizes what Raz considers the "social" institutional basis of the nature of law. To accept the thrust of Raz's theory of legal authority, in other words, idealizes artificial reasoning – this time, the second-order executive stage of legal reasoning – to such a point as to divorce 'the law' from social experience, the lived meanings of which officials bring into their statements about institutional roles. What Raz takes as "intelligible facts" is a metaphysics that distances the law from the very "attitudes of respect" that Raz privileges as the ultimate experiential origins of a modern legal order.

8. Forgetting the Act of Forgetting

More, Raz's sense of legal reasoning in the "intelligible facts" of a legal point of view reinforces a naivety about the nature of law. Hans Kelsen, alone in the tradition of legal positivism, impresses upon us that it is the institution's *statement* of the will, not the will itself, that constitutes law. Raz privileges several elements: the cognitive objects of moral reasoning, the institutional source of the posit of a value, and the detached legal point of view. His argument is misdirected if it is, indeed, a social realism with which he wishes to build his theory of law, as he claims. Raz projects the nature of law into some speculative metaphysics. It is this very metaphysics that Raz takes as "social fact."

One point needs emphasis in appreciating the thrust of Raz's contribution to the resilient tradition of legal positivism. Theories of legal positivism have associated binding laws of a modern state with writing. And the written word has signified cognitive referents, doctrines, rules, principles, and other standards. Raz insists that the project of the legal official is a conceptual enterprise, just as it is with the philosopher of law. In *Practical Reason and Norms*, for example, Raz begins by distinguishing substantive practical philosophy from conceptual analysis. Substantive practical philosophy studies the justice and morality of the deliberative

122 *Reference re Anti-Inflation* [1976] 2 SCR 373; 68 DLR (3d) 452.
123 See generally, Conklin, *Images of a Constitution*.
124 Raz, *Practical Reason and Norms*, 10.

stage of moral reasoning. Practical philosophy asks whether the choice of a value at the end of moral reasoning is instrumental for the good life. What values should an individual or community pursue? What arguments should be considered as reason for action? Which norms are morally binding? Though he admits that the substantive and the conceptual do overlap to some extent, Raz states that his is "primarily an essay in conceptual analysis."[125] Here, one asks 'what are the logical features of value?' 'the reasons for action?' 'the norms?' 'and the nature of rules of inference for practical reasoning?' And here, Raz aims to develop "a unified logic of all the concepts" that addresses which institution ought to determine the content of this or that value. Raz calls the latter project normative theory.

When Raz distinguishes between first-order and second-order reasons, for example, he claims to be making a *conceptual* distinction. Raz privileges the cognitive when he elaborates the detached legal point of view. Raz is determined to accurately represent the "*structure* of reasoning" that characterizes authoritative norms.[126] So too, he claims to be making conceptual distinctions when he distinguishes between the deliberative arm and the executive arm of reasoning, between law creation and law applying, between the incorporation thesis and the separation thesis, between moral reasoning and a judicial decision, between the committed and the legal point of view, and between language and the cognitive. Raz emphasizes the role of conceptual analysis in the important statement of his legal theory in "Authority, Law and Morality."[127] The role of legal theory, he writes, is "to pick up" on those concepts that are "central and significant to the way the concept plays its role in people's understanding of society, to elaborate and explain them."[128] What is important is the shared understanding of the concept of law. Consistent with each element of his legal theory, concepts are said to possess authority and concepts mediate individuals with institutions.

The paradox is that the legal official, working from the legal point of view, embarks upon a quest to locate the institutional source of any norm alleged to be legal, all the while haunted by the unrecognized and unrecognizable authorizing origin of his or her quest for an authoritative norm. The official realizes, though, that to be an authorizing origin of the institutional structure, the organization must fundamentally differ from an orderly posited norm. And to differ in such a manner, the origin must be external to binding norms. The officials on the structure must define an outside to the institutional structure. That outside, the world of non-law, locates the origin of the institutional structure. But because it is outside

---

125 Raz, *Practical Reason and Norms*, 193.
126 Raz, "Authority, Law and Morality," in *Ethics in the Public Domain*, 210-37.
127 Raz, "Authority, Law and Morality," 237.
128 Raz, *The Authority of Law*, 97.

the structure, the origin is not recognizable nor justicible. As Raz himself notes in *The Authority of Law*, nothing is part of the normative legal structure unless it is a norm that the institutional structure will recognize as legally binding.[129] As he explained:

> The fact that a rule is an ultimate legal rule means no more than that there is no legal ground, no legal justification for its validity. It does not imply that there is no ground or justification for the rule, only that if such ground exists it is not a legal one.... By definition ultimate legal rules are not similarly grounded on legal reasons. The absence of a further law determining the grounds of validity of the ultimate rules is precisely what makes them *ultimate* legal rules.[130]

Although Raz claims that such an absent origin can only aid in the identification of what norms are members of the legal structure, even here, the deliberation about membership in the legal structure lops off the experiential world that Raz attributes to the origin. "Every legal system rests on its ultimate laws, which commonly means on a set of ultimate laws of recognition and laws of discretion."[131] That is, the ultimate grounding of a legal order, according to Raz, are laws, binding laws, laws located inside a normative structure. As with Hart, Raz continues in the *Authority of Law*, the justicible rules begin the trace of authority in a normative structure: "[n]othing is part of a legal system unless either it is a rule of recognition of the system, or the courts ought to recognize and apply it." If the institutional structure's self-definition of social life ends, so too does the existence of the legal structure.[132] The institutional bureaucratic structure is an indispensable assumption of Raz's theory of law, as he himself admits. And although the structure directs an official to include changing values[133] and non-legal values from other legal structures, the structure remains the starting point for the official's legal analysis.

Raz does recognize that there is some such absent ultimate 'rule' that authorizes the legal structure. The ultimate origin is a belief, an "attitude," which manifests the "bonding" or immediacy between individual and institution. But Raz explicitly rejects any such attitude from reasons for action. When he elaborates the nature of a binding law, he forgets the experiential origin and he describes how officials do indeed and ought to forget the origins from the legal point of view. This is precisely what the official expels as legally non-existent. Since the expelled attitudes are non-existent, they are also a non-truth because truth only

129 Raz, *The Authority of Law*, 69.
130 Raz, *The Authority of Law*, 97.
131 Raz, *The Authority of Law*, 99.
132 Raz, *The Authority of Law*, 98.
133 Raz, *The Authority of Law*, 69.

relates to legal existence and legal existence only relates to the autonomous institutional structure, Raz claims. The authorizing origin of legal reasoning ultimately rests in the pre-legal world, despite the fact that the autonomous legal structure, on Raz's terms, authorizes itself to posit binding norms. A binding norm begins with the autonomous institutional structure. Such a structure logically precedes the authority conferring rules that endorse the institutions' acts.

The ultimate source of the authority of the institutions, however, is absent from the structure and, as such, cannot be a reason for action. Nor can it be a ground for the authority of the rule. An ultimate *legal* rule can only be located inside the legal structure and its power-conferring norms. With an ultimate legal rule, one can go no further than the institutional structure: "[t]he fact that a rule is an ultimate legal rule means no more than that there is no legal ground, no legal justification for its validity."[134] The institutional structure does possess an ultimate origin. But the origin dwells in the realm juridically defined as non-law.

The authorizing ground or *arche* for the rule is absent from the structure. The *arche* is projected into an objectless realm – that is, into a realm without recognizable or 'existing' objects. The institutional structure defines what is non-law as well as what is law. The ultimate authorizing ground of the structure, as with Dworkin and his predecessors, dwells in non-law: "[b]y definition ultimate legal rules are not similarly grounded on legal reasons. The absence of a further rule determining the grounds of validity of the ultimate rules is precisely what makes them *ultimate* legal rules."[135] The ultimate rules are *absent* from binding legal rules: Raz is clear about this point. They are excluded from (legal) existence.

As a consequence, a *differend* or untranslatable gap protrudes as legal officials, in their quest for exclusionary rules from the legal point of view, begin to exclude an outside from an inside, non-law from law, deliberation from a decision, and morality from authority. So, once again, the institutional structure defines its own authority and, therefore, its own existence. 'The people' exists for the structure, not the structure for the people. For the people remain legally non-existent and, therefore, a non-truth unless the structure's institutions define the people as juridically recognizable persons, as 'the people.' It is not surprising that Raz would end *Ethics in the Public Domain* with the admission that "to some extent" there is no escape from the "blemish" of the alienation of the citizenry from the law.[136] Indeed, Raz is correct that there is no such escape, for both Raz and his legal officials define the world in such a manner as to conceive of such a blemish. The social alienation is the consequence of Raz's positivism rather than of some un-

134 Raz, *The Authority of Law*.

135 Raz, "The Politics of the Rule of Law," 378.

controllable social fact that the legal official must accept as a 'given.'

The absent origin of legal positivism is pre-deliberative, pre-analytic and even pre-scriptive in Raz's own sense of the deliberative, analytic and scriptive. The official believes in the analytic and moral goodness of the institutional structure. That belief is an act of faith, on Raz's own admission, that an institution's decisions, more often than not, will be better than decisions that continually (re)interpreted. The act of faith contradicts the possibility that the official confers meaning *into* the detached, value-free statements by institutions, something which Kelsen himself acknowledged.

Even the act of faith, though, is forgotten as officials "artificially" reason about the proper roles of institutions that claim authority. For the institutions *claim* the authority to define (legal) existence and therefore (legal) truth. But the institution's norms are cognitively produced and, as such, risk the "blemish" of being dead abstractions estranged from social life. The institutions claim an authority that displaces the need for an authorizing origin. Norms 'exist' by virtue of their juridical recognition. To be binding, the normative structure must exclude the lived meanings that the officials confer *into* statements about the institutional structure. The experiential attitudes of respect are non-existent and therefore non-truth. The attitudes of respect towards the institutions are invisible to the officials who decide from the legal point of view. Since the experiential is invisible, the experiential and physical bodies of the officials and non-officials alike are expendable. The blemish of social alienation does, indeed, become inescapable. The authority-conferring norms and the mandatory norms of the institutional structure become dead abstractions interdependent with other dead abstractions. Only a faith that the structure is authorized by the invisible can save the structure.

The king's institutions are dead. Only the invisible can save the king.

Conclusion: The End of Legal Positivism

The tradition of legal positivism has faced a critical problem. How can a humanly posited norm or rule be binding unless there is some finality to legal reasoning? In order to maintain that the humanly posited norm/rule is authoritative, officials have, since Roman times, referred the grounding of the norm/rule to some authorizing origin. The reference to some authorizing origin of legal reasoning has allowed officials to become detached from their reasoning and, further, to objectify what one might otherwise consider the subjective posit of values and norms over others. The reference to the origin has unified the posited norms. The origin has ended the trace of one grounding to another, of one institution to another. Legal reasoning has, as a consequence, taken on a linear direction towards the origin.

The origin, to bring finality to the human posit of norms/rules, is invisible to the written statements about the rules. What is 'written' are statutes and judicial decisions that have been authored. The authors are special authors. They are not the authors that one ordinarily associates with poetry or novels or academic treatises. They are authors who can be located on an institutional pyramidal hierarchy. The act of authorship can be identified with precision in terms of a quantifiable place and time. Although officials may well make statements that common law judges consider the 'unwritten' part of the law (what Austin calls law "improperly so called"), only those statements which can be traced to the institutional authors of the sovereign state are considered binding. What finalizes the trace of writing is the inaccessible character of the authorizing origin of the writing.

Accordingly, the authorizing origin of humanly posited norms has taken on the character of an invisible *arche* not unlike the unmoved mover of Aristotle and Aquinas. Philosophers of the natural law tradition have postulated the *arche* as self-starting, as 'out there' beyond the human posit of ordinary norms. And yet, though postulated as self-starting, officials must possess a faith that the origin actually exists. For existence has been understood as circumscribed by the binding norms. And officials may not attribute the origin as a part of legal existence in order to render finality to the binding norms.

Unlike the claims of Augustine and Aquinas, though, the tradition of legal positivism has held that the self-starting origin is humanly produced. An unmoved

Author, believed to pre-exist and to transcend human behaviour, does not authorize the humanly posited norms.

Having acknowledged the need for an inaccessible authorizing origin in order to maintain the authority of binding norms, officials (especially lawyers and judges) forget the need for the origin. They must forget the need for the origin as they trace the cognitive grounding of one norm to another in their quest for the authority of their posited norms. When something is forgotten, though, it may be later remembered. The tradition of legal positivism becomes air-tight, it seems, because officials, as they reason about the trace of the grounding of their norms, forget that they had forgotten something.

1. The Finality of the Trace of *Auctoritas*

The Tradition has faced a critical problem in the demarcation of an inside from an outside, an 'is' from an 'ought.' In order to be posited, a norm/rule must possess some fixity in time and space. Unless fixed, the norm is a mere transient and isolated fragment. If a mere scriptive fragment, it can hardly be said to be posited. But how can a norm be considered fixed? Moreover, how can a fixed norm be considered binding if a legal structure only includes ordinarily posited norms?

The tradition of legal positivism has responded to these questions by acknowledging that some different 'norm' finalizes the trace of authority. The possibility that there is a final origin or grounding or *arche* elevates what one might understand as the arbitrary, subjective posit of a norm into an objective realm. In the trace of the grounding of one posited norm to another, the legal official can act impartially because the origin, not the judge's subjective values, ultimately grounds the human posit of norms.

What brings finality to the reasoning about posited norms/rules, however one defines a norm/rule? Can human agents posit the origin? Or must the human agent postulate a source or ground that legal positivism considers as non-legal? How can an ordinarily posited rule or justification finalize the trace of statements unless the finality is located exterior to the language of the legal structure? If the *arche* were an ordinarily posited rule, then the trace of authority from one category to another and from one institutional source to another would continue *ad infinitum*. And one would be hard pressed to describe any rule as posited in that it would lack the fixity in a quantifiable time and space that one needs in order to describe the rule as posited. So, the foremost philosophers and legal officials have attempted to explain the nature of the origin or *arche* of the legal structure. During moments of constitutional crisis, legal officials especially try to identify the origin.[1]

1 William E. Conklin, *Images of a Constitution* (Toronto: University of Toronto Press, 1989).

In order to bring unity to the structure, the quest has taken a direction towards a *single* unifying origin (Joseph Raz, though, has argued that there may be several, presumably because a heterology of voices are expressed in the pre-legal realm of non-law, the ultimate grounding being an "attitude" of bonding). But the Tradition has acknowledged that in order to terminate the *ad infinitum* trace of the language of the structure, the *arche* must differ from ordinarily posited rules/norms. What renders such a difference between an ordinarily posited rule and its origin is the invisibility of the origin vis-à-vis the language of the humanly posited norms/rules.

Allow me to recount the various responses to the problematic of finality. Thomas Hobbes's response was to hypothesize a natural condition that preceded language *per se*. When creatures began to take on conventions as the signification of marks and sounds, they became authors of expression. The authors, for Hobbes, were the first human beings who had acquired a language. They pre-existed their product, a contract. Pursuant to their contract, they promised never to return to the natural condition. Independent of such a promise, though, they never could return to the natural condition because, having acquired a language, one cannot escape from the language. Jean-Jacques Rousseau carried this notion of an invisible author further by claiming that one invisible author alone transcended the civil institutions and the humanly posited rules.

And John Austin continued the theme even further by insisting that the institutional structure was composed of historically contingent authors. For Austin, though, the justicible laws of the historical authors depended upon the non-justicible habits of the bulk of the people. So, with his distinction between authored laws (authored by civil institutions) and the unwritten habits of the people, Austin could distinguish between legality and constitutionality, written from unwritten laws, law from morality, is from ought, and laws properly so called from laws improperly so called.

Hans Kelsen acknowledged that the basic norm in the all-inclusive system of norms was non-posited. Indeed, he insisted that the final norm could not be articulated in language. If articulated, it would no longer be final for it would be incorporated into the authoritative "ought statements," which constitute "legal existence." Even H.L.A. Hart, though considered by others as advocating posited "social conventions" as the *arche* of the authoritative structure, differentiated between the rule of recognition, the critical "foundation" of "the legal," and the unwritten experiential moment of bonding that the rule of recognition could only re-present as a thought-statement. For Hart, the experiential moment preceded the legal language of primary and secondary rules. And Joseph Raz, although he privileged a decision as excluding any consideration of the merits of the decision, claimed that the obligation to obey such a binding decision depended upon an emotional (and cognitive) "attitude" of respect towards the institutions that he also described as the ultimate "normative facts." That very "attitude" emanated, he claimed, from non-law.

In sum, with each jurist, rules/norms are considered posited only if one acknowledges the possibility that there is an origin that lies inaccessible to the written statements about the humanly posited will, the statements being what Kelsen considers norms.

The quest for the authorizing origin of authored laws lies within a long and deep tradition. Rooted in the works of Thomas Hobbes and Jean-Jacques Rousseau, the tradition of legal positivism has identified authority with the Roman sense of *auctoritas*. Such a sense of *auctoritas* projects authoritative rules, because of the possibility of the invisible Object as their ultimate referent, as impersonal. Hobbes and Rousseau believed that the *arche* of posited rules rested in the state of nature that pre-existed the legislated rules. The creatures in Hobbes' natural condition lacked a language through which one could deliberate. And, when authors acquired a language, their promises transcended their Representer's legislation. Rousseau's General Will, nested in a state of nature, also preceded a deliberation that was only possible once one had acquired a language. In a sense, we officials only "find" the identity of the origin when we deliberate, reflect and articulate our newly acquired official language.

Just as Kafka describes the old man standing before the doors of the castle of Law, though, there always remains another legal ground or source or principle behind every statement about a posited rule. Working internally through the written statements, juridical officials cannot possibly recognize the ultimate origin. Why not? Because officials may only recognize an object through a language: a sign represents such an object. But if the authorizing origin, unrepresented by a sign, precedes the written statements (which the tradition of legal positivism consistently considers the constituents of legal language), the origin cannot be accessed. The origin is invisible vis-à-vis the language of the officials. Belief, not empirically ascertained evidence or logic, produces the origin. The belief relies upon an act of faith that the origin dwells 'out there.' For an untranslatable gap persists between the official language and the origin, even when one asserts that the origin is a "brute fact." To try to persuade an official that the origin does not exist – after all we admit that it *pre*-exists and that it is non-justicible because it rests outside the language of the legal structure – is not persuasive. We officials *believe* that it exists. The origin, to be an origin, is absent from the binding rules, norms, principles, arguments and other discursive sources. For Hobbes, the absent source is a plurality of authors who promise never to return to the natural condition and who thereupon lose a role as actors create the institutional structure; for Rousseau the General Will; for Kant, the pure will; for Austin, the People; for Kelsen, the *Grundnorm*; for Hart, the unstated judicial practices; and for Joseph Raz, the "attitude" of respect towards legal institutions and their decisions. Even when Kant and Kelsen consider the *arche* of synthetic *a priori* reasoning, they recognize that the origin of pure practical reasoning transcends such reasoning and that juridical officials forget the invisibility of the origin in order to make sense of the totality and autonomy of the legal structure.

H.L.A. Hart attempts to bring realism into legal positivism by going to the unstated practices of judges. Joseph Raz goes further, as do a series of contemporary legal theorists, by postulating the given structure of institutions as the ultimate sociological fact of legal analysis. But even here, the moment of recognition of the authorizing origin of a posited decision comes *after* juridical officials posit their decisions. That is, a consciousness of the ultimate origin of juridical discourse enters the written statements retrospectively.

And yet, from the legal point of view (Raz's use of the term), analytic reasoning assumes that the authorizing origin precedes the reasoning. The origin is projected as absent from the analytic project. The origin is unsignifiable. The origin rests external to the official statements about the posited rules. The language of the origin, if there is such a language of the origin (and Kelsen claims that there is no such language, as the *Grundnorm* is a pure concept without a sign to represent it), cannot be signified by the official language. The origin, to be an origin, remains unrecognized through our official language. We cannot enforce something that is unsignifiable. For an official cannot recognize the origin in order to enforce it. Thus, posited rules, if the rules are to be authoritative, produce the need for an absence from the official language. The rules are then superimposed upon that absence during the positing act. But in the very act of positing the rule, legal statements transcend the origin. The posited rules become primary, not supplemental to the origin. And both the origin and the authority of the posited rules exists on faith during the posit of a rule/norm. The origin is a mere possibility because it dwells outside (legal) existence. What pre-exists from the positivist view of legal language are posited scriptive fragments, unrelated to each other, unsystematic and manifesting a heterology of voices.

Hart himself realizes that officials effectively create the identity of the rule(s) of recognition when they posit primary rules. But because the written statement about the rule of recognition merely "approximates" a still more ultimate origin, an origin of the origin, officials must *believe* in a non-knowledge, a non-recognized and non-recognizable knowledge, as the origin of the humanly posited rules. Their belief, again, is a matter of faith. The invisible origin of posited rules/norms is unspoken and unwritten, unspeakable and non-scribable in the official language of the structure. We officials must *believe* as an act of faith that it pre-exists our language in order that our speech and writing be considered posited and in order that our posited rules be considered authoritative.

2. The Invisible Origin

With Hart and Raz, legal reasoning possesses two origins. The one, recognized by the legal officials, is justicible in that it is signified in the written statements about posited rules. The rule(s) of recognition is described as such a justicible origin. The second, preceding the language of the structure, is the origin of such an origin. Hobbes and Kelsen describe the origin of the origin as a singular source. Because of its singularity, the originary moment is believed to unify the structure of humanly posited fragments. What was arbitrary (a fragment, one script unrelated with the other) now becomes rationally interrelated into a cohesive whole. Although Raz claims that there may be several rules of recognition, he too argues that an adjudicative coherency renders unconnected decisions coherent. The important point, though, is that, because the origin of the rules of recognition cannot be accessed through the writing of binding rules (the origin of the rule[s] of recognition preceding legal existence), a void persists between the ultimate origin and the recognizable official language.

The languageless character of the natural condition, for example, underplays why civil institutions must not and cannot return to the origin, according to Hobbes. Actors play with the shared conventions about what signs signify. They can never directly access the former intent of the authors who created the Representer and its institutional structure. The origin, for Kelsen, is an *in itself* that needs no third factor for its existence. For Hart, the origin is a bondedness that an official immediately feels towards a social convention. As language can only represent – not present – the immediacy, the language can never return to the moment of bondedness except through a once removed chain of marks and signs.

More generally, with each philosopher of legal positivism, the origin finalizes the trace of authority because the origin lacks a referent (and a sign that officials may recognize as binding). The origin, that is, does not refer to another object that would be recognizable through legal language. The origin is believed to start the trace of legal reasoning, although the origin is retrospectively constructed. If the origin referred to a further object, the origin's referent would be the origin. The trace of authority would continue. Though postulated as self-starting, the origin exceeds the written statements whose cognitive referents officials recognize as binding. The origin is a remainder or left over from the written statements. Philosophers and officials must intellectually jump, as an act of faith, from the authored statements to the origin. For how does one know that there is an origin if the origin cannot be accessed through legal language? And how can the identity of the origin be knowable if the binding norms themselves define the origin as radically foreign, as pre-legal, as non-law and, therefore, as excluded from the efficacious and justicible laws properly so called or, at least, from what officials consider authoritative?

Hobbes, Rousseau, Austin, and Kelsen suggest that there must just be one invisible origin to the whole system of humanly stipulated laws. That one origin provides the focal point that functions to unify a multiplicity of private wills. What is taken as 'law' is traced in the direction of the origin. But, as Hart emphasizes, such an originating moment is "pre-modern" for it is an anthropologically felt experience rather than an articulated justification through written statements. The trace immunizes juridical officials from the power relations that characterize the posit of norms upon the outsider who does not know the cognitive doctrines to which legal writing refers. As Raz says, we must respect the self-legitimizing intelligible sociological fact of an institutional structure. The authority of the technical rules flow from that fact.

Kant and Kelsen carry the tracing project one step further. For Kant and Kelsen, the origin of the origin is neither an unstated judicial practice nor an invisible author nor a primordial nature. Rather, the primordial moment is an *a priori* concept. The concept too cannot be accessed through legal language because the concept is understood as a pure thought in isolation from any sign to signify the thought. The thought dwells, perhaps, in the legal unconscious, though even this may not be so for even the unconscious is arguably represented through a language. Whether an author or a concept, the authorizing origin of posited norms is invisible to the officials who express their binding norms through the writing authored by institutions on the sovereign state's pyramidal hierarchy.

The originating moment of human laws is ultimately an invisibility that juridical agents can only later re-present, in the act of faith, through a language whose configurations of signs and marks are recognizable by officials who claim to represent the legal structure. The origin is projected as primordial. Hobbes, Kelsen, and Hart describe it as "natural," "primitive," and "pre-legal." Despite its unknowability through written statements of the sovereign's institutions, jurists and officials define legality in terms of its opposite: the "primitive." They characterize the quantifiable time and place of the unknowable as before speech, before writing, without power, and without deliberation. The unknowable, that is, is primordial. At best, they acknowledge that the "primitive" is a revealed immediacy, without an interceding language. Haunted by the possibility of this invisible author/thought/experience, we officials have insisted upon constructing an absolute representative of the originating source/*arche*: the Leviathan, the General Will, the basic norm, the rule of recognition, the sources, and the sovereign state. We have thereby named the unnameable. Having done so, we have thereupon proceeded to forget the importance of the unsignifiable origin as our own creation. We officials have been content with the mere name. We have erroneously defined the authorizing origin of the legal structure as once removed from the invisible. And we have named that once removed origin as 'the Rule of Law,' 'Justice,' 'The Law,' 'the

Framers' Intent,' and the like. These names function as symbols, not signs, because they become an end without a referent to signify. Written statements can access the unknowable no further than the symbol. One can deliberate and dialogue only after a narrative has been constructed in the name of the symbol. The symbol functions as an end in itself rather than as a sign that represents a referent. The symbol cannot bridge the gulf between the language of the humanly created structure and the unknowable invisible, which is attributed to the primordial origin before the symbol is named in space and time. The symbol can refer to no further object, even the invisible Object, which the tradition of legal positivism recognizes as the authorizing origin of the humanly posited laws. If the symbol did refer to the invisible, then, as Kant notes, the symbol would no longer finalize the trace of authority. And yet, the untranslatable gulf between symbol and the invisible would remain.

3. The Violence of the Juridical Production of the Origin

This returns one to the very 'authorized' coercion to which my analysis of the tradition of legal positivism has repeatedly turned. The trace of the grounding of authoritative rules terminates in an origin which, officials postulate, gives form to the trace. This origin authorizes all institutions to posit rules, according to the Tradition. The postulate of the origin permits legal officials to insist that their interpretation of texts is impersonal and objective, above politics and above history. From what Raz calls "the legal point of view," the official resolves a legal issue in terms of the official's role on the institutional structure: that is, did the right official in the right institution make the decision? The substantive moral content of the rule, though inevitably incorporated into the content of binding rules, is considered a separate issue from the issue of institutional function and, more generally, the issue of the authority of the rules. Indeed, if an official departs from the statements about the posited rules, the official commits, in Kelsen's view at least, an unethical and unjust conduct. It makes sense, then, that the tradition of legal positivism considers as violent any conduct that contravenes the laws of the institutional structure. One who lacks a desire to complete and to fulfil the requirements of the authoritative structure is an out-law, a foreigner, an alien. This characterization of what is violent comes to pass because of the postulated 'existence' of the invisible authorizing origin of humanly authored laws.

At the same time that the written statements about humanly posited rules define what is anti-social or 'violent,' the very nature of law carries a violent character with it. The thrust of this violence arises from the exclusion of the authorizing origin from the structure of humanly posited binding norms/rules. For the postulate of the origin as a transcendent non-knowable Object in an objectless realm excludes competing claimants to authority. Antigone's was such a claim. By enforcing a *plenum dominion*, the cognitive referents of humanly posited rules enclose all such competing claimants. An enclosure constitutes the nature of binding laws in a modern state. This violence arises from a particular sense of authority associated with the Roman quest for an authorizing grounding or origin of human laws. The violence of the *auctoritas* is doubled as the written statements about the grounding of the legal doctrines and other categories overtake and systematize arbitrary fragments. For as officials so reason, they forget their dependence upon the invisible origin and then they forget that they had even forgotten their dependence.

This necessary violence in the very constitution of binding laws arises from three circumstances: first, the officials' loss of memory of the authorizing origin as they trace the grounding of one law to another grounding; second, as they forget the act of forgetting through the trace of a grounding; and third, as the resulting structure encloses all human acts. This necessary violence to the authority of posited binding laws sustains the authority of posited rules. Historical authors and officials aim to retrieve an origin that the jurists and officials of legal positivism postulate. The postulate is necessary for the continuity and coherence of binding norms. Without the postulate of the invisible origin, one cannot claim that rules are posited, that the authority of posited rules is separate from the deliberation about morals, that law's truth claims lie in the trace for the authority of posited laws, and that this trace must terminate with an invisible origin that transcends the trace. Again, there must be an ultimate invisible grounding in order to end the *ad infinitum* tracing activity of legal reasoning. The positivist enterprise may remain positivist only by postulating an epistemological origin before civil institutions take form and before rules/norms are posited.

Yet, the figurative sense of laws as "a second nature," to use Plato's term, so important to the early totemic legal culture of the Greeks, vividly exposes that the invisible authorizing origin, so essential to the authority of posited laws in a modern legal structure, is entangled in a culturally contingent meaning of legal authority. Ironically, the modern sense of legal authority depends upon the belief in a fixed, certain, and universal Object, notwithstanding the tradition of legal positivism's postulate, induced through an act of faith, that the origin is inaccessible through what officials take as legal language: the written statements about the grounding of cognitive objects. The official gazes backwards and upwards, beyond the writing, to a transcendent source. Unable to articulate the unknowable, the spirit of the origin haunts the interpreter. A spirit (perhaps it is better to call it a ghost) haunts every act of every juridical official. The official is the agent of the spirit, a spirit created by the agent, excluded from the analytic enterprise, and then forgotten as an exclusion. No wonder judges speak of the 'spirit of the law' or 'the intent of the Founding Fathers' all the while that they exclude evidence of what the historically contingent writers actually contemplated when they wrote certain terms of a constitutional text. The belief in the transcendent origin renders unity, coherence, and finality to the willed laws and interpretations. This origin magnetically attracts the officials when, to the non-lawyer, the structure may well appear incoherent, inconsistent, purposeless, and nakedly violent.

4. The Contradiction

Although this effort to retrieve the unretrievable occurs *after* the juridical official begins to experience his or her quest for the authorizing origin of a binding posited rule, the official acts as if the ultimate origin pre-existed the interpretive act, logically, epistemologically, and phenomenologically. The official thereby oversees the analytic and tracing project as if Truth and Justice preceded the interpretive act. But, despite this postulate in the pre-existence of the origin, the absent origin takes on an identity *after* the official retrospectively traces and analyzes the writing. In addition, the interpretation of the texts (re)constructs the 'original intent' of the 'founding fathers' of the whole civil structure. Positivism claims that binding posited rules never did access the origin. For the origin does not dwell in the writing. Writing cannot access the origin. Only authoritative norms constitute (legal) existence. And legal existence comes *after* the pre-existence.

Accordingly, the tradition of legal positivism describes how officials deceive themselves in that officials believe that they have lost what the canons of the positivist tradition realize the officials never had. Contrary to the claims of Hobbes, Rousseau, Austin, and Hart, the legal officials and institutions could never experience an immediacy or bonding with the originary moment because, to be ultimate, such a bonding had to pre-exist (legal) existence. The interpreter only 'knows' – or, more correctly, can only claim to know – the written sign that refers to a cognitive object. An unsignifiable author, judicial practice or *Grundnorm* never does enclose our reasoning because, until the nostalgic moment of signification, the origin is a no-thing, a non-object in an objectless exteriority.

Juridical officials create in the name of this emptiness. Indeed, Austin, Hart and Raz acknowledge that authoritative interpreters actually construct the will of the Absent "Commander," to use Bentham's term, of posited rules. The official's own search for the originary self-reflection creates the absent origin: expert knowers 'recognize' the creation of the absent origin as ultimate or foundational after its absence has attracted the official to link the grounding of one posited rule with another. The official retro*spective*ly imagines an original intent of the founding fathers of a civil legal structure. The attributions projected into the original intent, though neither true nor real, are necessary for legal reasoning and necessary for the posit of authoritative rules, according to the positivist tradition.

Thus, the realism of Hart and Raz is built upon an unrealism. Contrary to Rousseau's and Austin's claim, did actual peoples previously possess what the binding norms tried to recover? The officials who work through juridical discourse never had what their rules of recognition believe they had lost: a language-less condition, an *a priori* concept, or a social bonding with institutions externalized as non-existent, existence being constituted from written statements authored by institutions on a pyramidal hierarchy. The loss precedes what is being lost. Put differently, the unstated and unwritten origin (by their exclusion of the origin from membership in legal existence) precedes the act of forgetting as officials, working from the legal point of view, posit binding norms. But the phenomenon of the loss of memory itself is forgotten once juridical officials proceed to ground the authored statements about legal doctrines.

That is, for a scriptive fragment to be considered authoritative, officials must presuppose or recognize that written statements may only hang together as a system if the act of forgetting itself is forgotten as they signify legal doctrines. Cognitive doctrines, rules, norms, principles, and other standards become the referents of the legal statements. Legal reasoning forgets the importance of the pre-existence, pre-legal, primitive, savage, anthropological, or non-law – call it what you will – as the originating source for the authority of the legal structure. This loss of memory, according to the canons, enters legal reasoning *after* juridical agents have begun their quest for the authority of a binding rule. In this manner, juridical officials are responsible for the creation of the authorizing origin. This juridical creation of the need for the forgotten origin, though, must be forgotten for the humanly authored laws to be considered posited. And this forgetting of the pre-existing origin occurs even though contemporary theorists, such as Joseph Raz, claim that the ultimate 'fact,' a phenomenal event, is the primordial experiential respect towards legal institutions, even though officials claim the normative system objective and value-neutral, and even though juridical officials aspire to be impartial and "distancing" technical scientists.

5. Forgetting the Origin

In the act of tracing posited fragments to some postulated origin through the official language, juridical officers encloak the origin with a written signification. Being a sign, the writing cannot access the signless origin. The officials fail – and fail they must – to rediscover the languageless authorizing origin. In the act of positing, constrained by the language of the structure, officials enclothe the possibility of the origin with the significations with which they are familiar. The origin, if it exists, is rejected as pre-legal, as non-law, and, therefore, as legally non-existent. The origin is forgotten and, as officials aspire to complete the comprehensiveness or totality of the structure of a modern sovereign state, they forget that their invisible origin was indispensable for their binding norms. When the judge or other legal official reasons through the written statements about the humanly posited norms from a legal point of view, he or she forgets the invisible character of the authorizing origin that he or she must postulate in order to resolve the problematic of finality of the trace of an objective, value-neutral *auctoritas*. The origin is universal, transcendent, omnipresent, omniscient and unknowable. So the analytic project succeeds in justifying the total comprehensiveness and autonomy of the posited legal structure at the very moment that it fails to reach its necessary authorizing origin. For, in order to succeed, legal officials must act as if they can succeed in completing the totality of the structure. They may succeed in closing any perceived gap in the structure. The consequential enclosure ensures an autonomy and totality to the structure.

But that success ensures that officials forget that they had even forgotten anything as they searched for the grounding through the statements about posited norms/rules. In the act of positing a rule, the official fails because, in the claim that the act of enclosure is authoritative, all official agents desire to gain access to a foreign source or *arche*-point. However the canons name the unnameable – the Leviathan, the Sovereign, the General Will, the People, the Rule of Recognition, the Source, the Rule of Law, the Administration of Justice, the Founding Fathers – the official desires the final grounding that one project necessitates that one forget. One aspires to complete a project that one can never access through the official language. What privileges the legal official's act as authoritative is one's claim to know the legally non-existent, to know, that is, the unknowable. The origin is unknowable because it dwells in an objectless realm that the language (that is, the written statements) about the posited rules/norms cannot access.

Moreover, the officials cannot succeed in completing the structure because, having forgotten that they desire to access an invisible origin, the officials, working internally through the authored statements, forget that their reasoning had constructed the need for the origin in the first place. They forget that legal positivism had resolved the problematic of the nature of law – the need for a finality in the quest for a grounding – by postulating an invisible *arche*. And the officials must forget their creation of the origin in order to insist that their laws are humanly posited. The officials themselves have created the invisible *arche*-point. Their creation of the invisible origin is an intentional phenomenon. That is, unlike Augustine or Aquinas, the officials *intend* or confer the need for the creation of the invisible origin. Posited binding rules/norms do not follow or comply with an independently existent or unmoved invisible origin, as Augustine and Aquinas believed. The origin is not self-starting, though the tradition of legal positivism postulates the need and existence of a self-starting origin. Like Augustine and Aquinas, though, the officials believe, as an act of faith, that the origin exists through the writing. The official builds a magnificient structure, attributes a mind, body, and personality to the structure, accepts its founding framer(s) as having had a complete thought-design of the structure, and aspires to plug gaps in the boundary between law and non-law in order to sustain the authority of the structure. The official, not the invisible origin, comes first in time and space: this is the point of difference between Aquinas, say, and the tradition of legal positivism.

All this is forgotten by the legal officials and philosophers of the tradition of legal positivism, as they proceed to create and justify a total and autonomous structure through a familiar language. So long as the officials and philosophers fail to recognize the phenomenon of their own authorship of the authorizing origin and so long as they act in the name of an invisible origin that finalizes the trace of the language of the structure, the language of the structure will remain monologic vis-à-vis the foreigners who speak through a non-recognizable language, the language of non-law, of popular morality. An untranslatable gulf persists between the officials and the foreigners because the officials have structured a language that paradoxically defines the foreigners as necessary foreigners for the cohesion and integrity of the structure. That gulf necessitates that the officials and the tradition of legal positivism believe in the origin as an act of faith. It is a belief, and not some empirically induced nor rationally deduced rule, that magnetically draws the official to the origin. As a consequence, the language of the structure is monologic and, therefore violent, against the heterology of voices of all living subjects. The monologue constrains all the while that the monologue's officials claim to be value-neutral, impartial, apolitical, and objective. The law is law in an ironic sense.

What exactly has been forgotten? To be a grounding for authored laws, the authorizing origin must be said to exist phenomenologically, logically, and epistemologically prior to posited rules. We officials forget the origin because we exclude it from legality. We juridical agents of the origin forget that we had forgotten something – the pre-*scriptive* or pre-language character of the origin of *auctoritas* – as we embarked upon legal reasoning. We officials remain entrapped inside the genre and structure that we – not the authorizing origin – have created. In Hobbes' case, the forgotten is a natural condition where "beasts" cannot speak to each other. With Rousseau, the forgotten is an inaccessible divine Will, which the legislatures may only approximate through their statutes. With Austin, the forgotten is the will of the people, which officials exclude from existence. In Kelsen's case, the forgotten is an 'in itself' hidden behind the norms. For Hart, the forgotten rests with a bonding that juridical agents will never and can never access except as an after-the-event phenomenon. Hart realizes that claimants to legal knowledge retrospectively create the origin as they recognize it through legal language. Hart acknowledges that the forgotten moment exists as the real origin for the official language. And Joseph Raz emphasizes the forgotten in the experiential attitude of respect that people share towards the institutional sources. Each canon in the Tradition realizes that the invisible origin is essential in order to finalize the trace of binding rules/norms through written legal statements. But the origin is forgotten as legally non-existent, as non-justicible, as outside the written language that officials of the origin have structured. The origin must be forgotten since it is so alien to the legal structure, a radical other, before time and place, before legal language. The origin is forgotten. But the forgetting is doubled.

Officials must forget two critical aspects for laws to be considered posited, then. First, the philosophers who have examined legal positivism are conscious of the need for an authorizing origin of all humanly posited laws. And they claim that officials act as if there were an origin as the officials search for the groundings of their posited norms/rules. And yet, the philosophers also realize that, as officials work internally through written statements, legal officials forget that the origin is invisible to the language. The forgetting is necessary for the officials to maintain the totality and autonomy of the structure of posited norms/rules. So the philosophers of legal positivism exclude the invisible origin from binding rules/norms as "savage," "primitive," "natural," "pre-legal," "law improperly so called," and "beliefs." Officials, simply, exclude the origin as subjective or non-law or an 'ought' world.

Secondly, what is forgotten is the experiential body. We even forget that our belief in the origin was a *belief*, a non-cognitive experiential phenomenon. We forget that, in the quest for the cognitive, we forget the belief and pretend that legal existence excludes it. Legal language is considered to signify cognitive creations. The official's very forgetting distinguishes the cognitive of the modern from the bodily of the pre-modern legal culture. In Chapter Two, I explained how important the body was to the totemic legal culture. All objects beyond the majestic doors of our modern castle of law are unrecognizable through the castle's language. As such, the objects are unknowable. Indeed, we cannot even know that they are objects in that our legal language projects them as dwelling in an objectless realm for which we have no names to assign to them.

While acting in the name of this forgotten origin – in the name of the unnameable, that is – we officials displace the lost origin with our written statements, which we, as officials of given legal institutions, author. The statements come to represent legal *existence*. The statements come to represent a rationally cohesive identity. We try to name the unnameable. We construct a picture or image of the unnameable. But we officials attribute an identity to the origin at the very moment that we expel the origin from our (legal) existence. Moreover, we lose our own personal identity as we believe we are (re)constructing the identity of the invisible origin. We lose our identity because we exclude our bodily experiences as non-law, as 'oughts' rather than as the 'is' of a legal existence. We remain "haunted," to use Hart's term in this context, by the possibility that there is some authorizing origin that is more real than the marks with which we recognize the origin. Even the interpreter, the judge or lawyer or officer, is transformed from a living being with embodied experiences into a juridical person, a cognitive object, which we 'understand' as an abstraction. The official, as much as the authoritative discourse, loses a human face. Even the official becomes a thing.

6. The Crisis

Why must we legal officials, working internally through the written statements, subvert our own positivist project when we postulate that there is an invisible authorizing origin to the trace of *auctoritas*. It is not surprising that Kant would consider as seditious any questioning of the origin, for example. For to question the existence of origin poses the possibility that the authority of the human posit of particular binding laws can no longer be taken for granted. But in Chapter Two I described a sense of authority radically different from that of the modern sense of an *arche*, a sense that renders the acceptance of the 'givenness' of legal institutions suspect. To suggest that the founding fathers of a constitution or the basic text itself does not originate a particular constitution requires that the curious official transverse the boundary between law and non-law. And that brings into question the very 'existence' of the legal structure unless, in an act of faith, one accepts that an invisible origin does, indeed, authorize the structure. That admission, though, brings into question the very autonomy and comprehensiveness of the structure of humanly posited binding norms. The official re-reads the historical circumstances surrounding the primordial moment of the structure. The invisible origin, however emptied of signs and particulars, remains the same. Such a sameness offers an ultimate referent for officials to explain historical events.

Officials still compete to better signify the invisible origin through the public language of civil institutions. But the sustained challenge arising from the question, 'what is the identity of the authorizing origin of posited laws?' places the written statements about the grounding of norms in continual crisis. The impartiality and objectivity of the structure is always under question. One need only look to the collapse of many sovereign states in order to appreciate the inevitable character of such a crisis. To question what institutions or officials or symbols best represent the origin destabilizes the authority of posited laws. The officials' belief in certainty about the ultimate origin, though invisible to the institutionally authored statements, is essential to finalize *auctoritas*. And that finality brings with it a fixity, unity, and rational coherence to the posited binding rules/norms themselves. Such a fixity, certainty, unity, and coherence is brought into question when the symbols of the origin are questioned. Even to question the symbolic trappings of the judge or legislature has, until recently in many common law countries, been considered contemptuous and even seditious in that the criticism has brought the administration of the structure into disrepute. Even laughter in the courtroom is sometimes considered contemptuous.

However, it is one thing to replace one group of representatives of the origin with another. It is another issue to question the 'existence' of the authoritative structure itself. In the latter context, authority remains located in an authorizing origin. But the new officials imagine the identity of the authorizing origin very differently. The new officials represent the origin with different founding fathers. The symbols of the authority of legal institutions differ. The jurisdiction of the institutional offices differ. History begins differently. But the officials' reference to the new identity, symbols, institutions, history and the like has the effect of forgetting that the authorizing origin, an invisible origin, preceded the phenomenology and the logic of the new officials' legal reasoning.

Indeed, if all officials were conscious that the ultimate authorizing origin of their posited binding norms nested in an objectless invisible realm and if all citizens knew that all officials were conscious of the invisible character of the origin, then there could no longer be a belief in the authorizing origin of posited laws. For the origin would no longer be forgotten. Nor would the officials have lost their memory about their having forgotten something. The officials' faith in a pre-existence would collapse. The loss of memory, I have argued, is essential for the continuity, totality, and autonomy of the binding quality of humanly posited norms/rules. The enclosing structure of the modern state would open out to the objectless realm of non-law. Juridical officials could no longer presuppose the fixity of posited laws. Because the postulate of an invisible origin and then the forgetting of that postulate is so indispensable to the tradition of legal positivism, the officials' retrieval of a self-consciousness about the invisibility of the origin would end the tradition of legal positivism.

It does not help the cause of the tradition of legal positivism that the belief in the invisibility of the authorizing origin rests upon an act of faith. If the dependence of posited laws upon an invisible originary moment were questioned, the whole structure would collapse, built as it is upon the forgetting by the officials who work through the writing from the legal point of view. Kant realized the portent of this possibility. So did common law judges of days past. That explains why, to question the origin, has, until relatively recently, constituted sedition in common law jurisdictions. Though the interpreter's experience has been excluded as non-law, terror would overwhelm the official's interpretive experience because one would recognize what has hitherto been forgotten: that the authorizing origin of legal knowledge is a non-knowledge, a non-law. This non-law is the situs for the *arche* with which we knowers have sought to ground our binding rules/norms. Juridical officials are content only if we remain within the familiar language of binding rules/norms and only if we forget about the postulate necessary to continue our enterprise of legal positivism.

The origin controls and posits the boundaries of my discretion, if the haunting of the spirit of the origin allows me to feel such a discretion. The official, who works internally through the language of the structure, analyzes the cognitive objects – the doctrines, the rules, the principles – of the language as if the origin gazed down upon the official from afar. The gaze of the origin points in a linear direction. The gaze reinforces our self-image of impersonality, which I traced to the Roman sense of *auctoritas*. The absence of the origin takes on invisible-like traits.

The origin dwells external to our control in contingent circumstances, before the start of our legal history, external to social circumstance. All this lack of control suggests a divinity to the origin not unlike the divinity of Aquinas' natural laws, except perhaps that, in our case, *we*, not some unmoved mover, created the invisible origin. This invisibility arises precisely at the moment that the tradition of legal positivism insists upon the impersonality of the interpretive act. The origin is a radical other to the written authorized statements of juridical officials. An untranslatable gap dwells between the two. Against the background of the gaze of the radical other towards us juridical officials, we analyze the differentiating categories that our language signifies. We hierarchize the weight of our categories in terms of their presupposed proximity with the origin of the gaze.

And yet we leave the origin just as we signify in its name. We analyze and trace one stipulated rule from another, one justification from another, and, in doing so, we mask the absence of the *arche* through our language. The authoritatively situated official may enjoy the analysis and trace only because he or she forgets about the absence of the *arche*. Indeed, we may reject questions about the originary *arche*, as with Hart, as an issue of morality, not law. That is, we forget that the *arche* pre-'exists' the language through which we come to know our cognitive objects. We rest content with representations about the originary moment. The representations overtake our quest. And, again, we forget what we have forgotten: namely the pre*scriptive* character of the originary moment of the rules, principles, and other standards that we posit. Officials enjoy playing with the language of the structure at the ironic expense of hiding the invisible origin from authority. One gains legal knowledge only if one presupposes that the most fundamental element of the structure is non-knowledge. For the ultimate originating moment is an *art*: a terrifying objectless, limitless darkness that we project as immeasurable in space and time.

Hobbes, Rousseau, Kant, Kelsen, Hart, and Raz unite in their view that juridical officials deliberate about the identity of the origin of legal reasoning only *after* the interpretative act signifies the authority of an act. Indeed, Kant, Kelsen, Hart, and

Raz acknowledge that the origin of legal reasoning is unknown during the moment of legal signification. Legal reasoning would otherwise deduce one stipulated rule from the absent existent origin. Nor does legal reasoning induce conclusions from human experience, according to Kant, Kelsen, and Hart. Unlike the Newtonian view of science where a natural cause is believed to chronologically precede an effect, the tradition of legal positivism describes an interpreter who posits a cause after the interpreter posits a rule. The retrospective character of the interpretive act thereby idealizes the ground or reason for the posited law. The ground is presupposed in that it arrives on the scene, if it does, *after* the origin of the quest, not before the quest. This is even so for Joseph Raz, the most 'realist' of contemporary legal positivists, who acknowledges that, constituted from an "attitude" of loyalty towards legal institutions, the "ultimate" or primordial origin is unknown as legally existent, as unconscious, and as unwritten. The legal scholar or authoritative interpreter comes to "recognize" the ground of a posited rule after the rule has made an effect. At that moment, the jurisprude, situated from an external point of view, consciously locates the ground in a narrative about the stipulated law. One may trace this narrative from one discourse about one area of law to another until one reaches the basic text at which point the text itself is grounded or founded in a natural condition, in a further originating moment, in inaccessible authors, in an unstated judicial practice, in a *Grundnorm*, in an 'ultimate source,' or in an *a priori* concept which is purified of all socially contingent contradictions. The origin is signified in a language *after* its surrogate has realized the need for the invisible origin in order to ensure rational coherence and authority.

The official produces a signification about a humanly posited law on the postulate that an authorizing origin for the law exists. The judge traces a text to a ground, distinguishes the ground from other competing grounds, and situates the ground in the trace of authoritatively deeper intermediate grounds. We finally reach the ground, or so we believe. That finality allows the judge to sense a fixity or definiteness to his or her signs about the posited law. The interpretive act thereby reproduces a configuration of signs about the stipulated law. The stipulated law is believed to be posited, just as the interpretive act may be said to posit a new rule through the act of tracing, interpretation, analysis, and grounding the trace. The continual search for a ground presupposes that there is some ultimate source, external to the trace, that finalizes the trace.

7. The End of a Tradition

We have finally reached the end of a tradition. The tradition of legal positivism ends by annihilating its own basic postulate: namely, that there must be a final authorizing origin for reasoning about binding humanly posited norms/rules and that, to be an origin, it must be invisible to the writing with which the norms/rules are signified. Legal officials attempt to reach the origin by tracing one ground to another, one historical institution to another. Legal reasoning is practical in that it draws from third factors to synthetically reach a conclusion, which, rather than being left in the clouds, encloses social events. Such synthetic *a priori* practical reasoning, though, can carry the agent only so far until the agent reaches the limits of an objectless realm. Beyond the limits of such reasoning, there is believed to dwell Justice, the Rule of Law, the perfectly Good Will, a natural condition, invisible authors, the *Grundnorm*, the unstated judicial practices. The juridical official 'knows' inscribed laws by grounding them through practical reasoning in the name of a groundless Justice. And all this takes place in an effort to close the autonomous and comprehensive legal structure of a modern state.

The closest that the official can come to the origin is through metaphor. Again and again, metaphor colours the acts of the historical genesis of contingent rules and institutions. Why is metaphor so necessary to practical juridical reasoning? Because posited rules, to be posited as laws, must be finalized. To be final, the rule must stand for or represent the origin. Yet, the origin must not refer to some further end to be an origin. If it did, the origin would no longer be an origin. Thus, an origin must be presupposed or unconscious. At best, as Raz suggests, that presupposed origin can be symbolized in a metonym such as a crown or a rock or a flag or 'the Constitution.'

The ultimate origin of legal positivism 'exists' without either an associated sign or a form that the sign can signify. Without particulars, in turn, posited rules cannot possibly represent the origin as an absence or a loss. Indeed, practical legal reasoning cannot represent its origin since the origin is external to the boundary of the legal language of the origin. How would it be possible for one to represent what is not? All interpretive acts of authoritatively situated authors are necessarily metaphorical, there being no sign to represent the origin, the origin being expelled to the objectless realm of non-law. The juridical agents claim a knowledge of what is not. Without such a claim, we could not recognize our inscriptive fragments as authoritative. So we must glorify the origin, sing hymns in its praise, bow to it, salute it, defer to it, dress for it and speak in its name. The Rule of Law, Justice, Law, Order: juridical officials rightly shroud these names with the magical sanctity of the end of the trace.

Yet, by being preoccupied with the trace of posited rules, the knower disguises the absence through signs that represent other signs. The authoritatively situated interpreter must act as if the origin – perhaps it is best that we capitalize the Origin because of its invisibility or divinity – leaves the official with no choice in deciding one way over another. Constrained by the gaze of a transcendent source in an objectless realm of thought, the official must interpret posited rules with impartiality and political neutrality. One may not judge the policy, the wisdom, or the justice of the particulars of the binding rules/norms. The official may insist upon such a neutrality only by forgetting the absent origin as pre-legal. The forgotten origin must be enforced, if need be, against those who, like Antigone, question that there is even such an authorizing origin of laws.

The tradition of legal positivism must acculturate a belief that historically contingent founding fathers started a particular legal order. In acculturating this belief, it is not surprising that the *arche* would be associated with historical *auctorae* such as John A. Macdonald, Thomas Jefferson, William of Orange, Lenin, Mao Zedong, or whomever. Sometimes, as in the case of John Austin, the *auctor* is believed to be an historical institution such as parliament. When Bentham and Austin give a pre-eminent role to parliamentary sovereignty or the people, though, they still appeal to a further origin, an *a priori* concept of the 'greatest good'(Bentham), which is believed to transcend historically contingent events. Kant described such an absent Origin as flowing from synthetic *a priori* reasoning. He called it the 'pure will' and the 'perfectly good will.' Hans Kelsen recognized that the absent origin must remain presupposed in order for there to be finality to posited norms. H.L.A. Hart recognized that the absent Origin must remain an unrecognizable secret until after primary rules have been posited. And Joseph Raz, after acknowledging the importance of the Origin, excised the Origin from the nature of binding laws. The presupposed unrecognized absent Origin conditions the Truth and the Justice of the administration of stipulated rules. The absence of the Origin drives juridical officials onwards in their never-ending quest for a grounding of their inscribed rules.

In this retrospective quest, the authoritatively situated interpreters of the language of binding rules/norms conceal a violence. The violence lies concealed inside the apparently impersonal, politically neutral interpretive acts. The violence surrounds the deference to authority. The violence colours the posit of a binding norm that is believed to be authorized by an origin. The violence imbues the posit of the norm upon other religious beliefs, including beliefs about contradictory senses of legal authority such as that of the totemic legal culture. The violence infuses legal reasoning in the very posit of a cognitive doctrine or rule, an intellectualism that expels the experiential body. Metonym and symbol cloak the violence with an impersonality. The Roman sense of *auctoritas* reigns. No wonder that human beings have experienced such a barbaric violence during the same century when the tradition of legal positivism has been practised throughout the planet. Of course, deep centuries-old racism, ethnic loyalties, and religious animosities add fuel to the fire. And, of course, modern technology has magnified the scope with which weapons may penetrate into the daily lives of civilians. But it is difficult to understand the brutal and open destruction of cities – Hiroshima, Nagasaki, Dresden, Priština, – and the horrendous liquidation of whole communities and their cultures during the past century without appreciating that the quest for *auctoritas* just cannot allow for a competing pyramidal hierarchy of surrogates. The peaceful dissolution of a state is the exception, not the rule. It is difficult to understand the monstrous atrocities of the twentieth century without appreciating that juridical officials claim a *plenum dominion* by virtue of the postulate of an invisible authorizing origin. Like the *plenum dominion*, the origin is boundless, without limits.

Kant adamantly insisted that subjects should not question the 'givenness' of the dark loss of memory in modern legal reasoning. The forgotten origin must remain forgotten because the originating moment's alien, yet presupposed, estrangement from the writing about norms/rules functions to preserve the rational unity of the structure's monologue. The origin of the legal reasoning process is forever inaccessible, notwithstanding the sustained reference to its existence and the existence of its surrogates (the founding fathers of the constitution) as the *arche* of all binding posited rules and notwithstanding the claim of the tradition of legal positivism that all law is posited. Posited through a seemingly transparent language, the cognitive objects of the familiar secondary scripts become the primary factor in the construction of the identity of the invisible *auctor or*, if the *auctor*'s invisibility is recognized as with Kelsen, in the retro*spective* construction of the absent Origin of synthetic *a priori* reasoning. The trace to the hidden loss of memory, in a sense, turns a crime into an *author*itative law. And, as we observed with Kelsen, the unreal becomes the real; the empty, formless origin of the language becomes the formed; the absent Origin becomes the *arche*. The supplementary apolitical, amoral, ahistorical, impersonal, scientistic project of legal reasoning, according to the Tradition, ends the need for the very presupposed origin, let alone the image of the origin as a spirit whose gaze haunts the memory of officials. The invisible Origin functions within a network of conditions that the juridical officers construct. Juridical officials construct rules, which, instead of supplementing the invisible origin, become *primary* and *must* become primary because of the very *absence* of the *arche* from juridical discourse. Juridical discourse ends by enclosing all competing discourses.

The leading theorists of legal positivism during the past century have recognized the demise of the historical *auctor*, just as Bentham, Austin, and now Raz recognize the supplementarity of legal institutions to the 'greatest good' or 'common good,' which transcends legal institutions. Kelsen did his best to erase from juridical discourse what he projected as the *auctor* of Nature, failing to realize that the invisible *Auctor* of which he wrote most certainly had a very little part to play either in Aristotle's sense of the 'natural' or Antigone's sense of the authority of unwritten customs. Yet, Kelsen himself could not part with the originary moment. The retrospective trace of the grounding of posited norms just had to have such an absent Origin in order to remain coherent and unitary. All norms had to be posited in the quest for a foundational *Grundnorm*, an unrecognizable moment of bonding or, from an earlier moment in the Tradition, the *auctors* in a natural condition. Expert knowers, immersed in the official writing of the civil institutions, claim to recognize the end through their familiar, transparent signs. The officials pretend to be situated in unison with the Origin in their quest for a grounding of posited norms. The unreal has become the real.

But juridical officers may retrace the signs that represent the Origin only by expelling the Origin as *pre*-scriptive, unsignified, and unsignifiable. In the act of positing rules, officials forget that the authorizing Origin is invisible to their language. And then, preoccupied with the legal point of view, they forget that they have forgotten the invisibility of the authorizing origin. And in the act of forgetting, the posit of a binding rule annihilates its own postulated positivism. The forgotten invisibility of the authorizing origin of binding posited rules ends the grand tradition of legal positivism.

The King has been found dead. Only the Invisible can save the King.

Bibliography

Primary Sources

Aquinas, Thomas. [1266-73] 1945. *Treatise on Law*, 1266-73. Translated from the First Part of the Second Part of the *Summa Theologica* in *Basic Writings of Saint Thomas Aquinas*. Ed. Anton C. Pegis. New York: Random House.

Aristotle. 1984. Ed. Jonathan Barnes, *The Collected Works of Aristotle*, 2 vols. Princeton: Princeton University Press.

Austin, John. [1861] 1971. *Lectures on Jurisprudence*. New York: Burt Franklin.

___.[1861, 1985] 1971. Excursus on Analogy (Analogical Reasoning and Syllogism). In *Lectures on Jurisprudence*, 249-72. New York: Burt Franklin. Reprint from ed. Robert Campbell. 1985, 5th ed. revd. London: John Murray. Originally published in 1861.

___. [1861] 1971. Note on Interpretation (Proper and Improper). In *Lectures on Jurisprudence*. 231-46. New York: Burt Franklin.

___. [1832, 1863] 1954. *The Province of Jurisprudence Determined and the Uses*. Intro. H.L.A. Hart. London: Weidenfeld & Nicolson.

Bentham, Jeremy. 1945. *The Limits of Jurisprudence Defined, Being Part Two of An Introduction to the Principles of Morals and Legislation*. Intro. Charles Warren Everett. Westport, Conn.: Greenwood Press.

___. [1789] 1948. *An Introduction to the Principles of Morals and Legislation*. Intro. by Laurence J. LaFleur. New York: Hafner Publ. and in 1970. Eds. J.H. Burns and H.L.A. Hart, London: University of London Athlone Press. Reprinted in 1996 in *Collected Works*. With Intro. by F. Rosen and Interpretive Essay by H.L.A. Hart. Oxford: Clarendon Press.

___. 1962. Essay on Language. In gen. ed. John Bowring, *Works of Jeremy Bentham*, vol. 8, 295-338. New York: Russell & Russell.

___. 1970. *Of Laws in General*. Ed. H.L.A. Hart. In *Collected Works of Jeremy Bentham*. Gen. ed. J.H. Burns. London: University of London Press.

___. 1977. *Fragment of Government*. Eds. J.H. Burns and H.L.A. Hart, Intro. by Ross Harrison; Cambridge: Cambridge University Press.

___. [1930] 1983a. *Constitutional Code*, vol. 1. Eds. F. Rosen and J.H. Burns. Oxford: Clarendon Press/New York: Oxford University Press. In *Collected Works of Jeremy Bentham*, vol. 1. Gen. ed. J.R. Dinwiddy. Oxford: Clarendon Press/New York: Oxford University Press.

___. 1983b. *Utilitarianism*. Ed. Amnon Goldworth. Oxford: Clarendon Press. In *Collected Works*. Gen. ed. J.R. Dinwiddy.

___. 1983c. *Deontology: Together with a Table of The Springs of Action & Article on Utilitarianism*. Ed. Amnon Goldworth. In *Collected Works*. Oxford/New York: Clarendon Press.

___. 1989. *First Principles Preparatory to Constitutional Code*. Ed. Philip Schofield. Oxford: Clarendon Press. *Collected Works of Jeremy Bentham*. Gen. ed. J.H. Burns. London: University of London Press.

Hart, H.L.A. 1952. Signs and Words. In *The Philosophical Quarterly* **2**: 59-62. Review article on John Holloway, *Language and Intelligence* (1951).

___. 1953. Definition and Theory in Jurisprudence. In *Law Quarterly Review* **70** (1954): 37-60. Reprinted in 1983 in Hart, *Essays in Jurisprudence and Philosophy* , 21-48. Oxford: Clarendon.

___. 1955. Are There Any Natural Rights? In *Philosophical Review* **64**: 175-91. Reprinted in 1970 in ed. A.I. Melden *Human Rights*, 77-90. Belmont, CA: Wadsworth.

___. 1956. Book Review: Hans Kelsen, *The Communist Theory of Law* (New York: Frederick A. Praeger, 1955) in *Harvard Law Review* **69** (1955-56): 772-78.

___. 1956-57. Analytical Jurisprudence in Mid-Twentieth Century: A Reply to Professor Bodenheimer. In *University of Pennsylvania Law Review* **105**: 953-75.

___. 1958. Positivism and the Separation of Law and Morals in *Harvard Law Review*, 593-629. Reprinted in 1961 in ed. Frederick A. Olafson, *Society, Law and Morality: Readings in Social Philosophy from Classical and Contemporary Philosophy*, 439-70. Englewood Cliffs, NJ: Prentice-Hall, and in 1983 in Hart, *Essays in Jurisprudence and Philosophy*. Oxford: Clarendon.

___. [1961] 1994, 2d. *The Concept of Law*. Oxford: Clarendon Press.

___. 1963. *Law, Liberty and Morality*. London: Oxford University Press; and Stanford: Stanford University Press.

___. 1964. Self-Referring Laws. In ed. Fritjof Lejman et al., *Festskrift till Karl Olivecrina*, 307-16. Stockholm: P.A. Norstedt & Soner. Reprinted in 1983 in Hart, *Essays in Jurisprudence and Philosophy*, 170-78. Oxford: Clarendon.

___. 1965a. *The Morality of the Criminal Law: Two Lectures*. London: Oxford University Press.

___. 1965b. Book review: Lon Fuller, *The Morality of Law* (1964). In *Harvard Law Review* **78** (1964-65): 1281-96. Reprinted in Hart, *Essays in Jurisprudence and Philosophy* (see 1983 below).

___. 1967a. Problems of Philosophy of Law. In ed. Paul Edwards, *Encyclopaedia of Philosophy*, vol 6, 264-76. London: Macmillan. Reprinted in 1983 in Hart, *Essays in Jurisprudence and Philosophy*, 88-119. Oxford: Clarendon.

___.1967b. Legal Positivism. In ed. Paul Edwards, *Encyclopaedia of Philosophy*, vol 4, 418-20. New York: Macmillan and Free Press; London: Collier-Macmillan.

___. 1967c. Bentham of Sovereignty. *Irish Jurist* **2**:327-35.

___. 1970. Kelsen's Doctrine of the Unity of Law. In eds. Howard E. Kiefer and Milton K. Munitz, *Ethics and Social Justice*, 171-99. Albany: State University of New York Press.

___. 1971. Immorality and Treason. In ed. Richard A. Wasserstrom, *Morality and the Law*, 49-54. Belmont, CA: Wadsworth.

___. 1982a. *Essays on Bentham*. Oxford: Clarendon Press.

___. 1982b. Sovereignty and Legally Limited Government. In *Essays on Bentham*, 220-42. Oxford: Clarendon Press.

___. 1982c. Commands and Authoritative Reasons. In *Essays on Bentham*, 242-68. Oxford: Clarendon Press.

___. 1983. *Essays in Jurisprudence and Philosophy*. Oxford: Clarendon Press.

___. 1994. Postscript in *Concept of Law*. In 2d ed., 241-60. Eds. P. Bulloch and J. Raz. Oxford: Clarendon Press.

Hegel, Georg Frederick. [1807] 1977. *The Phenomenology of Spirit*. Trans. A.V. Miller. Analysis of text and fwd. by J.N. Finday. Oxford: Oxford University Press. Translated from *Phänomenologie des Geistes*. 1952. Edited by J. Hoffmeister.

___. 1975. *Natural Law*. Trans. T. M. Knox. Oxford: Oxford University Press.

___. [1821] 1952. Philosophy of Right. Trans. T. M. Knox. Oxford: Oxford University Press. Also translated by S.W. Dyde. In [1896] 1996. London: Bell; New York: Prometheus.

___. [1802] 1977. *Faith and Knowledge*. Trans. Walter Cerf and H.S. Harris. Albany: State University of New York Press.

___. [1962] 1988. Lectures on the Philosophy of Religion: One Volume Edition, the lectures of 1827. Ed. Peter C. Hodgson, trans. R.F. Brown, P.C. Hodgson, and J.M. Stewart with aid of H.S. Harris. Berkeley: University of California Press.

Hobbes, Thomas. [1640a, 1889] 1969. *Elements of Law: Natural and Politic*. Ed. with pref. and critical notes by Ferdinand Tonnies. New intro by M.M. Goldsmith in 2d ed., 1969. New York/London: Frank Cass. Critical ed. by Howard Warrender. 1983. Oxford: Clarendon Press.

___. [1640b, 1928] 1983. *Elements of Law*. Introd. to 2nd edn M.M. Goldsmith, Critical Ed'n, Howard Warrender. Oxford: Clarendon Press.

___. [1642c, 1651] 1983. *De Cive*. In *Philosophical Works of Thomas Hobbes*, vol. 3. Oxford: Oxford University Press. Entitled in 1st edn as *Philosophical Rudiments concerning Government and Society*.

___. [1650] 1994. *De Corpore Politico*. Intro. G.A.J. Rogers, pt. 2 of *The Elements of Law*. Reprint Bristol: Thoemmes.

___. [1650] 1994. *Human Nature*. Intro. G.A.J. Rogers, pt. 1 of *The Elements of Law*. Reprint Bristol: Thoemmes.

___. [1651] 1957. *Leviathan*. Ed. with intro. essay and notes by Michael Oakeshott. Oxford: Basil Blackwell. The same, but with an intro. by R.S. Peters. 1962. *Hobbes*. New York: Collier Books. The same, but with an intro. by C.B. Macpherson. 1968. *Leviathan; or, The Matter, Forme, and Power of a Common-wealth Ecclesiasticall and Civill*. Harmondsworth: Penguin.

___. [1681] 1971. *A Dialogue between a Philosopher and a Student of the Common Laws of England*. Ed. and intro. Joseph Cropsey. Chicago: University of Chicago Press.

___. 1840. An Answer to a Book published by Dr. Bramhall called the Catching of the Leviathan. In *English Works of Thomas Hobbes* vol. 4, 279-384.

___. [1839-45] 1962. *The English Works of Thomas Hobbes of Malmesbury*. Ed. William Molesworth, 11 vols. Germany: Scienta Verlag Aalen. 2d reprint, 1968. Originally published in London: John Bohn.

___. 1995. *Three Discourses: A critical modern edition of newly identified work of the young Hobbes*. Ed. Noel B. Reynolds and Arlene Saxonhouse. Chicago: University of Chicago Press.

Kant, Immanuel. [1785] 1981, 2d. *Grounding for the Metaphysics of Morals*. Trans. James W. Ellington. Indianapolis: Hackett.

___. [1788] 1949. *Critique of Practical Reason*. Trans. Lewis W. Beck. Chicago: University of Chicago Press.

___. [1790] 1987. *Critique of Judgement*. Trans. Werner S. Pluher. Indianapolis: Hackett.

___. [1793] 1970 1977. On the Common Saying. In *Kant's Political Writings*, 61-92. Ed. Hans Reins. Cambridge: Cambridge University Press.

___. [1793, 1794 2d.] 1934, 1960. *Religion within the Limits of Reason Alone*. Trans. Theodore M. Greene and Hoyt H. Hudson. New York: Harper.

___. [1797] 1985. *The Metaphysical Elements of Justice*. Trans. John Ladd. New York: Macmillan. Also published in1971 as *The Philosophy of Law*. Trans. W. Hastie. Clifton, NJ: Augustus M. Kelley.

Kelsen, Hans. [1922/23] 1973. God and the State. In ed. Ota Weinberger, *Essays in Legal and Moral Philosophy*, 61-82. Trans. Peter Heath. Dordrecht and Boston: D. Reidel.

___. 1923. Kelsen, Foreword to the Second Printing of *Main Problems in the Theory of Public Law*, 3-22. Translated by Stanley L. Paulson and Bonnie Litschewski Paulson in *Normativity and Norms*.

___. [1928] 1973. The Idea of Natural Law. In *Essays in Legal and Moral Philosophy*. Ed. Ota Weinberger; trans. Peter Heath, 27-60. Dordrecht and Boston: D. Reidel.

___. 1933. Letter to Renato Treves dated 3 August 1933. In eds. Stanley L. Paulson and Bonnie Litschewski Paulson, *Normativity and Norms*, 169-75. Trans. Bonnie Litschewski Paulson, Stanley L. Paulson and Michael Sherberg, intro. Stanley L. Paulson. Oxford: Clarendon Press.

___. [1934a] 1992. *Introduction to the Problems of Legal Theory*. Trans. Bonnie Litschewski Paulson and Stanley L. Paulson of 1st ed. of *Reine Rechtslehre*. Oxford: Clarendon.

___. [1934b] 1967. *The Pure Theory of Law*. Trans. Max Knight. Berkeley: University of California Press. Originally published as *Reine Rechtslehre*. Vienna: Deuticke).

___. 1934c. The Pure Theory. Its Method and Fundamental Concepts: Pt. 1 in *Law Quarterly Review* **50**: 474-98. The second part of the essay is in *Law Quarterly Review* **51**: 517-35.

___. [1934d] 1990. On the Theory of Interpretation in *Legal Studies* **10** (1990): 289-97. Trans. Bonnie Litschewski and Stanley Paulson.

___. 1936. The Party-Dictatorship in *Politica* **2**: 19-32.

___. [1933, 1937-38] 1957. Platonic Justice. Trans. Glenn Negley. In *What is Justice? Justice, Law & Politics in the Mirror of Science*, 82-109. Berkeley and Los Angeles: University of California Press. Reprinted from *Ethics* **48**: 367-400.

___. 1937-38. The Philosophy of Aristotle and the Hellenic-Macedonian Policy in *Ethics* **48**: 1-64.

___. [1939] 1973. The Emergence of the Causal Law from the Principle of Retribution. In ed. Ota Weinberger, *Essays in Legal and Moral Philosophy*, 165-215. Trans. Peter Heath. Dordrecht and Boston: D. Reidel.

___. [1941a] 1971. The Law as a Specific Social Technique. In *What is Justice? Justice, Law & Politics in the Mirror of Science*, 231-36. Berkeley and Los Angeles: University of California Press.

___. [1941b] 1971. The Pure Theory of Law and Analytical Jurisprudence. In *Harvard Law Journal* **55** (1941): 44-70; reprinted in Kelsen, *What is Justice? Justice, Law & Politics in the Mirror of Science*, 266-87. Berkeley and Los Angeles: University of California Press.

___. 1941c. Causality and Retribution. In *What is Justice? Justice, Law & Politics in the Mirror of Science*, 303-23. Berkeley and Los Angeles: University of California Press.

___. 1942. Value Judgments in the Science of Law. In *What is Justice? Justice, Law & Politics in the Mirror of Science*, 209-30. Berkeley and Los Angeles: University of California Press.

___. [1946] 1974. Natural and Social Science. In *Society and Nature*, 263-66. New York: Arno Press.

___. [1948a] 1957. Law, State, and Justice in the Pure Theory of Law. In *Yale Law Journal* **59** (1947-48): 377-90. Reprinted in *What is Justice? Justice, Law & Politics in the Mirror of Science*, 288-302. Berkeley and Los Angeles: University of California Press.

___. [1948b] 1971. Absolutism and Relativism in Philosophy and Politics. In *What is Justice? Justice, Law & Politics in the Mirror of Science*, 198-208. Berkeley and Los Angeles: University of California Press.

___. [1949] 1971. The Natural-Law Doctrine before the Tribunal of Science. In *What is Justice? Justice, Law & Politics in the Mirror of Science*, 137-73. Berkeley and Los Angeles: University of California Press.

___. [1950] 1971. Causality and Imputation. In *What is Justice? Justice, Law & Politics in the Mirror of Science*, 324-49. Berkeley and Los Angeles: University of California Press.

___. [1951] 1971. Science and Politics. In *What is Justice? Justice, Law & Politics in the Mirror of Science*, 350-75. Berkeley and Los Angeles: University of California Press.

___. [1952a] 1971. What is Justice? In *What is Justice? Justice, Law and Politics in the Mirror of Science*, 1-24. Berkeley and Los Angeles: University of California Press.

___. [1952b] 1984. What is a Legal Act? In *American Journal of Jurisprudence* **29**: 199-212. Trans. Bonnie Paulson and Stanley L. Paulson.

___. [1952-53] 1971. The Idea of Justice in the Holy Scriptures. In *What is Justice? Justice, Law and Politics in the Mirror of Science*, 25-81. Berkeley and Los Angeles: University of California Press.

___. 1953. Political Absolutism. In *Encyclopaedia Britanica* **1**: 65-6.

___. 1956. A Dynamic Theory of Natural Law. In *What is Justice? Justice, Law and Politics in the Mirror of Science*, 175-97. Berkeley and Los Angeles: University of California Press.

___. [1957] 1960. Plato and the Doctrine of Natural Law. In *Vanderbilt Law Review*. **14**: 23-64. Trans. Richard N. Porter.

___. 1959. On the Basic Norm. In *California Law Review* **47**: 107-10.

___. 1960a. Causality and Accounting. In ed. Ota Weinberger, *Essays in Legal and Moral Philosophy*, 154-64. Trans. Peter Heath. Dordrecht and Boston: D. Reidel.

___. 1960b. Law and Morality. In ed. Ota Weinberger, *Essays in Legal and Moral Philosophy*, 154-64. Trans. Peter Heath. Dordrecht and Boston: D. Reidel.

___. 1961. *General Theory of Law and State*. Trans. Anders Wedberg. New York: Russell & Russell.

___. [1964] 1973. The Foundation of the Theory of Natural Law. In ed. Ota Weinberger, *Essays in Legal and Moral Philosophy*, 114-53. Trans. Peter Heath. Dordrecht and Boston: D. Reidel.

___. [1965] 1973. On the Concept of the Norm. In ed. Ota Weinberger, *Essays in Legal and Moral Philosophy*, 216-27. Trans. Peter Heath. Dordrecht and Boston: D. Reidel.

___. 1966. Norm and Value. In *California Law Review* 1624-29.

___. [1965] 1973. Law and Logic. In ed. Ota Weinberger, *Essays in Legal and Moral Philosophy*, 216-27. Trans. Peter Heath. Dordrecht and Boston: D. Reidel.

___. 1965. Professor Stone and the Pure Theory of Law. In *Stanford Law Review* **17**: 1130-1157.

___. 1971. Aristotles' Doctrine of Justice. In *What is Justice? Justice, Law & Politics in the Mirror of Science*, 110-36. Berkeley and Los Angeles: University of California Press.

___. 1973a. The Idea of Natural Law. In *Essays in Legal and Moral Philosophy*. Ed. and intro. Ota Weinberger. Trans. Peter Heath. Dordrecht and Boston: D. Reidel.

___. 1973b. The Foundation of the Theory of Natural Law. In *Essays in Legal and Moral Philosophy*, 114-53. Ed. and intro. Ota Weinberger. Trans. Peter Heath. Dordrecht and Boston: D. Reidel.

___. 1974a. *Society and Nature: a sociological inquiry*. New York: Arno Press.

___. 1974b. The Law of Causality in Modern Natural Science. In *Society and Nature*, 249-62. New York: Arno Press.

___. 1974c. The Law of Causality and the Principle of Retribution in the Greek Philosophy of Nature. In *Society and Nature*, 233-48. New York: Arno Press.

___. [1979] 1991 (English edn). *General Theory of Norms*. Trans. Michael Hartney. Oxford: Clarendon Press.

___. 1986. The Function of a Constitution. In eds. Richard Tur and William Twining, *Essays on Kelsen*, 109-22. Oxford: Clarendon Press.

Plato. 1961. *The Collected Dialogues of Plato, including the Letters*. Ed. Edith Hamilton and Huntington Cairns. Princeton: Princeton University Press.

Raz, Joseph. [1970] 1980 2d. *The Concept of a Legal System: An Introduction to the Theory of the Legal System* . Oxford: Clarendon.

___. 1971. The Identity of Legal Systems. In *California Law Review* **59**: 795-815. Reprinted in California Law Review, *Essays in Honor of Hans Kelse* ·, 795-815.

___. 1972. Legal Principles and the Limits of Law. In *Yale Law Journal* **81**: 823-54. Reprinted in 1984 in ed. Marshall Cohen, *Ronald Dworkin and Contemporary Jurisprudence*, 295-324. Totowa, New Jersey: Rowman and Allanheld.

___. 1973. On the Functions of Law. In *Oxford Essays in Jurisprudence* 2d Series, 278-304. Oxford: Clarendon Press.

___. 1977. Promises and obligations. In eds. P.M.S. Hacker and Joseph Raz, *Law, Morality and Society: Essays in Honour of H.L.A. Hart*, 210-28 Oxford: Clarendon.

___. 1978. Reasons for Action, Decisions and Norms. In ed. Joseph Raz, *Practical Reasoning*, 128-43. Oxford: Clarendon Press.

___. 1979. *The Authority of Law: Essays on Law and Morality*. Oxford: Clarendon.

___. 1980. *The Concept of a Legal System: An Introduction to the Theory of Legal System*. 2d ed. Oxford: Clarendon Press.

___. 1981. On the Basis of Legal Validity. In *American Journal of Jurisprudence*. **26**: 178-89. Trans. Stanley L. Paulson.

___. 1983. The Problem about the Nature of Law. In *University of Western Ontario Law Review* **21**: 203-18.

___. 1984a. Hart on Moral Rights and Legal Duties. *Oxford Journal of Legal Studies* **4**: 123-31.

___. 1984b. Right-Based Moralities. In ed. Jeremy Waldron, *Theories of Rights*, 182-200. Oxford: Oxford University Press.

___. 1985. Authority, Law and Morality. In *Monist* **68**: 295-324.

___. 1986. *The Morality of Freedom*. Oxford: Clarendon Press.

___. 1986. The Purity of the Pure Theory. In eds. Richard Tur and William Twining, *Essays on Kelsen*. Oxford: Clarendon Press.

___. 1990. *Practical Reason and Norms*. 2d ed. Princeton: Princeton University Press.

___. [1975] 1990. Postscript to the second edition: Rethinking exclusionary reasons in *Practical Reason and Norms*, 178-99. 2d. Princeton: Princeton University Press.

___. 1994. *Ethics in the Public Domain, Public Domain: Essays in the Morality of Law and Politics*. Oxford: Clarendon.

___. 1998. On the Authority and Interpretation of Constitutions. In ed. Larry Alexander, *Constitutionalism: Philosophical Foundations*, 152-93. Cambridge: Cambridge University Press.

___. 1999. *Engaging Reason*. Oxford: Clarendon.

Rousseau, Jean-Jacques. [1750a, 1755] 1913. A Discourse on the Origin of Inequality in *The Social Contract and Discourses*, 143-229. Trans. with intro. G.D.H. Cole. London/New York: Everyman's Library.

___. [1750b] 1913. A Discourse on the Moral Effects of the Arts and Sciences. In *The Social Contract and the Discourses*, 117-42. Trans. with intro. G.D.H. Cole. London/New York: Everyman's Library.

___. [1750c] 1958, 1913. A Discourse on Political Economy. In *The Social Contract and the Discourses*, 233-69. Trans. with intro. G.D.H. Cole. London/New York: Everyman's Library.

___. [1762, 1790] 1968. *Social Contract*. Ed. Maurice Cranston. London: Penguin.

Secondary Sources

Aarnio, Aulis, Robert Alexy, and Alexsander Peczenik. 1981. The Foundation of Legal Reasoning. In *Rechtstheorie* **12**: 133-48. Berlin: Duncker & Humblot.

___. With Akzin, Benjamin. 1964. Analysis of State and Law Structure. In Salo Engel. With Rudolf A. Metall. *Law, State and International Legal Order: Essays in Honor of Hans Kelsen*, 1-20. Knoxville: University of Tennessee Press.

Alexy, Robert. 1989. *A Theory of Legal Argumentation: The Theory of Rational Discourse as a Theory of Legal Justification*. Trans. Ruth Adler and Neil MacCormick. Oxford: Clarendon Press.

Allen, R.E. 1980. *Socrates and Legal Obligation*. Minneapolis: University of Minnesota Press.

Alexander, Larry, ed. 1998. *Constitutionalism: Philosophical Foundations*. Cambridge: Cambridge University Press.

Amslek, Paul, and MacCormick, Neil. 1991. *Controversies about Law's Ontology*. Edinburgh: Edinburgh University Press.

Andrews, A. 1962. The Growth of the City-State. In ed. H. Lloyd-Jones, *The Greeks*, 15-55. London: A.C. Watts.

Anscombe, Elizabeth. 1978. On the Source of the Authority of the State. In *Ratio* **20**: 1-28.

Arendt, Hannah. 1961. What is Authority? In *Between Past and Future: Six Exercises in Political Thought*, 91-141. New York: Meridan.

Arthur, Marylin. 1973. Early Greece: The Origins of the Western Attitude towards Women. In *Arethusia* **6**: 7-58.

___. [1977] 1987, 2d. From Medusa to Cleopatra: Women in the Ancient World. In eds. Renate Bridenthal, Claudia Koonz, and Susan Stuard, *Becoming Visible - Women in European History*, 79-105. Boston: Houghton Mifflin.

Axonhouse, Arlene W. 1995. Hobbes and the Beginnings of Modern Political Thought. In Hobbes, *Three Discourses*, 123-54. Ed. Arlene Saxonhouse. Chicago: University of Chicago Press.

Bakhtin, Mikhail. 1981. *The Dialogic Imagination*. Ed. Michael Holquist, trans. Caryl Emerson and Michael Holquist. Austin: University of Texas Press.

___. 1986. *Speech Genres and other Late Essays*. Trans. Vern W. McGee. Austin: University of Texas Press.

___. 1990. *Art and Answerability: Early Philosophical Essays*. Trans. Vadim Liapunov, supp. trans. Kenneth Boston. Austin: University of Texas Press.

Barth, Karl. 1959. *From Rousseau to Ritschl: Protestant Theology in the Nineteenth Century*. London: SCM Press.

Barthes, Roland. [1957, 1972] 1981. Myth Today. In *Mythologies*, 109-59. Trans. Anette Lavers; New York: Noonday Press.

___. 1979. From Work to Text. In Josu, U. Harari ed, *Textual Strategies: Perspectives in Post Structuralist Criticism*, 73-81. Ithaca: Cornell University Press.

___. 1981. The Theory of the Text. In ed. Robert Young, *Untying the Text: A Post Structuralist Reader*, 31-47. Boston: Routledge & Kegan Paul.

___. 1985. Rhetoric of the Image. In ed. Robert E. Innis. *Semiotics: An Introductory Anthology*, 190-205. Bloomington: Indiana University Press.

Barton, Thomas D. 1992. The Structure of legal Systems. In *American Journal of Jurisprudence*, **37**: 291-317.

Baumgardt, David. 1952. *Bentham and the Ethics of Today: with Bentham Manuscripts Hitherto Unpublished*. Princeton: Princeton University Press.

Bell. David R. 1969-70. Authority in Royal Institute of Philosophy, *The Proper Study*, *Lectures* **4**: 190-203.

Berkovits, Eliezer. 1989. *Not in Heaven: The Nature and Function of Halakha*. New York: Ktav Publishing House.

Berns, Laurence. 1972. 2d. ed. Thomas Hobbes. In *History of Political Philosophy*, ed. Leo Strauss and Joseph Cropsey, 370-94. Chicago & London: University of Chicago Press.

Beyleveld, Deryck. 1993. From the Middle-Way to Normative Individualism. In *Modern Law Review* **56**: 104-19.

___. 1985. With Roger Brownsword. The Practical Difference between Natural-Law Theory and Legal Positivism in *Oxford Journal of Legal Studies* **5** (1): 1-32.

Bix, Brian Bill. 1993. [1996a] 1999. *Jurisprudence: Theory and Context*. Boulder, Colorado: Westview Press; London: Sweet & Maxwell.

___. 1996b. Legal Positivism. With Brian Leiter in ed. D. Patterson, *A Companion to Philosphy of Law and Legal Theory*, 241-60. Oxford: Clarendon Press.

___. ed. 1998. *Analyzing Law: New Essays in Legal Theory*. Oxford: Clarendon Press.

Bobbio, Norberto. 1970. *Sein* and *Sollen* in Legal Science. In *Archiv für Rechts- und Sozialphilosophie* **61**: 7-30.

___. 1993. *Thomas Hobbes and the Natural Law Tradition*. Trans. Daniela Gobetti. Chicago: University of Chicago Press.

Bodenheimer, Edgar. 1958. Analytical Positivism, Legal Realism, and the Future of Legal Method. In *Virginia Law Review* **44**: 365-78.

Bowie, Norman E. 1974. The War between Natural Law Philosophy and Legal Positivism. In *Idealistic Studies* **4**: 145-59. With a Comment by Edward Kent: 156-59.

Boyle, Joseph. 1992. Natural Law and the Ethics of Traditions. In ed. Robert P. George, *Natural Law Theory: Contemporary Essays*, 3-30. Oxford: Clarendon.

Bradley, A.C. 1962. Hegel's Theory of Tragedy. In ed. Anne and Henry Paolucci, *Hegel on Tragedy*, 367-88. Garden City, New York: Doubleday.

Bretall, R. W. 1962. Kant's Theory of the Sublime. In ed. George Tapley Whitney and David S. Bowers, *The Heritage of Kant*,, 379-402. New York: Russell & Russell.

Brink, David O. 1985. Legal Positivism and Natural Law Reconsidered. In *Monist* **68** (1985): 364-87.

Brown, Robert. 1984. *The Nature of Social Laws: Machiavelli to Mill*. Cambridge: Cambridge University Press.

Brown, K.C. 1965. The Taylor Thesis: Some Objections in Hobbes Studies. *Hobbes Studies*, 57-71. Oxford: Basil Blackwell.

Brown, Stuart M. 1962. Has Kant a Philosophy of Law? In *The Heritage of Kant*, 33-48. Ed. George Tapley Whitney and David F. Bowers. New York: Russell & Russell.

Bulygin, Eugenio. 1995. Cognition and Interpretation of Law. In eds. Letizia Gianformaggio and Stanley L. Paulson, *Cognition and Interpretation of Law*, 11-35. Torino: g. diappichelli editore.

Burcell, Graham, Colin Gordon, and Peter Miller, eds. 1991. *The Foucault Effect: Studies in Governmentality*. Chicago: University of Chicago Press.

Burns, J.H. 1973. Bentham on Sovereignty: An Exploration in *Northern Ireland Legal Quarterly* **24**, no. 3: 399-416.

Butler, Judith. 1990. *Gender Trouble*. London: Routledge.

Burnet, John. 1896-97. Law and Nature in Greek Ethics. In *International J. Ethics* **7** #3: 328-33.

___. 1930, 4th ed. *Early Greek Philosophy*. London: A. & C. Black.

Campbell, Tom D. 1996. *The Legal Theory of Ethical Positivism* (Aldershot, England: Dartmouth.

___. 1998. The Point of Legal Positivism. *Kings College Law Journal* **9**: 63-87.

Caputo, John D. 1997. *The Prayers and Tears of Jacques Derrida: Religion without Religion*. Bloomington: Indiana University Press.

Carty, Anthony, ed. 1990. *Post-Modern Law: Enlightenment, Revolution and the Death of Man*. Edinburgh: Edinburgh University Press.

Cassirer, Ernst. 1951. *The Philosophy of the Enlightenment*. Ed. Fritz C.A. Koelln, trans. James P. Pettegrove. Princeton: Princeton University Press.

Cheah, Pheng, David Fraser, and Judith Grbich, eds. 1996. *Thinking Through the Body of the Law*. New York: New York University Press.

Chloros, A.G. 1955. Some Aspects of the Social and Ethical Element in Analytical Jurisprudence. In *Juridical Review* **67**: 79-102.

Cohen, Morris R. 1962. A Critique of Kant's Philosophy of Law. In eds. George Tapley Whitney and David F. Bowers, *The Heritage of Kant*, 279-302. New York: Russell & Russell.

Coleman, Jules L. 1982. Negative and Positive Positivism. In *Journal of Legal Studies* **11**: 139-64. Reprinted in 1984 in *Ronald Dworkin and Contemporary Jurisprudence*, 28-48. Ed. M. Cohen. Totowa, N.J.: Rowman & Allanhead. Also reprinted in Jules L. Coleman, *Market Morals and the Law*, 3-27. Cambridge: Cambridge University Press.

___. 1989. On the Relationship between Law and Morality. In *Ratio Juris* **2** (1): 66-78.

___. 1991. Rules and Social Facts. In *Harvard Journal of Law and Public Policy* **14**: 7-3-25.

___. 1992. Authority and Reason. In ed. Robert P. George, *Natural Law*, 287-319. Oxford: Clarendon Press. Reprinted in 1996 in ed. Robert P. George, *The Autonomy of Law: Essays on Legal Positivism*, 287-313. Oxford: Clarendon Press.

___. 1993. With Brian Leiter. Determinacy, Objectivity, and Authority. In *University of Pennsylvania Law Review* **142**: 549-637.

___. 1994. *Jurisprudence*. With Anthony Sebok. New York: Garland.

___. 1995. Truth and Objectivity in Law. In *Legal Theory* **1**: 33-68.

___. 1996. Authority and Reason. In *The Autonomy of Law: Essays on Legal Positivism*, 287-313. Oxford: Clarendon Press.

___. 1998a. Second Thoughts and Other First Impressions. In ed. Brian Bix, *Analyzing Law*, 257-322. Oxford: Clarendon Press.

___. 1998b. Incorporationism, Conventionality, and the Practical Difference Thesis. In *Legal Theory* **4**: 381-425.

Conklin, William. 1992. The End of Judicial Review. In *Current Legal Theory* **10** (1992): 1-16. Reprinted with revisions in ed. Bert van Roermund, *Constitutional Review, Verfassungsgerichtsbarkeit, Constitutionele Toetsing*, 33-54. Zwolle: Kluwer.

___. 1996. The Invisible Author of Legal Authority. In *Law and Critique* **7** (2): 173-92.

___. 1997. Hegel, the Author and Authority in Sophocles *Antigone*. In ed. Leslie Rubin, *Justice v. Law in Greek Political Thought*, 129-51. New York: Rowman & Littlefield.

___. 1998a. The Secret Foundation of Sovereignty in Legal Positivism. In *Rechtstheorie Beiheft* **17**: 83-92.

___. 1998b. *The Phenomenology of Modern Legal Discourse: The Juridical Production and the Unconcealment of Suffering*. Aldershot,U.K./Brookfield, U.S.A./Singapore/Sydney: Dartmouth/Ashgate.

___. 1998c. Alternatives to the Study of Legal Texts: An Annotated Bibliography of Legal Phenomenology and Legal Semiotics. In *Current Legal Theory* **16** (2): 3-61.

Cooper John M. 1976-77. Aristotle on the Forms of Friendship. In *Review of Metaphysics* **30**: 619-48.

____. 1980. Aristotle on Friendship. In ed. Amelie O. Rorty, *Essays on Aristotle's Ethics*, 301-40. Berkeley: University of California Press.

____. 1996. Justice and Rights in Aristotle's *Politics*. In *Review of Metaphysics* **49**: 850-72.

Copleston, Frederick. [1946] 1985. *A History of Philosophy: Late Medieval and Renaissance Philosophy*. Westminster, MD: Newman; New York/London: Doubleday.

___. 1950-77. *A History of Philosophy*. 9 vols. New York: Doubleday.

Cornford, Francis Macdonald. 1957. *From Religion to Philosophy: A Study in the Origins of Western Speculation*. New York: Harper & Sons.

Cowan, Thomas A. 1971. Law without Force. In *California Law Review* **59**: 683-714. Reprinted in California Law Review, *Essays in Honour of Hans Kelsen*, 683-714. South Hackensack: Rothman & Co.

Cranston, Maurice, ed. 1972. *Hobbes and Rousseau: A Collection of Critical Essays*. With Richard S. Peters. Garden City, NY: Doubleday.

Day, John. 1963. Authority. In *Political Studies* **11**: 257-71.

Derrida, Jacques. 1982a. Plato's Pharmacy. In *Dissemination*, 61-171. Trans. with notes, Barbara Johnson. Chicago: University of Chicago Press.

___. 1982b. The Ends of Man. *Margins of Philosophy*. Trans. Alan Bass, 109-36. Chicago: University of Chicago Press.

___. 1982c. Form and Meaning: A Note on the Phenomenology of Language. *Margins oj Philosophy*. Trans. Alan Bass, 155-73. Chicago: University of Chicago Press.

___. 1982d. The Pit and the Pyramid: Introduction to Hegel's Semiology. *Margins of Philosophy*, 69-108. Trans. Alan Bass. Chicago: University of Chicago Press.

___. 1982c. Sending: on Representation. In *Social Research* **49** #2: 294-326. Trans. Peter Caws and Mary Ann Caws.

___. 1990a. *Du droit à la philosophie*. Paris: Galilee.

___. 1990b. Force of Law: The 'Mystical Foundation of Authority.' In *Cardozo Law Review*, **11**: 919-1045. Trans. Mary Quaintance.

___. 1994. *Specters of Marx: The State of the Debt, the Work of Mourning, and the New International*. Trans. Peggy Kamuf, intro. Bernd Magnus & Stephen Cullenberg, New York/ London: Routledge.

___. [1996] 1998. Ed. with Gianni Vattimo. *Religion*. Stanford: Stanford University Press.

Dias, R.W.M. 1968. Legal Politics: Norms behind the *Grundnorm*. In *Cambridge Law Journal*: 233-59.

Dickerson, John. 1929. The Law behind the Law. In *Columbia Law Review* **29**: 113-46; **30**: 285-319.

Dietrich, B. C. 1974. *The Origins of Greek Religion*. Berlin: Walter de Gruyter.

Donougho, Martin. 1989-90. The Woman in White: On the Reception of Hegel's *Antigone*. In *Owl of Minerva* **21**: 65-89.

Dorff, Eliot N. and Arthur Rosett. 1988. *A Living Tree: The Roots and Growth of Jewish Law*, 346-57, 421-34. Albany, New York: State University of New York.

Dummett, Michael. 1978. *Truth and Other Enigmas*. Cambridge: Cambridge University Press.

Duxbury, Neil. 1993. Faith in Reason: the Process Tradition in American Jurisprudence. In *Cardozo Law Review* **15**: 601-705.

Dworkin, Ronald. 1968. Comment on the Unity of Law's Doctrine in *Ethics and Social Justice*, eds. Howard E. Kiefer and Milton K. Munitz, 200-06. Albany: State University of New York Press.

___. 1975. The Original Position. In ed. Norman Daniels, *Reading Rawls: Critical Studies on Rawls' A Theory of Justice*, 16-53. Oxford: Basil Blackwell.

___. 1977. Is Law a System of Rules? In ed. R.M. Dworkin, *The Philosophy of Law*, 38-65. Oxford: Oxford University Press.

___. 1982. Natural Law Revisited. In *University of Florida Law Review* **34**: 165-88.

___. 1984. A Reply by Ronald Dworkin. In ed. M. Cohen, *Ronald Dworkin and Contemporary Jurisprudence*, 247-300. Totowa, N.J.: Rowman & Allanhead.

___. 1985. Law's Ambition for Itself. In *Virginia Law Review* **71**: 173-87.

___. 1986a. *A Matter of Principle*. Oxford: Clarendon Press.

___. 1986b. *Law's Empire*. Cambridge: Harvard University Press.

___. 1986c. The Form of principle. In *A Matter of Principle*, 33-71. Oxford: Clarendon.

___. 1986d. Is There Really No Right Answer in Hard Cases? In *A Matter of Principle*, 119-45. Oxford: Clarendon Press.

___. 1991. On Gaps in the Law. In eds. Paul Amslek and Neil MacCormick *Controversies about Law's Ontology*, 84-90. Edinburgh: Edinburgh University Press.

___. 1992. On Open Texture in Law. In ed. Paul Amslek and Neil MacCormick, *Controversies about Law's Ontology*. Edinburgh: Edinburgh University Press.

___. 1994. *Life's Dominion: An Argument about Abortion, Euthanasia, and Individual Freedom.* New York: Vintage Books.

___. 1995. Authority and Reason. In ed. R. George, *The Autonomy of Law: Essays on Legal Positivism*, 287-319. Oxford: Clarendon Press.

___. 1996. *Freedom's Law*. Cambridge Mass: Harvard University Press.

Dyzenhaus, David. 1992. Why Positivism is Authoritarian. In *American Journal of Jurisprudence*, 83-112.

___. 1996. Hermann Heller and the Legitimacy of Legality. In *Oxford Journal of Legal Studies* **16**: 641-65.

Ebenstein, William. [1945] 1969. *The Pure Theory of Law*. New York: Augustus M. Kelley; South Hackensack, NJ: Rothman Reprints.

___. 1971. The Pure Theory of Law: Demythologizing Legal Thought. In *California Law Review* **59**: 617-82. Reprinted in California Law Review, *Essays in Honour of Hans Kelsen*, 617-82. South Hackensack: Rothman & Co.

Eckhoff, Torstein, and Nils Kristian Sundby. 1975. The Notion of Basic Norm(s) in Jurisprudence. In ed Folke Schmidt, *Scandanavian Studies in Law* **19**: 123-51

Edelman, Murray. 1964. The Political Language of the Helping Professions. In *Politics and Society* **4**: 295-310.

Edgeworth, Brendan. 1986. Legal Positivism and the Philosophy of Language: A Critique of H.L.A. Hart's Descriptive Sociology. In *Legal Studies* **6** (2): 115-39.

Eisenach, Eldon J. 1982. Hobbes on Church, State and Religion. In *History of Political Thought.* **3**: 215-43.

d'Entrèves, Alexander Passerin. 1967. *The Notion of the State: An Introduction to Political Theory*. Oxford: Clarendon Press.

Engel, Salo. 1964. With Rudolf A. Metall. *Law, State and International Legal order: Essays in Honor of Hans Kelsen.* Knoxville: University of Tennessee Press.

Finnis, John. 1987. Comment. In *Issues in Contemporary Legal Philosophy: The Influence of H.L.A. Hart*, 62-75. Oxford: Clarendon Press.

___. 1987. On Reason and Authority in *Law's Empire.* In *Law and Philosophy* **6**: 357-80.

___. 1996. The Truth in Legal Positivism. In ed. Robert P. George, *The Autonomy of Law: Essays on Legal Positivism*, 195-214. Oxford: Clarendon.

Fish, Stanley. 1980. *Is There a Text in the Classroom?: The Authority of Interpretative Communities*. Cambridge Mass.: Harvard University Press.

___. 1989. *Doing What Comes Naturally: Change, Rhetoric and the Practice of Theory in Literary and Legal Studies*. Durham, NC: Duke University Press.

Fitzgerald, P.J. 1966. *Salmond on Jurisprudence.* 12th ed. London: Sweet and Maxwell.

Frank Fleerackers, Frank, Evert van Leeuwan, and Bert van Roermund, eds. 1996. *Law, Life and Images of Man: Modes of Thought in Modern Legal Theory*. Berlin: Duncker & Humblot.

Flew, Antony. 1955. Divine Omnipotence and Human Freedom. In *New Essays in Philosophical Theology*, 144-69. Eds. Anthony Flew and Alasdair MacIntyre. London: SCM Press.

Foster, Hal, ed. 1983. *The Anti-Aesthetic: Essays on Postmodern Condition.* Seattle: Bay Press.

Foucault, Michel. 1970. *The Order of Things: an Archeology of the Human Sciences.* New York: Vintage Books.

___. 1972. The Discourse on Language. In *The Archeology of Knowledge* Trans. A. M. Sheridan Smith. New York: Pantheon. Reprinted in ed. Robert Young. 1981. *Untying the Text: A Post Structuralist Reader*, 48-78. Boston: Routledge and Kegan Paul. Another translation of the essay is under the title The Order of Discourse. 1984. In ed. Michael Shapiro, *Language and Politics* 48-78. London: Basil Blackwell.

___. 1979. My Body, This Paper, This Fire. In *Oxford Literary Review* **4**: 9-28.

___. 1980. Two Lectures. In ed. Colin Gordon, *Power/Knowledge: Selected Interviews & Other Writings, 1972-1977*, 91-7. New York: Pantheon.

___. 1982. The Subject and Power. In *Critical Theory* **8**: 777-795.

___. 1984. What is an Author? In ed. Paul Rabinow, *The Foucault Reader*, 101-20. New York: Pantheon.

___. 1991. Governmentality. In eds. Graham Burchell, Colin Gordon, and Peter Miller, *The Foucault Effect: Studies in Governmentality*, 87-104. Chicago: University of Chicago Press.

Frankfort, H., H.A. Frankfort, John A. Wilson, and Thorkild Jacobsen, eds. 1949. *Before Philosophy: The Intellectual Adventure of Ancient Man.* Harmondsworth: Penguin.

Frankfort, H.A. 1949. Myth and Reality. In H. and H.A. Frankfort, John A. Wilson, Thorkild Jacobsen, *Before Philosophy: The Intellectual Adventures of Ancient Man*, 11-36. Harmondsworth: Penguin.

Friedman, Richard B. 1969. An Introduction to Mill's Theory of Authority. In ed. J.B. Schneewind, *Mill: A Collection of Critical Essays*,, 379-425. Notre Dame/London: University of Notre Dame Press.

___. 1989. Oakeshott on the Authority of Law. In *Ratio Juris* **2** (1): 27-40.

Friedmann, Wolfgang. 1957. *Legal Theory.* 5th ed. New York: Columbia University.

Friedrich, C.J. 1958. *Authority.* Cambridge, Mass.: Harvard University Press.

Fuber, Klaus. 1996. Farewell to Legal Positivism: the Separation Thesis Unravelling. In ed. Robert P. George, *The Autonomy of Law: Essays on Legal Positivism*, 119-62. Oxford: Clarendon.

Fuller, Lon. [1940] 1966. *The Law in Quest of Itself* London: Beacon.

___. 1956a. Human Purpose and Natural Law. In *Journal of Philosophy* **53**: 697. Reprinted in *Natural Law Forum* (1958) **3**: 68-76.

___. 1956b. A Rejoinder to Professor Nagel. In *Natural Law Forum* (1958) **3**: 83-104.

___. 1958. Positivism and Fidelity to Law – A Reply to Professor Hart. In *Harvard Law Review* **71**:630-72.

___. [1964] 1969. *The Morality of Law.* Rev. ed. New Haven: Yale University Press.

___. 1968. *Anatomy of Law.* New York/London: New American Library/Mentors; New York: Praeger.

Gadamer, Hans-Georg. 1975. *Truth and Method.* Trans. David E. Linge. New York: Crossroads.

Gauthier, David. 1969. *The Logic of Leviathan: the Moral and Political Theory of Thomas Hobbes.* Oxford: Clarendon Press.

Gavison, Ruth. 1982. Natural Law, Positivism, and the Limits of Jurisprudence: A Modern Round in *Yale Law Journal* **91**: 1250-85.

___. 1987. *Issues in Contemporary Legal Philosophy: The Influence of H.L.A. Hart.* Oxford: Clarendon Press.

George, Robert P. 1992. *Natural Law Theory: Contemporary Essays*. Oxford: Clarendon.

___. 1996a. *The Autonomy of Law: Essays on Legal Positivism* Oxford: Clarendon Press.

___. 1996b. Does Positivism Matter? In *The Autonomy of Law: Essays on Legal Positivism*, 57-78. Oxford: Clarendon Press.

___. 1996c. Natural Law and Positive Law. In *The Autonomy of Law: Essays on Legal Positivism*, 321-34. Oxford: Clarendon Press.

___. 1999. *In Defence of Natural Law*. Oxford: Clarendon.

Gierke, Otto. [1900], 1958. *Political Theories of the Middle Ages*. Trans. with intro. Frederic William Maitland, 76-100 Beacon Hill/Boston: Beacon Press.

Gilson, Etienne. 1941. *God and Philosophy*. New Haven:Yale University Press.

Glover, Willis B. 1965. God and Thomas Hobbes. In ed. K.C. Brown, *Hobbes Studies*, 141-68. Oxford: Basil Blackwell.

Golding, Martin P. 1986. Jurisprudence and Legal Philosophy in Twentieth Century America – Major Themes and Developments. In *Journal of Legal Education* **36**: 441-84.

Goldsmith, M.M. 1966. *Hobbes' Science of Politics*. New York and London.

___. 1980. Hobbes Mortal God: Is There a Fallacy in Hobbes Theory of Sovereignty? In *History of Political Thought* **1**: 33-50.

Goldworth, Amnon. 1969. The Meaning of Bentham's Greatest Happiness Principle. In *Journal of the History of Philosophy*. **7**: 315-21.

Goodrich, Peter. 1990. Contractions: Rousseau in the Year Two Thousand. In ed. Anthony Carty. *Post Modern Law: Enlightenment, Revolution and the Death of Man*, 40-70. Edinburgh: Edinburgh University Press.

Gray, John Chapman. [1909, rev. ed. 1921] 1963. *Nature and Sources of the Law*. New York: Columbia University Press.

Greenleaf, W.H. 1972. Hobbes: The Problem of Interpretation. In ed. Maurice Cranston and Richard S. Peters, *Hobbes and Rousseau: A Collection of Critical Essays*, 5-36. Garden City, New York: Doubleday.

Golding, M.P. 1971. Kelsen and the Concept of legal system. In ed. Robert S. Summers, *More Essays in Legal Philosophy: General Assessments of Legal Philosophers*, 69-100. Oxford: Basil Blackwell.

Gradbruch, Gustav. 1936. Anglo-American Jurisprudence Through Continental Eyes. In *Law Quarterly Review* **52**: 530-45.

Greenawalt, Kent. 1987a. *Conflicts of Law and Morality*. Oxford: Oxford University Press.

___. 1987b. The Rule of Recognition and the Constitution. In *Columbia Law Review* **85**: 621-71.

___. 1988. Hart's Rule of Recognition and the United States. In *Ratio Juris* **1**: 40-57.

___. 1996. Too Thin and Too Rich: Distinguishing Features of Legal Positivism. In ed. Robert P. George, *The Autonomy of Law: Essays on legal Positivism*, 1-29. Oxford: Oxford University Press.

Grzegorczyk, Christophe; Françoise Michaut, and Michel Troper. 1992. *Le positivisme juridique*. Paris: L.G.D.J.

Guest, Stephen. 1992. *Ronald Dworkin* Edinburgh: Edinburgh University Press.

___, ed. 1996. *Positivism Today*. Aldershot/Brookfield, USA, Singapore/Sydney: Dartmouth.

Guthrie, W.G.C. 1950. *The Greeks and their Gods*. London: Methuen.

___. 1957. *In the Beginning: Some Greek Views on the Origins of Life and the Early State oj Man*. London/Ithaca: Methuen/Cornell University Press.

___. 1969. *A History of Greek Philosophy* vol. 3, 55-131. 6 vols. Cambridge: Cambridge University Press.

Hacker, P.M.S., and Joseph Raz. 1977. *Law, Morality, and Society: Essays in Honour of H.L.A. Hart*. Oxford: Clarendon Press.

Hall, Jerome. 1964. From Legal Theory to Integrative Jurisprudence. In *University of Cincinnati Law Review* **33** (2): 153-205.

Halliday, R. J., T. Kenyon, and A. Reeve. Hobbes Belief in God. In *Political Studies* **31**: 418-33.

Hamburger, Lotte, and Joseph Hamburger. 1985. *Troubled Lives: John and Sarah Austin*. Toronto: University of Toronto Press.

Hand, Sean, ed. 1989. *The Levinas Reader*. London: Basil Blackwell.

Harris, H.S. 1995. *Hegel: Phenomenology and System*. Indianapolis/Cambridge: Hackett.

Harris, J.W. 1977a. Kelsen's Concept of Authority. In *Cambridge Law Journal* **36**: 353-63.

___. 1977b. The Concept of the Sovereign Will. In *Acta Juridica*: 1-15.

Harrison, Ross. 1983. *Bentham*. London: Routledge and Kegan Paul.

Heinze, R. 1925. Auctoris. In *Hermes* **9**: 348-66.

Heuston, R.F.V. 1961. Sovereignty. In ed. A. G. Guest *Oxford Essays in Jurisprudence*, 198-222. Oxford: Clarendon Press.

Hittinger, Russell. 1992. Natural Law and Virtue: Theories at Cross Purposes. In ed. Robert P. George, *Natural Law Theory: Contemporary Essays*, 42-70. Oxford: Clarendon.

Horowitz, Asher. 1987. *Rousseau, Nature and History*. Toronto: University of Toronto

Hood, F.C. 1964. *The Divine Politics of Thomas Hobbes: an Interpretation of Leviathan*. Oxford: Clarendon Press.

Howe, Mark DeWolfe, 1951a. The Positivism of Mr. Justice Holmes. In *Harvard Law Review*, **64**: 529-89.

___. 1951. A Brief Rejoinder. In *Harvard Law Review* **64**: 537-39.

Hughes, Graham. 1971. Validity and the Basic Norm. In ed. California Law Review, *Essays in Honour of Hans Kelsen*, **59**: 695-714. South Hackensack: Rothman.

Huizinga J. 1950. *Homo Ludens: A Study of the Play-Element in Culture*. Boston: Beacon.

Hunt, Alan. 1992a. Law's Empire or Legal Imperialism? In Hunt, *Reading Dworkin Critically*, 9-43. New York/Oxford: Berg.

___. 1992b. *Reading Dworkin Critically*. New York/Oxford: Berg.

Ingraffia, Brian D. 1995. *Postmodern Theory and Biblical Theology:Vanquishing God's Shadow*. Cambridge/New York: Cambridge University Press.

Inwood, M. J. 1989. Hegel, Plato and Greek *Sittlichkeit*. In ed. Z. A. Pelczynski. *The State and Civil Society: Studies in Hegel's Political Philosophy*. Cambridge: Cambridge University Press.

Irigary, Luce. 1985. *Speculum of the Other Woman*. Ithaca, N.Y.: Cornell University Press.

Jacoff, Rachel. 1993. *The Cambridge Companion to Dante*. Cambridge: Cambridge University Press.

Jebb, Richard C. 1962. Introduction. In *Sophocles: The Plays and Fragments: Pt III. The Antigone*. Amsterdam: Servio.

Johnston, David. 1989. Hobbes Mortalism. In *History of Political Thought* **10** (4): 647-663.

Kamuf, Peggy. 1986. Floating Authorship. In *Diacritics* **16**: 3-13.

Kaufmann, Walter. 1971. Hegel's Ideas about Tragedy. In ed. Warren E. Steinkraus. *New Studies in Hegel's Philosophy*. 201-22. New York: Holt, Rinehard & Winston.

Kearney, Richard, ed. 1984. *Dialogue with Contemporary Continental thinkers: The Phenomenological Tradition*. Manchester: Manchester University Press.

Kiefer, Howard E., and K. Munitz. 1970. *Ethics and Social Justice*. Albany, NY: State University of New York Press.

King, B.E. 1963. The Basic Concept of professor Harts Jurisprudence in *Cambridge Law Journal*, 270-303.

Koestler, Arthur. 1967. *The Ghost in the Machine*. London: Hutchinson.

Kraft, Julius. 1993. On the Methodical relationship between Jurisprudence and Theology. In *Law and Critique* **4** (1): 117-23.

Kranenburg, Joke Klein. 1997. Legal Positivism Divided. In *Current Legal Theory* **15**: 3-23.

Kraut, Richard. 1996. Are there Natural Rights in Aristotle? In *Review of Metaphysics* **49**: 755-74.

Kretschmann, M. 1962. An Exposition of Kant's Philosophy of Law. In *The Heritage of Kant*. Eds. George Tapley Whitney and David F. Bowers, 245-76. New York: Russell and Russell.

Kriegel, Blandine. 1994. Rights and Natural Law. In ed. Mark Lilla. *New French Thought: Political Philosophy*, 155-73. Princeton: Princeton University Press.

Krieger, Leonard. 1962. Kant and the Crisis of Natural law. In eds. George Tapley Whitney and David S. Bowers, *The Heritage of Kant*, 191-210. New York: Russell & Russell.

___. [1968] 1973. Authority. In ed. Philip P. Weiner, *Dictionary of the History of Ideas: Studies of Selected Pivotal Ideas*, vol. 1, 141-62. New York: Charles Scribner's Sons.

Krieger, Murray, ed. 1987. *The Aims of Representation: Subject/Text/History*. Irvine Studies in the Humanities. New York: Columbia University Press.

Kripke, Saul A. 1982. *Wittgenstein: On Rules and Private Language*. Oxford: Basil Blackwell.

Kroner, Richard. 1966. *Between Faith and Thought*. New York: Oxford University Press.

___. 1981. *Kant to Hegel: Introduction to Hegel's Early Theological Writings*. Aufl. Tübingen: JCB Mohr [Siebeck].

Lacan, Jacques. 1977. *Ecrits*. Trans. Alan Sheridan. New York: W.W. Norton.

Lauterpacht, H. [1933] 1963. Kelsen's Pure Science of Law. In ed. H. Milford, *Modern Theories of Law*, 105-38. Oxford: Oxford University Press.

Learner, Gerda. 1986. *The Creation of Patriarchy*. Oxford: Oxford University Press.

Levinas, Emmanuel. 1969. *Totality and Infinity: An Essay on Exteriority*. Trans. Alphonso Lingis. Pittsburgh: Duquesne University Press.

___. 1985. *Ethics and Infinity*. Trans. Richard A. Cohen. Pittsburgh: Duquesne University Press.

___. 1986a. Dialogue with Emmanuel Levinas. In ed. Richard A Cohen, Face to Face with Levinas, 13-33. With Richard Kearney. Albany: State University of New York.

___. 1986b. The Trace of the Other. In ed. Mark C. Taylor, *Deconstruction in Context: Literature and Philosophy*, 345-59. Chicago & London: University of Chicago Press.

___. 1989. Time and the Other. In ed. Sean Hand, *The Levinas Reader*, 37-58. Oxford: Basil Blackwell.

Lilla, Mark. 1994. *New French Thought: Political Philosophy*. Princeton: Princeton University Press.

Lindahl, Hans. 1996. Law and Cartesianism. In eds. Frank Fleerackers, Evert van Leeuwa,n and Bert van Roermund, eds., *Law, Life and Images of Man: Modes of Thought in Modern Legal Theory*, 139-68. Berlin: Duncker & Humblot.

Llewelyn, John. 1985. *Beyond Metaphysics: the Hermeneutic Circle in Contemporary Continental Philosophy*. New Jersey: Humanities Press.

Lloyd-Jones, Hugh. 1962. *The Greeks*. London: A.C. Watts.

___. [1971] 1983, 2d. *The Justice of Zeus*. Berkeley: University of Califorbnia Press.

van Loon, Jan F. Glastra. 1996. The Metaphysical Foundation of Hans Kelsen's Legal Theory and the Husteron-Prooteron Fallacy. In eds. Frank Fleerackers, Evert van Leeuwan, and Bert van Roermund. *Law, Life and Images of Man: Modes of Thought in Modern Legal Theory*, 95-108. Berlin: Duncker & Humblot, 1996.

Lyotard, Jean-François. 1988. *The Differand: Phrases in Dispute*. Trans. Georges van den Abbeele. Theory and History of Literature, **40**. Minneapolis: University of Minnesota Press.

MacCormick, Neil. 1978. *Legal Reasoning and Legal Theory*. Oxford:Clarendon.

___. 1985. A Moralistic Case for A-Moralistic Law? In *Valparaiso University Law Review* **20** (1): 1-41.

___. 1986a. *An Institutional Theory of Law: New Approaches to Legal Positivism*. With Ota Weinberger. Dordrecht: D. Reidel.

___. 1986b. With Zenon Bankowski. Speech Acts, Legal Institutions and Real Laws. In MacCormick and Peter Birks, *The Legal Mind: Essays for Tony Honore*, 121-33. Oxford: Clarendon Press.

___. 1986c. With Peter Birks. *The Legal Mind: Essays for Tony Honore* (Oxford: Clarendon Press.

___. 1986d. With Zenon Bankowski. 1986. Speech Acts, Legal Institutions, and Real Laws. In Neil MacCormick and Peter Birks *The Legal Mind: Essays for Tony Honore*, 121-33. Oxford: Clarendon Press.

___. 1987. Why Cases have Rationes and What these Are. In ed. Laurence Goldstein, *Precedent in Law*. Oxford: Clarendon Press.

___. 1989. Spontaneous order and the Rule of Law: Some Problems. In *Ratio Juris* **2** (1): 41-54.

___. 1991. On Open Texture in Law. In Paul Amslek and Neil MacCormick, *Controversies about Law's Ontology*, 72-83. Edinburgh: Edinburgh University Press.

___. 1992. Natural Law and the Separation of Law and Morals. In ed. Robert P. George, *Natural Law Theory: Contemporary Essays*, 105-33. Oxford: Clarendon Press.

___. 1993. Beyond the Sovereign State. In *Modern Law Review* **56**: 1-18.

___. 1996. The Concept of Law and the Concept of Law. In ed. Robert P. George, *The Autonomy of Law*, 163-93. Oxford: Clarendon Press.

___. 1999. My Philosophy of Law. In Wintgens, *The Law in Philosophical Perspectives* ,120-45. Dordrecht/Boston/London: Kluwer.

___. 2000. *Questioning Sovereignty: Law, State and Nation in the European Commonwealth*. Oxford: Oxford University Press.

Macpherson, C.B. 1962. *The Political Theory of Possessive Individualism: Hobbes to Locke*. Oxford: Clarendon Press.

Manin, Bernard. 1994. On Legitimacy and Political Deliberation. In ed. Mark Lilla. *New French Thought: Political Philosophy*, 186-200. Princeton: Princeton University Press.

Manning, C.A.W. 1962. *The Nature of International Society*. London: Bell.

___. [1933] 1963. Austin To-day: Or 'The Province of Jurisprudence Re-examined. In ed. H. Milford, *Modern Theories of Law*, 180-226. Oxford: Oxford University Press.

Marion, Jean-Luc. 1994. Metaphysics and Phenomenology: A Relief for Theology. In *Critical Inquiry* **20**: 572-91.

Marmor, Andrei. 1992. *Interpretation and Legal Theory* Oxford: Clarendon Press.

___. 1998. An Essay on The Objectivity of Law. In ed. Brian Bix, *Analyzing Law: New Essays in Legal Theory*, 3-31. Oxford: Clarendon Press.

Martin, Michael. 1987. *The Legal Philosophy of HLA Hart: A Critical Appraisal*. Philadelphia: Temple University Press.

Martinich, A.P. 1992. *The Two Gods of Leviathan: Thomas Hobbes on Religion and Politics*. Cambridge: Cambridge University Press.

McBride, William. 1984. The Fetishism of Illegality and the Mystifications of Authority and Legitimacy. In *Georgia Law Review* **18**: 862-91.

McGrade, A.S. ~~????~~ Aristotle's Place in the history of Natural Rights. In *Review of Metaphysics* **49**: 803-29.

McIlwain, C.H. 1969. *Constitutionalism and the Changing World*, 26-46. Cambridge: Cambridge University Press.

McLaughlin, Robert N. 1989. On a Similarity between Natural Law Theories and English Legal Positivism in *The Philosophical Quarterly* **39** (157): 445-62.

Meerbote, Ralf. 1972. The Unknowability of Things in Themselves. In ed. Lewis White Beck, *Proceedings of the Third International Kant Congress*, 415-23. Dordrecht: D. Reidel.

Metz, Johann Baptist. 1994. Suffering unto God. In *Critical Inquiry* **20**: 611-23.

Michelman, Frank. 1998. Constitutional Authorship. In ed. Larry Alexander, *Constitutionalism: Philosophical Foundations*, 64-91. Cambridge: Cambridge University Press.

Miller, Fred D. 1996. Aristotle and the Origins of Natural Rights. In *Review of Metaphysics* **49**: 873-907.

Mills, Patricia Jagentowicz. 1986. Hegel's *Antigone*. In *The Owl of Minerva* **17** (2): 131-52.

Miller, Walter B. 1955. Two Concepts of Authority. In *American Anthropologist* **57**: 271-89.

Morgan, Michael L. 1988. Authorship and the History of Philosophy. In *Review of Metaphysics* **42**: 327-55.

Murray, Gilbert. 1951. *Five Stages of Greek Religion* . New York: Doubleday.

Miller, Fred D., Aristotle and the Origins of Natural Rights. In *Review of Metaphysics* **49**: 873-907.

Morison, W.L. *John Austin*. 1982. London: Edward Arnold.

Morrison, Wayne. 1999. *Jurisprudence: From the Greek to post-modernism*. London: Cavendish.

Morrow, Glenn R. 1948. Plato and the Law of Nature. In eds. Milton R. Konvitz and Arthur E. Murphy, *Essays in Political Theory*, 17-44. New York: Kennikat Press.

Murphy, Mark C. 1995. Was Hobbes a Legal Positivist? In *Ethics* **105**: 846-73.

Murray, Gilbert. 1957. *Five Stages in Ancient Greek Society: A Study of the Origins of Western Speculation*. New York: Harper & Bros.

Nagel, Ernst. 1958. On the Fusion of Fact and Value: A Reply to Professor Fuller. In *Natural Law Forum* **3**: 77-82.

___. 1959. Fact, Value and Human Purpose. In *Natural Law Forum*, **4**: 26-43.

Nancy, Jean-Luc. 1991. *The Inoperative Community*. Ed. Peter Connor, trans. Peter Connor et al. Theory and History of Literature, **76**. Minneapolis: University of Minnesota Press.

Nehemas, Alexander. 1981-82. The Postulated Author: Critical Monism as a Regulative Ideal. In *Critical Inquiry* **8**: 133-49.

___. 1986. What an Author Is. In *Journal of Philosophy*, **83**: 685-91.

___. 1987. Writer, Text and Author. In ed. Anthony J. Cascadi, *Literature and the Quest of Philosophy* 265-91. Baltimore, Johns Hopkins University Press.

Nissim-Sabat, Marilyn. 1990. Autonomy, Empathy, and Transcendence in Sophocles *Antigone*: A Phenomenological Perspective. In *Listening* **25**: 225-250.

Nussbaum, Martha C. 1986. *The Fragility of Goodness: Luck and Ethics in Greek Tragedy and Philosophy*. Cambridge: Cambridge University Press.

Oakeshott, Michael. [1937] 1975. *Hobbes on Civil Association*. Oxford: Basil Blackwell.

___. 1938. The Concept of a Philosophical Jurisprudence. In *Politica* **3**: 203.

___. 1975a. Introduction. *Hobbes on Civil Association*, 1-74. Oxford: Basil Blackwell. Original edn in Hobbes.1946. *Leviathan*, vii-lxvi. Ed. Michael Oakeshott. Oxford: Blackwell. References are to the *Civil Association* reprint.

___. 1975b. The Moral Life in the Writings of Thomas Hobbes. In *Hobbes on Civil Association*, 103-13. Oxford: Basil Blackwell.

___. 1975c. A Myth. In *Hobbes on Civil Association*, 150-54. Oxford: Basil Blackwell.

Oakley, Francis. 1961. Christian Theology and the Newtonian Science: The Rise of the concept of the Laws of Nature. In *Church History* **30**: 433-57.

___. 1984. *Omnipotence, Covenant & Order: An excursion in the history of ideas from Abelard to Leibniz*. Ithaca & London: Cornell University Press.

Olivecrona, Karl. 1975. The Will of the Sovereign: Some Reflections on Bentham's Concept of A Law. In *American Journal of Jurisprudence* **20**: 95-110.

___. 1978. Benthams Veil of Mystery. In *Current Legal Problems* **31**: 227-37.

Oppenheim, Felix E. 1957. The Natural Law Thesis, Affirmation or Denial? In *American Political Science Review* **1**: 41-53.

Paulson, Stanley L. 1980. Material and Formal Authorisation in Kelsen's Pure Theory. In *Cambridge Law Journal* **39** (1): 172-93.

___. 1986. On the Status of the *Lex Posterior* Derogating Rule. In ed. Richard Tur and William Twining, *Essays on Kelsen*, 229-47. Oxford: Clarendon Press.

___. 1990. Kelsen on Legal Interpretation. In *Legal Studies* **10**: 136-52.

___. 1992. The Neo-Kantian Dimension of Kelsens Pure Theory of Law. In *Oxford Journal of Legal Studies* **12**: 311-32.

___. 1994. Lon Fuller, Gustav Radbruch, and the Positivist Theses. In *Law and Philosophy* **13**: 313-59.

___. 1996. On the Early Development of the *Grundnorm* In eds. Frank Kleerackers, Evert van Leeuwan, and Bert van Roermund, *Law, Life and Images of Man: Modes of Thought in Modern Legal Theory*, 217-30. Berlin: Duncker & Humblot.

___. 1998. Four Phases in Hans Kelsens Legal Theory? Reflections on a Periodization. In *Oxford Journal of Legal Studies* **18**:153-66.

Paulson, Bonnie Litschewski, and Stanley Paulson. 1992. Short Annotated Bibliography of Secondary Literature in English. In Hans Kelsen, *Introduction to the Problems of Legal Theory* , 145-53. Oxford Clarendon Press.

Perry, Michael J. 1998. What is the Constitution? (and other Fundamental Questions). In ed. Larry Alexander, *Constitutionalism: Philosophical Foundations*, 99-151. Cambridge: Cambridge University Press.

Peters, R.S., P.G. Winch, and A.E. Duncan-Jones. 1958. Symposium: Authority. In Aristotelian Society, *Proceedings* **32**: 207-60.

Pocock, J.G.A. 1957. *The Ancient Constitution and the Feudal Law*. Cambridge: Cambridge University Press.

Pomeroy, Sarah. 1997. *Families in Classical and Hellenistic Greece: Representations and Realities*. Oxford: Clarendon.

Postema, Gerald J. 1982. Coordination and Convention at the Foundations of Law. In *Journal of Legal Studies*. **11**: 165-203.

___. 1986. *Bentham and the Common Law Tradition*. Oxford: Clarenden Press.

Pound, Roscoe. 1959. *Jurisprudence* 5 vols. St Paul: West.

Ravven, Heidi M. 1988. Has Hegel Anything to Say to Feminists? In *The Owl of Minerva* **19**: 149-68.

Reynolds, Barney. 1993. Natural Law versus Positivism: The Fundamental Conflict. In *Oxford Journal of Legal Studies* **13** (4): 441-56.

Ricoeur, Paul. 1974. *The Conflict of Interpretations*, ed. Don Ihde. Evanston: Northwestern University Press.

___. 1981. *Hermeneutics & the Human Sciences*, ed. and trans. John B. Thompson. Cambridge: Cambridge University Press.

Ross, Alf. 1969. On Self-reference and a Puzzle in Constitutional Law in *Mind* **78**: 1-24.

___. 1961. Validity and Conflict between Legal Positivism and Natural Law. In *Revista Juridica de Buernos Aires*, 46-93.

Rotman, Brian. 1993. *Taking God Out of Mathematics and Putting the Body Back In: An Essay in Corporeal Semiotics* . Stanford: Stanford University Press.

Rumble, Wilfrid E. 1979. Divine Law, Utilitarian Ethics and Positvist Jurisprudence: A Study of the Legal Philosophy of John Austin. In *American Journal of Jurisprudence*, **24**: 139-80.

___. 1985. *The Thought of John Austin: Jurisprudence, Colonial Reform, and the British Constitution*. London & Dover, New Hampshire: Athlone Press.

Sacks, Sheldon, ed. 1979. *On Metaphor*. Chicago and London: University of Chicago Press.

Sampford, Charles. 1989. *The Disorder of Law: A Critique of Legal Theory*. London: Basil Blackwell

Sartorius, Rolf. 1971. Hart's Concept of Law. In ed. Robert S. Summers, *More Essays in Legal Philosophy: General Assessments of Legal Philosophers*, 131-61. Oxford: Basil Blackwell.

___. 1987. Positivism and the Foundations of legal Authority. In ed. Ruth Gavison, *Issues in Contemporary Legal Philosophy: The Influence of H.L.A. Hart*, 43-61. Oxford: Clarendon Press.

Scarpelli, Uberto. [1965] 1996. *Qu'est-ce que le positivisme juridique?* Trans. from Italian by Colette Clavreul, pref. by Letizia Gianformaggio. Bruylant: L.G.D.J.

___. 1968. Legal Philosophy Today: An Introduction. In ed. Robert S. Summers, *Essays in Legal Philosophy*, vol. 1, 1-21. Berkeley: University of California Press.

Schauer, Frederick. 1991a. The Authority of Legal Scholarship. In *University of Pennsylvania Law Review* **139**: 1003-17.

___. 1991. Rules and the Rule of Law. In *Harvard Journal of Law and Public Policy*. **14**: 645-94.

___. 1993. Constitutional Positivism. In *Connecticut Law Review* **25**: 797-828.

___. 1998. Positivism Through Thick and Thin. In ed. Brian Bix, *Analyzing Law: New Essays in Legal Theory*, 65-78. Oxford: Clarendon Press.

Schofield, Malcolm. 1996. Sharing in the Constitution. In *Review of Metaphysics* **49**: 831-58.

Schwartz, Joel. 1985. Hobbes and the Two Kingdoms of God. In *Polity* **18**: 7-24.

Schwarz, Wolfgang. 1962-63. Kant's Philosophy of Law and International Peace. In *Philosophy and Phenomenological Research* **23**: 71-80.

Schapiro, Scott J. 1998. On Harts Way Out. In *Legal Theory* **4**: 469-507.

Shuman, Samuel I. 1963. *Legal Positivism: Its Scope and Illustrations*. Detroit: Wayne State University Press.

Shiner, Roger A. 1992. *Norm and Nature: The Movements of Legal Thought*. Oxford: Clarendon Press.

Soper, Philip. 1992. Some Natural Confusions about Natural Law. In *Michigan Law Review* **90**: 2393-2423.

Schofield, Malcolm. 1996. Sharing in the Constitution. In *Review of Metaphysics* **49**: 831-58.

Sebok, Anthony J. 1995. Misunderstanding Positivism. In *Michigan Law Review* **93**: 2054-132.

___. 1998. *Legal Positivism in American Jurisprudence*. Cambridge: Cambridge University Press.

Segal, Charles. 1953. From Religion to Philosophy. In *Journal of Hellenic Studies* **73**: 77-84

___. *Interpreting Greek Tragedy: Myth, Poetry, Text*. 1986. Ithaca & London: Cornell University Press.

Shapiro, Scott J. 1998. On Hart's Way Out. In *Legal Theory* **4**: 469-507.

Shiner, Roger A. 1992. *Norm and Nature: The Movements of Legal Thought*. Oxford: Clarendon Press.

Shklar, Judith. 1964. *Legalism: Law, Morals and Political Trials*. Cambridge, Mass/London: Harvard University Press.

___. [1964] 1972. Rousseaus Images of Authority. In *Hobbes and Rousseau: A Collection of Critical Essays*, Maurice Cranston and Richard S. Peters, 333-65. Garden City, New York: Anchor Books. Originally published in 1966 in *American Political Science Review* **58**.

___. [1969] 1985. *Man and Citizen: A Study of Rousseau's Social Theory*. Cambridge: University of Cambridge Press.

Sigmund, Paul E. 1971, 2d. *Natural Law in Political Thought*. London: University Press of America.

Silving, Helen. 1964. The Lasting Value of Kelsenism. In Salo Engel with Rudolf A. Metall. *Law, State and International Legal Order: Essays in Honor of Hans Kelsen*, 297-346. Knoxville: University of Tennessee Press.

Simpson, A.W.B. 1964. The Analysis of Legal Concepts. In *Law Quarterly Review*, **80**: 535-58.

Skinner, Quentin. 1988. Warrender and Skinner on Hobbes: A Reply. In *Political Studies* **36**: 692-95.

___. 1992. Liberty and Legal Obligation in Hobbes Leviathan. In ed. Hyman Gross and Ross Harrison, *Jurisprudence: Cambridge Essays*, 231-56. Oxford: Clarendon Press.

Springborg, Patricia. 1995. Hobbes Biblical Beasts: *Leviathan* and *Behemoth*. In *Political Theory* **23**: 353-75.

Summers, Robert S. 1963. Professor H.L.A. Hart's Concept of Law. In *Duke Law Journal*, 629-70.

___. 1966. The *New* Analytical Jurists. In *New York University Law Review* **41**: 861-96.

Starr, Chester G. 1961. The Decline of Early Greek Kings. In *Historia* **10**: 129-38.

Stecker, Robert. 1987. Apparent, Implied, and Postulated Authors, In *Philosophy and Literature* **1**: 258-71.

Stewart, Iain. 1987. Closure and Legal Norm. In *Modern Law Review*, 908-33.

Steinrager, James. 1977. *Bentham*. London/Ithaca: George Allen & Unwin.

Stout, Jeffrey. 1992. Truth, Natural Law and Ethical Theory. In ed. Robert P. George, *Natural Law Theory: Contemporary Essays*, 71-102. Oxford: Clarendon.

Stewart, Ian. 1986. Kelsen and the Exegetical Tradition. In eds. Richard Tur and William Twining, *Essays on Kelsen*, 123-47. Oxford: Clarendon Press.

Stone, Julius. 1963. Mystery and Mystique in the Basic Norm. In *Modern Law Review* **26**: 34-50.

Stout, Jeffrey. 1992. Truth, Natural Law and Ethical Theory. In ed. Robert P. George, *Natural Law Theory: Contemporary Essays*, 71-102. Oxford: Clarendon.

Strauss, Leo. 1936. *The Political Philosophy of Hobbes: Its Basis and Genesis*. Trans. Elsa M. Sinclair. Chicago: University of Chicago Press.

___. 1953. *Natural Right and History*. Chicago: University of Chicago Press.

___. 1965. The Spirit of Hobbes Political Philosophy. In *Hobbes' Studies*, ed. K. C. Brown, 1-30. Oxford: Basil Blackwell.

Summers, Robert. 1966. The New Analytical Jurists. In *New York University Law Review* **41**: 861-96.

Taliaferro, Charles. 1996. Gods Natural Laws. In ed. Robert P. George, *Natural Law, Liberalism, and Morality: Contemporary Essays*, 283-301. Oxford: Clarendon.

Tarnas, Richard. 1991. *The Passions of the Western Mind*. New York: Ballantine.

Taylor, A.E. [1938] 1965. The Ethical Doctrine of Hobbes. In *Philosophy* (1938) **13**: 406-24. Reprinted in ed. K.C. Brown, *Hobbes' Studies*, 35-55. Oxford: Basil Blackwell.

Taylor, Mark C. 1994. Denegating God. In *Critical Inquiry* **20**: 592-609.

Thomas, Philip A. 1996. *Legal Frontiers*. Aldershot: Dartmouth.

Thomas, C. G. 1973. Matriarchy in Early Greece: The Bronze and Dark Ages. In *Arethusa* **6**: 173 -95

Thomson, George. [1949] 1954. *Studies in Ancient Greek Society: the Prehistoric Aegean*. London: Lawrence & Wishart.

Tierney, Brian. 1989. The Origins of Natural Rights Language. In *History of Political Thought* **10** (4): 615-46.

Tuck, Richard. 1972. Why is Authority Such a Problem? In eds. Peter Laslett, W. G. Runciman, and Quinton Skinner, *Philosophy, Politics and Society*, 4th ser., 174-207. Oxford: Basil Blackwell.

Tuebner, Gunther. 1993. *Law as an Autopoietic System*. Oxford: Basil Blackwell.

Tur, Richard and William Twining, eds. 1986. *Essays on Kelsen*. Oxford: Clarendon Press.

Trainor, Brian T. 1988. Warrender and Skinner on Hobbes. *Political Studies* **36**: 680-91.

Vattimo, Gianni. 1988. *The End of Modernity: Nihilism and Hermeneutics in Postmodern Culture*. Baltimore: Johns Hopkins University Press.

Vernant, Jean-Pierre. 1972. With Pierre Vidal-Naquet. *Tragedy and Myth in Ancient Greece*. New Jersey: Humanities Press.

___. 1974. *Myth and Society in Ancient Greece*. Trans. Janet Lloyd. New Jersey: Humanities Press.

___. 1982. *The Origins of Greek Thought*. Ithaca, NY: Cornell University Press.

Vernengo, Roberto J. 1986. Kelsens *Rechtssatze* as Detached Statements. In eds. Richard Tur and William Twining, *Essays on Kelsen*, 99-108. Oxford: Clarendon.

Visker, Rudi. 1995. *Michel Foucault: Geneology as Critique*. London: Verso.

Vlastos, Gregory. 1946. Solonian Justice. In *Classical Philology* **41**: 65-83.

___. 1947. Equality and Justice in Early Greek Cosmologies. In *Classical Philology*, 156-78.

___ . 1952. Theology and Philosophy in Early Greek Thought. In *Philosophical Quarterly*, 97-123.

Waldon, Jeremy, 1996. Kants Legal Positivism. In *Harvard Law Review* **109**: 1535-66.

Waluchow, Wilfrid. 1994. *Inclusive Legal Positivism*. Oxford: Clarendon Press.

Ward, Graham. 1995. *Barth, Derrida and the Language of Theology*. Cambridge: Cambridge University Press.

Ward, Ian. 1997. *Kantianism, Postmodern and Critical Legal Thought*. Dordrecht/Boston/ London: Kluwer. Law and Philosophy Library.

Warrender, Howard. 1960. The Place of God in Hobbes Philosophy: A Rely to Mr. Plamenatz. In *Hobbes' Studies*, ed. K.C. Brown, 89-100. Oxford: Basil Blackwell. Originally published in *Political Studies* **8**: 48-57.

___. [1957, 1961] 1966. *The Political Philosophy of Hobbes: His Theory of Obligation*. Oxford: Clarendon Press.

Wroblewski, Jerzy. 1991. On the Unstated in Law: Implicit Presuppositions and Conventions. In *Controversies about Law's Ontology*. Ed. Paul Amslek and Neil MacCormick, 91-106. Edinburgh: Edinburgh University Press.

Weber, Samuel. 1987. The Limits of Professionalism. In Weber *Institution and Interpretation*, 18-32. Afterword Wlad Godzich. Theory and History of Literature, **31**. Minneapolis: University of Minnesota Press.

___. 1990. In the Name of the Law. In *Cardozo Law Review* **11**: 1515-1538.

Weibe, Donald. 1976. Explanation and Theological Method. *Zygon* **11**: 35-49.

___. 1978. Science and Religion: Is Compatibility Possible? In *Journal of the American Scientific Affiliation*, 169-76.

___. 1987. The Prelogical Mentality Revisited. In *Religion* **17**: 29-61.

___. 1989. Is Science an Implicit Religion? In *Studies in Religion* **18** (2): 171-83.

Weinberger, Ota. 1973. Introduction: Hans Kelsen as Philosopher. In *Essays in Legal and Moral Philosophy*, ix-xxvi. Ed. Ota Weinberger, trans. Peter Heath. Dordrecht and Boston: D. Reidel.

___. 1986. With Neil MacCormick. *An Institutional Theory of Law: New Approaches to Legal Positivism*. Dordrecht: D. Reidel.

___. Weinberger, Ota. 1991a. Institutionalist Theories of Law. In Paul Amslek and Neil MacCormick, *Controversies about Law's Ontology*. Edinburgh: Edinburgh University Press.

___. 1991b. *Law, Institution and Legal Politics: Fundamental Problems of Legal Theory and Social Philosophy*. Dordrecht: Kluwer.

___. 1999. Neo-Institutionalism: My Views on the Philosophy of Law. In ed. Luc J. Wintgens, *The Law in Philosophical Perspectives*, 253-72. Dordrecht/Boston/London: Kluwer.

Weinrib, Ernst. 1995. *The Idea of Private Law*. Cambridge: Harvard University Press.

Whitemore, Raymond C. 1956. In God We Live: A Critical History of Pantheism. In *Philosophy* **31**: 36-54.

Whitney, George Tapley, and David F. Bowers, eds. 1962. *The Heritage of Kant*. New York: Russell & Russell.

Williamson, Raymond Keith. 1984. *Introduction to Hegel's Philosophy of Religion*. Albany: State University of New York.

Winnington-Ingram, R.P. 1980. *Sophocles: An Interpretation*. Cambridge: Cambridge University Press.

Woodmansee, Martha. 1983-84. The Genious and the Copyright: Economic and Legal Conditions of the Emergence of the Author. In *Eighteenth Century Studies* **17**: 425-48.

Wroblewski, Jerzy. 1991. On the Unstated in Law: Implicit presuppositions and Conventions. In Paul Amslek and Neil MacCormick, eds., *Controversies about Law's Ontology*. Edinburgh: Edinburgh University Press.

Yntema, Hessel, E. 1941. Jurisprudence on Parade. In *Michigan Law Review* **39**: 1154-1181.

Zizek, Slavoj. 1989. *The Sublime Object of Ideology*. London/New York: Verso.

___. 1990. Beyond Discourse-Analysis. In *New Reflections of Our Time*. Ed. Ernesto Laclau, 249-60. London/New York: Verso.

___. 1991. *For they know not what they do: Enjoyment as a Political Factor*. London/New York: Verso.

___. 1993. *Tarrying with the Negative: Kant, Hegel and the Critique of Ideology*. Durham: Duke University Press.

Index

Law and Philosophy Library

1. E. Bulygin, J.-L. Gardies and I. Niiniluoto (eds.): *Man, Law and Modern Forms of Life*. With an Introduction by M.D. Bayles. 1985 ISBN 90-277-1869-5
2. W. Sadurski: *Giving Desert Its Due*. Social Justice and Legal Theory. 1985 ISBN 90-277-1941-1
3. N. MacCormick and O. Weinberger: *An Institutional Theory of Law*. New Approaches to Legal Positivism. 1986 ISBN 90-277-2079-7
4. A. Aarnio: *The Rational as Reasonable*. A Treatise on Legal Justification. 1987 ISBN 90-277-2276-5
5. M.D. Bayles: *Principles of Law*. A Normative Analysis. 1987 ISBN 90-277-2412-1; Pb: 90-277-2413-X
6. A. Soeteman: *Logic in Law*. Remarks on Logic and Rationality in Normative Reasoning, Especially in Law. 1989 ISBN 0-7923-0042-4
7. C.T. Sistare: *Responsibility and Criminal Liability*. 1989 ISBN 0-7923-0396-2
8. A. Peczenik: *On Law and Reason*. 1989 ISBN 0-7923-0444-6
9. W. Sadurski: *Moral Pluralism and Legal Neutrality*. 1990 ISBN 0-7923-0565-5
10. M.D. Bayles: *Procedural Justice*. Allocating to Individuals. 1990 ISBN 0-7923-0567-1
11. P. Nerhot (ed.): *Law, Interpretation and Reality*. Essays in Epistemology, Hermeneutics and Jurisprudence. 1990 ISBN 0-7923-0593-0
12. A.W. Norrie: *Law, Ideology and Punishment*. Retrieval and Critique of the Liberal Ideal of Criminal Justice. 1991 ISBN 0-7923-1013-6
13. P. Nerhot (ed.): *Legal Knowledge and Analogy*. Fragments of Legal Epistemology, Hermeneutics and Linguistics. 1991 ISBN 0-7923-1065-9
14. O. Weinberger: *Law, Institution and Legal Politics*. Fundamental Problems of Legal Theory and Social Philosophy. 1991 ISBN 0-7923-1143-4
15. J. Wróblewski: *The Judicial Application of Law*. Edited by Z. Bańkowski and N. MacCormick. 1992 ISBN 0-7923-1569-3
16. T. Wilhelmsson: *Critical Studies in Private Law*. A Treatise on Need-Rational Principles in Modern Law. 1992 ISBN 0-7923-1659-2
17. M.D. Bayles: *Hart's Legal Philosophy*. An Examination. 1992 ISBN 0-7923-1981-8
18. D.W.P. Ruiter: *Institutional Legal Facts*. Legal Powers and their Effects. 1993 ISBN 0-7923-2441-2
19. J. Schonsheck: *On Criminalization*. An Essay in the Philosophy of the Criminal Law. 1994 ISBN 0-7923-2663-6
20. R.P. Malloy and J. Evensky (eds.): *Adam Smith and the Philosophy of Law and Economics*. 1994 ISBN 0-7923-2796-9
21. Z. Bańkowski, I. White and U. Hahn (eds.): *Informatics and the Foundations of Legal Reasoning*. 1995 ISBN 0-7923-3455-8

Law and Philosophy Library

22. E. Lagerspetz: *The Opposite Mirrors*. An Essay on the Conventionalist Theory of Institutions. 1995 ISBN 0-7923-3325-X
23. M. van Hees: *Rights and Decisions*. Formal Models of Law and Liberalism. 1995 ISBN 0-7923-3754-9
24. B. Anderson: *"Discovery" in Legal Decision-Making*. 1996 ISBN 0-7923-3981-9
25. S. Urbina: *Reason, Democracy, Society*. A Study on the Basis of Legal Thinking. 1996 ISBN 0-7923-4262-3
26. E. Attwooll: *The Tapestry of the Law*. Scotland, Legal Culture and Legal Theory. 1997 ISBN 0-7923-4310-7
27. J.C. Hage: *Reasoning with Rules*. An Essay on Legal Reasoning and Its Underlying Logic. 1997 ISBN 0-7923-4325-5
28. R.A. Hillman: *The Richness of Contract Law*. An Analysis and Critique of Contemporary Theories of Contract Law. 1997 ISBN 0-7923-4336-0; 0-7923-5063-4 (Pb)
29. C. Wellman: *An Approach to Rights*. Studies in the Philosophy of Law and Morals. 1997 ISBN 0-7923-4467-7
30. B. van Roermund: *Law, Narrative and Reality*. An Essay in Intercepting Politics. 1997 ISBN 0-7923-4621-1
31. I. Ward: *Kantianism, Postmodernism and Critical Legal Thought*. 1997 ISBN 0-7923-4745-5
32. H. Prakken: *Logical Tools for Modelling Legal Argument*. A Study of Defeasible Reasoning in Law. 1997 ISBN 0-7923-4776-5
33. T. May: *Autonomy, Authority and Moral Responsibility*. 1998 ISBN 0-7923-4851-6
34. M. Atienza and J.R. Manero: *A Theory of Legal Sentences*. 1998 ISBN 0-7923-4856-7
35. E.A. Christodoulidis: *Law and Reflexive Politics*. 1998 ISBN 0-7923-4954-7
36. L.M.M. Royakkers: *Extending Deontic Logic for the Formalisation of Legal Rules*. 1998 ISBN 0-7923-4982-2
37. J.J. Moreso: *Legal Indeterminacy and Constitutional Interpretation*. 1998 ISBN 0-7923-5156-8
38. W. Sadurski: *Freedom of Speech and Its Limits*. 1999 ISBN 0-7923-5523-7
39. J. Wolenski (ed.): *Kazimierz Opalek Selected Papers in Legal Philosophy*. 1999 ISBN 0-7923-5732-9
40. H.P. Visser 't Hooft: *Justice to Future Generations and the Environment*. 1999 ISBN 0-7923-5756-6
41. L.J. Wintgens (ed.): *The Law in Philosophical Perspectives*. My Philosophy of Law. 1999 ISBN 0-7923-5796-5
42. A.R. Lodder: *DiaLaw*. On Legal Justification and Dialogical Models of Argumentation. 1999 ISBN 0-7923-5830-9
43. C. Redondo: *Reasons for Action and the Law*. 1999 ISBN 0-7923-5912-7

Law and Philosophy Library

44. M. Friedman, L. May, K. Parsons and J. Stiff (eds.): *Rights and Reason*. Essays in Honor of Carl Wellman. 2000 ISBN 0-7923-6198-9
45. G.C. Christie: *The Notion of an Ideal Audience in Legal Argument*. 2000 ISBN 0-7923-6283-7
46. R.S. Summers: *Essays in Legal Theory*. 2000 ISBN 0-7923-6367-1
47. M. van Hees: *Legal Reductionism and Freedom*. 2000 ISBN 0-7923-6491-0
48. R. Gargarella: *The Scepter of Reason*. Public Discussion and Political Radicalism in the Origins of Constitutionalism. 2000 ISBN 0-7923-6508-9
49. M. Iglesias Vila: *Facing Judicial Discretion*. Legal Knowledge and Right Answers Revisited. 2001 ISBN 0-7923-6778-2
50. M. Kiikeri: *Comparative Legal Reasoning and European Law*. 2001 ISBN 0-7923-6884-3
51. A.J. Menéndez: *Justifying Taxes*. Some Elements for a General Theory of Democratic Tax Law. 2001 ISBN 0-7923-7052-X
52. W.E. Conklin: *The Invisible Origins of Legal Positivism*. A Re-Reading of a Tradition. 2001 ISBN 0-7923-7101-1

KLUWER ACADEMIC PUBLISHERS – DORDRECHT / BOSTON / LONDON

MIX
Papier aus verantwortungsvollen Quellen
Paper from responsible sources
FSC® C105338
FSC
www.fsc.org

If you have any concerns about our products,
you can contact us on
ProductSafety@springernature.com

In case Publisher is established outside the EU,
the EU authorized representative is:
Springer Nature Customer Service Center GmbH
Europaplatz 3, 69115 Heidelberg, Germany

Printed by Libri Plureos GmbH
in Hamburg, Germany